SUPERMAN VS. ZOD

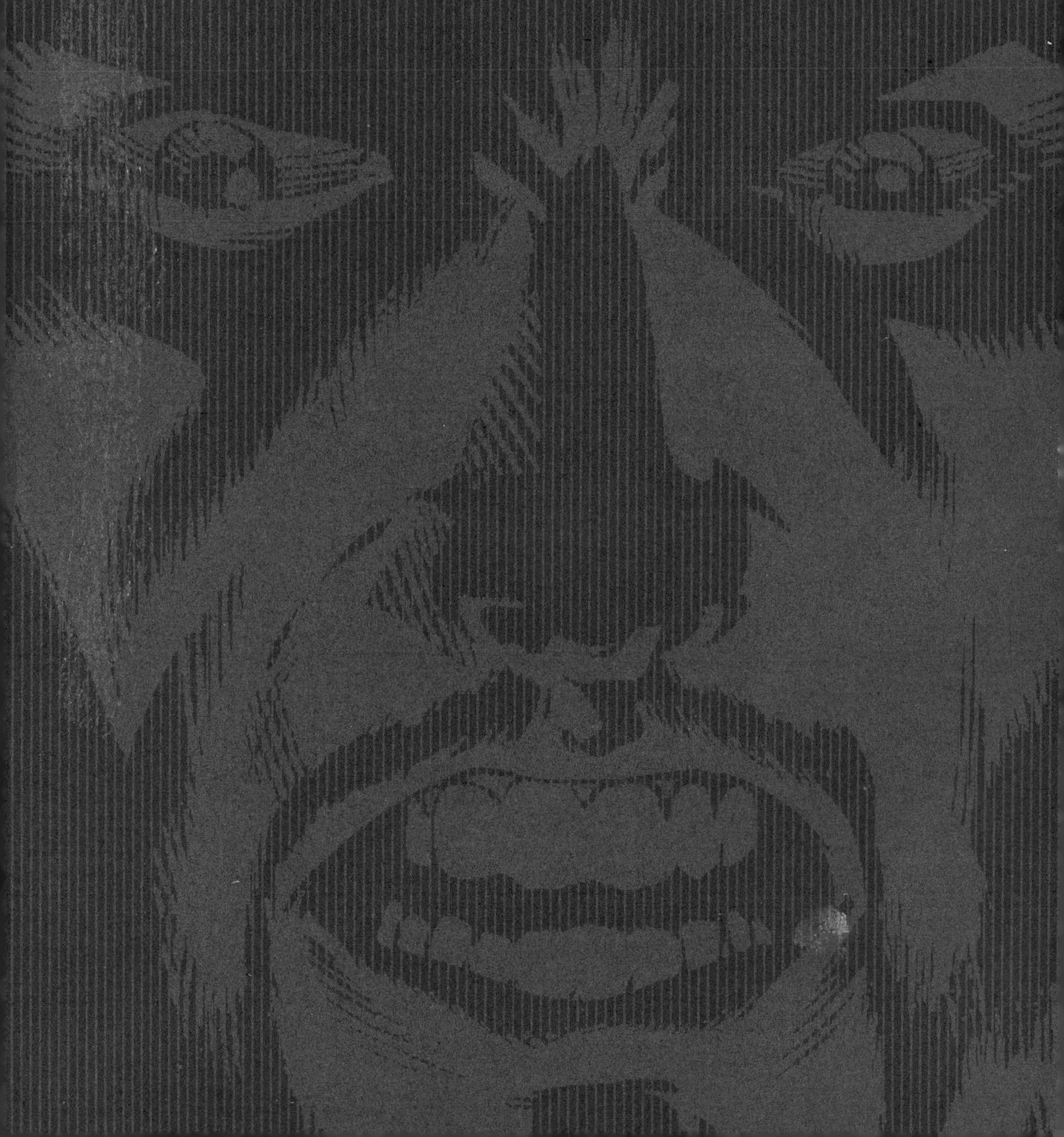

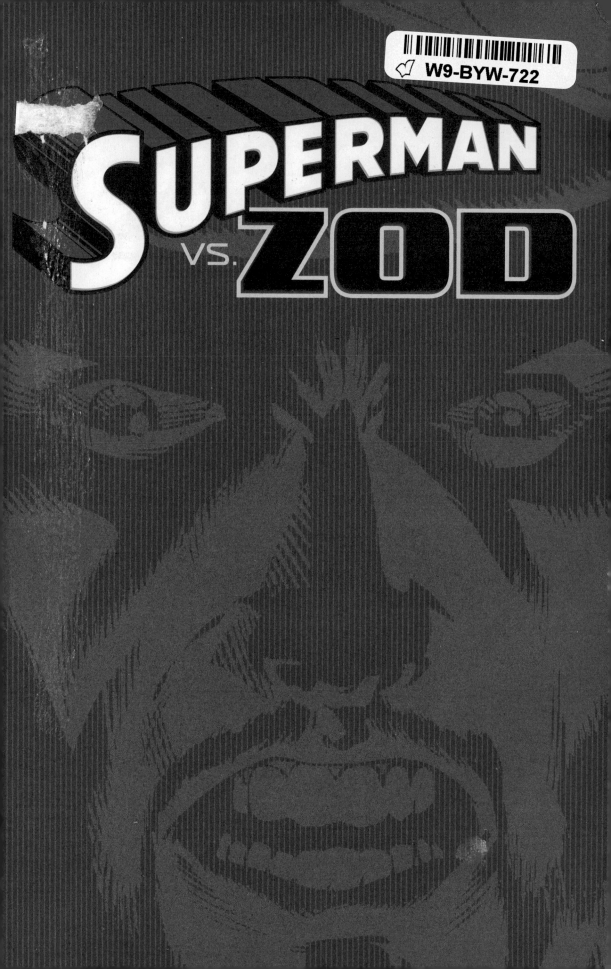

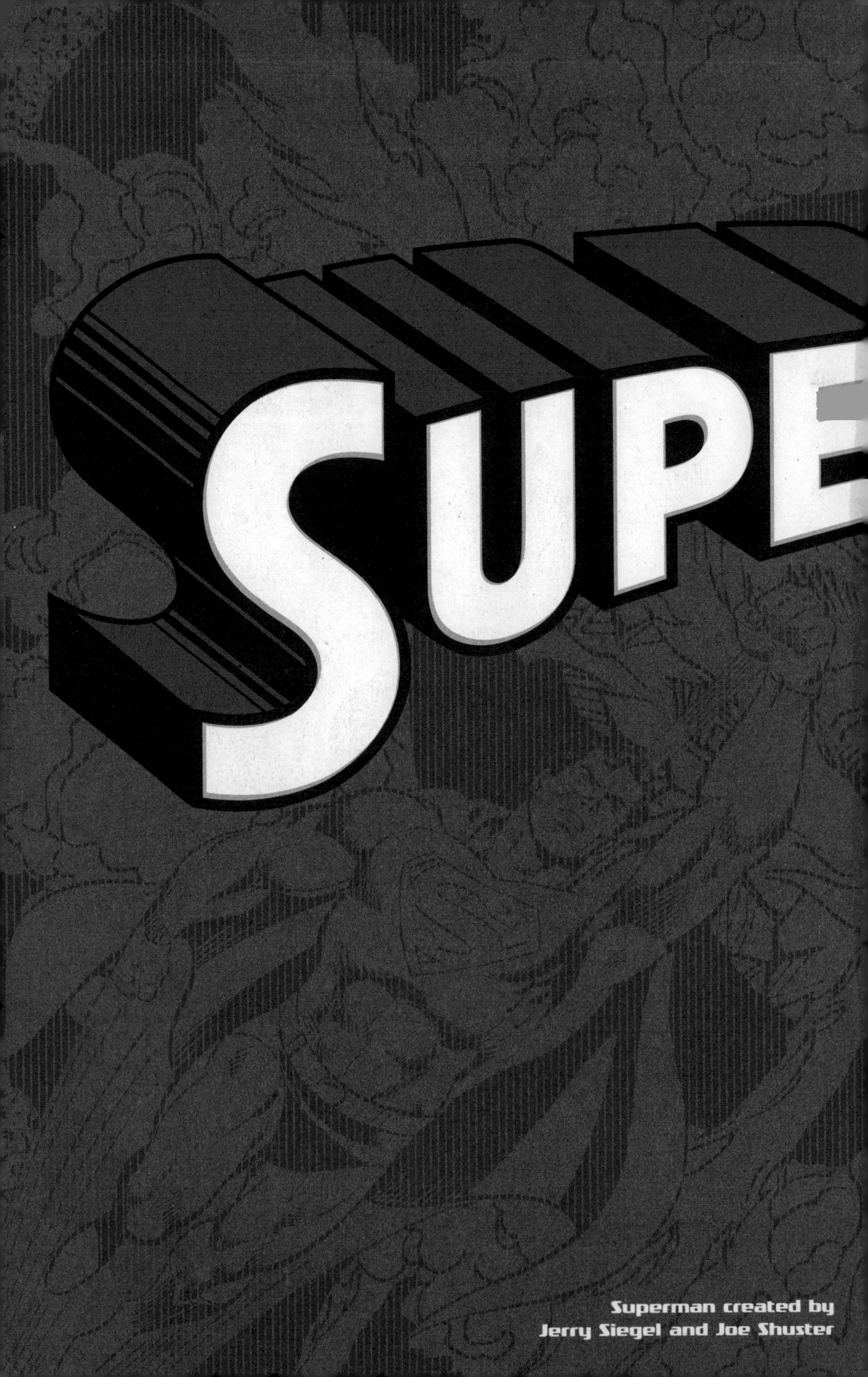

Superman created by
Jerry Siegel and Joe Shuster

RMAN VS. ZOD

Julius Schwartz
Mort Weisinger
Matt Idelson Editors – Original Series

E. Nelson Bridwell
Nachie Castro Associate Editors – Original Series

Peter Hamboussi Editor

Robbin Brosterman Design Director – Books

Curtis King Jr. Publication Design

Bob Harras VP – Editor-in-Chief

Diane Nelson President

Dan DiDio and Jim Lee Co-Publishers

Geoff Johns Chief Creative Officer

John Rood Executive VP – Sales, Marketing and Business Development

Amy Genkins Senior VP – Business and Legal Affairs

Nairi Gardiner Senior VP – Finance

Jeff Boison VP – Publishing Operations

Mark Chiarello VP – Art Direction and Design

John Cunningham VP – Marketing

Terri Cunningham VP – Talent Relations and Services

Alison Gill Senior VP – Manufacturing and Operations

Hank Kanalz Senior VP – Digital

Jay Kogan VP – Business and Legal Affairs, Publishing

Jack Mahan VP – Business Affairs, Talent

Nick Napolitano VP – Manufacturing Administration

Sue Pohja VP – Book Sales

Courtney Simmons Senior VP – Publicity

Bob Wayne Senior VP – Sales

SUPERMAN VS. ZOD
Published by DC Comics. Cover and compilation Copyright © 2013
DC Comics. All Rights Reserved.
Originally published in single magazine form in ADVENTURE COMICS
283, ACTION COMICS 473, 548-549, DC COMICS PRESENTS 97,
ACTION COMICS ANNUAL 10 Copyright © 1961, 1977, 1983, 1986,
2007 DC Comics. All Rights Reserved. All characters, their distinctive
likenesses and related elements featured in this publication are
trademarks of DC Comics. The stories, characters and incidents
featured in this publication are entirely fictional. DC Comics does not
read or accept unsolicited ideas, stories or artwork.

DC Comics, 1700 Broadway, New York, NY 10019
A Warner Bros. Entertainment Company.
Printed by RR Donnelley, Salem, VA, USA. 3/8/13. First Printing.
ISBN: 978-1-4012-3849-0

Library of Congress Cataloging-in-Publication Data

Donner, Richard, author.
  Superman vs. Zod / [Richard Donner, Robert Bernstein].
    pages cm
  "Originally published in single magazine form in Adventure Comics 283,
Action Comics 473, 548-549, DC Comics Presents 97, Action Comics Annual 10."
  ISBN 978-1-4012-3849-0
  1. Graphic novels. I. Bernstein, Robert, 1919-1988, author. II. Title.
  PN6728.S9D66 2013
  741.5'973—dc23
                                    2012046496

SUSTAINABLE
FORESTRY
INITIATIVE

Certified Chain of Custody
Promoting Sustainable Forestry
www.sfiprogram.org
SFI-01042
APPLIES TO TEXT STOCK ONLY

"THE PHANTOM SUPERBOY" 5
(From ADVENTURE COMICS #283, 1961)
Writer: Robert Bernstein   Artist: George Papp
Cover: Curt Swan & Stan Kaye

"THE GREAT PHANTOM PERIL" 21
(From ACTION COMICS #473, 1977)
Writer: Cary Bates   Penciller: Curt Swan
Inker: Text Blaisdell   *Cover: Curt Swan & Neal Adams*

"ESCAPE FROM THE PHANTOM ZONE" 39
(From ACTION COMICS #548, 1983)
Writer: Cary Bates   Penciller: Alex Saviuk
Inkers: Vince Colletta & Pablo Marcos   *Cover: Gil Kane*

"SUPERMAN MEETS THE ZOD SQUAD" 65
(From ACTION COMICS #549, 1983)
Writer: Cary Bates   Penciller: Alex Saviuk
Inkers: Vince Colletta & Pablo Marcos   *Cover: Gil Kane*

"PHANTOM ZONE: THE FINAL CHAPTER" 89
(From DC COMICS PRESENTS #97, 1986)
Writer: Steve Gerber   Penciller: Rick Veitch
Inker: Bob Smith   *Cover: Rick Veitch & Bob Smith*

"THE CRIMINALS OF KRYPTON" 128
(From ACTION COMICS ANNUAL #10, 2007)
Writers: Geoff Johns and Richard Donner
Penciller: Rags Morales   Inker: Mark Farmer

Cover art by Eddy Barrows, J.P. Mayer and Rod Reis

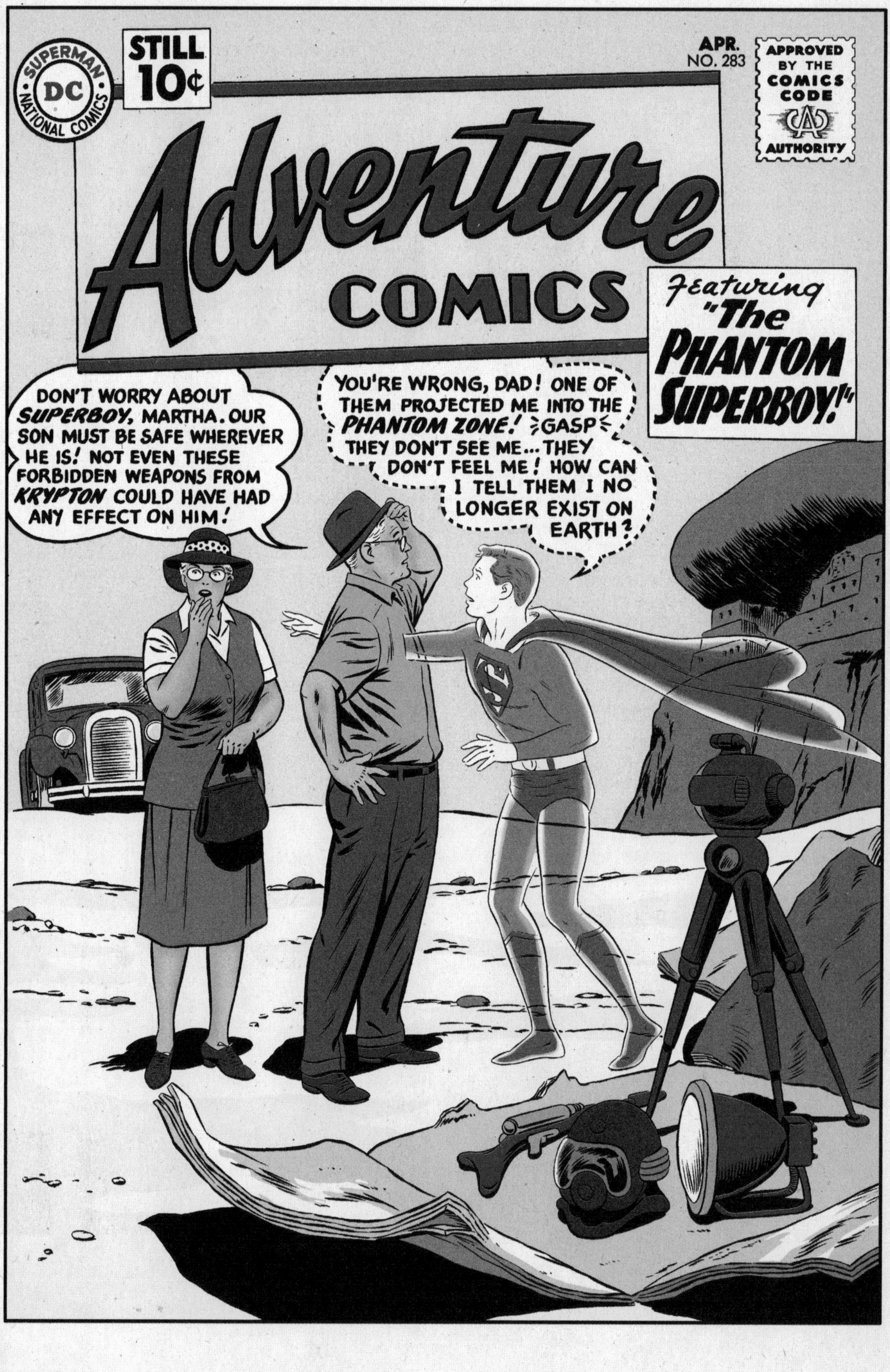
SUPERMAN DC NATIONAL COMICS
STILL 10¢
APR. NO. 283
APPROVED BY THE COMICS CODE AUTHORITY
Adventure COMICS
Featuring "The PHANTOM SUPERBOY!"
DON'T WORRY ABOUT SUPERBOY, MARTHA. OUR SON MUST BE SAFE WHEREVER HE IS! NOT EVEN THESE FORBIDDEN WEAPONS FROM KRYPTON COULD HAVE HAD ANY EFFECT ON HIM!
YOU'RE WRONG, DAD! ONE OF THEM PROJECTED ME INTO THE PHANTOM ZONE! GASP THEY DON'T SEE ME... THEY DON'T FEEL ME! HOW CAN I TELL THEM I NO LONGER EXIST ON EARTH?

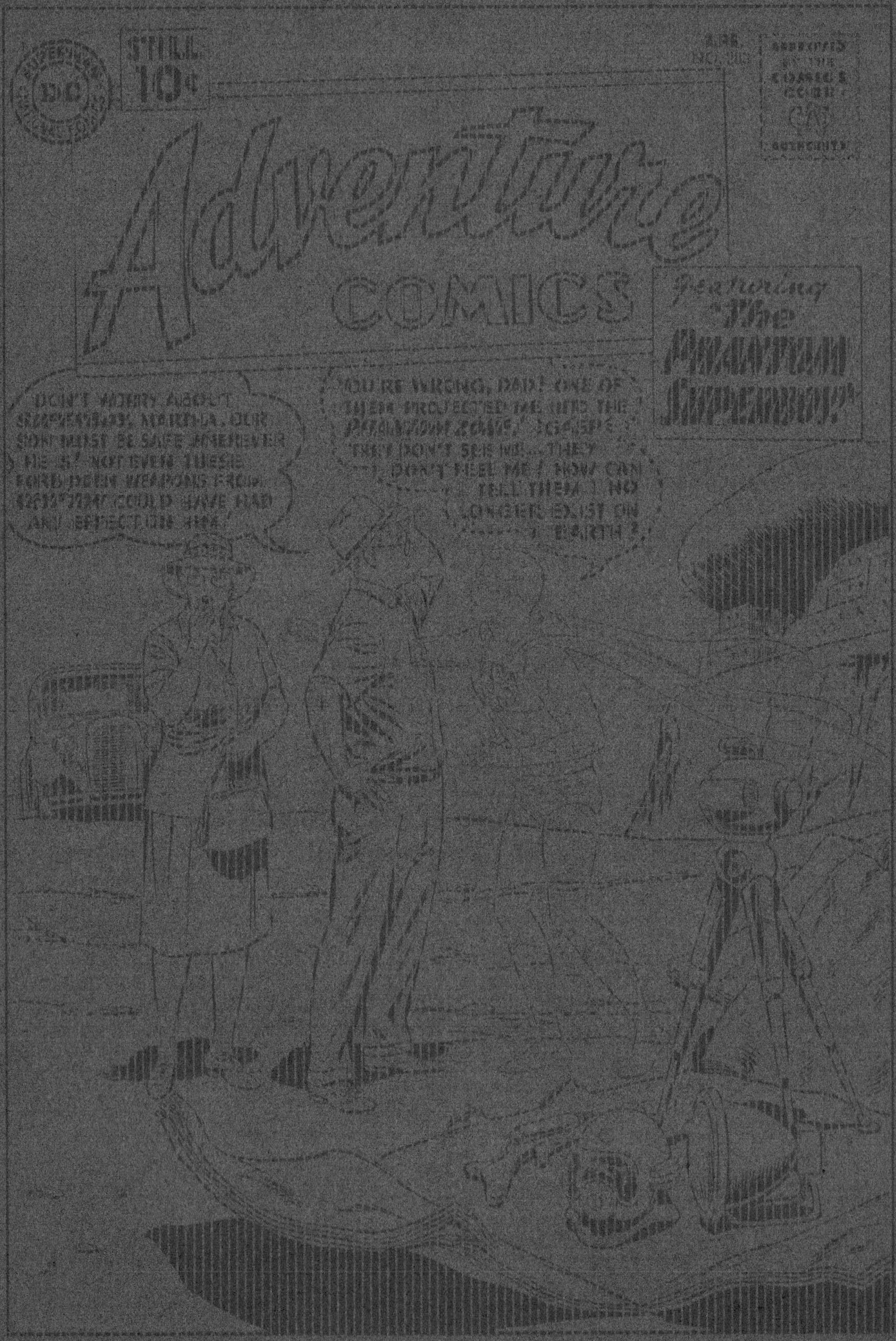

STILL 10¢
Adventure
COMICS
featuring
"The Phantom Superboy!"
DON'T WORRY ABOUT
YOU'RE WRONG, DAD! ONE OF
TELL THEM I NO
LONGER EXIST ON
EARTH?

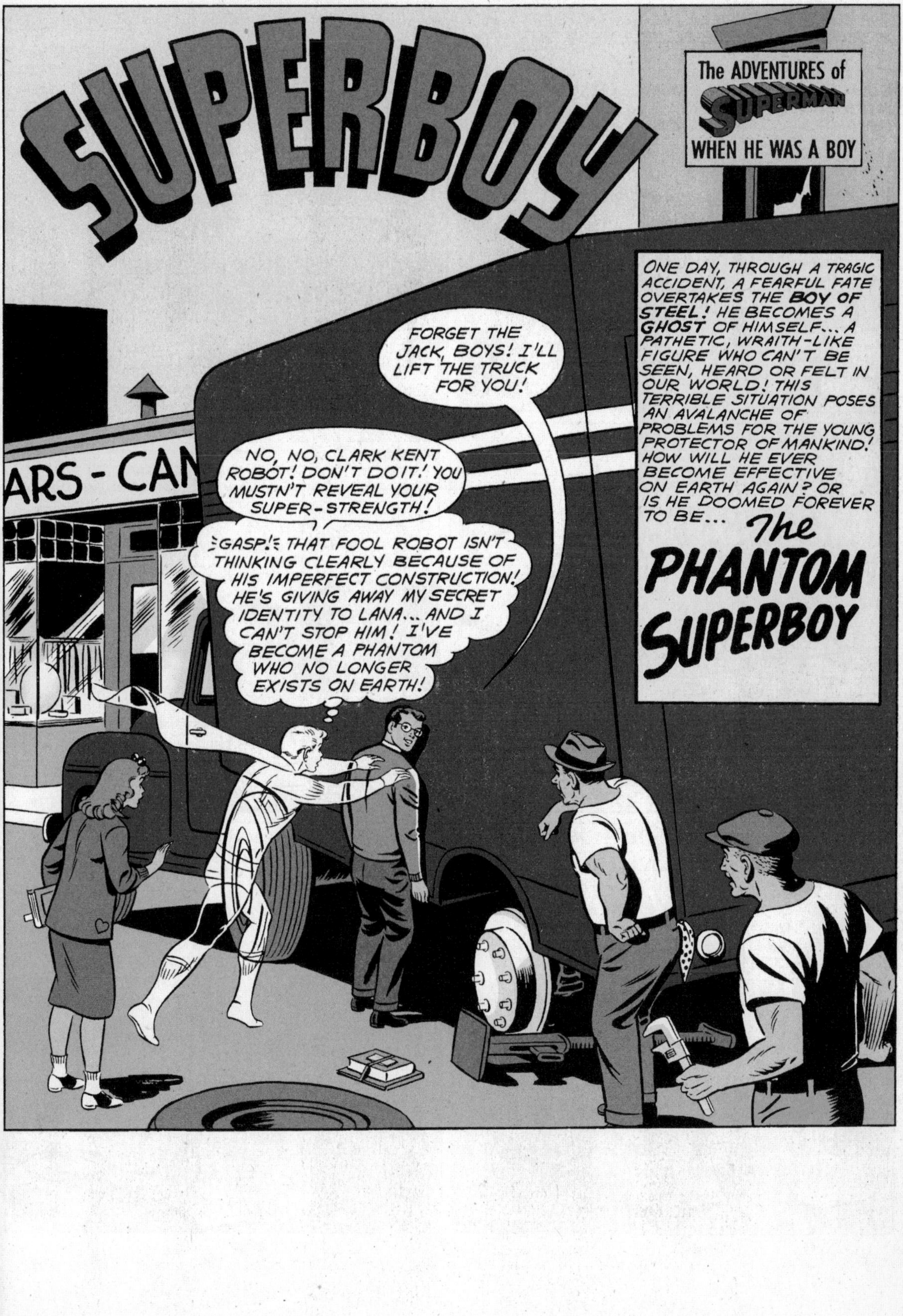
SUPERBOY
The ADVENTURES of SUPERMAN WHEN HE WAS A BOY
ONE DAY, THROUGH A TRAGIC ACCIDENT, A FEARFUL FATE OVERTAKES THE BOY OF STEEL! HE BECOMES A GHOST OF HIMSELF... A PATHETIC, WRAITH-LIKE FIGURE WHO CAN'T BE SEEN, HEARD OR FELT IN OUR WORLD! THIS TERRIBLE SITUATION POSES AN AVALANCHE OF PROBLEMS FOR THE YOUNG PROTECTOR OF MANKIND! HOW WILL HE EVER BECOME EFFECTIVE ON EARTH AGAIN? OR IS HE DOOMED FOREVER TO BE... The PHANTOM SUPERBOY
FORGET THE JACK, BOYS! I'LL LIFT THE TRUCK FOR YOU!
NO, NO, CLARK KENT ROBOT! DON'T DO IT! YOU MUSTN'T REVEAL YOUR SUPER-STRENGTH!
GASP! THAT FOOL ROBOT ISN'T THINKING CLEARLY BECAUSE OF HIS IMPERFECT CONSTRUCTION! HE'S GIVING AWAY MY SECRET IDENTITY TO LANA... AND I CAN'T STOP HIM! I'VE BECOME A PHANTOM WHO NO LONGER EXISTS ON EARTH!
ARS - CAN

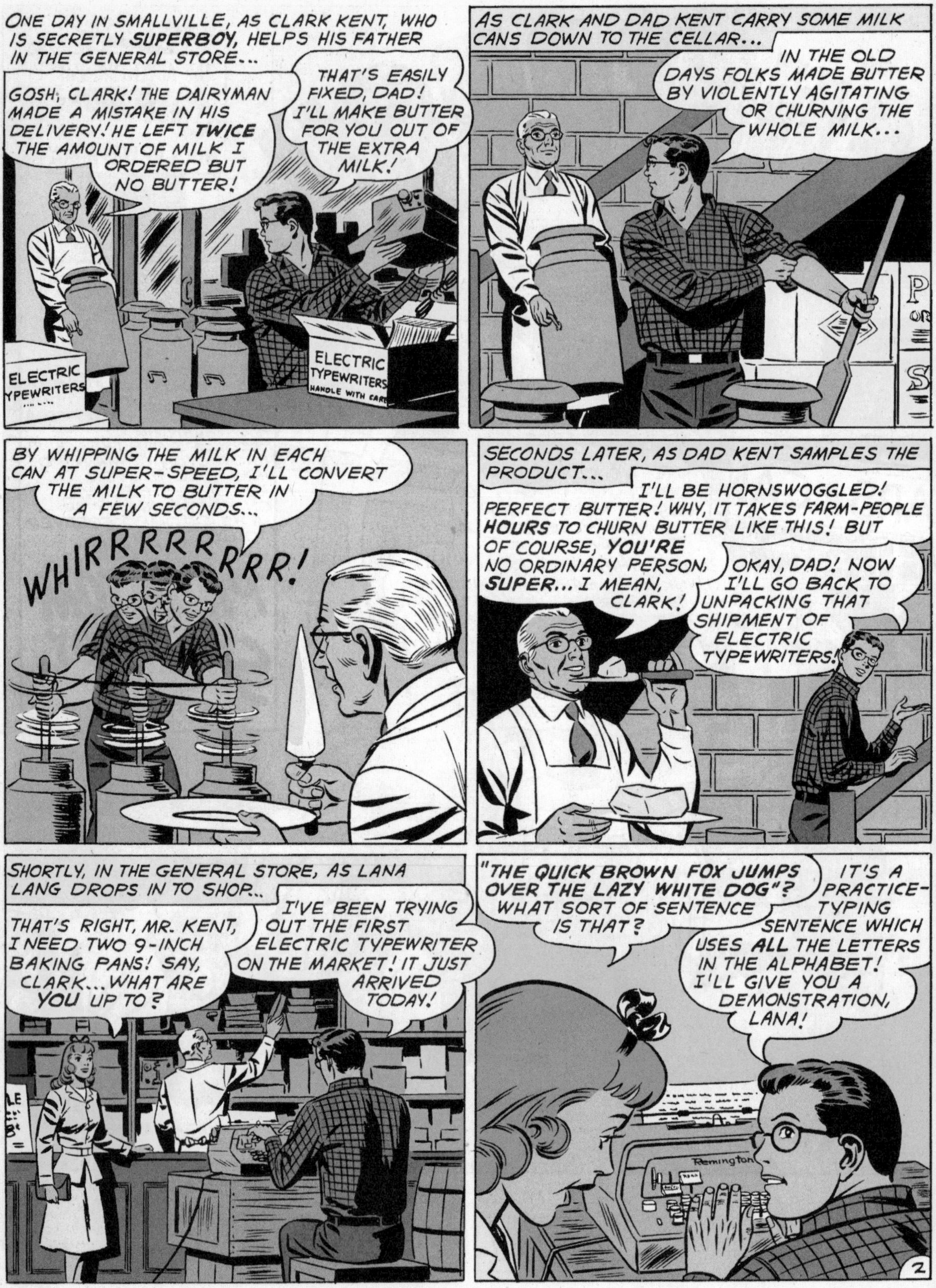

ONE DAY IN SMALLVILLE, AS CLARK KENT, WHO IS SECRETLY SUPERBOY, HELPS HIS FATHER IN THE GENERAL STORE...
GOSH, CLARK! THE DAIRYMAN MADE A MISTAKE IN HIS DELIVERY! HE LEFT TWICE THE AMOUNT OF MILK I ORDERED BUT NO BUTTER!
THAT'S EASILY FIXED, DAD! I'LL MAKE BUTTER FOR YOU OUT OF THE EXTRA MILK!
ELECTRIC TYPEWRITERS
ELECTRIC TYPEWRITERS HANDLE WITH CARE
AS CLARK AND DAD KENT CARRY SOME MILK CANS DOWN TO THE CELLAR...
IN THE OLD DAYS FOLKS MADE BUTTER BY VIOLENTLY AGITATING OR CHURNING THE WHOLE MILK...
BY WHIPPING THE MILK IN EACH CAN AT SUPER-SPEED, I'LL CONVERT THE MILK TO BUTTER IN A FEW SECONDS...
WHIRRRRRRRRR!
SECONDS LATER, AS DAD KENT SAMPLES THE PRODUCT...
I'LL BE HORNSWOGGLED! PERFECT BUTTER! WHY, IT TAKES FARM-PEOPLE HOURS TO CHURN BUTTER LIKE THIS! BUT OF COURSE, YOU'RE NO ORDINARY PERSON, SUPER... I MEAN, CLARK!
OKAY, DAD! NOW I'LL GO BACK TO UNPACKING THAT SHIPMENT OF ELECTRIC TYPEWRITERS!
SHORTLY, IN THE GENERAL STORE, AS LANA LANG DROPS IN TO SHOP...
THAT'S RIGHT, MR. KENT, I NEED TWO 9-INCH BAKING PANS! SAY, CLARK... WHAT ARE YOU UP TO?
I'VE BEEN TRYING OUT THE FIRST ELECTRIC TYPEWRITER ON THE MARKET! IT JUST ARRIVED TODAY!
"THE QUICK BROWN FOX JUMPS OVER THE LAZY WHITE DOG"? WHAT SORT OF SENTENCE IS THAT?
IT'S A PRACTICE-TYPING SENTENCE WHICH USES ALL THE LETTERS IN THE ALPHABET! I'LL GIVE YOU A DEMONSTRATION, LANA!
Remington
2

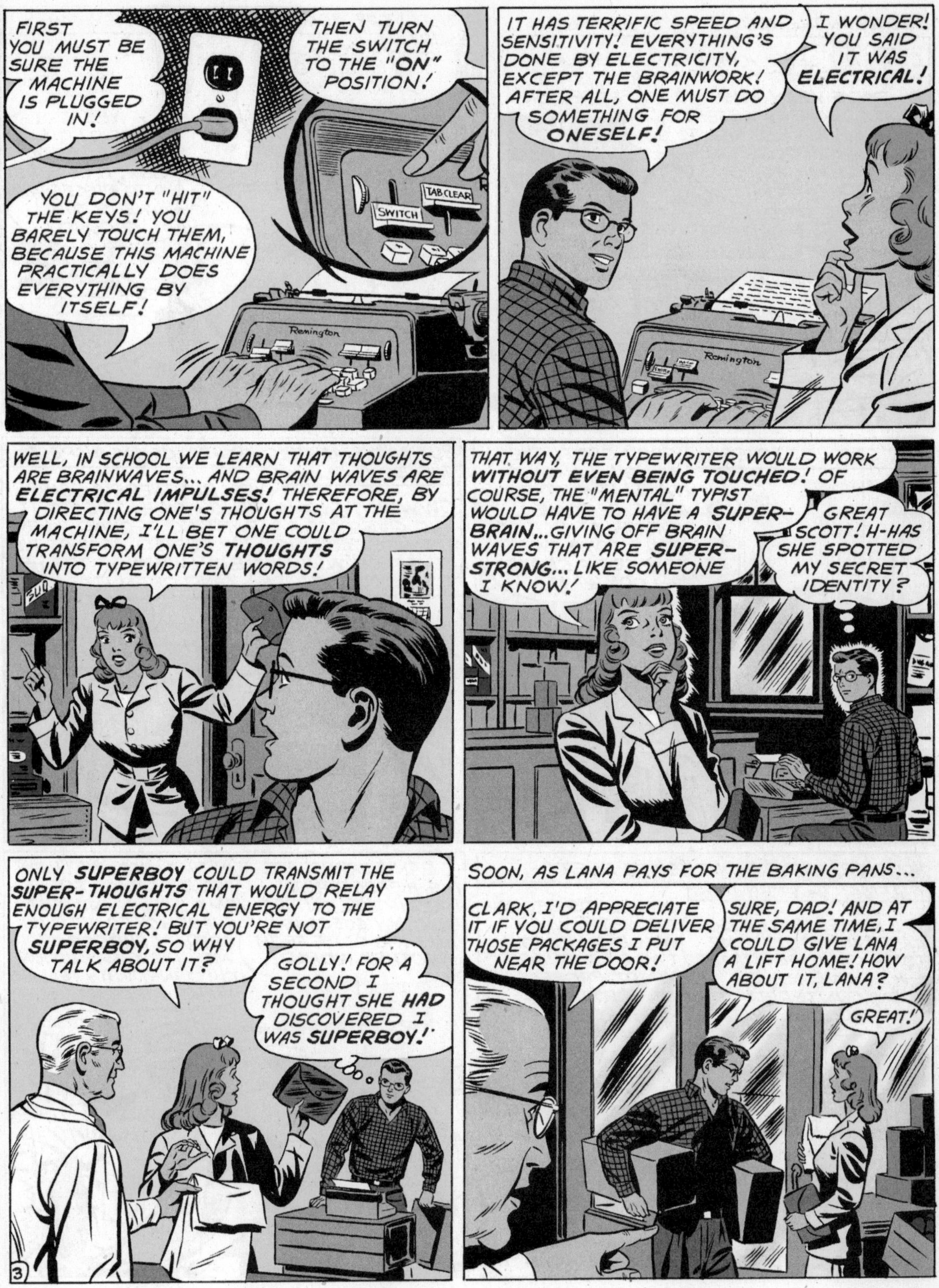
FIRST YOU MUST BE SURE THE MACHINE IS PLUGGED IN!
THEN TURN THE SWITCH TO THE "ON" POSITION!
TAB CLEAR
SWITCH
YOU DON'T "HIT" THE KEYS! YOU BARELY TOUCH THEM, BECAUSE THIS MACHINE PRACTICALLY DOES EVERYTHING BY ITSELF!
Remington
IT HAS TERRIFIC SPEED AND SENSITIVITY! EVERYTHING'S DONE BY ELECTRICITY, EXCEPT THE BRAINWORK! AFTER ALL, ONE MUST DO SOMETHING FOR ONESELF!
I WONDER! YOU SAID IT WAS ELECTRICAL!
Remington
WELL, IN SCHOOL WE LEARN THAT THOUGHTS ARE BRAINWAVES... AND BRAIN WAVES ARE ELECTRICAL IMPULSES! THEREFORE, BY DIRECTING ONE'S THOUGHTS AT THE MACHINE, I'LL BET ONE COULD TRANSFORM ONE'S THOUGHTS INTO TYPEWRITTEN WORDS!
THAT WAY, THE TYPEWRITER WOULD WORK WITHOUT EVEN BEING TOUCHED! OF COURSE, THE "MENTAL" TYPIST WOULD HAVE TO HAVE A SUPER-BRAIN...GIVING OFF BRAIN WAVES THAT ARE SUPER-STRONG... LIKE SOMEONE I KNOW!
GREAT SCOTT! H-HAS SHE SPOTTED MY SECRET IDENTITY?
ONLY SUPERBOY COULD TRANSMIT THE SUPER-THOUGHTS THAT WOULD RELAY ENOUGH ELECTRICAL ENERGY TO THE TYPEWRITER! BUT YOU'RE NOT SUPERBOY, SO WHY TALK ABOUT IT?
GOLLY! FOR A SECOND I THOUGHT SHE HAD DISCOVERED I WAS SUPERBOY!
3
SOON, AS LANA PAYS FOR THE BAKING PANS...
CLARK, I'D APPRECIATE IT IF YOU COULD DELIVER THOSE PACKAGES I PUT NEAR THE DOOR!
SURE, DAD! AND AT THE SAME TIME, I COULD GIVE LANA A LIFT HOME! HOW ABOUT IT, LANA?
GREAT!

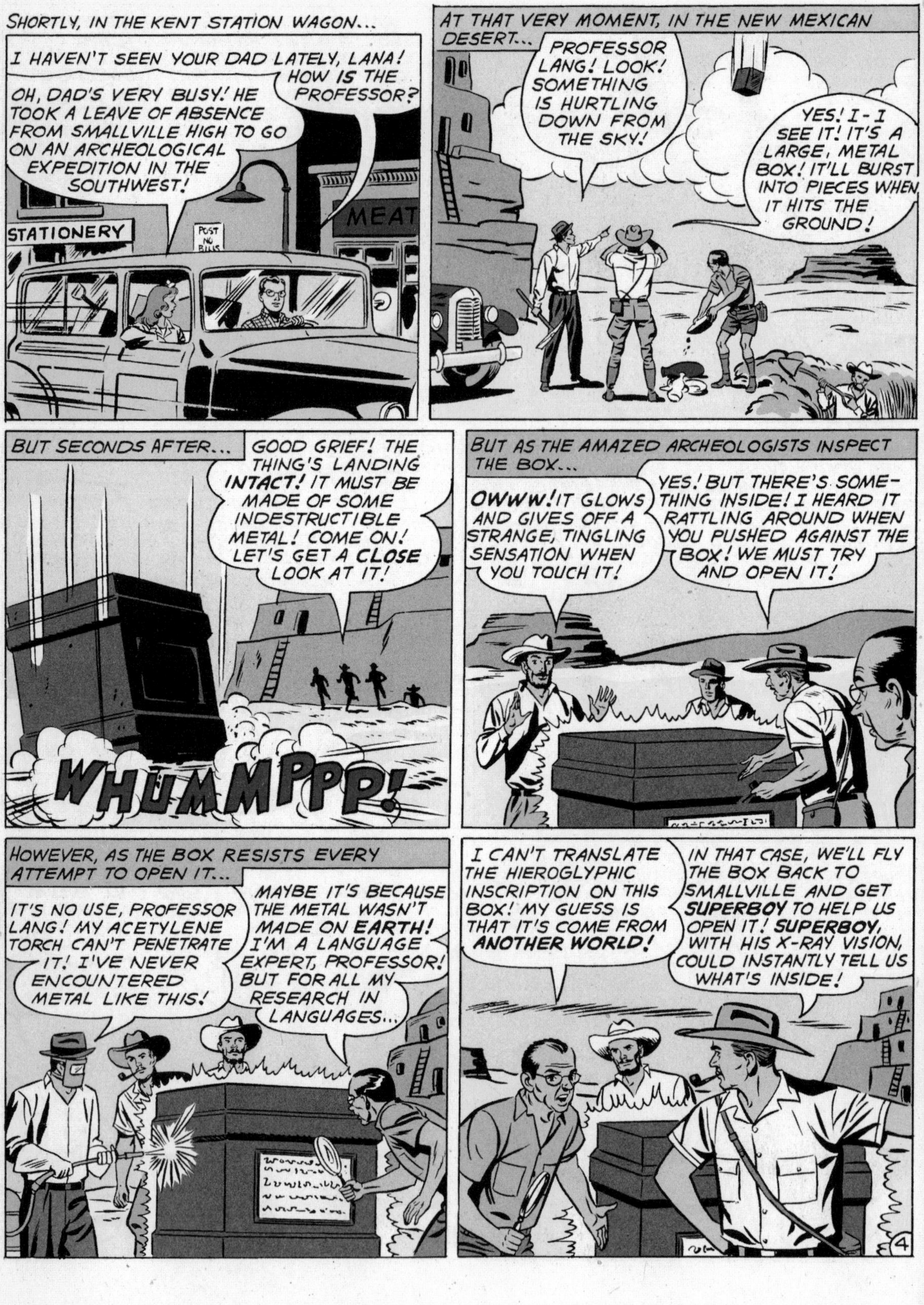
SHORTLY, IN THE KENT STATION WAGON...
I HAVEN'T SEEN YOUR DAD LATELY, LANA! HOW IS THE PROFESSOR?
OH, DAD'S VERY BUSY! HE TOOK A LEAVE OF ABSENCE FROM SMALLVILLE HIGH TO GO ON AN ARCHEOLOGICAL EXPEDITION IN THE SOUTHWEST!
STATIONERY
POST NO BILLS
MEAT
AT THAT VERY MOMENT, IN THE NEW MEXICAN DESERT...
PROFESSOR LANG! LOOK! SOMETHING IS HURTLING DOWN FROM THE SKY!
YES! I - I SEE IT! IT'S A LARGE, METAL BOX! IT'LL BURST INTO PIECES WHEN IT HITS THE GROUND!
BUT SECONDS AFTER...
GOOD GRIEF! THE THING'S LANDING INTACT! IT MUST BE MADE OF SOME INDESTRUCTIBLE METAL! COME ON! LET'S GET A CLOSE LOOK AT IT!
WHUMMPPP!
BUT AS THE AMAZED ARCHEOLOGISTS INSPECT THE BOX...
OWWW! IT GLOWS AND GIVES OFF A STRANGE, TINGLING SENSATION WHEN YOU TOUCH IT!
YES! BUT THERE'S SOMETHING INSIDE! I HEARD IT RATTLING AROUND WHEN YOU PUSHED AGAINST THE BOX! WE MUST TRY AND OPEN IT!
HOWEVER, AS THE BOX RESISTS EVERY ATTEMPT TO OPEN IT...
IT'S NO USE, PROFESSOR LANG! MY ACETYLENE TORCH CAN'T PENETRATE IT! I'VE NEVER ENCOUNTERED METAL LIKE THIS!
MAYBE IT'S BECAUSE THE METAL WASN'T MADE ON EARTH! I'M A LANGUAGE EXPERT, PROFESSOR! BUT FOR ALL MY RESEARCH IN LANGUAGES...
I CAN'T TRANSLATE THE HIEROGLYPHIC INSCRIPTION ON THIS BOX! MY GUESS IS THAT IT'S COME FROM ANOTHER WORLD!
IN THAT CASE, WE'LL FLY THE BOX BACK TO SMALLVILLE AND GET SUPERBOY TO HELP US OPEN IT! SUPERBOY, WITH HIS X-RAY VISION, COULD INSTANTLY TELL US WHAT'S INSIDE!
4

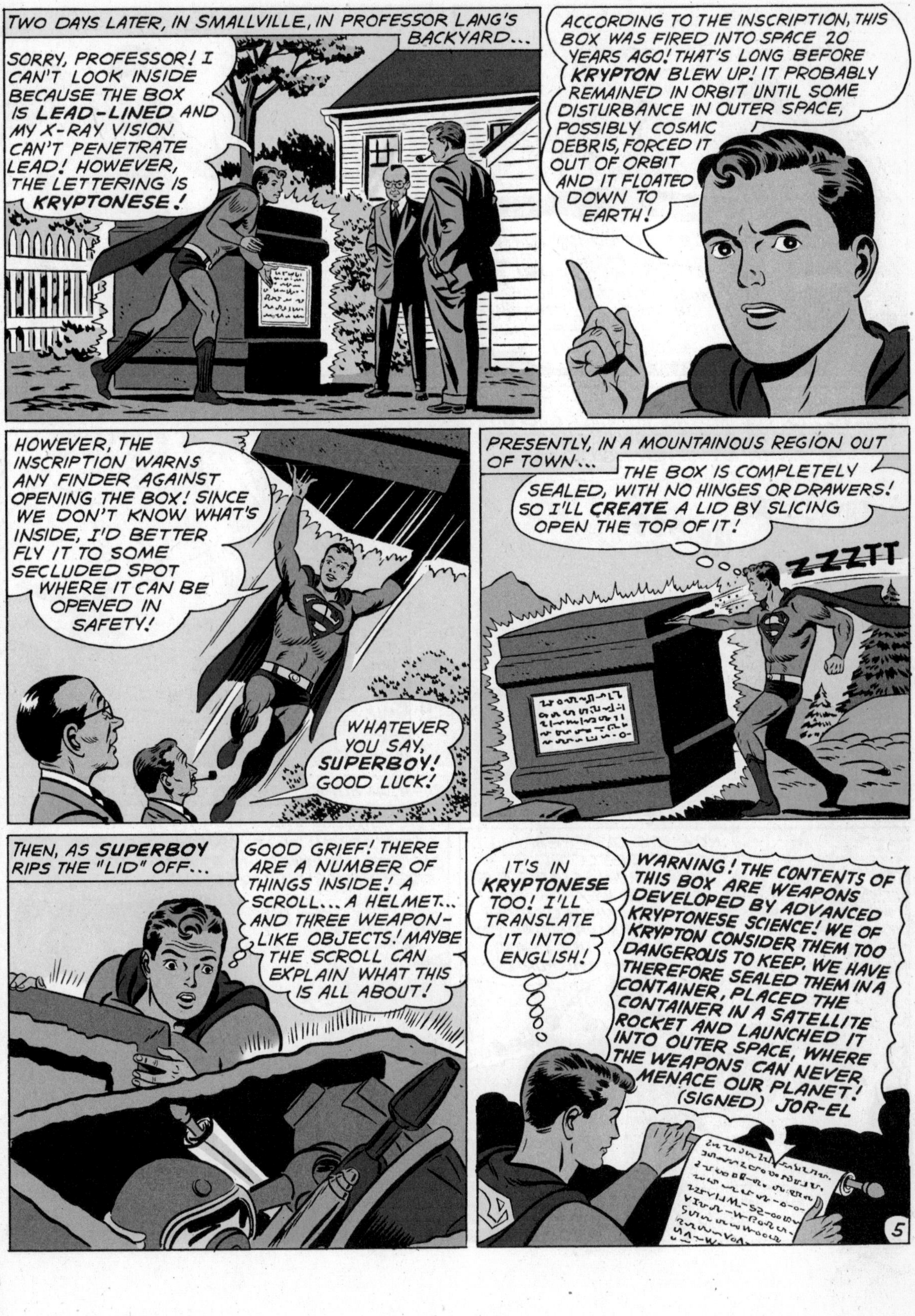

TWO DAYS LATER, IN SMALLVILLE, IN PROFESSOR LANG'S BACKYARD...
SORRY, PROFESSOR! I CAN'T LOOK INSIDE BECAUSE THE BOX IS LEAD-LINED AND MY X-RAY VISION CAN'T PENETRATE LEAD! HOWEVER, THE LETTERING IS KRYPTONESE!
ACCORDING TO THE INSCRIPTION, THIS BOX WAS FIRED INTO SPACE 20 YEARS AGO! THAT'S LONG BEFORE KRYPTON BLEW UP! IT PROBABLY REMAINED IN ORBIT UNTIL SOME DISTURBANCE IN OUTER SPACE, POSSIBLY COSMIC DEBRIS, FORCED IT OUT OF ORBIT AND IT FLOATED DOWN TO EARTH!
HOWEVER, THE INSCRIPTION WARNS ANY FINDER AGAINST OPENING THE BOX! SINCE WE DON'T KNOW WHAT'S INSIDE, I'D BETTER FLY IT TO SOME SECLUDED SPOT WHERE IT CAN BE OPENED IN SAFETY!
WHATEVER YOU SAY, SUPERBOY! GOOD LUCK!
PRESENTLY, IN A MOUNTAINOUS REGION OUT OF TOWN...
THE BOX IS COMPLETELY SEALED, WITH NO HINGES OR DRAWERS! SO I'LL CREATE A LID BY SLICING OPEN THE TOP OF IT!
ZZZTT
THEN, AS SUPERBOY RIPS THE "LID" OFF...
GOOD GRIEF! THERE ARE A NUMBER OF THINGS INSIDE! A SCROLL... A HELMET... AND THREE WEAPON-LIKE OBJECTS! MAYBE THE SCROLL CAN EXPLAIN WHAT THIS IS ALL ABOUT!
IT'S IN KRYPTONESE TOO! I'LL TRANSLATE IT INTO ENGLISH!
WARNING! THE CONTENTS OF THIS BOX ARE WEAPONS DEVELOPED BY ADVANCED KRYPTONESE SCIENCE! WE OF KRYPTON CONSIDER THEM TOO DANGEROUS TO KEEP. WE HAVE THEREFORE SEALED THEM IN A CONTAINER, PLACED THE CONTAINER IN A SATELLITE ROCKET AND LAUNCHED IT INTO OUTER SPACE, WHERE THE WEAPONS CAN NEVER MENACE OUR PLANET! (SIGNED) JOR-EL
5

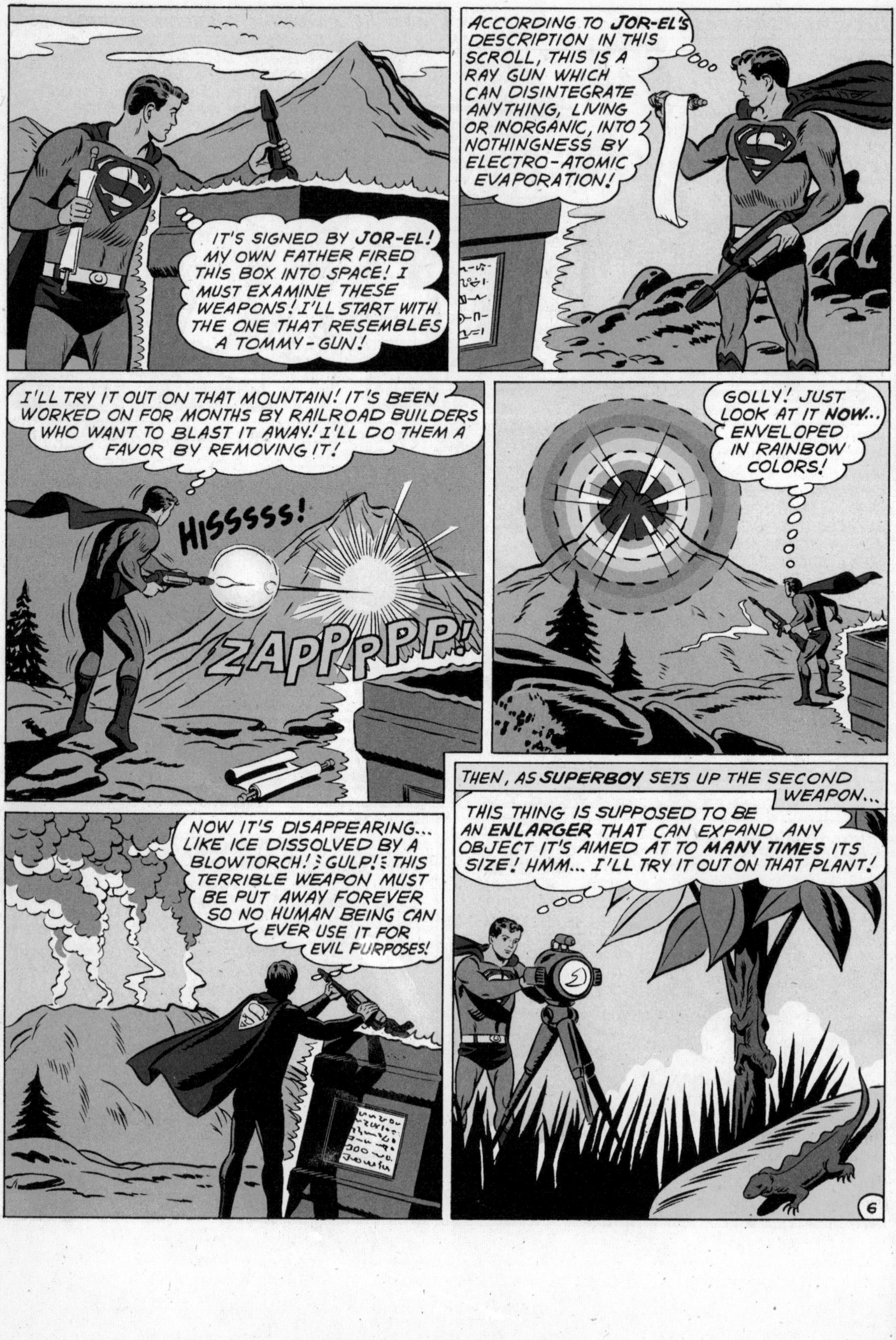
IT'S SIGNED BY JOR-EL! MY OWN FATHER FIRED THIS BOX INTO SPACE! I MUST EXAMINE THESE WEAPONS! I'LL START WITH THE ONE THAT RESEMBLES A TOMMY-GUN!
ACCORDING TO JOR-EL'S DESCRIPTION IN THIS SCROLL, THIS IS A RAY GUN WHICH CAN DISINTEGRATE ANYTHING, LIVING OR INORGANIC, INTO NOTHINGNESS BY ELECTRO-ATOMIC EVAPORATION!
I'LL TRY IT OUT ON THAT MOUNTAIN! IT'S BEEN WORKED ON FOR MONTHS BY RAILROAD BUILDERS WHO WANT TO BLAST IT AWAY! I'LL DO THEM A FAVOR BY REMOVING IT!
HISSSSS!
ZAPPPPPP!
GOLLY! JUST LOOK AT IT NOW... ENVELOPED IN RAINBOW COLORS!
NOW IT'S DISAPPEARING... LIKE ICE DISSOLVED BY A BLOWTORCH! GULP! THIS TERRIBLE WEAPON MUST BE PUT AWAY FOREVER SO NO HUMAN BEING CAN EVER USE IT FOR EVIL PURPOSES!
THEN, AS SUPERBOY SETS UP THE SECOND WEAPON...
THIS THING IS SUPPOSED TO BE AN ENLARGER THAT CAN EXPAND ANY OBJECT IT'S AIMED AT TO MANY TIMES ITS SIZE! HMM... I'LL TRY IT OUT ON THAT PLANT!
6

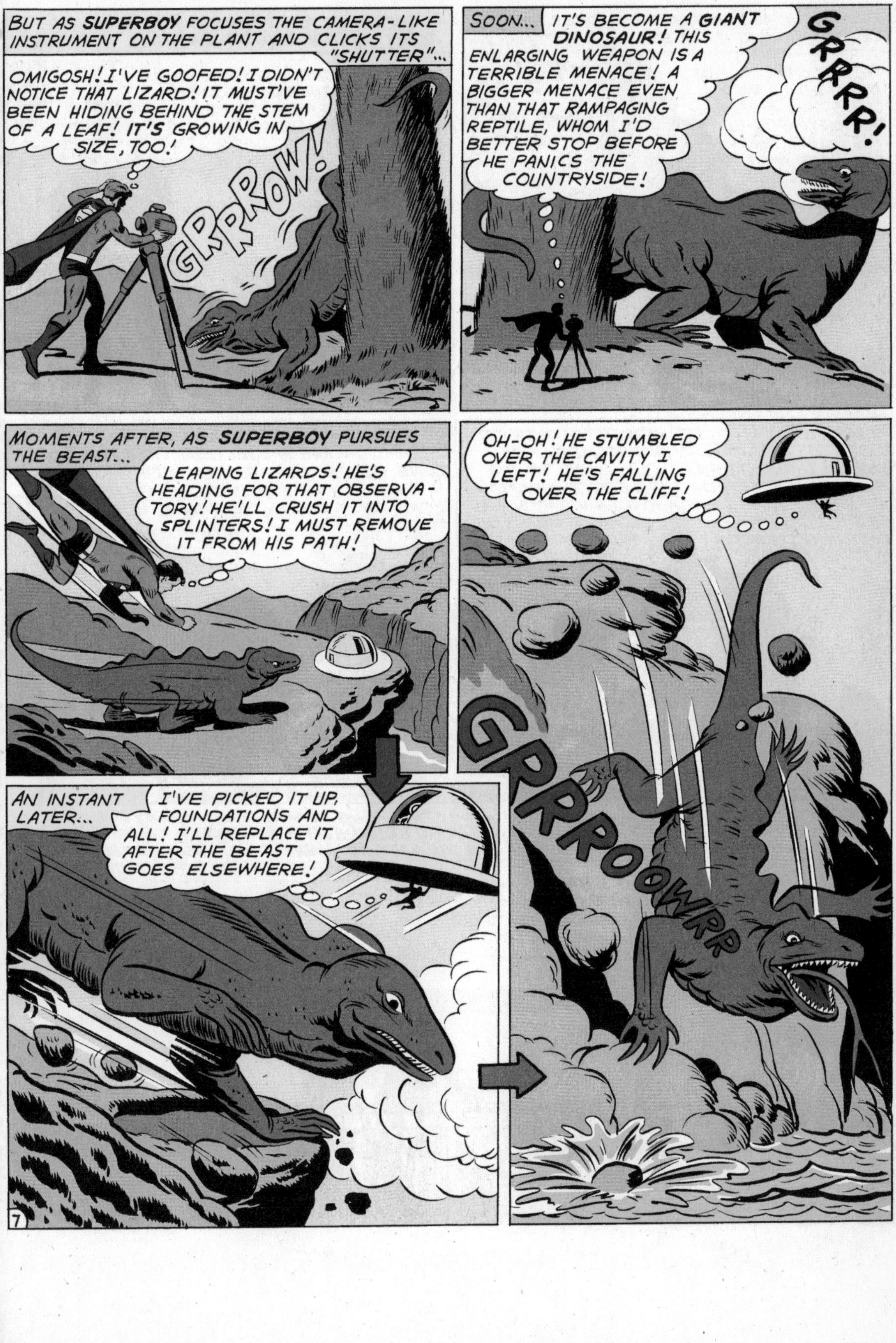

BUT AS SUPERBOY FOCUSES THE CAMERA-LIKE INSTRUMENT ON THE PLANT AND CLICKS ITS "SHUTTER"...
OMIGOSH! I'VE GOOFED! I DIDN'T NOTICE THAT LIZARD! IT MUST'VE BEEN HIDING BEHIND THE STEM OF A LEAF! IT'S GROWING IN SIZE, TOO!
GRRROW!
SOON...
IT'S BECOME A GIANT DINOSAUR! THIS ENLARGING WEAPON IS A TERRIBLE MENACE! A BIGGER MENACE EVEN THAN THAT RAMPAGING REPTILE, WHOM I'D BETTER STOP BEFORE HE PANICS THE COUNTRYSIDE!
GRRRR!
MOMENTS AFTER, AS SUPERBOY PURSUES THE BEAST...
LEAPING LIZARDS! HE'S HEADING FOR THAT OBSERVATORY! HE'LL CRUSH IT INTO SPLINTERS! I MUST REMOVE IT FROM HIS PATH!
AN INSTANT LATER...
I'VE PICKED IT UP, FOUNDATIONS AND ALL! I'LL REPLACE IT AFTER THE BEAST GOES ELSEWHERE!
7
OH-OH! HE STUMBLED OVER THE CAVITY I LEFT! HE'S FALLING OVER THE CLIFF!
GRRROOWRR

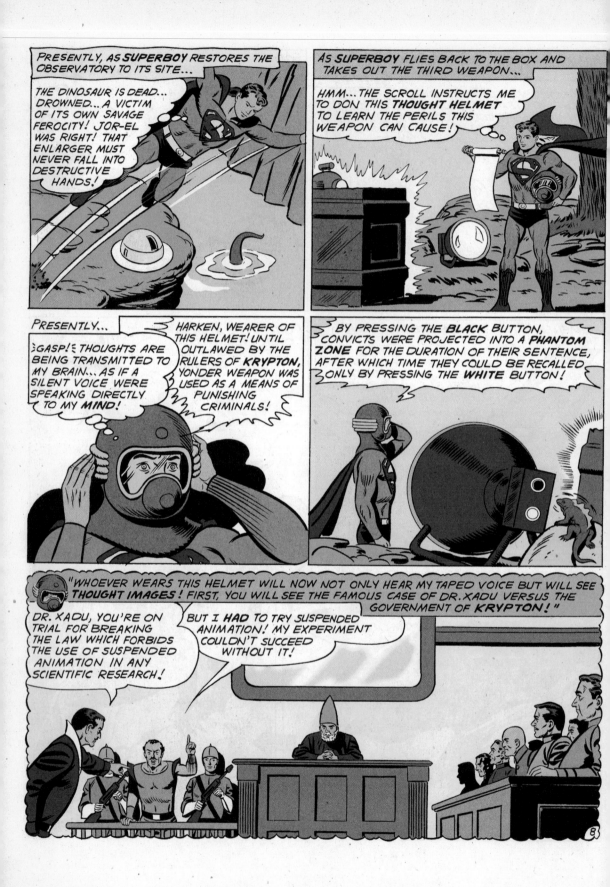

PRESENTLY, AS **SUPERBOY** RESTORES THE OBSERVATORY TO ITS SITE...

THE DINOSAUR IS DEAD... DROWNED... A VICTIM OF ITS OWN SAVAGE FEROCITY! JOR-EL WAS RIGHT! THAT ENLARGER MUST NEVER FALL INTO DESTRUCTIVE HANDS!

AS **SUPERBOY** FLIES BACK TO THE BOX AND TAKES OUT THE THIRD WEAPON...

HMM... THE SCROLL INSTRUCTS ME TO DON THIS **THOUGHT HELMET** TO LEARN THE PERILS THIS WEAPON CAN CAUSE!

PRESENTLY...

GASP! THOUGHTS ARE BEING TRANSMITTED TO MY BRAIN... AS IF A SILENT VOICE WERE SPEAKING DIRECTLY TO MY **MIND**!

HARKEN, WEARER OF THIS HELMET! UNTIL OUTLAWED BY THE RULERS OF **KRYPTON**, YONDER WEAPON WAS USED AS A MEANS OF PUNISHING CRIMINALS!

BY PRESSING THE **BLACK** BUTTON, CONVICTS WERE PROJECTED INTO A **PHANTOM ZONE** FOR THE DURATION OF THEIR SENTENCE, AFTER WHICH TIME THEY COULD BE RECALLED ONLY BY PRESSING THE **WHITE** BUTTON!

"WHOEVER WEARS THIS HELMET WILL NOW NOT ONLY HEAR MY TAPED VOICE BUT WILL SEE **THOUGHT IMAGES**! FIRST, YOU WILL SEE THE FAMOUS CASE OF DR. XADU VERSUS THE GOVERNMENT OF **KRYPTON**!"

DR. XADU, YOU'RE ON TRIAL FOR BREAKING THE LAW WHICH FORBIDS THE USE OF SUSPENDED ANIMATION IN ANY SCIENTIFIC RESEARCH!

BUT I **HAD** TO TRY SUSPENDED ANIMATION! MY EXPERIMENT COULDN'T SUCCEED WITHOUT IT!

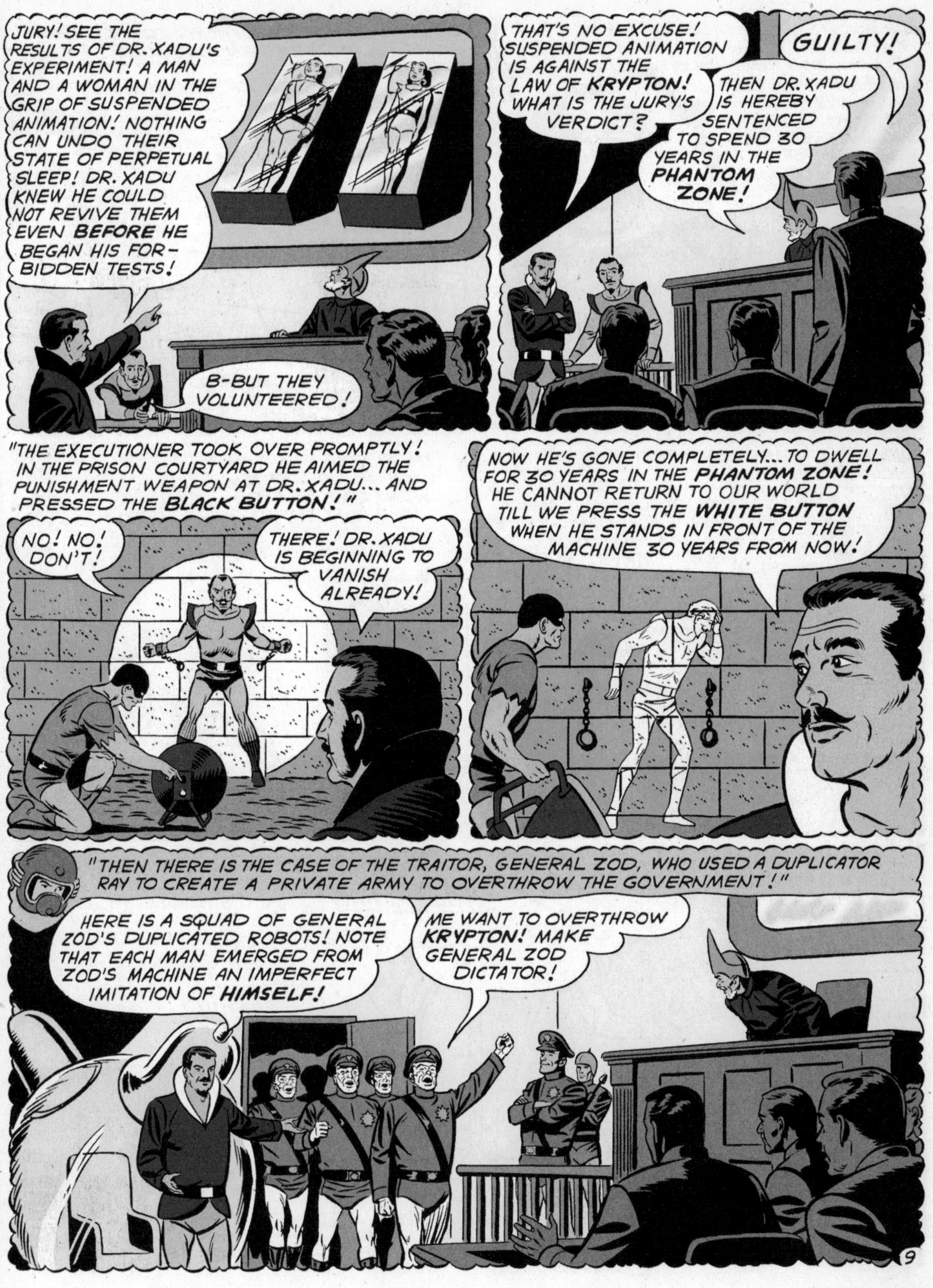
JURY! SEE THE RESULTS OF DR. XADU'S EXPERIMENT! A MAN AND A WOMAN IN THE GRIP OF SUSPENDED ANIMATION! NOTHING CAN UNDO THEIR STATE OF PERPETUAL SLEEP! DR. XADU KNEW HE COULD NOT REVIVE THEM EVEN BEFORE HE BEGAN HIS FOR-BIDDEN TESTS!
B-BUT THEY VOLUNTEERED!
THAT'S NO EXCUSE! SUSPENDED ANIMATION IS AGAINST THE LAW OF KRYPTON! WHAT IS THE JURY'S VERDICT?
GUILTY!
THEN DR. XADU IS HEREBY SENTENCED TO SPEND 30 YEARS IN THE PHANTOM ZONE!
"THE EXECUTIONER TOOK OVER PROMPTLY! IN THE PRISON COURTYARD HE AIMED THE PUNISHMENT WEAPON AT DR. XADU... AND PRESSED THE BLACK BUTTON!"
NO! NO! DON'T!
THERE! DR. XADU IS BEGINNING TO VANISH ALREADY!
NOW HE'S GONE COMPLETELY... TO DWELL FOR 30 YEARS IN THE PHANTOM ZONE! HE CANNOT RETURN TO OUR WORLD TILL WE PRESS THE WHITE BUTTON WHEN HE STANDS IN FRONT OF THE MACHINE 30 YEARS FROM NOW!
"THEN THERE IS THE CASE OF THE TRAITOR, GENERAL ZOD, WHO USED A DUPLICATOR RAY TO CREATE A PRIVATE ARMY TO OVERTHROW THE GOVERNMENT!"
HERE IS A SQUAD OF GENERAL ZOD'S DUPLICATED ROBOTS! NOTE THAT EACH MAN EMERGED FROM ZOD'S MACHINE AN IMPERFECT IMITATION OF HIMSELF!
ME WANT TO OVERTHROW KRYPTON! MAKE GENERAL ZOD DICTATOR!
9

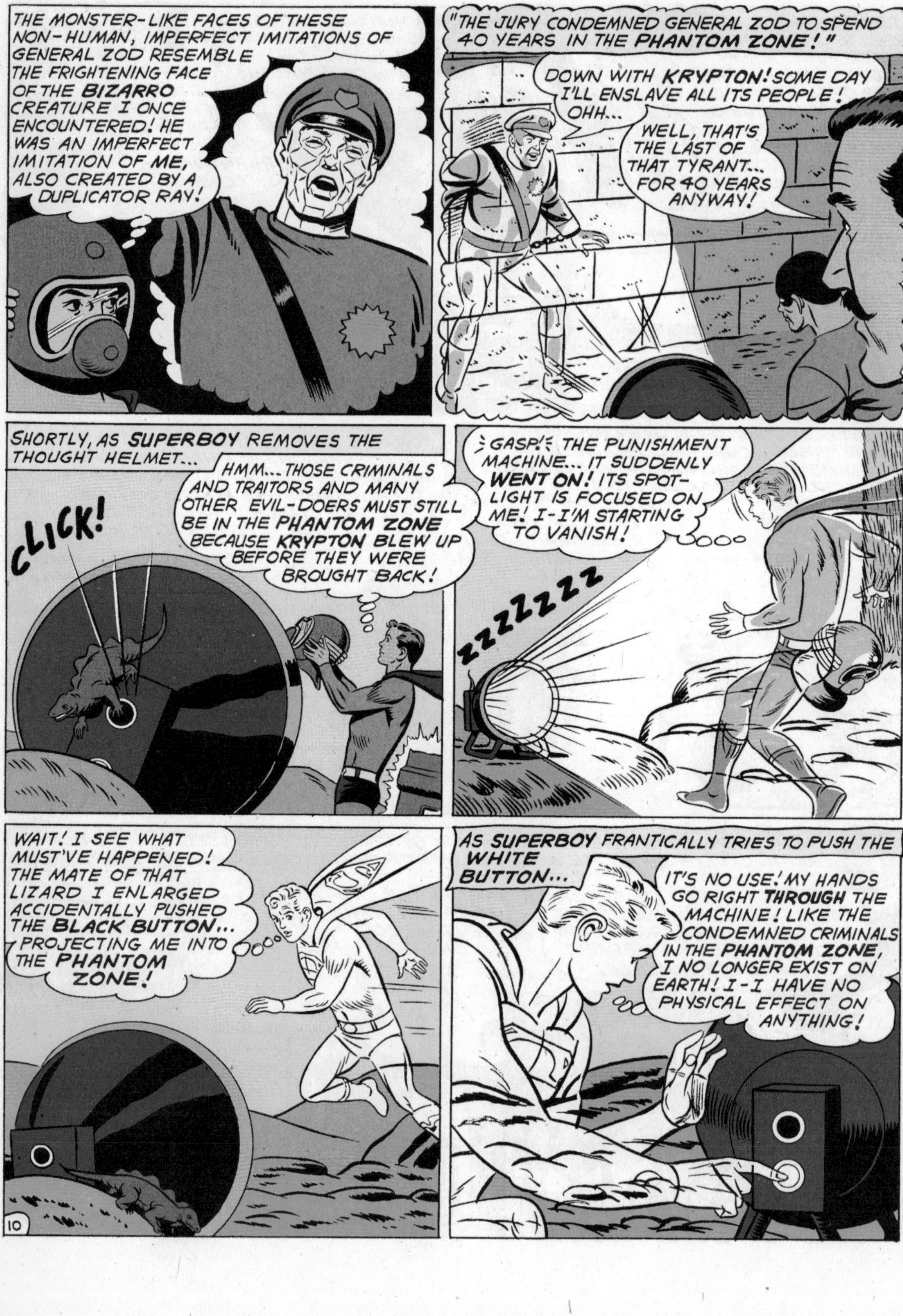
THE MONSTER-LIKE FACES OF THESE NON-HUMAN, IMPERFECT IMITATIONS OF GENERAL ZOD RESEMBLE THE FRIGHTENING FACE OF THE BIZARRO CREATURE I ONCE ENCOUNTERED! HE WAS AN IMPERFECT IMITATION OF ME, ALSO CREATED BY A DUPLICATOR RAY!
"THE JURY CONDEMNED GENERAL ZOD TO SPEND 40 YEARS IN THE PHANTOM ZONE!"
DOWN WITH KRYPTON! SOME DAY I'LL ENSLAVE ALL ITS PEOPLE! OHH...
WELL, THAT'S THE LAST OF THAT TYRANT... FOR 40 YEARS ANYWAY!
SHORTLY, AS SUPERBOY REMOVES THE THOUGHT HELMET...
HMM... THOSE CRIMINALS AND TRAITORS AND MANY OTHER EVIL-DOERS MUST STILL BE IN THE PHANTOM ZONE BECAUSE KRYPTON BLEW UP BEFORE THEY WERE BROUGHT BACK!
CLICK!
GASP! THE PUNISHMENT MACHINE... IT SUDDENLY WENT ON! ITS SPOT-LIGHT IS FOCUSED ON ME! I-I'M STARTING TO VANISH!
ZZZZZZZ
WAIT! I SEE WHAT MUST'VE HAPPENED! THE MATE OF THAT LIZARD I ENLARGED ACCIDENTALLY PUSHED THE BLACK BUTTON... PROJECTING ME INTO THE PHANTOM ZONE!
AS SUPERBOY FRANTICALLY TRIES TO PUSH THE WHITE BUTTON...
IT'S NO USE! MY HANDS GO RIGHT THROUGH THE MACHINE! LIKE THE CONDEMNED CRIMINALS IN THE PHANTOM ZONE, I NO LONGER EXIST ON EARTH! I-I HAVE NO PHYSICAL EFFECT ON ANYTHING!
10

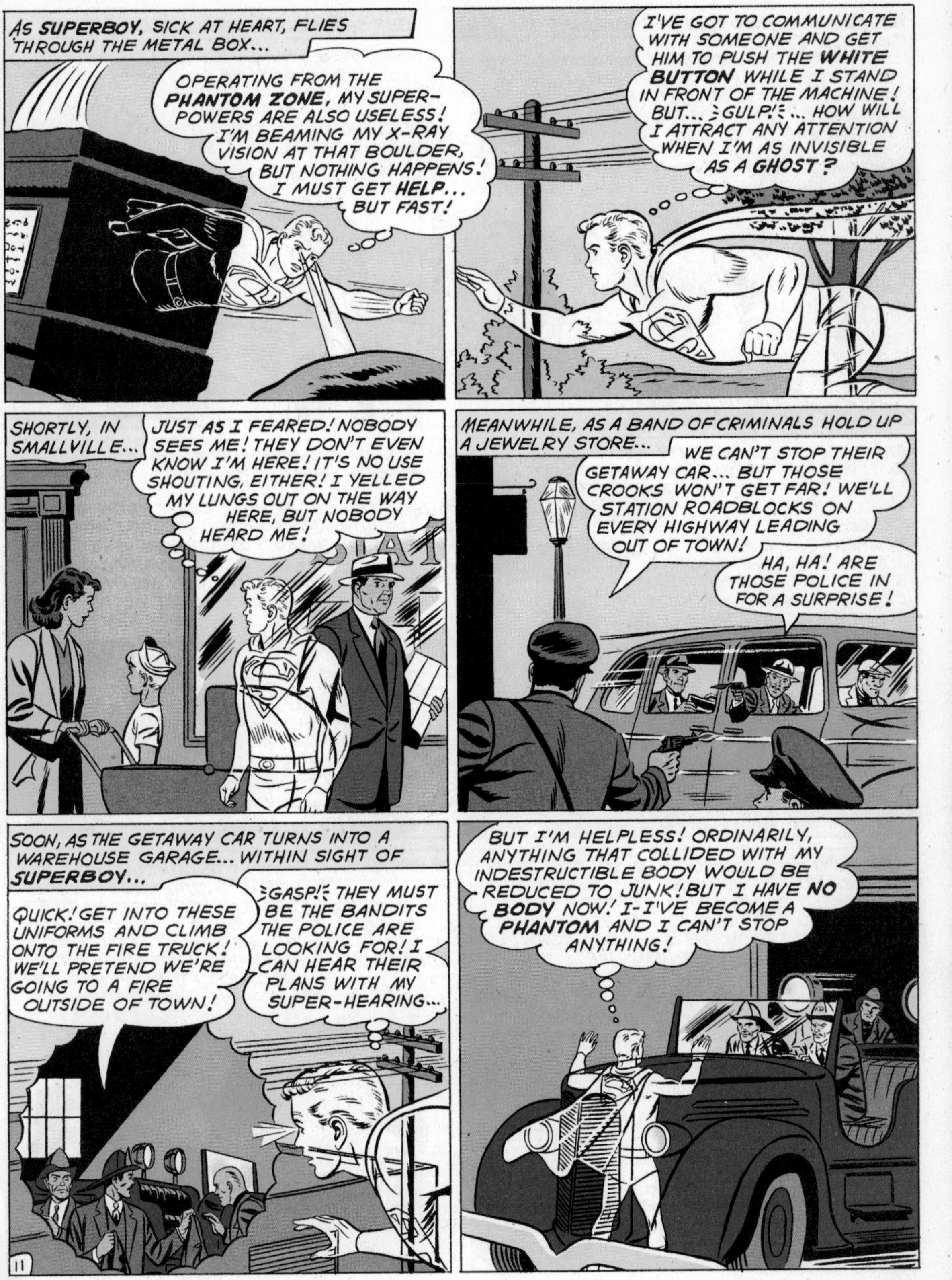
AS SUPERBOY, SICK AT HEART, FLIES THROUGH THE METAL BOX...
OPERATING FROM THE PHANTOM ZONE, MY SUPER-POWERS ARE ALSO USELESS! I'M BEAMING MY X-RAY VISION AT THAT BOULDER, BUT NOTHING HAPPENS! I MUST GET HELP... BUT FAST!
I'VE GOT TO COMMUNICATE WITH SOMEONE AND GET HIM TO PUSH THE WHITE BUTTON WHILE I STAND IN FRONT OF THE MACHINE! BUT... GULP! ... HOW WILL I ATTRACT ANY ATTENTION WHEN I'M AS INVISIBLE AS A GHOST?
SHORTLY, IN SMALLVILLE...
JUST AS I FEARED! NOBODY SEES ME! THEY DON'T EVEN KNOW I'M HERE! IT'S NO USE SHOUTING, EITHER! I YELLED MY LUNGS OUT ON THE WAY HERE, BUT NOBODY HEARD ME!
MEANWHILE, AS A BAND OF CRIMINALS HOLD UP A JEWELRY STORE...
WE CAN'T STOP THEIR GETAWAY CAR... BUT THOSE CROOKS WON'T GET FAR! WE'LL STATION ROADBLOCKS ON EVERY HIGHWAY LEADING OUT OF TOWN!
HA, HA! ARE THOSE POLICE IN FOR A SURPRISE!
SOON, AS THE GETAWAY CAR TURNS INTO A WAREHOUSE GARAGE... WITHIN SIGHT OF SUPERBOY...
QUICK! GET INTO THESE UNIFORMS AND CLIMB ONTO THE FIRE TRUCK! WE'LL PRETEND WE'RE GOING TO A FIRE OUTSIDE OF TOWN!
GASP! THEY MUST BE THE BANDITS THE POLICE ARE LOOKING FOR! I CAN HEAR THEIR PLANS WITH MY SUPER-HEARING...
11
BUT I'M HELPLESS! ORDINARILY, ANYTHING THAT COLLIDED WITH MY INDESTRUCTIBLE BODY WOULD BE REDUCED TO JUNK! BUT I HAVE NO BODY NOW! I-I'VE BECOME A PHANTOM AND I CAN'T STOP ANYTHING!

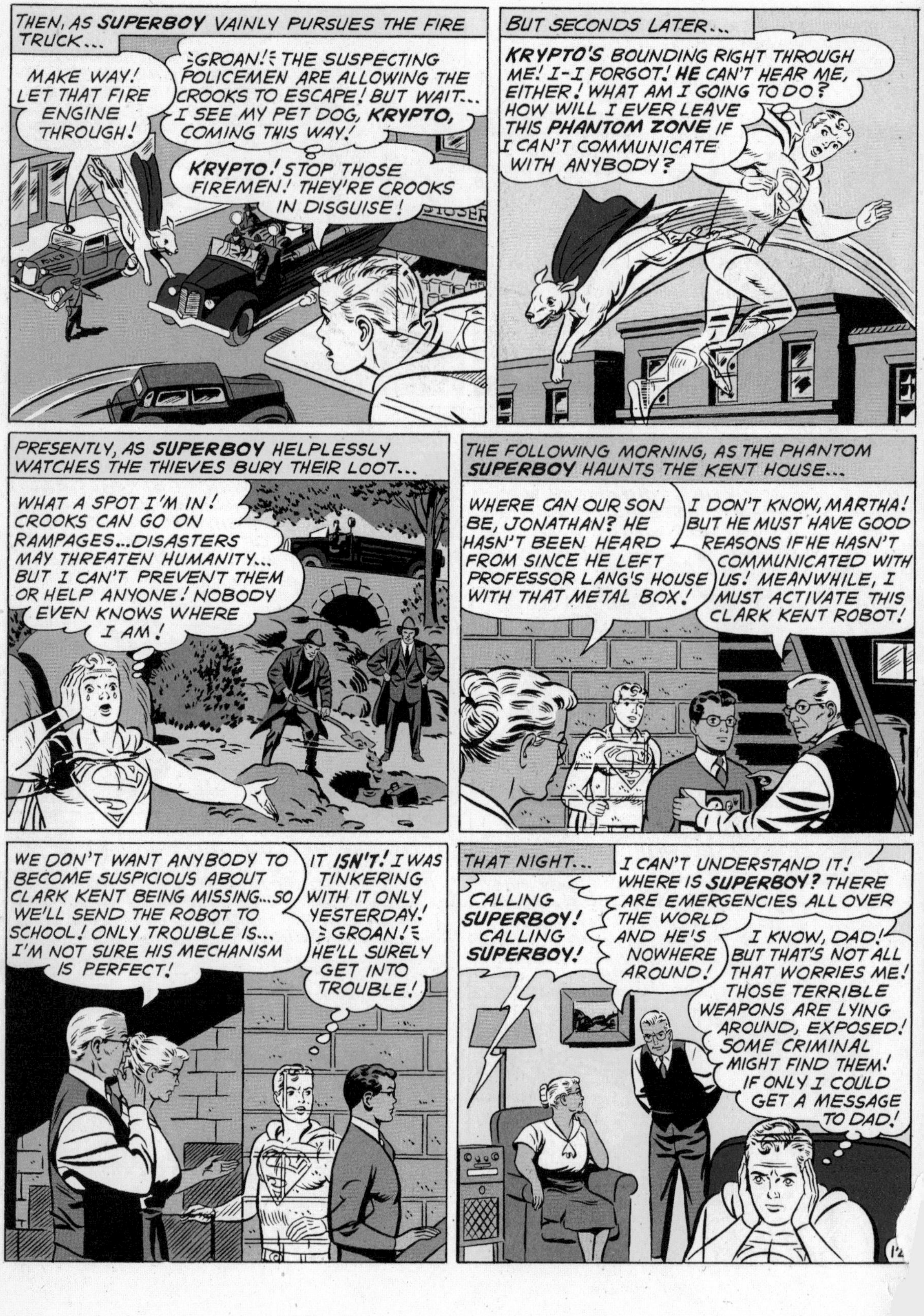
THEN, AS SUPERBOY VAINLY PURSUES THE FIRE TRUCK...
MAKE WAY! LET THAT FIRE ENGINE THROUGH!
GROAN! THE SUSPECTING POLICEMEN ARE ALLOWING THE CROOKS TO ESCAPE! BUT WAIT... I SEE MY PET DOG, KRYPTO, COMING THIS WAY!
KRYPTO! STOP THOSE FIREMEN! THEY'RE CROOKS IN DISGUISE!
BUT SECONDS LATER...
KRYPTO'S BOUNDING RIGHT THROUGH ME! I-I FORGOT! HE CAN'T HEAR ME, EITHER! WHAT AM I GOING TO DO? HOW WILL I EVER LEAVE THIS PHANTOM ZONE IF I CAN'T COMMUNICATE WITH ANYBODY?
PRESENTLY, AS SUPERBOY HELPLESSLY WATCHES THE THIEVES BURY THEIR LOOT...
WHAT A SPOT I'M IN! CROOKS CAN GO ON RAMPAGES...DISASTERS MAY THREATEN HUMANITY... BUT I CAN'T PREVENT THEM OR HELP ANYONE! NOBODY EVEN KNOWS WHERE I AM!
THE FOLLOWING MORNING, AS THE PHANTOM SUPERBOY HAUNTS THE KENT HOUSE...
WHERE CAN OUR SON BE, JONATHAN? HE HASN'T BEEN HEARD FROM SINCE HE LEFT PROFESSOR LANG'S HOUSE WITH THAT METAL BOX!
I DON'T KNOW, MARTHA! BUT HE MUST HAVE GOOD REASONS IF HE HASN'T COMMUNICATED WITH US! MEANWHILE, I MUST ACTIVATE THIS CLARK KENT ROBOT!
WE DON'T WANT ANYBODY TO BECOME SUSPICIOUS ABOUT CLARK KENT BEING MISSING...SO WE'LL SEND THE ROBOT TO SCHOOL! ONLY TROUBLE IS... I'M NOT SURE HIS MECHANISM IS PERFECT!
IT ISN'T! I WAS TINKERING WITH IT ONLY YESTERDAY! GROAN! HE'LL SURELY GET INTO TROUBLE!
THAT NIGHT...
CALLING SUPERBOY! CALLING SUPERBOY!
I CAN'T UNDERSTAND IT! WHERE IS SUPERBOY? THERE ARE EMERGENCIES ALL OVER THE WORLD AND HE'S NOWHERE AROUND!
I KNOW, DAD! BUT THAT'S NOT ALL THAT WORRIES ME! THOSE TERRIBLE WEAPONS ARE LYING AROUND, EXPOSED! SOME CRIMINAL MIGHT FIND THEM! IF ONLY I COULD GET A MESSAGE TO DAD!

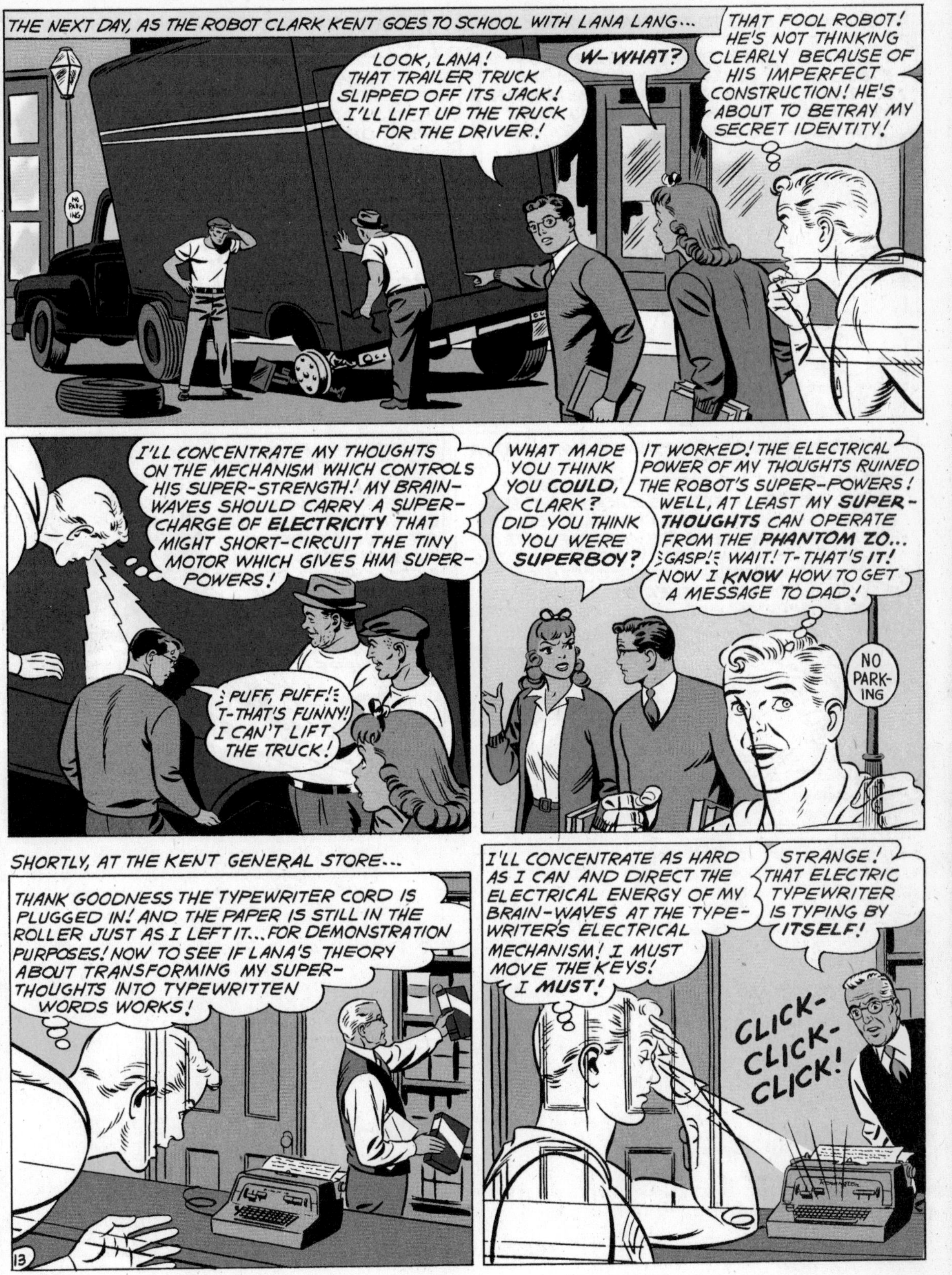
THE NEXT DAY, AS THE ROBOT CLARK KENT GOES TO SCHOOL WITH LANA LANG...
LOOK, LANA! THAT TRAILER TRUCK SLIPPED OFF ITS JACK! I'LL LIFT UP THE TRUCK FOR THE DRIVER!
W-WHAT?
THAT FOOL ROBOT! HE'S NOT THINKING CLEARLY BECAUSE OF HIS IMPERFECT CONSTRUCTION! HE'S ABOUT TO BETRAY MY SECRET IDENTITY!
I'LL CONCENTRATE MY THOUGHTS ON THE MECHANISM WHICH CONTROLS HIS SUPER-STRENGTH! MY BRAIN-WAVES SHOULD CARRY A SUPER-CHARGE OF ELECTRICITY THAT MIGHT SHORT-CIRCUIT THE TINY MOTOR WHICH GIVES HIM SUPER-POWERS!
PUFF, PUFF! T-THAT'S FUNNY! I CAN'T LIFT THE TRUCK!
WHAT MADE YOU THINK YOU COULD, CLARK? DID YOU THINK YOU WERE SUPERBOY?
IT WORKED! THE ELECTRICAL POWER OF MY THOUGHTS RUINED THE ROBOT'S SUPER-POWERS! WELL, AT LEAST MY SUPER-THOUGHTS CAN OPERATE FROM THE PHANTOM ZO... GASP! WAIT! T-THAT'S IT! NOW I KNOW HOW TO GET A MESSAGE TO DAD!
NO PARKING
SHORTLY, AT THE KENT GENERAL STORE...
THANK GOODNESS THE TYPEWRITER CORD IS PLUGGED IN! AND THE PAPER IS STILL IN THE ROLLER JUST AS I LEFT IT... FOR DEMONSTRATION PURPOSES! NOW TO SEE IF LANA'S THEORY ABOUT TRANSFORMING MY SUPER-THOUGHTS INTO TYPEWRITTEN WORDS WORKS!
13
I'LL CONCENTRATE AS HARD AS I CAN AND DIRECT THE ELECTRICAL ENERGY OF MY BRAIN-WAVES AT THE TYPE-WRITER'S ELECTRICAL MECHANISM! I MUST MOVE THE KEYS! I MUST!
STRANGE! THAT ELECTRIC TYPEWRITER IS TYPING BY ITSELF!
CLICK-CLICK-CLICK!

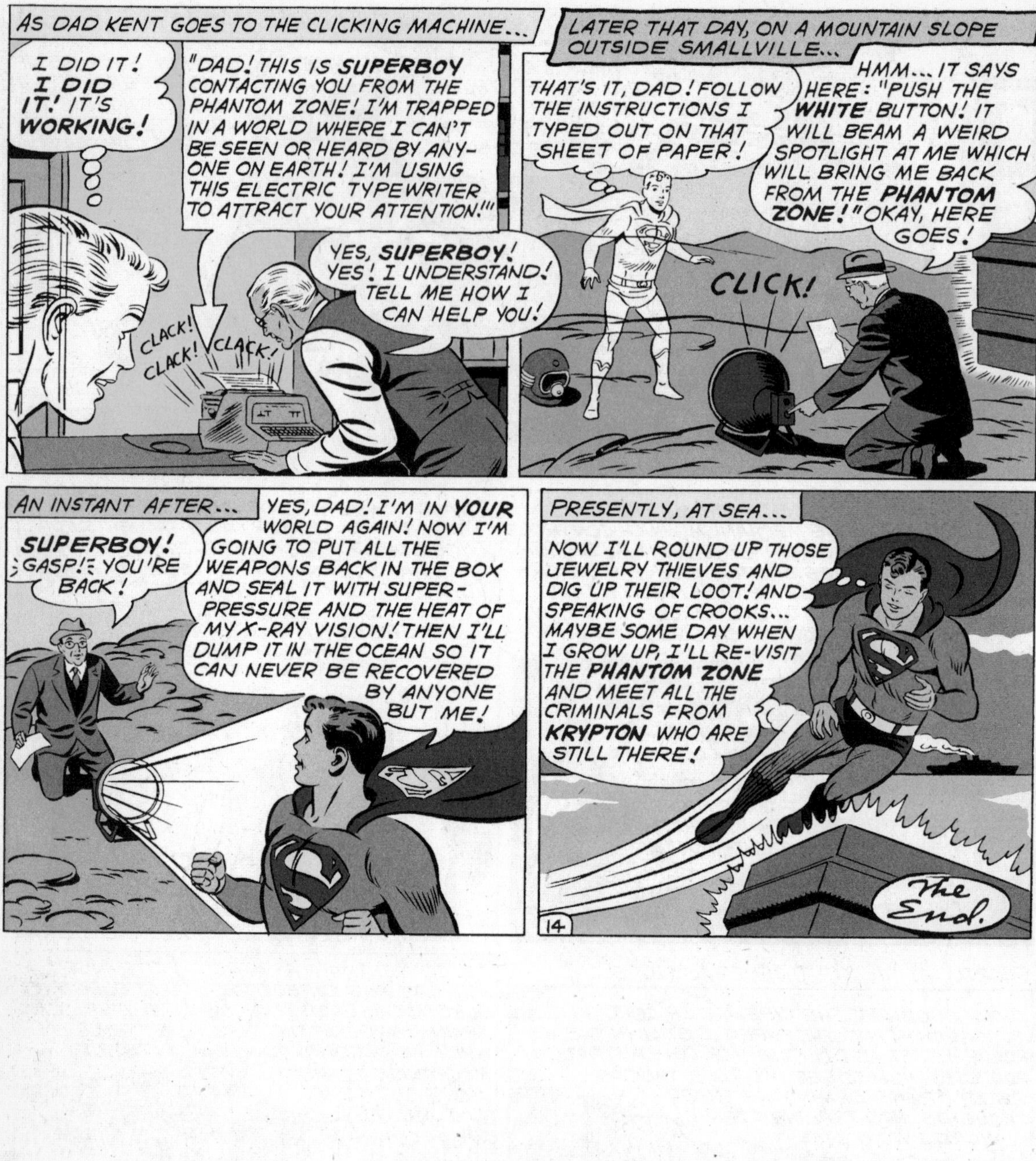
AS DAD KENT GOES TO THE CLICKING MACHINE...
I DID IT! I DID IT! IT'S WORKING!
"DAD! THIS IS SUPERBOY CONTACTING YOU FROM THE PHANTOM ZONE! I'M TRAPPED IN A WORLD WHERE I CAN'T BE SEEN OR HEARD BY ANYONE ON EARTH! I'M USING THIS ELECTRIC TYPEWRITER TO ATTRACT YOUR ATTENTION!"
YES, SUPERBOY! YES! I UNDERSTAND! TELL ME HOW I CAN HELP YOU!
CLACK! CLACK! CLACK!
LATER THAT DAY, ON A MOUNTAIN SLOPE OUTSIDE SMALLVILLE...
THAT'S IT, DAD! FOLLOW THE INSTRUCTIONS I TYPED OUT ON THAT SHEET OF PAPER!
HMM... IT SAYS HERE: "PUSH THE WHITE BUTTON! IT WILL BEAM A WEIRD SPOTLIGHT AT ME WHICH WILL BRING ME BACK FROM THE PHANTOM ZONE!" OKAY, HERE GOES!
CLICK!
AN INSTANT AFTER...
SUPERBOY! GASP! YOU'RE BACK!
YES, DAD! I'M IN YOUR WORLD AGAIN! NOW I'M GOING TO PUT ALL THE WEAPONS BACK IN THE BOX AND SEAL IT WITH SUPER-PRESSURE AND THE HEAT OF MY X-RAY VISION! THEN I'LL DUMP IT IN THE OCEAN SO IT CAN NEVER BE RECOVERED BY ANYONE BUT ME!
PRESENTLY, AT SEA...
NOW I'LL ROUND UP THOSE JEWELRY THIEVES AND DIG UP THEIR LOOT! AND SPEAKING OF CROOKS... MAYBE SOME DAY WHEN I GROW UP, I'LL RE-VISIT THE PHANTOM ZONE AND MEET ALL THE CRIMINALS FROM KRYPTON WHO ARE STILL THERE!
14
The End.

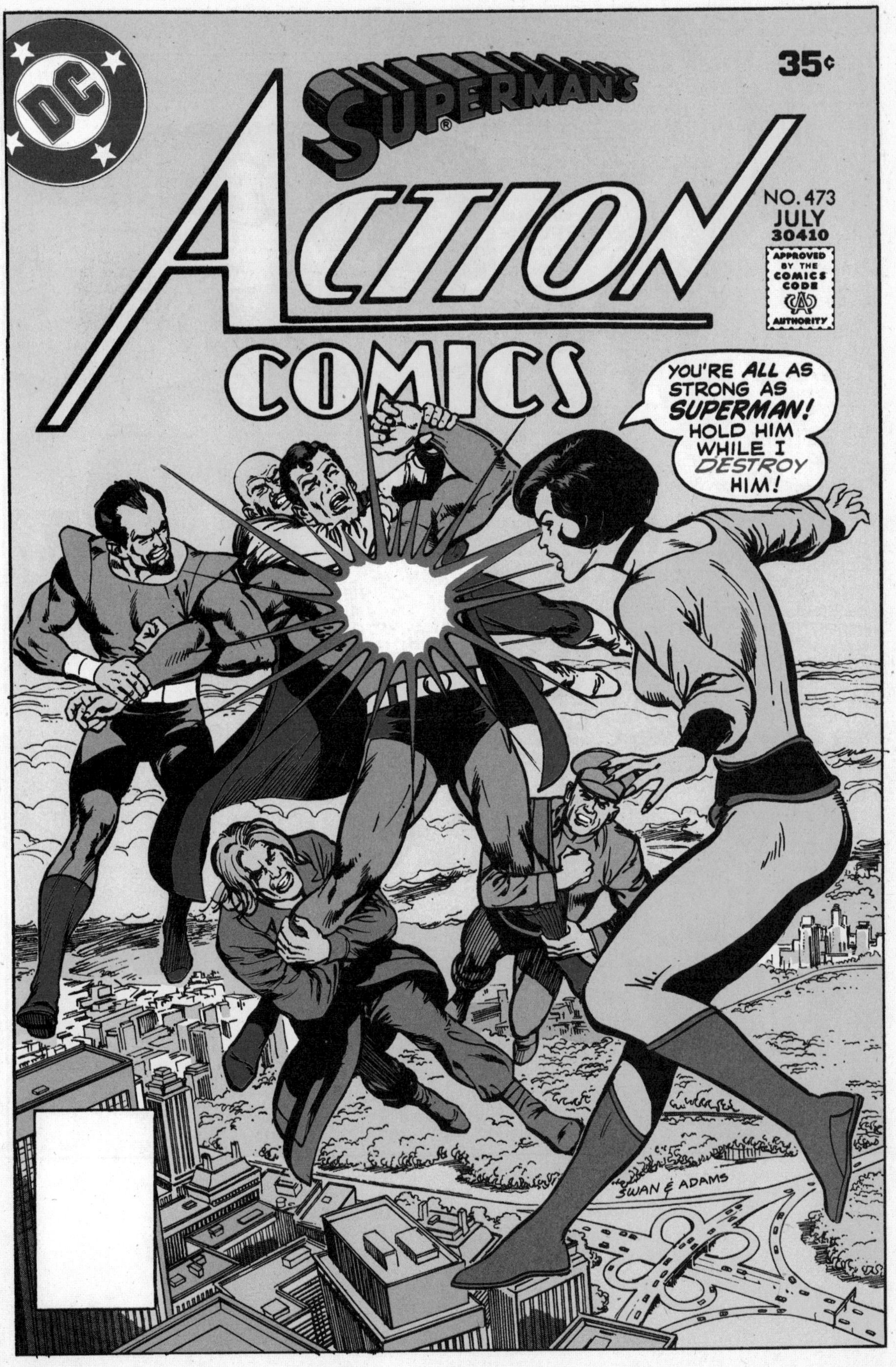
SUPERMAN'S
ACTION COMICS
35¢
NO. 473
JULY
30410
APPROVED BY THE COMICS CODE AUTHORITY
YOU'RE ALL AS STRONG AS SUPERMAN! HOLD HIM WHILE I DESTROY HIM!
SWAN & ADAMS

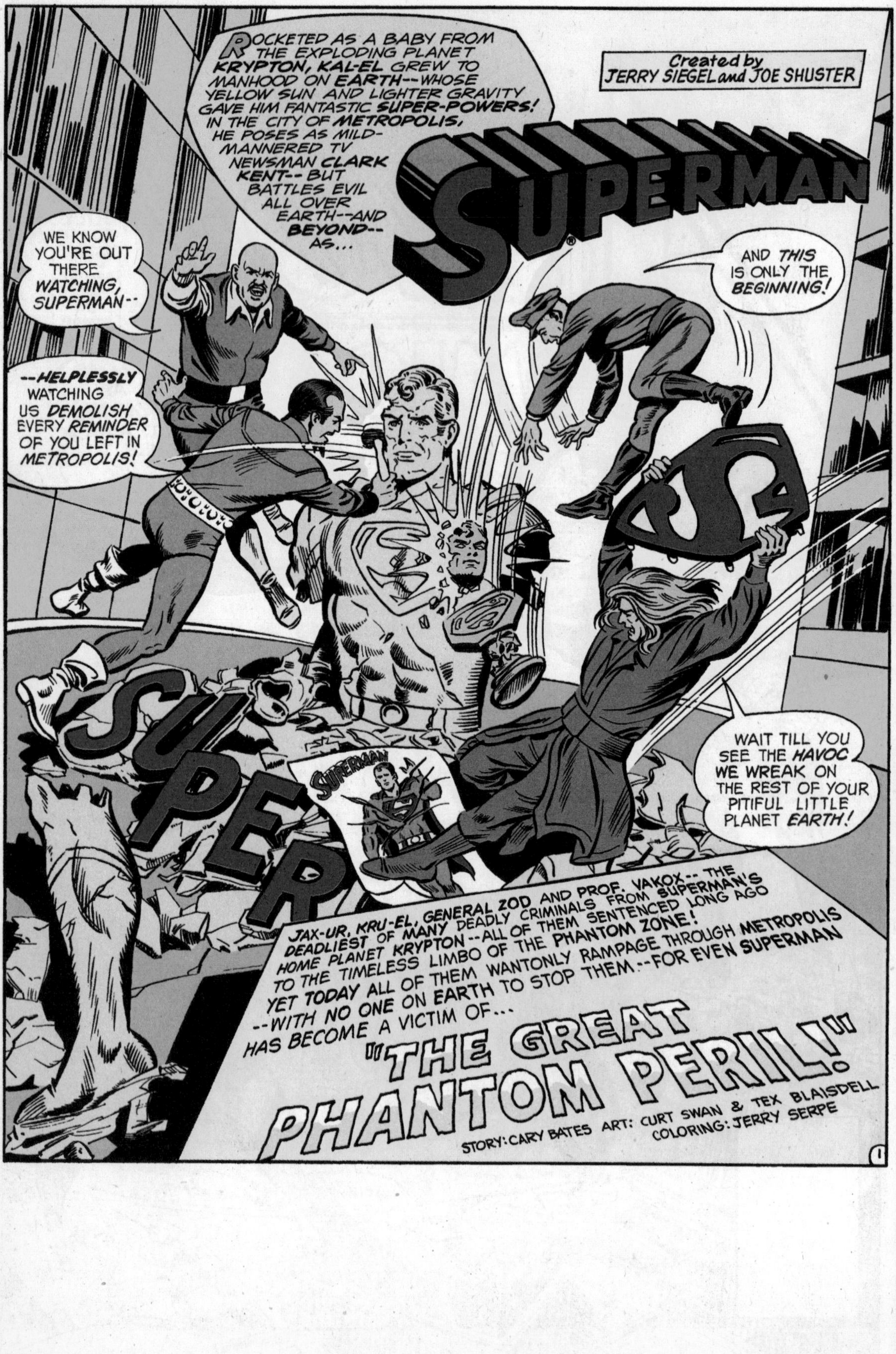

ROCKETED AS A BABY FROM THE EXPLODING PLANET KRYPTON, KAL-EL GREW TO MANHOOD ON EARTH--WHOSE YELLOW SUN AND LIGHTER GRAVITY GAVE HIM FANTASTIC SUPER-POWERS! IN THE CITY OF METROPOLIS, HE POSES AS MILD-MANNERED TV NEWSMAN CLARK KENT-- BUT BATTLES EVIL ALL OVER EARTH--AND BEYOND--AS...
Created by JERRY SIEGEL and JOE SHUSTER
SUPERMAN
WE KNOW YOU'RE OUT THERE WATCHING, SUPERMAN--
AND THIS IS ONLY THE BEGINNING!
--HELPLESSLY WATCHING US DEMOLISH EVERY REMINDER OF YOU LEFT IN METROPOLIS!
SUPER
WAIT TILL YOU SEE THE HAVOC WE WREAK ON THE REST OF YOUR PITIFUL LITTLE PLANET EARTH!
JAX-UR, KRU-EL, GENERAL ZOD AND PROF. VAKOX-- THE DEADLIEST OF MANY DEADLY CRIMINALS FROM SUPERMAN'S HOME PLANET KRYPTON--ALL OF THEM SENTENCED LONG AGO TO THE TIMELESS LIMBO OF THE PHANTOM ZONE! YET TODAY ALL OF THEM WANTONLY RAMPAGE THROUGH METROPOLIS --WITH NO ONE ON EARTH TO STOP THEM.--FOR EVEN SUPERMAN HAS BECOME A VICTIM OF...
"THE GREAT PHANTOM PERIL!"
STORY: CARY BATES ART: CURT SWAN & TEX BLAISDELL COLORING: JERRY SERPE
1

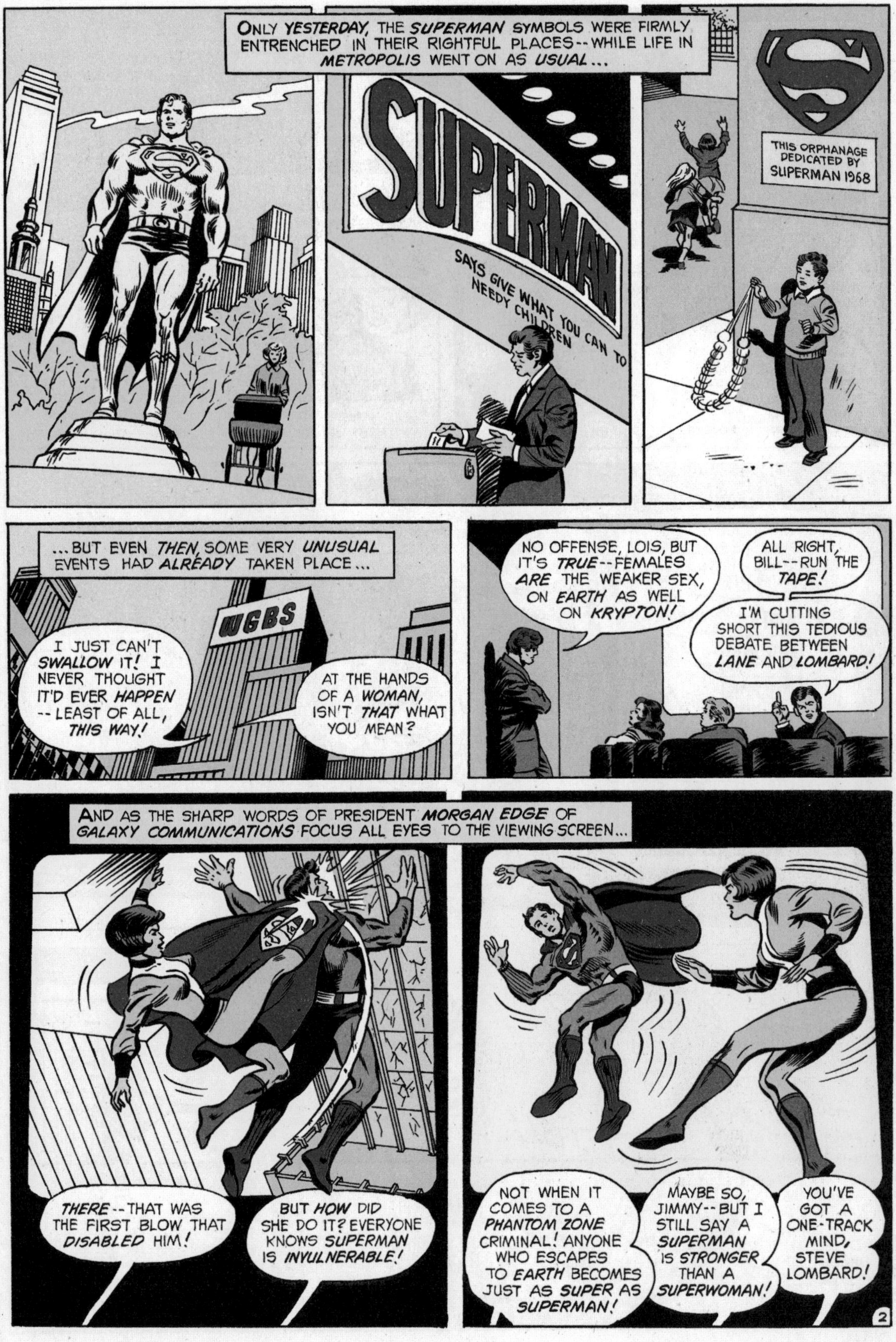

ONLY YESTERDAY, THE SUPERMAN SYMBOLS WERE FIRMLY ENTRENCHED IN THEIR RIGHTFUL PLACES--WHILE LIFE IN METROPOLIS WENT ON AS USUAL...
SUPERMAN
SUPERMAN SAYS GIVE WHAT YOU CAN TO NEEDY CHILDREN
THIS ORPHANAGE DEDICATED BY SUPERMAN 1968
...BUT EVEN THEN, SOME VERY UNUSUAL EVENTS HAD ALREADY TAKEN PLACE...
WGBS
I JUST CAN'T SWALLOW IT! I NEVER THOUGHT IT'D EVER HAPPEN --LEAST OF ALL, THIS WAY!
AT THE HANDS OF A WOMAN, ISN'T THAT WHAT YOU MEAN?
NO OFFENSE, LOIS, BUT IT'S TRUE--FEMALES ARE THE WEAKER SEX, ON EARTH AS WELL ON KRYPTON!
ALL RIGHT, BILL--RUN THE TAPE!
I'M CUTTING SHORT THIS TEDIOUS DEBATE BETWEEN LANE AND LOMBARD!
AND AS THE SHARP WORDS OF PRESIDENT MORGAN EDGE OF GALAXY COMMUNICATIONS FOCUS ALL EYES TO THE VIEWING SCREEN...
THERE--THAT WAS THE FIRST BLOW THAT DISABLED HIM!
BUT HOW DID SHE DO IT? EVERYONE KNOWS SUPERMAN IS INVULNERABLE!
NOT WHEN IT COMES TO A PHANTOM ZONE CRIMINAL! ANYONE WHO ESCAPES TO EARTH BECOMES JUST AS SUPER AS SUPERMAN!
MAYBE SO, JIMMY--BUT I STILL SAY A SUPERMAN IS STRONGER THAN A SUPERWOMAN!
YOU'VE GOT A ONE-TRACK MIND, STEVE LOMBARD!
2

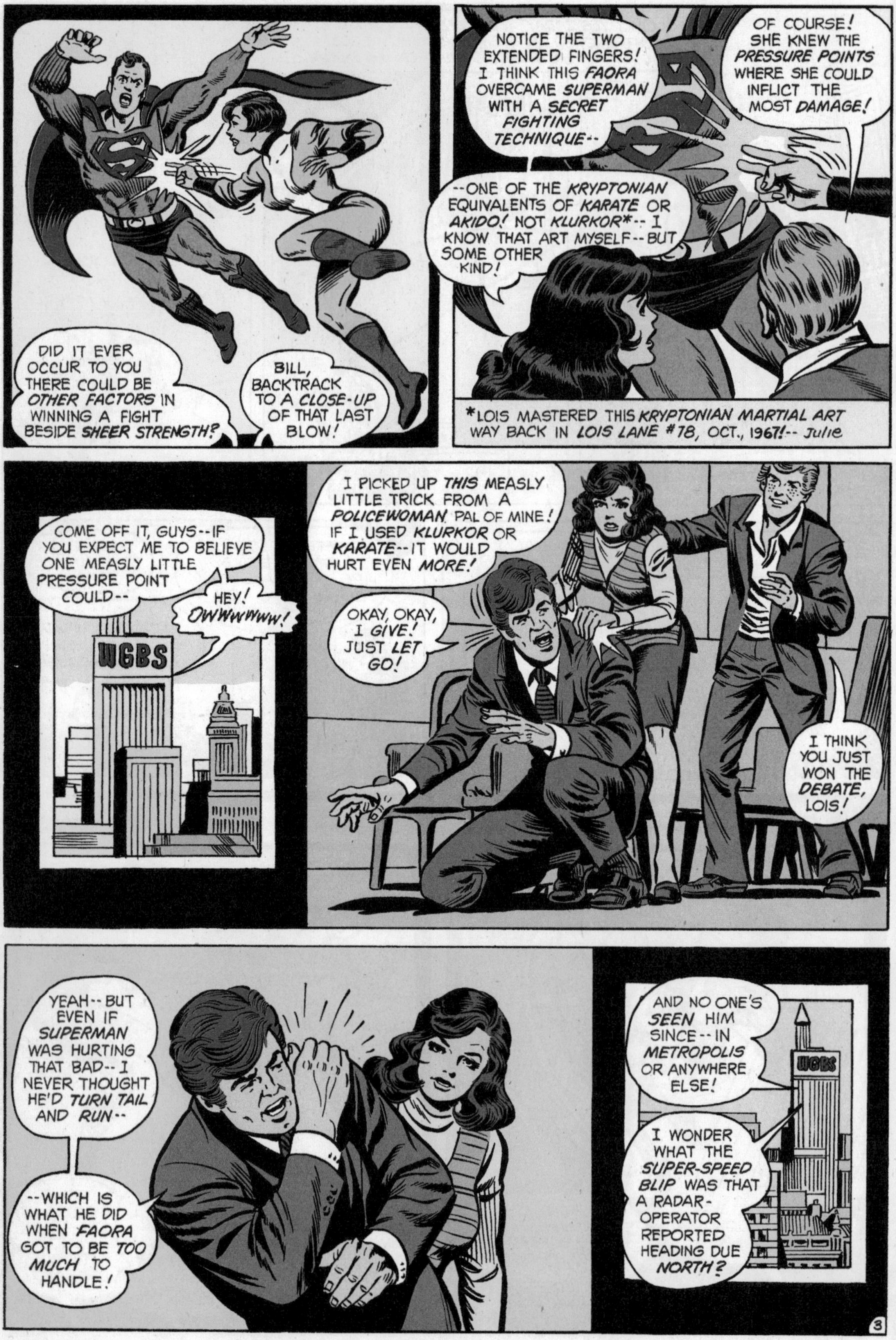

DID IT EVER OCCUR TO YOU THERE COULD BE OTHER FACTORS IN WINNING A FIGHT BESIDE SHEER STRENGTH?
BILL, BACKTRACK TO A CLOSE-UP OF THAT LAST BLOW!
NOTICE THE TWO EXTENDED FINGERS! I THINK THIS FAORA OVERCAME SUPERMAN WITH A SECRET FIGHTING TECHNIQUE--
--ONE OF THE KRYPTONIAN EQUIVALENTS OF KARATE OR AKIDO! NOT KLURKOR*-- I KNOW THAT ART MYSELF--BUT SOME OTHER KIND!
OF COURSE! SHE KNEW THE PRESSURE POINTS WHERE SHE COULD INFLICT THE MOST DAMAGE!
*LOIS MASTERED THIS KRYPTONIAN MARTIAL ART WAY BACK IN LOIS LANE #78, OCT., 1967!-- Julie
COME OFF IT, GUYS--IF YOU EXPECT ME TO BELIEVE ONE MEASLY LITTLE PRESSURE POINT COULD--
HEY! OWWWWWW!
WGBS
I PICKED UP THIS MEASLY LITTLE TRICK FROM A POLICEWOMAN PAL OF MINE! IF I USED KLURKOR OR KARATE--IT WOULD HURT EVEN MORE!
OKAY, OKAY, I GIVE! JUST LET GO!
I THINK YOU JUST WON THE DEBATE, LOIS!
YEAH--BUT EVEN IF SUPERMAN WAS HURTING THAT BAD--I NEVER THOUGHT HE'D TURN TAIL AND RUN--
--WHICH IS WHAT HE DID WHEN FAORA GOT TO BE TOO MUCH TO HANDLE!
AND NO ONE'S SEEN HIM SINCE--IN METROPOLIS OR ANYWHERE ELSE!
WGBS
I WONDER WHAT THE SUPER-SPEED BLIP WAS THAT A RADAR-OPERATOR REPORTED HEADING DUE NORTH?
3

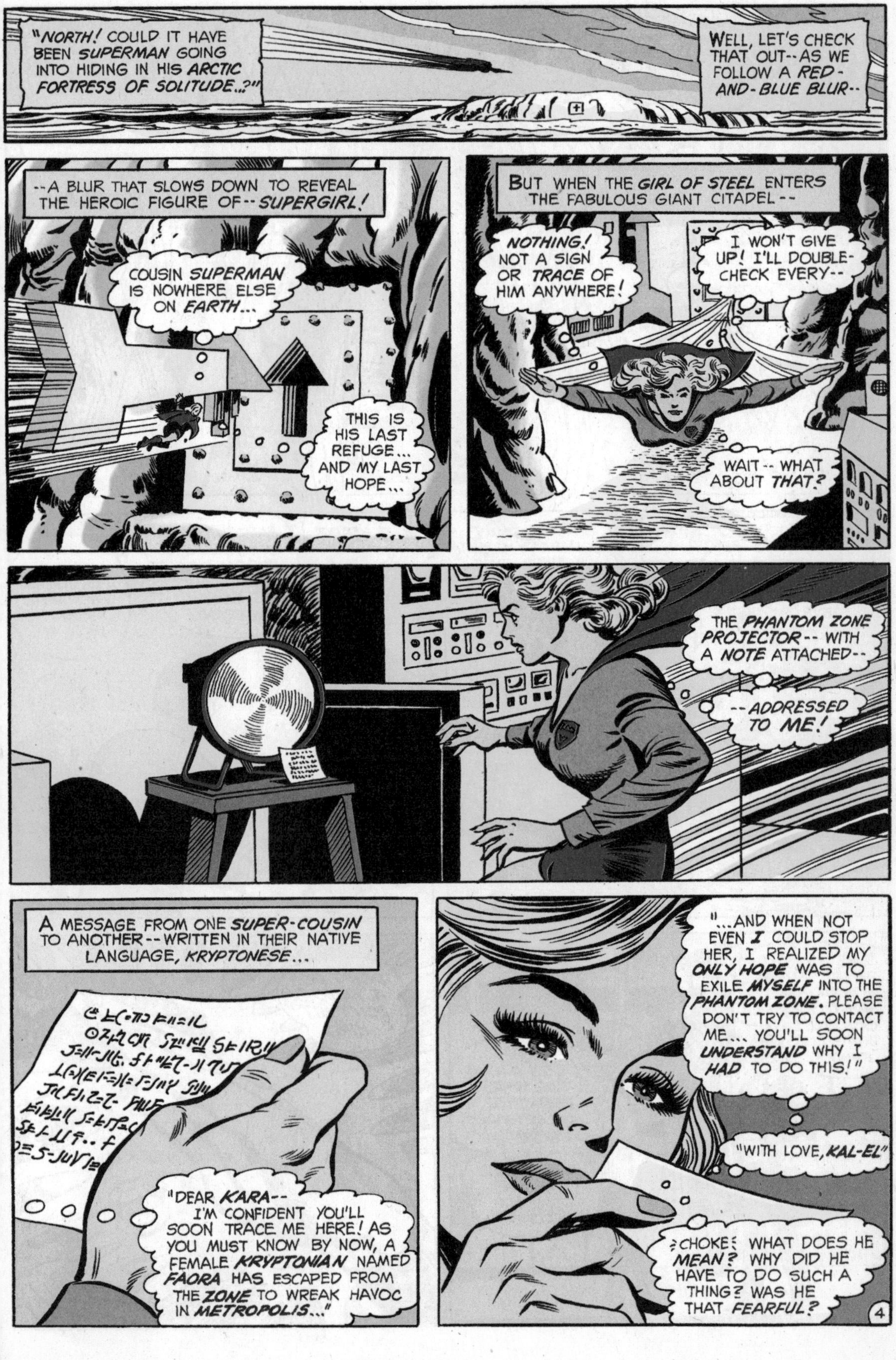
"NORTH! COULD IT HAVE BEEN SUPERMAN GOING INTO HIDING IN HIS ARCTIC FORTRESS OF SOLITUDE..?"
WELL, LET'S CHECK THAT OUT--AS WE FOLLOW A RED-AND-BLUE BLUR--
--A BLUR THAT SLOWS DOWN TO REVEAL THE HEROIC FIGURE OF--SUPERGIRL!
COUSIN SUPERMAN IS NOWHERE ELSE ON EARTH...
THIS IS HIS LAST REFUGE... AND MY LAST HOPE...
BUT WHEN THE GIRL OF STEEL ENTERS THE FABULOUS GIANT CITADEL--
NOTHING! NOT A SIGN OR TRACE OF HIM ANYWHERE!
I WON'T GIVE UP! I'LL DOUBLE-CHECK EVERY--
WAIT--WHAT ABOUT THAT?
THE PHANTOM ZONE PROJECTOR--WITH A NOTE ATTACHED--
--ADDRESSED TO ME!
A MESSAGE FROM ONE SUPER-COUSIN TO ANOTHER--WRITTEN IN THEIR NATIVE LANGUAGE, KRYPTONESE...
"DEAR KARA-- I'M CONFIDENT YOU'LL SOON TRACE ME HERE! AS YOU MUST KNOW BY NOW, A FEMALE KRYPTONIAN NAMED FAORA HAS ESCAPED FROM THE ZONE TO WREAK HAVOC IN METROPOLIS..."
"...AND WHEN NOT EVEN I COULD STOP HER, I REALIZED MY ONLY HOPE WAS TO EXILE MYSELF INTO THE PHANTOM ZONE. PLEASE DON'T TRY TO CONTACT ME... YOU'LL SOON UNDERSTAND WHY I HAD TO DO THIS!"
"WITH LOVE, KAL-EL"
CHOKE! WHAT DOES HE MEAN? WHY DID HE HAVE TO DO SUCH A THING? WAS HE THAT FEARFUL?
4

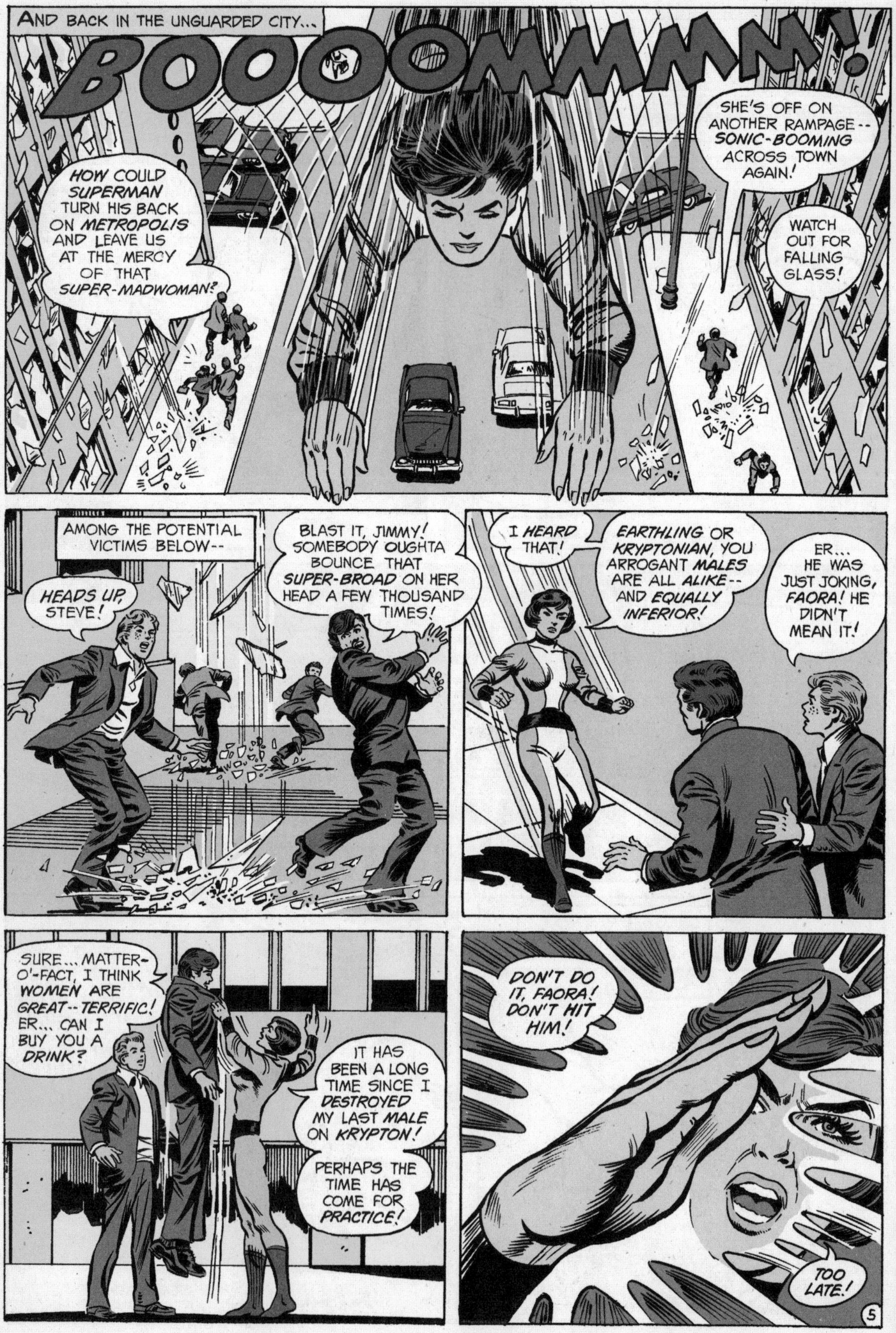
AND BACK IN THE UNGUARDED CITY...
BOOOOMMMM!
HOW COULD SUPERMAN TURN HIS BACK ON METROPOLIS AND LEAVE US AT THE MERCY OF THAT SUPER-MADWOMAN?
SHE'S OFF ON ANOTHER RAMPAGE -- SONIC-BOOMING ACROSS TOWN AGAIN!
WATCH OUT FOR FALLING GLASS!
AMONG THE POTENTIAL VICTIMS BELOW--
HEADS UP, STEVE!
BLAST IT, JIMMY! SOMEBODY OUGHTA BOUNCE THAT SUPER-BROAD ON HER HEAD A FEW THOUSAND TIMES!
I HEARD THAT!
EARTHLING OR KRYPTONIAN, YOU ARROGANT MALES ARE ALL ALIKE -- AND EQUALLY INFERIOR!
ER... HE WAS JUST JOKING, FAORA! HE DIDN'T MEAN IT!
SURE... MATTER-O'-FACT, I THINK WOMEN ARE GREAT -- TERRIFIC! ER... CAN I BUY YOU A DRINK?
IT HAS BEEN A LONG TIME SINCE I DESTROYED MY LAST MALE ON KRYPTON!
PERHAPS THE TIME HAS COME FOR PRACTICE!
DON'T DO IT, FAORA! DON'T HIT HIM!
TOO LATE!
5

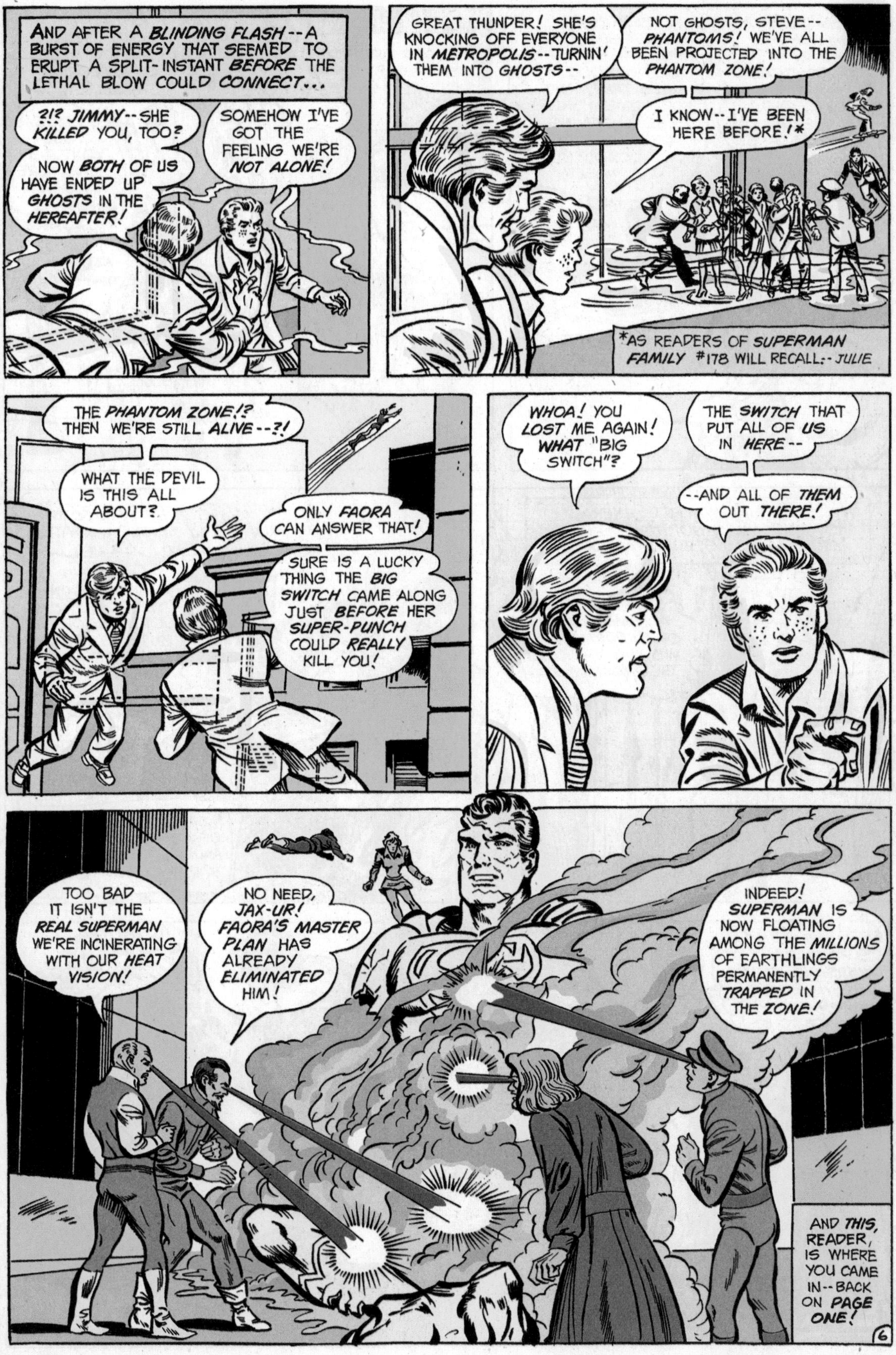
AND AFTER A BLINDING FLASH--A BURST OF ENERGY THAT SEEMED TO ERUPT A SPLIT-INSTANT BEFORE THE LETHAL BLOW COULD CONNECT...
?!? JIMMY--SHE KILLED YOU, TOO?
NOW BOTH OF US HAVE ENDED UP GHOSTS IN THE HEREAFTER!
SOMEHOW I'VE GOT THE FEELING WE'RE NOT ALONE!
GREAT THUNDER! SHE'S KNOCKING OFF EVERYONE IN METROPOLIS--TURNIN' THEM INTO GHOSTS--
NOT GHOSTS, STEVE--PHANTOMS! WE'VE ALL BEEN PROJECTED INTO THE PHANTOM ZONE!
I KNOW--I'VE BEEN HERE BEFORE!*
*AS READERS OF SUPERMAN FAMILY #178 WILL RECALL:-JULIE
THE PHANTOM ZONE!? THEN WE'RE STILL ALIVE--?!
WHAT THE DEVIL IS THIS ALL ABOUT?
ONLY FAORA CAN ANSWER THAT!
SURE IS A LUCKY THING THE BIG SWITCH CAME ALONG JUST BEFORE HER SUPER-PUNCH COULD REALLY KILL YOU!
WHOA! YOU LOST ME AGAIN! WHAT "BIG SWITCH"?
THE SWITCH THAT PUT ALL OF US IN HERE--
--AND ALL OF THEM OUT THERE!
TOO BAD IT ISN'T THE REAL SUPERMAN WE'RE INCINERATING WITH OUR HEAT VISION!
NO NEED, JAX-UR! FAORA'S MASTER PLAN HAS ALREADY ELIMINATED HIM!
INDEED! SUPERMAN IS NOW FLOATING AMONG THE MILLIONS OF EARTHLINGS PERMANENTLY TRAPPED IN THE ZONE!
AND THIS, READER, IS WHERE YOU CAME IN--BACK ON PAGE ONE!
6

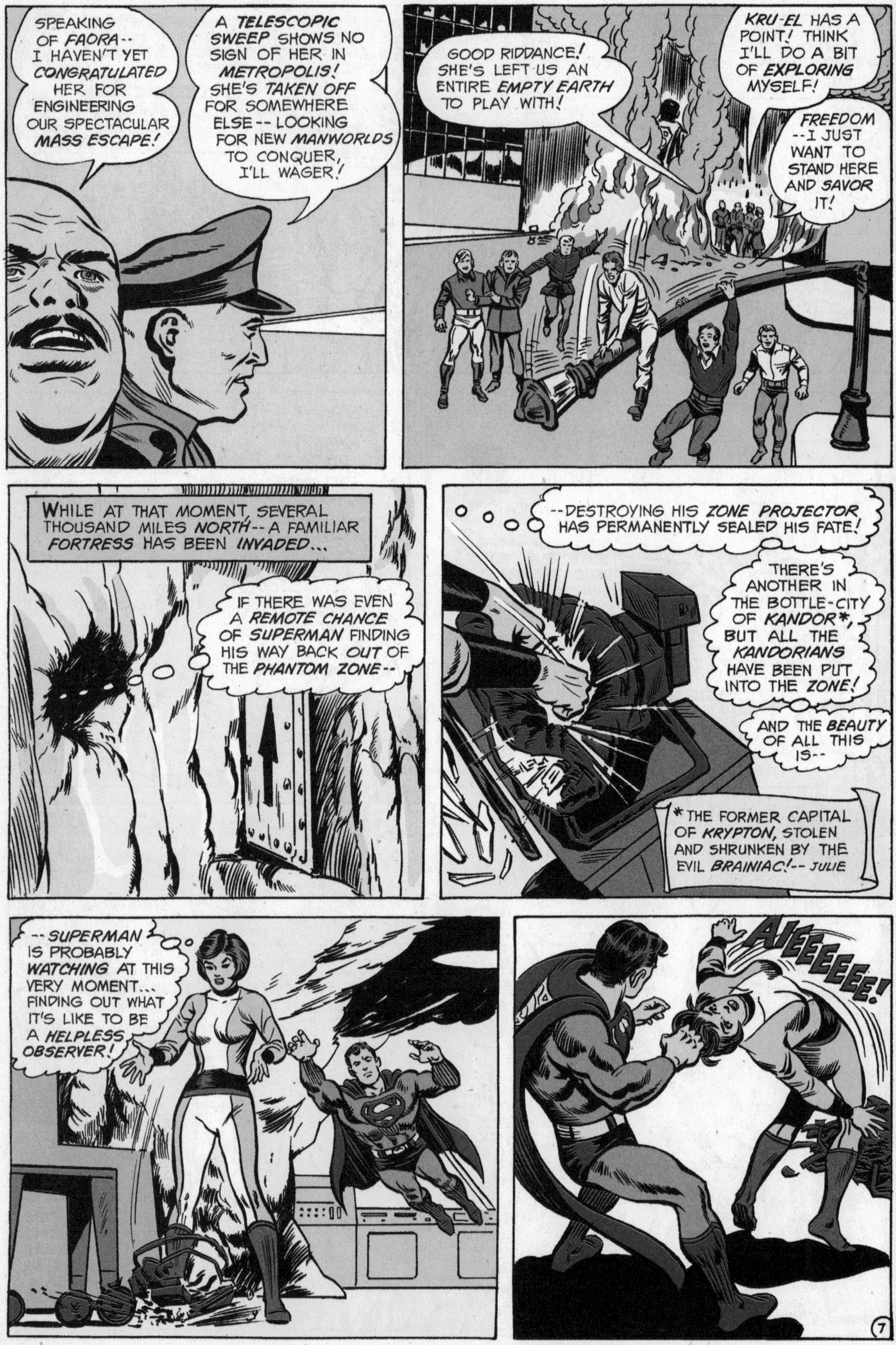
SPEAKING OF FAORA-- I HAVEN'T YET CONGRATULATED HER FOR ENGINEERING OUR SPECTACULAR MASS ESCAPE!
A TELESCOPIC SWEEP SHOWS NO SIGN OF HER IN METROPOLIS! SHE'S TAKEN OFF FOR SOMEWHERE ELSE -- LOOKING FOR NEW MANWORLDS TO CONQUER, I'LL WAGER!
GOOD RIDDANCE! SHE'S LEFT US AN ENTIRE EMPTY EARTH TO PLAY WITH!
KRU-EL HAS A POINT! THINK I'LL DO A BIT OF EXPLORING MYSELF!
FREEDOM --I JUST WANT TO STAND HERE AND SAVOR IT!
WHILE AT THAT MOMENT, SEVERAL THOUSAND MILES NORTH-- A FAMILIAR FORTRESS HAS BEEN INVADED...
IF THERE WAS EVEN A REMOTE CHANCE OF SUPERMAN FINDING HIS WAY BACK OUT OF THE PHANTOM ZONE--
--DESTROYING HIS ZONE PROJECTOR HAS PERMANENTLY SEALED HIS FATE!
THERE'S ANOTHER IN THE BOTTLE-CITY OF KANDOR*, BUT ALL THE KANDORIANS HAVE BEEN PUT INTO THE ZONE!
AND THE BEAUTY OF ALL THIS IS--
*THE FORMER CAPITAL OF KRYPTON, STOLEN AND SHRUNKEN BY THE EVIL BRAINIAC! -- JULIE
-- SUPERMAN IS PROBABLY WATCHING AT THIS VERY MOMENT... FINDING OUT WHAT IT'S LIKE TO BE A HELPLESS OBSERVER!
AIEEEEEEE!
7

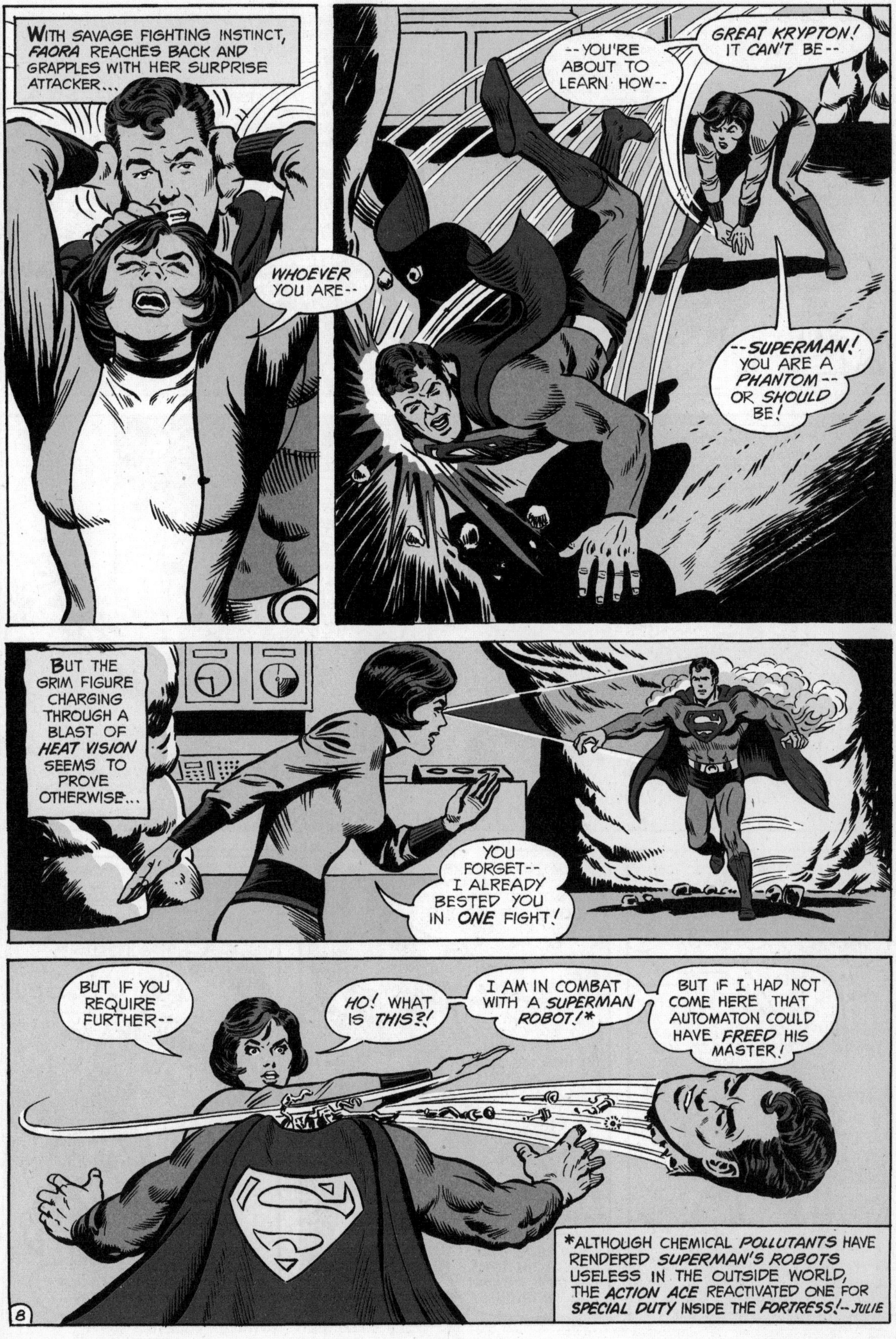

WITH SAVAGE FIGHTING INSTINCT, FAORA REACHES BACK AND GRAPPLES WITH HER SURPRISE ATTACKER...
WHOEVER YOU ARE--
--YOU'RE ABOUT TO LEARN HOW--
GREAT KRYPTON! IT CAN'T BE--
--SUPERMAN! YOU ARE A PHANTOM--OR SHOULD BE!
BUT THE GRIM FIGURE CHARGING THROUGH A BLAST OF HEAT VISION SEEMS TO PROVE OTHERWISE...
YOU FORGET--I ALREADY BESTED YOU IN ONE FIGHT!
BUT IF YOU REQUIRE FURTHER--
HO! WHAT IS THIS?!
I AM IN COMBAT WITH A SUPERMAN ROBOT!*
BUT IF I HAD NOT COME HERE THAT AUTOMATON COULD HAVE FREED HIS MASTER!
*ALTHOUGH CHEMICAL POLLUTANTS HAVE RENDERED SUPERMAN'S ROBOTS USELESS IN THE OUTSIDE WORLD, THE ACTION ACE REACTIVATED ONE FOR SPECIAL DUTY INSIDE THE FORTRESS!--JULIE
8

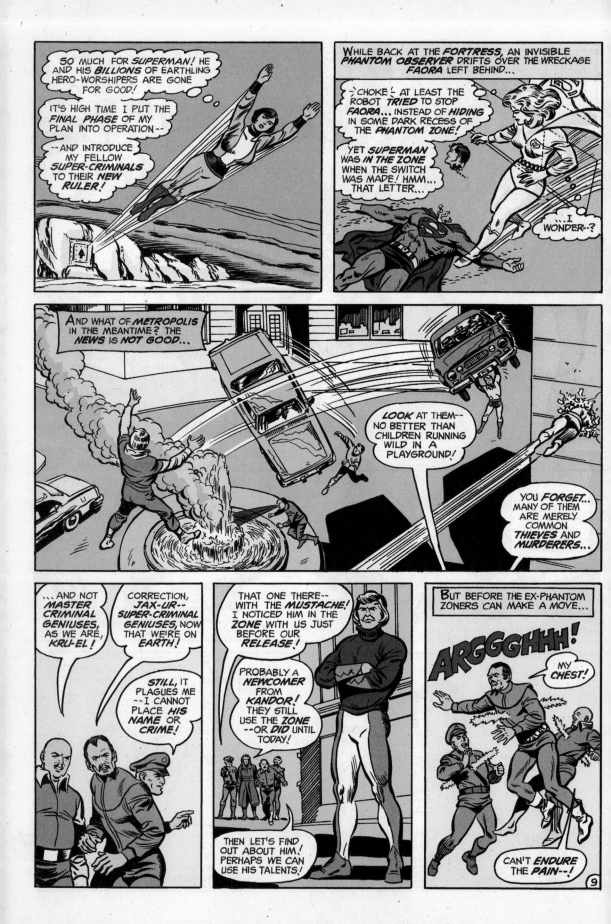

SO MUCH FOR *SUPERMAN!* HE AND HIS *BILLIONS* OF EARTHLING HERO-WORSHIPERS ARE GONE FOR GOOD!

IT'S HIGH TIME I PUT THE *FINAL PHASE* OF MY PLAN INTO OPERATION--

--AND INTRODUCE MY FELLOW *SUPER-CRIMINALS* TO THEIR *NEW RULER!*

WHILE BACK AT THE *FORTRESS,* AN INVISIBLE *PHANTOM OBSERVER* DRIFTS OVER THE WRECKAGE *FAORA* LEFT BEHIND...

--*CHOKE!*-- AT LEAST THE ROBOT *TRIED* TO STOP *FAORA*... INSTEAD OF *HIDING* IN SOME DARK RECESS OF THE *PHANTOM ZONE!*

YET *SUPERMAN* WAS *IN THE ZONE* WHEN THE SWITCH WAS MADE! HMM... THAT LETTER...

...I WONDER--?

AND WHAT OF *METROPOLIS* IN THE MEANTIME? THE *NEWS* IS *NOT GOOD*...

LOOK AT THEM-- NO BETTER THAN CHILDREN RUNNING WILD IN A PLAYGROUND!

YOU *FORGET*... MANY OF THEM ARE MERELY COMMON *THIEVES* AND *MURDERERS*...

...AND NOT *MASTER CRIMINAL GENIUSES,* AS WE ARE, *KRU-EL!*

CORRECTION, *JAX-UR*-- *SUPER-CRIMINAL GENIUSES,* NOW THAT WE'RE ON *EARTH!*

STILL, IT PLAGUES ME --I CANNOT PLACE *HIS* NAME OR *CRIME!*

THAT ONE THERE-- WITH THE *MUSTACHE!* I NOTICED HIM IN THE *ZONE* WITH US JUST BEFORE OUR *RELEASE!*

PROBABLY A *NEWCOMER* FROM *KANDOR!* THEY STILL USE THE *ZONE* --OR *DID* UNTIL TODAY!

THEN LET'S FIND OUT ABOUT HIM! PERHAPS WE CAN USE HIS *TALENTS!*

BUT BEFORE THE EX-PHANTOM ZONERS CAN MAKE A MOVE...

ARGGGHHH!

MY *CHEST!*

CAN'T *ENDURE* THE *PAIN*--!

9

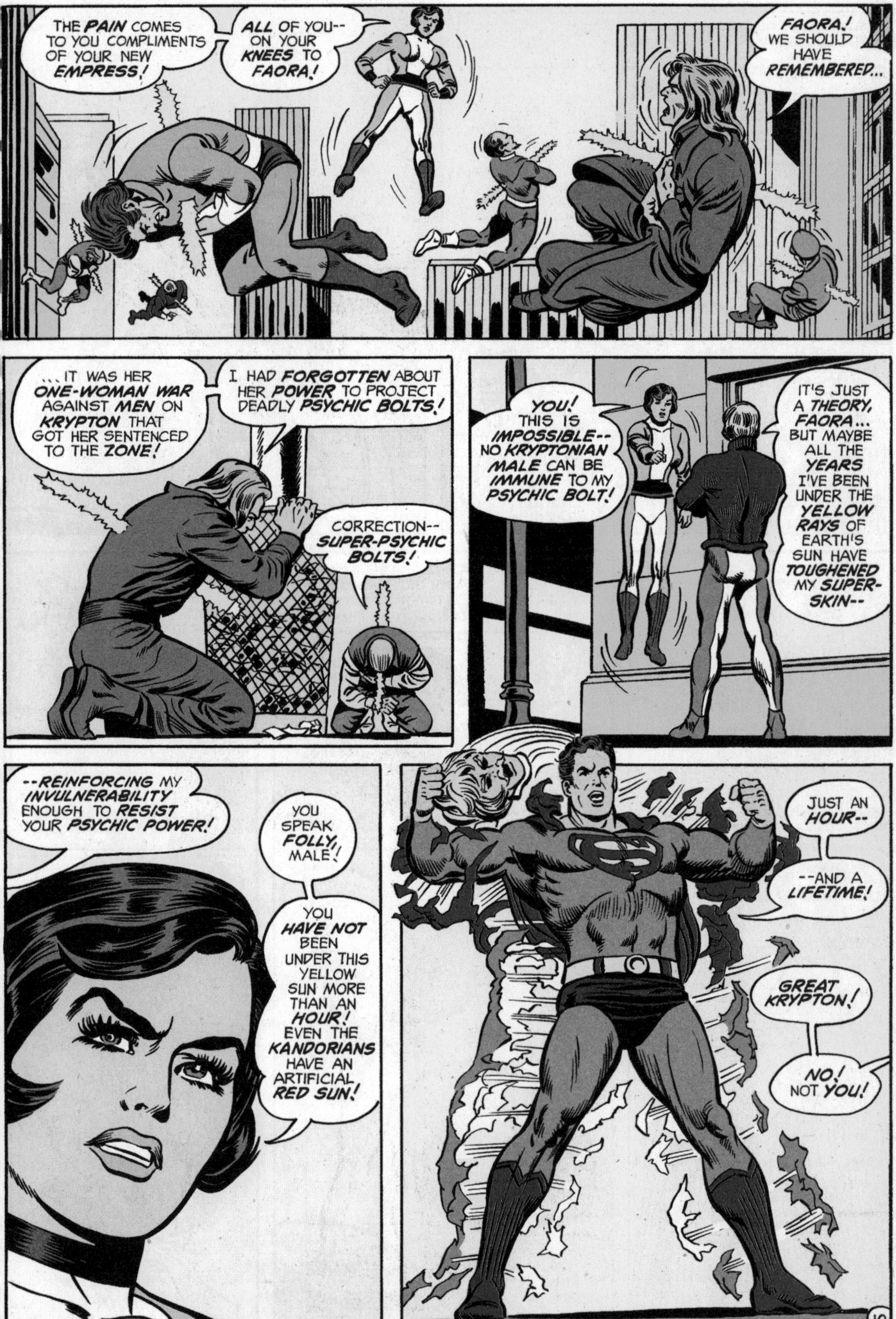
THE PAIN COMES TO YOU COMPLIMENTS OF YOUR NEW EMPRESS!
ALL OF YOU-- ON YOUR KNEES TO FAORA!
FAORA! WE SHOULD HAVE REMEMBERED...
...IT WAS HER ONE-WOMAN WAR AGAINST MEN ON KRYPTON THAT GOT HER SENTENCED TO THE ZONE!
I HAD FORGOTTEN ABOUT HER POWER TO PROJECT DEADLY PSYCHIC BOLTS!
CORRECTION-- SUPER-PSYCHIC BOLTS!
YOU! THIS IS IMPOSSIBLE-- NO KRYPTONIAN MALE CAN BE IMMUNE TO MY PSYCHIC BOLT!
IT'S JUST A THEORY, FAORA... BUT MAYBE ALL THE YEARS I'VE BEEN UNDER THE YELLOW RAYS OF EARTH'S SUN HAVE TOUGHENED MY SUPER-SKIN--
--REINFORCING MY INVULNERABILITY ENOUGH TO RESIST YOUR PSYCHIC POWER!
YOU SPEAK FOLLY, MALE!
YOU HAVE NOT BEEN UNDER THIS YELLOW SUN MORE THAN AN HOUR! EVEN THE KANDORIANS HAVE AN ARTIFICIAL RED SUN!
JUST AN HOUR--
--AND A LIFETIME!
GREAT KRYPTON!
NO! NOT YOU!
10

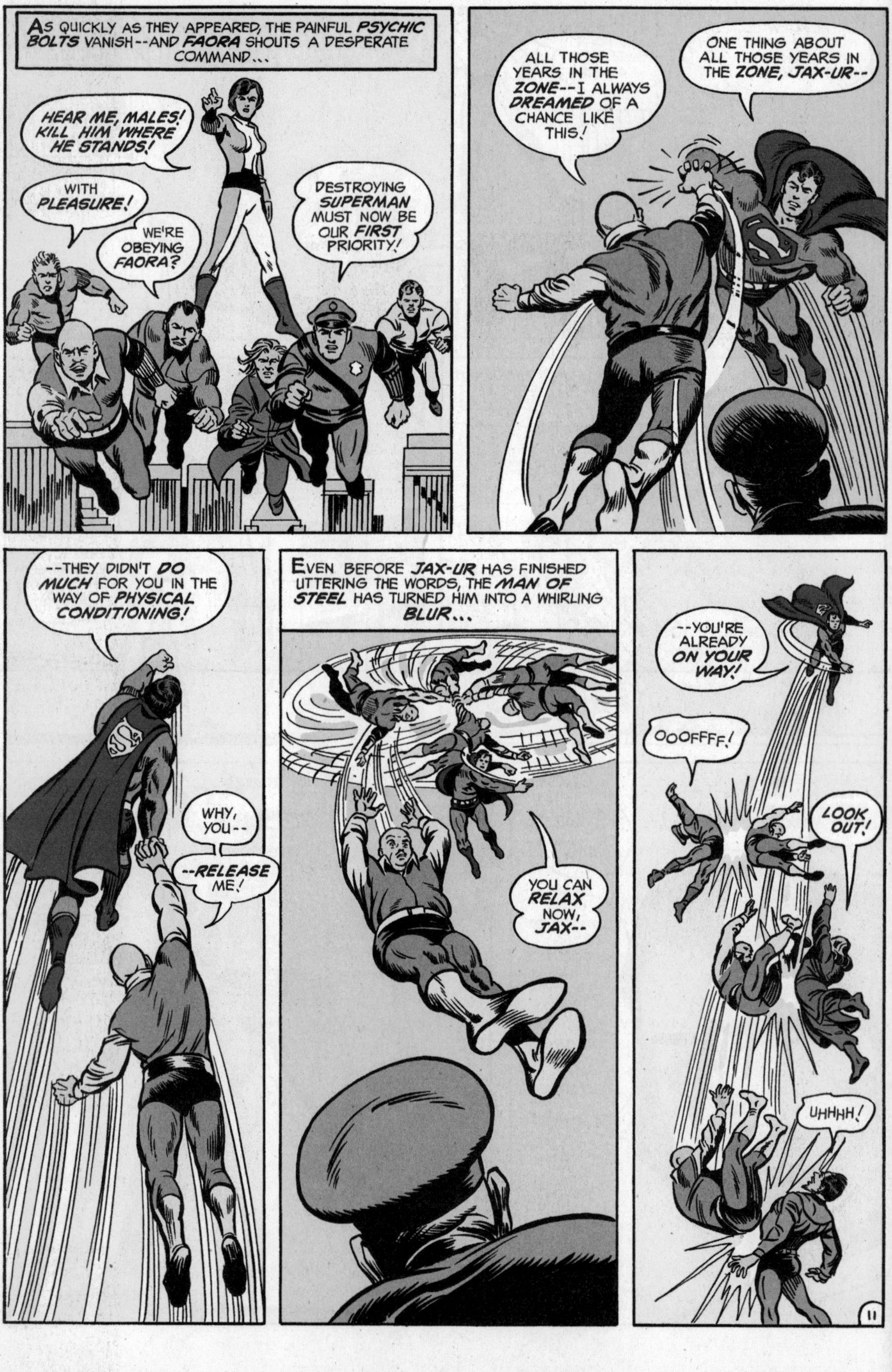
AS QUICKLY AS THEY APPEARED, THE PAINFUL PSYCHIC BOLTS VANISH--AND FAORA SHOUTS A DESPERATE COMMAND...
HEAR ME, MALES! KILL HIM WHERE HE STANDS!
WITH PLEASURE!
WE'RE OBEYING FAORA?
DESTROYING SUPERMAN MUST NOW BE OUR FIRST PRIORITY!
ALL THOSE YEARS IN THE ZONE--I ALWAYS DREAMED OF A CHANCE LIKE THIS!
ONE THING ABOUT ALL THOSE YEARS IN THE ZONE, JAX-UR--
--THEY DIDN'T DO MUCH FOR YOU IN THE WAY OF PHYSICAL CONDITIONING!
WHY, YOU--
--RELEASE ME!
EVEN BEFORE JAX-UR HAS FINISHED UTTERING THE WORDS, THE MAN OF STEEL HAS TURNED HIM INTO A WHIRLING BLUR...
YOU CAN RELAX NOW, JAX--
--YOU'RE ALREADY ON YOUR WAY!
OOOFFFF!
LOOK OUT!
UHHHH!
11

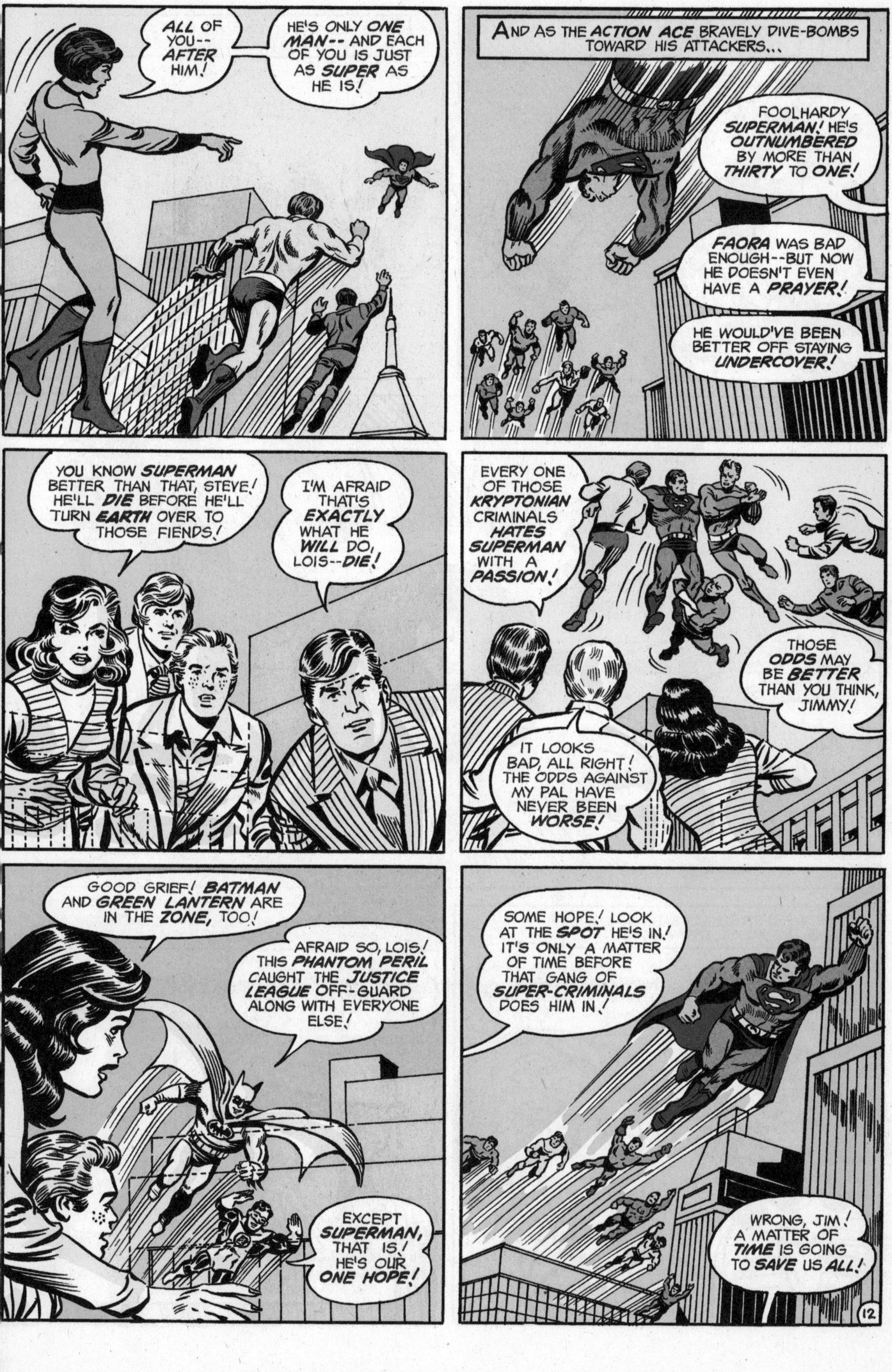
ALL OF YOU-- AFTER HIM!
HE'S ONLY ONE MAN-- AND EACH OF YOU IS JUST AS SUPER AS HE IS!
AND AS THE ACTION ACE BRAVELY DIVE-BOMBS TOWARD HIS ATTACKERS...
FOOLHARDY SUPERMAN! HE'S OUTNUMBERED BY MORE THAN THIRTY TO ONE!
FAORA WAS BAD ENOUGH--BUT NOW HE DOESN'T EVEN HAVE A PRAYER!
HE WOULD'VE BEEN BETTER OFF STAYING UNDERCOVER!
YOU KNOW SUPERMAN BETTER THAN THAT, STEVE! HE'LL DIE BEFORE HE'LL TURN EARTH OVER TO THOSE FIENDS!
I'M AFRAID THAT'S EXACTLY WHAT HE WILL DO, LOIS--DIE!
EVERY ONE OF THOSE KRYPTONIAN CRIMINALS HATES SUPERMAN WITH A PASSION!
IT LOOKS BAD, ALL RIGHT! THE ODDS AGAINST MY PAL HAVE NEVER BEEN WORSE!
THOSE ODDS MAY BE BETTER THAN YOU THINK, JIMMY!
GOOD GRIEF! BATMAN AND GREEN LANTERN ARE IN THE ZONE, TOO!
AFRAID SO, LOIS! THIS PHANTOM PERIL CAUGHT THE JUSTICE LEAGUE OFF-GUARD ALONG WITH EVERYONE ELSE!
EXCEPT SUPERMAN, THAT IS! HE'S OUR ONE HOPE!
SOME HOPE! LOOK AT THE SPOT HE'S IN! IT'S ONLY A MATTER OF TIME BEFORE THAT GANG OF SUPER-CRIMINALS DOES HIM IN!
WRONG, JIM! A MATTER OF TIME IS GOING TO SAVE US ALL!
12

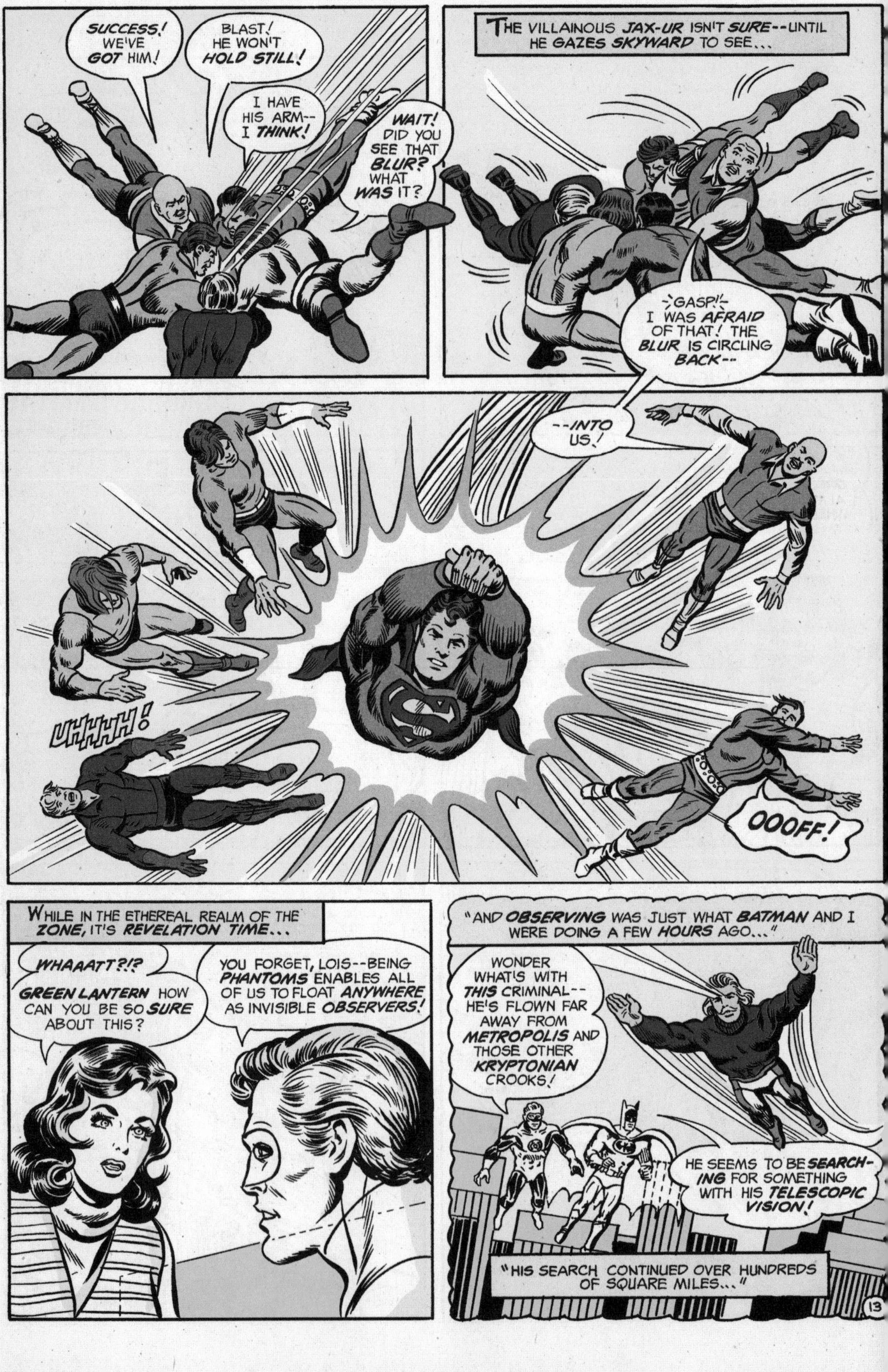
SUCCESS! WE'VE GOT HIM!
BLAST! HE WON'T HOLD STILL!
I HAVE HIS ARM-- I THINK!
WAIT! DID YOU SEE THAT BLUR? WHAT WAS IT?
THE VILLAINOUS JAX-UR ISN'T SURE--UNTIL HE GAZES SKYWARD TO SEE...
-GASP!- I WAS AFRAID OF THAT! THE BLUR IS CIRCLING BACK--
--INTO US!
UHHHH!
OOOFF!
WHILE IN THE ETHEREAL REALM OF THE ZONE, IT'S REVELATION TIME...
WHAAATT?!? GREEN LANTERN HOW CAN YOU BE SO SURE ABOUT THIS?
YOU FORGET, LOIS--BEING PHANTOMS ENABLES ALL OF US TO FLOAT ANYWHERE AS INVISIBLE OBSERVERS!
"AND OBSERVING WAS JUST WHAT BATMAN AND I WERE DOING A FEW HOURS AGO..."
WONDER WHAT'S WITH THIS CRIMINAL-- HE'S FLOWN FAR AWAY FROM METROPOLIS AND THOSE OTHER KRYPTONIAN CROOKS!
HE SEEMS TO BE SEARCHING FOR SOMETHING WITH HIS TELESCOPIC VISION!
"HIS SEARCH CONTINUED OVER HUNDREDS OF SQUARE MILES..."
13

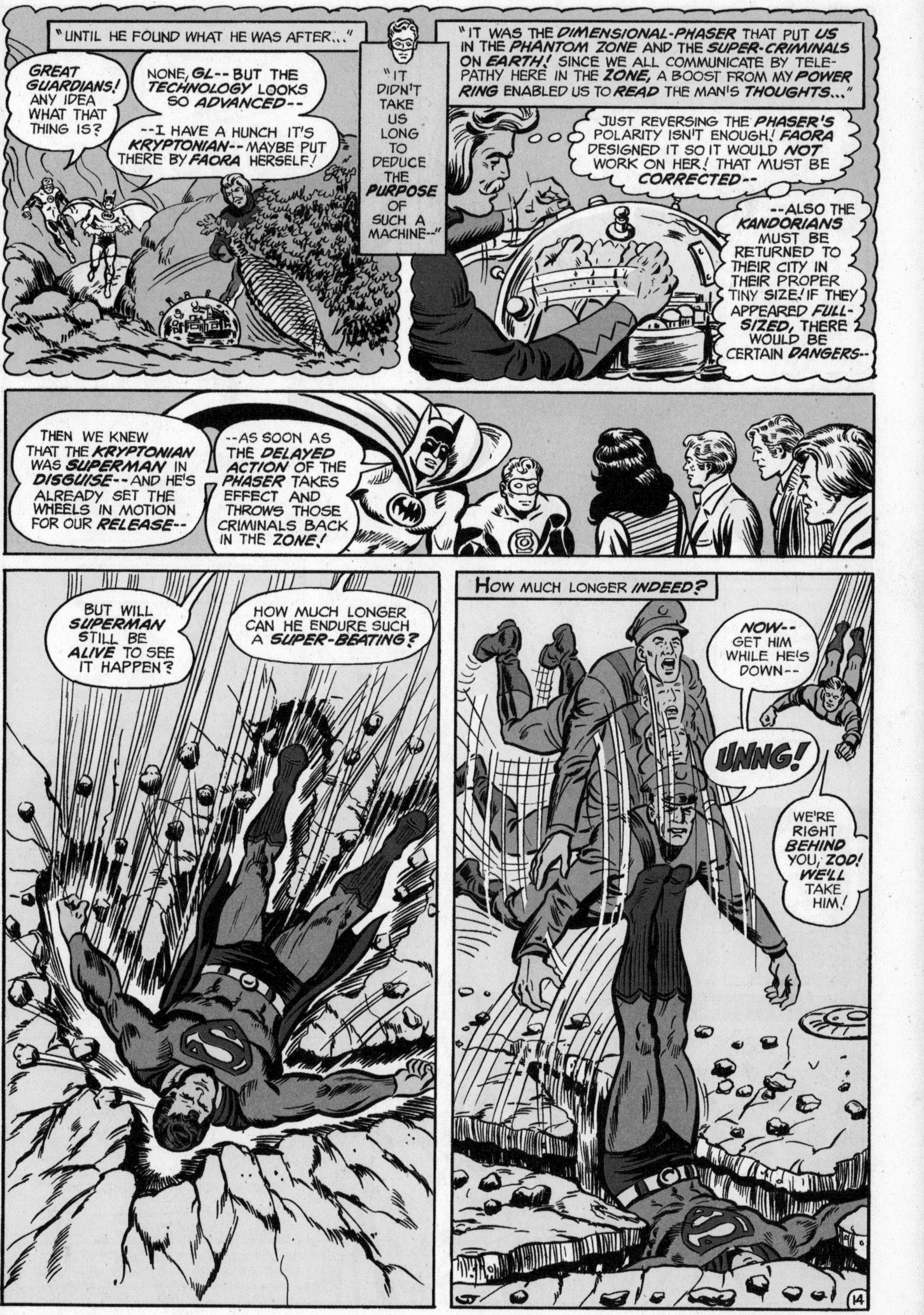
"UNTIL HE FOUND WHAT HE WAS AFTER..."
GREAT GUARDIANS! ANY IDEA WHAT THAT THING IS?
NONE, GL-- BUT THE TECHNOLOGY LOOKS SO ADVANCED--
--I HAVE A HUNCH IT'S KRYPTONIAN-- MAYBE PUT THERE BY FAORA HERSELF!
"IT DIDN'T TAKE US LONG TO DEDUCE THE PURPOSE OF SUCH A MACHINE--"
"IT WAS THE DIMENSIONAL-PHASER THAT PUT US IN THE PHANTOM ZONE AND THE SUPER-CRIMINALS ON EARTH! SINCE WE ALL COMMUNICATE BY TELEPATHY HERE IN THE ZONE, A BOOST FROM MY POWER RING ENABLED US TO READ THE MAN'S THOUGHTS..."
JUST REVERSING THE PHASER'S POLARITY ISN'T ENOUGH! FAORA DESIGNED IT SO IT WOULD NOT WORK ON HER! THAT MUST BE CORRECTED--
--ALSO THE KANDORIANS MUST BE RETURNED TO THEIR CITY IN THEIR PROPER TINY SIZE! IF THEY APPEARED FULL-SIZED, THERE WOULD BE CERTAIN DANGERS--
THEN WE KNEW THAT THE KRYPTONIAN WAS SUPERMAN IN DISGUISE-- AND HE'S ALREADY SET THE WHEELS IN MOTION FOR OUR RELEASE--
--AS SOON AS THE DELAYED ACTION OF THE PHASER TAKES EFFECT AND THROWS THOSE CRIMINALS BACK IN THE ZONE!
BUT WILL SUPERMAN STILL BE ALIVE TO SEE IT HAPPEN?
HOW MUCH LONGER CAN HE ENDURE SUCH A SUPER-BEATING?
HOW MUCH LONGER INDEED?
NOW-- GET HIM WHILE HE'S DOWN--
UNNG!
WE'RE RIGHT BEHIND YOU, ZOD! WE'LL TAKE HIM!
14

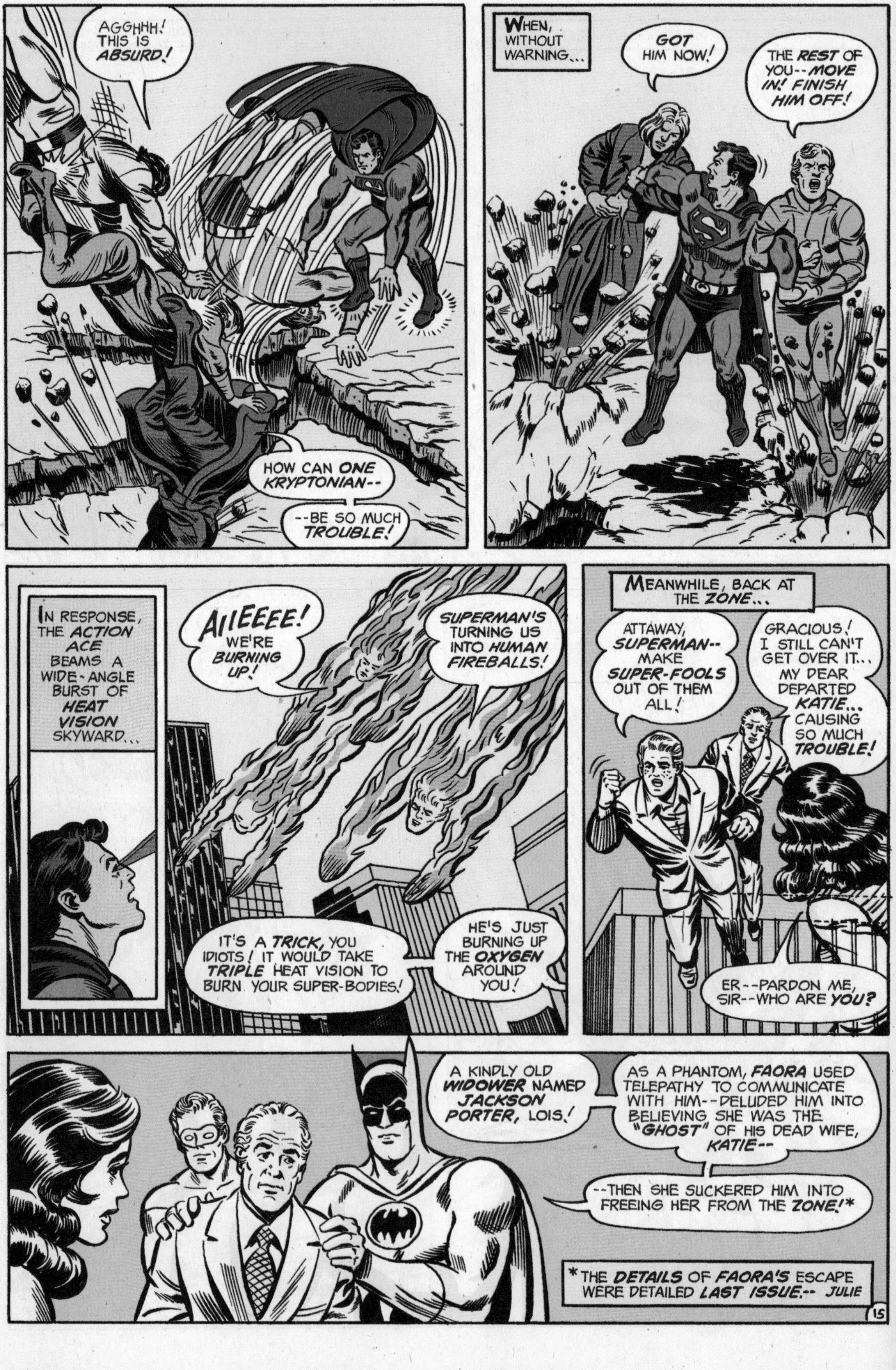
AGGHHH! THIS IS ABSURD!
HOW CAN ONE KRYPTONIAN--
--BE SO MUCH TROUBLE!
WHEN, WITHOUT WARNING...
GOT HIM NOW!
THE REST OF YOU--MOVE IN! FINISH HIM OFF!
IN RESPONSE, THE ACTION ACE BEAMS A WIDE-ANGLE BURST OF HEAT VISION SKYWARD...
AIIEEEE! WE'RE BURNING UP!
SUPERMAN'S TURNING US INTO HUMAN FIREBALLS!
IT'S A TRICK, YOU IDIOTS! IT WOULD TAKE TRIPLE HEAT VISION TO BURN YOUR SUPER-BODIES!
HE'S JUST BURNING UP THE OXYGEN AROUND YOU!
MEANWHILE, BACK AT THE ZONE...
ATTAWAY, SUPERMAN-- MAKE SUPER-FOOLS OUT OF THEM ALL!
GRACIOUS! I STILL CAN'T GET OVER IT... MY DEAR DEPARTED KATIE... CAUSING SO MUCH TROUBLE!
ER--PARDON ME, SIR--WHO ARE YOU?
A KINDLY OLD WIDOWER NAMED JACKSON PORTER, LOIS!
AS A PHANTOM, FAORA USED TELEPATHY TO COMMUNICATE WITH HIM--DELUDED HIM INTO BELIEVING SHE WAS THE "GHOST" OF HIS DEAD WIFE, KATIE--
--THEN SHE SUCKERED HIM INTO FREEING HER FROM THE ZONE!*
*THE DETAILS OF FAORA'S ESCAPE WERE DETAILED LAST ISSUE.-- JULIE
15

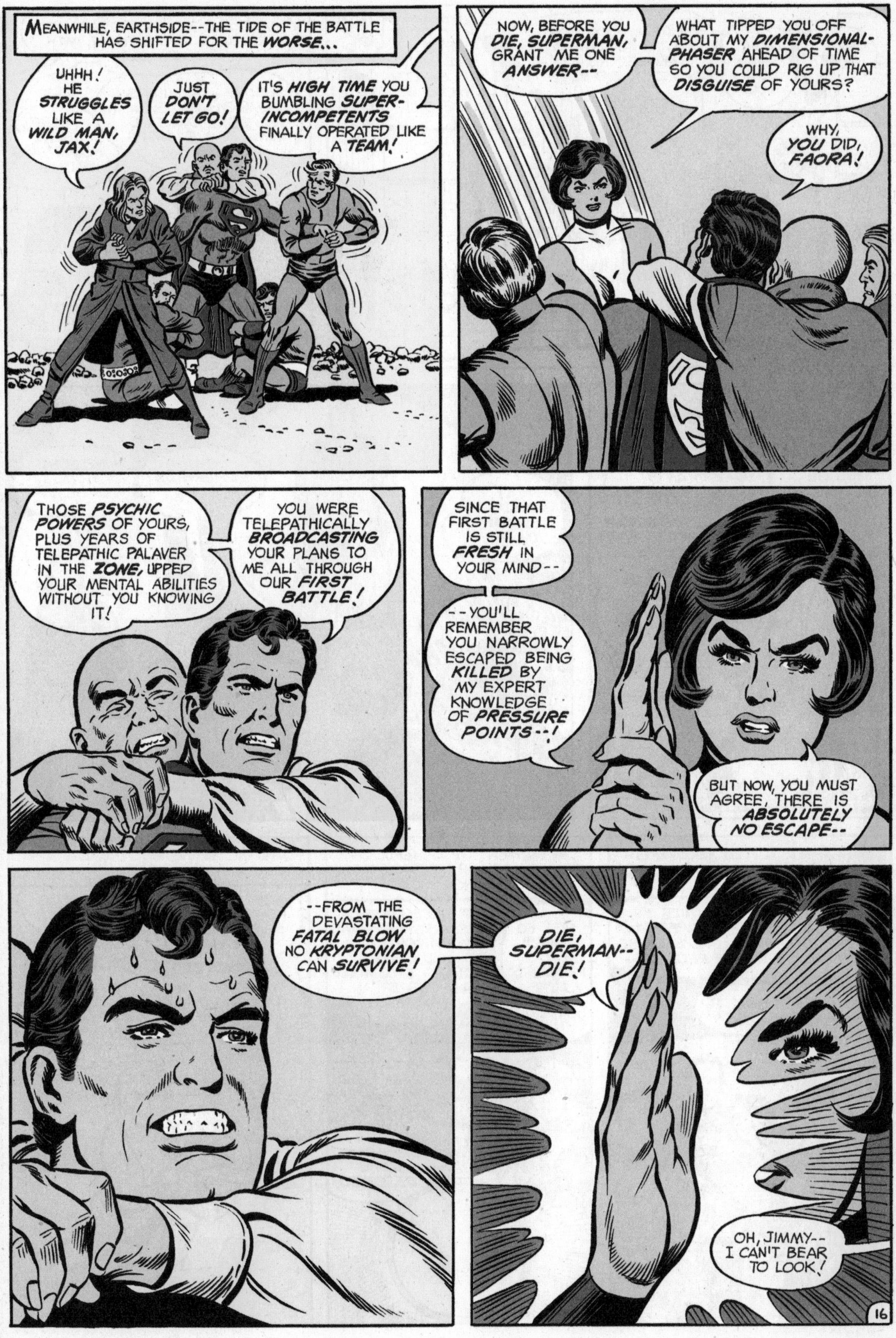
MEANWHILE, EARTHSIDE--THE TIDE OF THE BATTLE HAS SHIFTED FOR THE WORSE...
UHHH! HE STRUGGLES LIKE A WILD MAN, JAX!
JUST DON'T LET GO!
IT'S HIGH TIME YOU BUMBLING SUPER-INCOMPETENTS FINALLY OPERATED LIKE A TEAM!
NOW, BEFORE YOU DIE, SUPERMAN, GRANT ME ONE ANSWER--
WHAT TIPPED YOU OFF ABOUT MY DIMENSIONAL-PHASER AHEAD OF TIME SO YOU COULD RIG UP THAT DISGUISE OF YOURS?
WHY, YOU DID, FAORA!
THOSE PSYCHIC POWERS OF YOURS, PLUS YEARS OF TELEPATHIC PALAVER IN THE ZONE, UPPED YOUR MENTAL ABILITIES WITHOUT YOU KNOWING IT!
YOU WERE TELEPATHICALLY BROADCASTING YOUR PLANS TO ME ALL THROUGH OUR FIRST BATTLE!
SINCE THAT FIRST BATTLE IS STILL FRESH IN YOUR MIND--
--YOU'LL REMEMBER YOU NARROWLY ESCAPED BEING KILLED BY MY EXPERT KNOWLEDGE OF PRESSURE POINTS--!
BUT NOW, YOU MUST AGREE, THERE IS ABSOLUTELY NO ESCAPE--
--FROM THE DEVASTATING FATAL BLOW NO KRYPTONIAN CAN SURVIVE!
DIE, SUPERMAN--DIE!
OH, JIMMY-- I CAN'T BEAR TO LOOK!
16

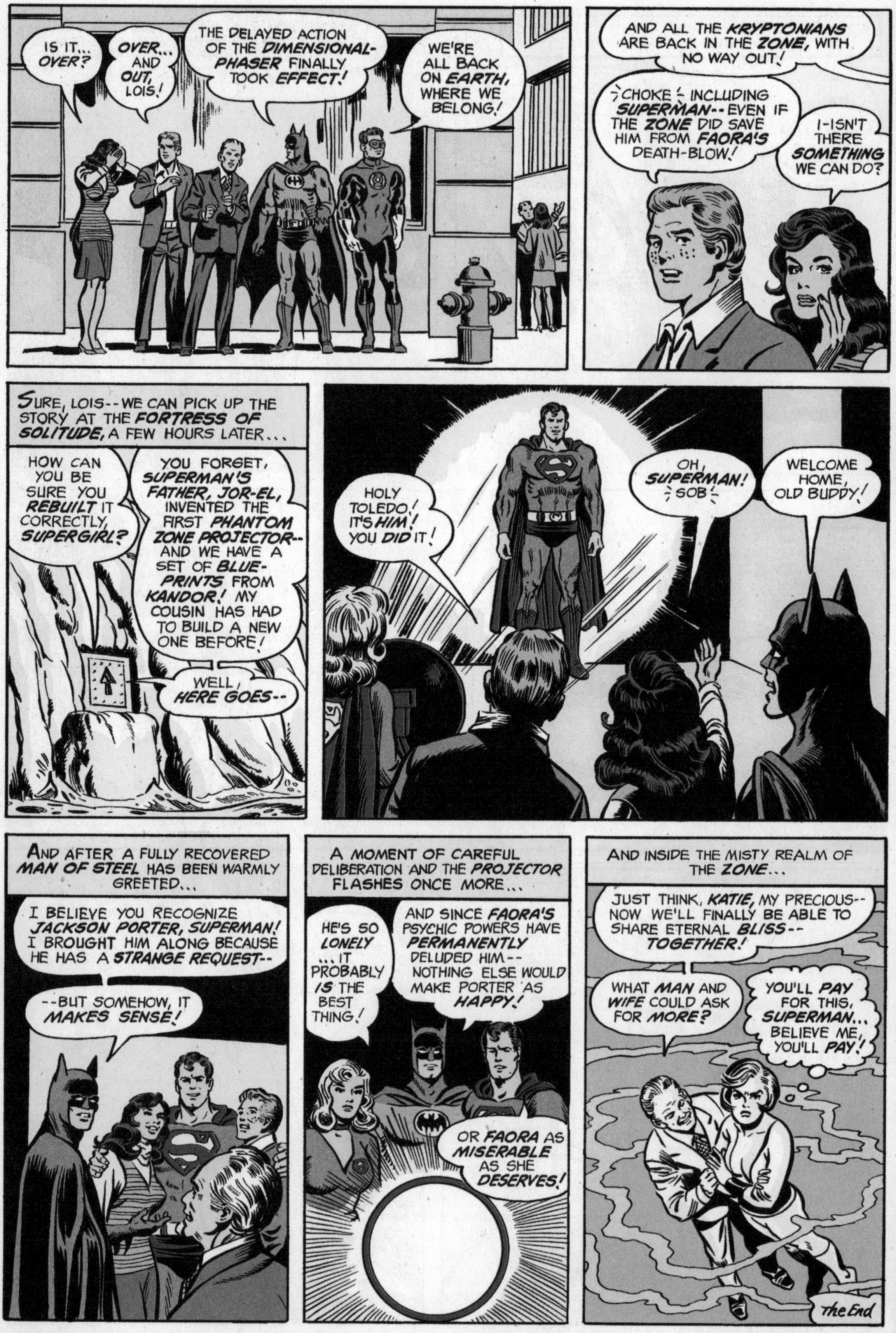
IS IT... OVER?
OVER... AND OUT, LOIS!
THE DELAYED ACTION OF THE DIMENSIONAL-PHASER FINALLY TOOK EFFECT!
WE'RE ALL BACK ON EARTH, WHERE WE BELONG!
AND ALL THE KRYPTONIANS ARE BACK IN THE ZONE, WITH NO WAY OUT!
-CHOKE- INCLUDING SUPERMAN-- EVEN IF THE ZONE DID SAVE HIM FROM FAORA'S DEATH-BLOW!
I-ISN'T THERE SOMETHING WE CAN DO?
SURE, LOIS-- WE CAN PICK UP THE STORY AT THE FORTRESS OF SOLITUDE, A FEW HOURS LATER...
HOW CAN YOU BE SURE YOU REBUILT IT CORRECTLY, SUPERGIRL?
YOU FORGET, SUPERMAN'S FATHER, JOR-EL, INVENTED THE FIRST PHANTOM ZONE PROJECTOR-- AND WE HAVE A SET OF BLUE-PRINTS FROM KANDOR! MY COUSIN HAS HAD TO BUILD A NEW ONE BEFORE!
WELL, HERE GOES--
HOLY TOLEDO! IT'S HIM! YOU DID IT!
OH, SUPERMAN! -SOB-
WELCOME HOME, OLD BUDDY!
AND AFTER A FULLY RECOVERED MAN OF STEEL HAS BEEN WARMLY GREETED...
I BELIEVE YOU RECOGNIZE JACKSON PORTER, SUPERMAN! I BROUGHT HIM ALONG BECAUSE HE HAS A STRANGE REQUEST--
--BUT SOMEHOW, IT MAKES SENSE!
A MOMENT OF CAREFUL DELIBERATION AND THE PROJECTOR FLASHES ONCE MORE...
HE'S SO LONELY ...IT PROBABLY IS THE BEST THING!
AND SINCE FAORA'S PSYCHIC POWERS HAVE PERMANENTLY DELUDED HIM-- NOTHING ELSE WOULD MAKE PORTER AS HAPPY!
OR FAORA AS MISERABLE AS SHE DESERVES!
AND INSIDE THE MISTY REALM OF THE ZONE...
JUST THINK, KATIE, MY PRECIOUS-- NOW WE'LL FINALLY BE ABLE TO SHARE ETERNAL BLISS-- TOGETHER!
WHAT MAN AND WIFE COULD ASK FOR MORE?
YOU'LL PAY FOR THIS, SUPERMAN... BELIEVE ME, YOU'LL PAY!
The End

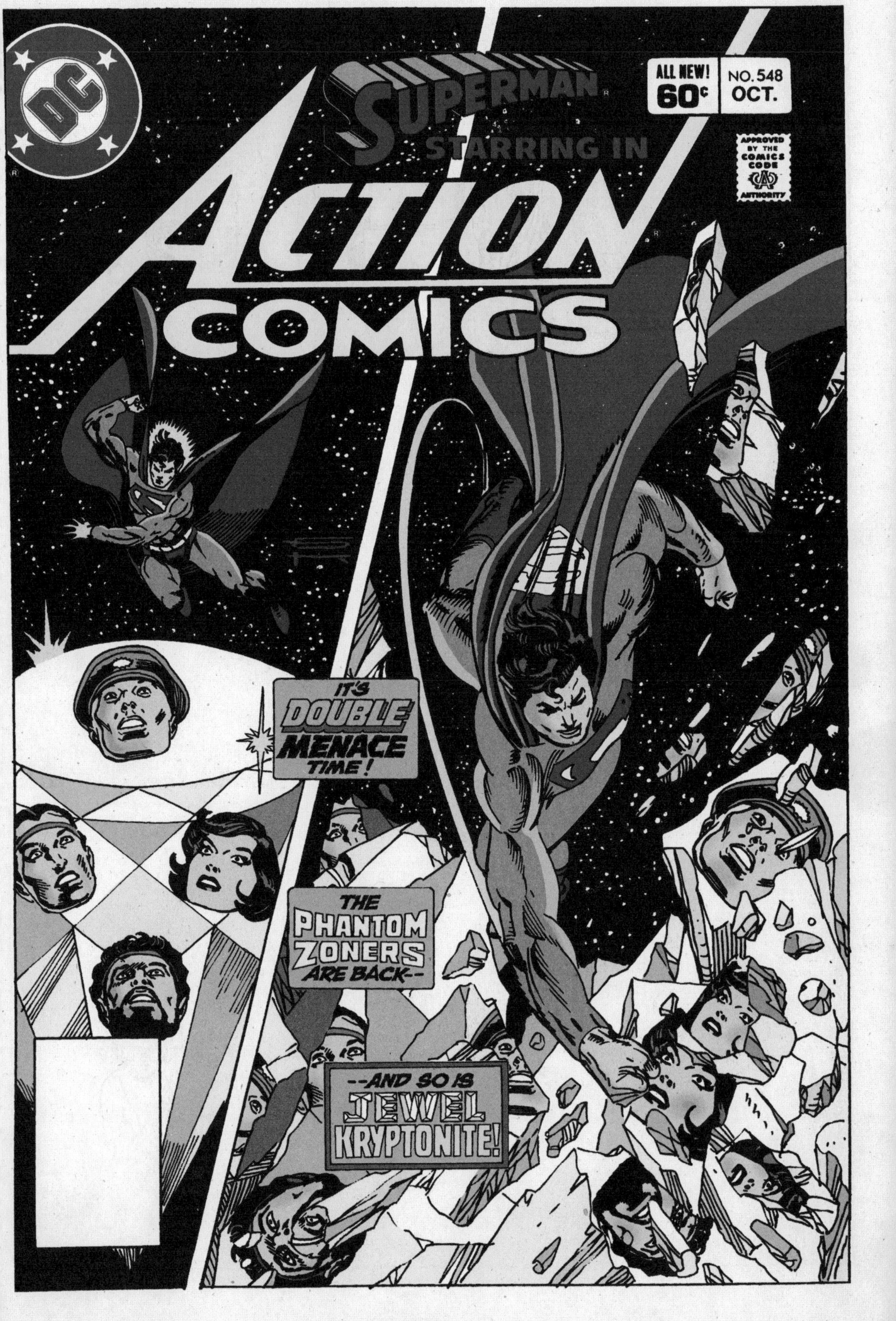
SUPERMAN
STARRING IN
ACTION COMICS
ALL NEW!
60¢
NO. 548
OCT.
APPROVED BY THE COMICS CODE AUTHORITY
IT'S DOUBLE MENACE TIME!
THE PHANTOM ZONERS ARE BACK--
--AND SO IS JEWEL KRYPTONITE!

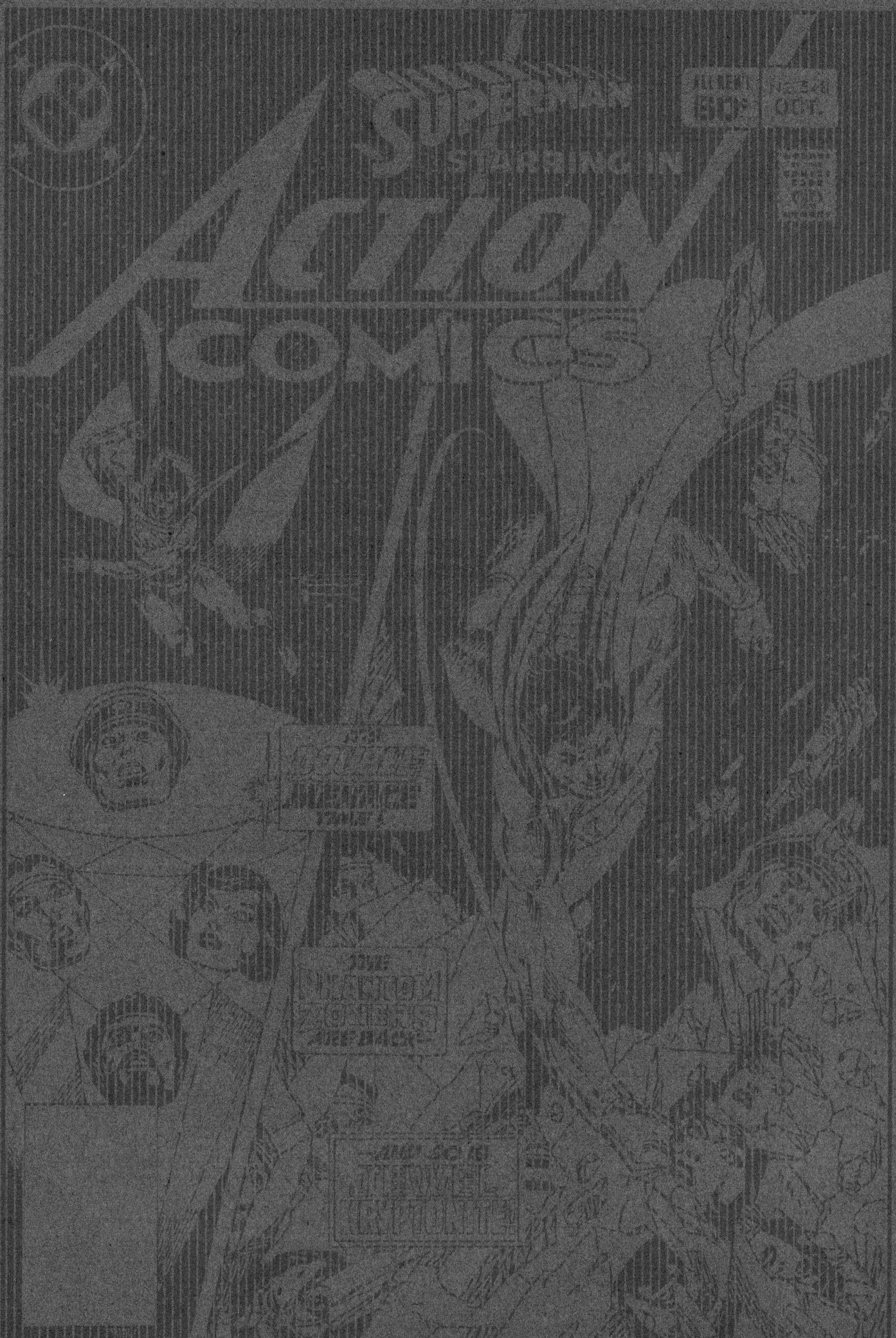
SUPERMAN
STARRING IN
ACTION
COMICS
OCT.

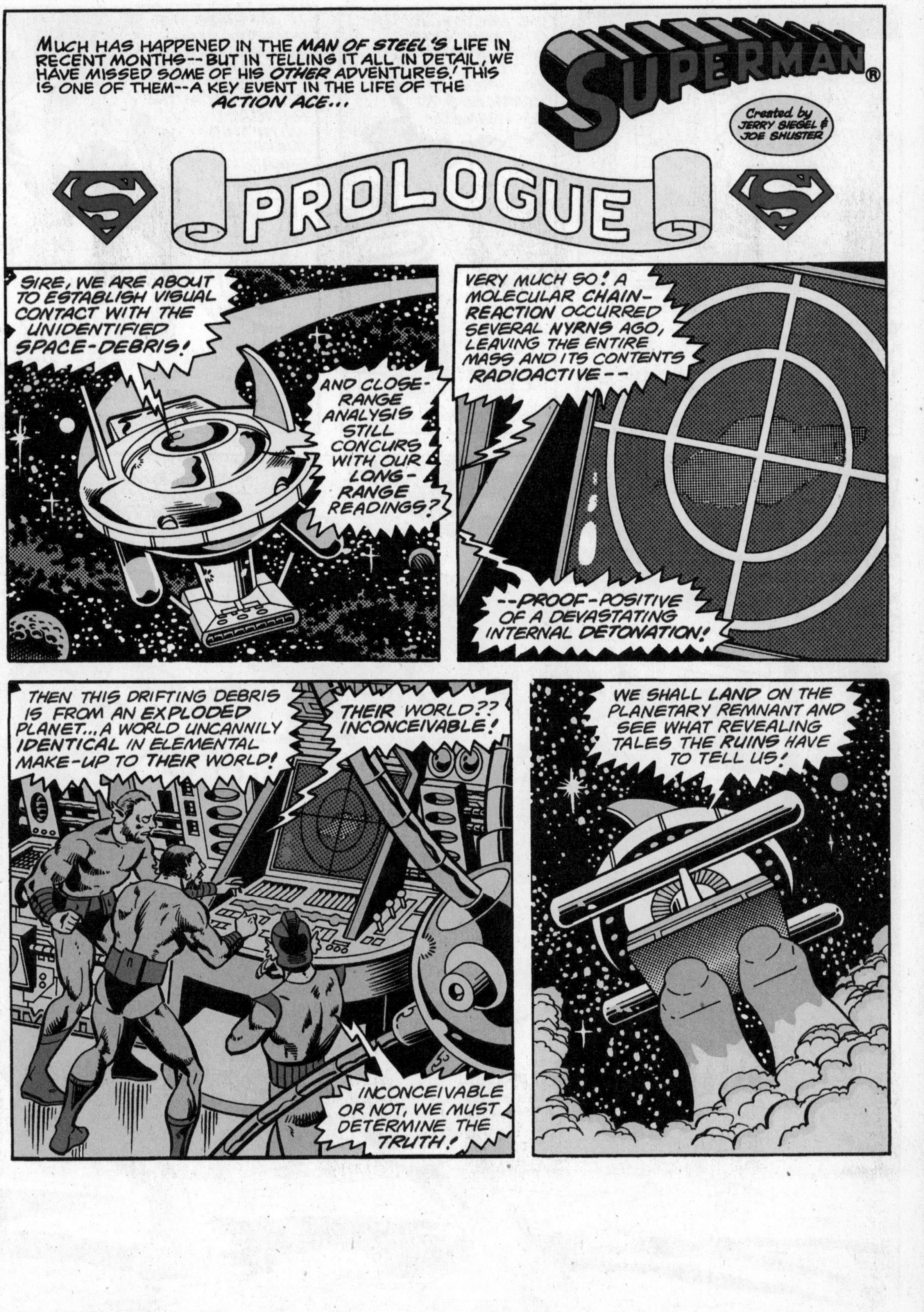
MUCH HAS HAPPENED IN THE MAN OF STEEL'S LIFE IN RECENT MONTHS-- BUT IN TELLING IT ALL IN DETAIL, WE HAVE MISSED SOME OF HIS OTHER ADVENTURES! THIS IS ONE OF THEM--A KEY EVENT IN THE LIFE OF THE ACTION ACE...
SUPERMAN®
Created by JERRY SIEGEL & JOE SHUSTER
PROLOGUE
SIRE, WE ARE ABOUT TO ESTABLISH VISUAL CONTACT WITH THE UNIDENTIFIED SPACE-DEBRIS!
AND CLOSE-RANGE ANALYSIS STILL CONCURS WITH OUR LONG-RANGE READINGS?
VERY MUCH SO! A MOLECULAR CHAIN-REACTION OCCURRED SEVERAL NYRNS AGO, LEAVING THE ENTIRE MASS AND ITS CONTENTS RADIOACTIVE--
--PROOF-POSITIVE OF A DEVASTATING INTERNAL DETONATION!
THEN THIS DRIFTING DEBRIS IS FROM AN EXPLODED PLANET...A WORLD UNCANNILY IDENTICAL IN ELEMENTAL MAKE-UP TO THEIR WORLD!
THEIR WORLD?? INCONCEIVABLE!
INCONCEIVABLE OR NOT, WE MUST DETERMINE THE TRUTH!
WE SHALL LAND ON THE PLANETARY REMNANT AND SEE WHAT REVEALING TALES THE RUINS HAVE TO TELL US!

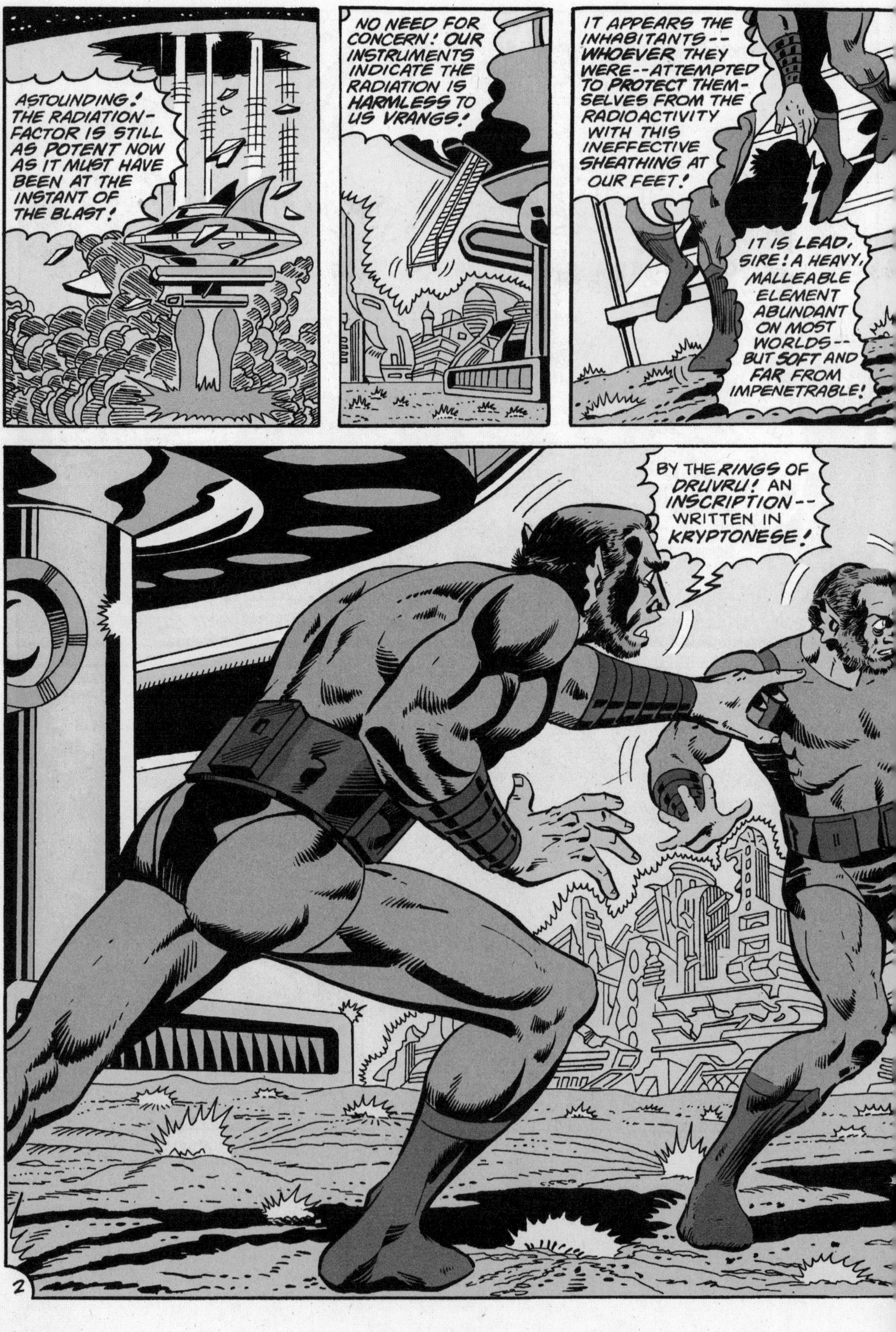

ASTOUNDING! THE RADIATION-FACTOR IS STILL AS POTENT NOW AS IT MUST HAVE BEEN AT THE INSTANT OF THE BLAST!
NO NEED FOR CONCERN! OUR INSTRUMENTS INDICATE THE RADIATION IS HARMLESS TO US VRANGS!
IT APPEARS THE INHABITANTS--WHOEVER THEY WERE--ATTEMPTED TO PROTECT THEMSELVES FROM THE RADIOACTIVITY WITH THIS INEFFECTIVE SHEATHING AT OUR FEET!
IT IS LEAD, SIRE! A HEAVY, MALLEABLE ELEMENT ABUNDANT ON MOST WORLDS--BUT SOFT AND FAR FROM IMPENETRABLE!
BY THE RINGS OF DRUVRU! AN INSCRIPTION--WRITTEN IN KRYPTONESE!
2

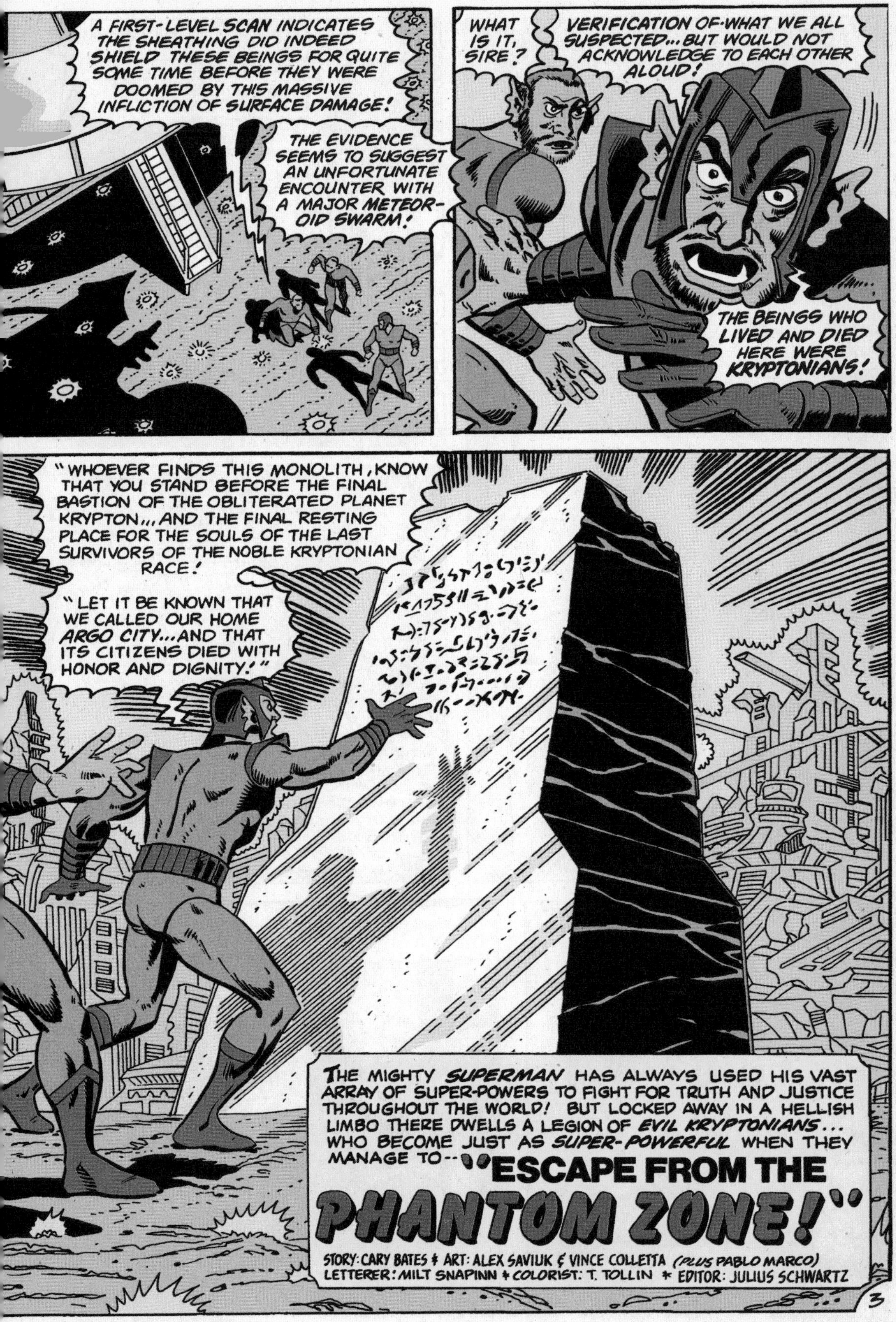
A FIRST-LEVEL SCAN INDICATES THE SHEATHING DID INDEED SHIELD THESE BEINGS FOR QUITE SOME TIME BEFORE THEY WERE DOOMED BY THIS MASSIVE INFLICTION OF SURFACE DAMAGE!
THE EVIDENCE SEEMS TO SUGGEST AN UNFORTUNATE ENCOUNTER WITH A MAJOR METEOR-OID SWARM!
WHAT IS IT, SIRE?
VERIFICATION OF WHAT WE ALL SUSPECTED... BUT WOULD NOT ACKNOWLEDGE TO EACH OTHER ALOUD!
THE BEINGS WHO LIVED AND DIED HERE WERE KRYPTONIANS!
"WHOEVER FINDS THIS MONOLITH, KNOW THAT YOU STAND BEFORE THE FINAL BASTION OF THE OBLITERATED PLANET KRYPTON... AND THE FINAL RESTING PLACE FOR THE SOULS OF THE LAST SURVIVORS OF THE NOBLE KRYPTONIAN RACE!
"LET IT BE KNOWN THAT WE CALLED OUR HOME ARGO CITY... AND THAT ITS CITIZENS DIED WITH HONOR AND DIGNITY!"
THE MIGHTY SUPERMAN HAS ALWAYS USED HIS VAST ARRAY OF SUPER-POWERS TO FIGHT FOR TRUTH AND JUSTICE THROUGHOUT THE WORLD! BUT LOCKED AWAY IN A HELLISH LIMBO THERE DWELLS A LEGION OF EVIL KRYPTONIANS... WHO BECOME JUST AS SUPER-POWERFUL WHEN THEY MANAGE TO--"ESCAPE FROM THE PHANTOM ZONE!"
STORY: CARY BATES & ART: ALEX SAVIUK & VINCE COLLETTA (PLUS PABLO MARCO)
LETTERER: MILT SNAPINN & COLORIST: T. TOLLIN * EDITOR: JULIUS SCHWARTZ
3

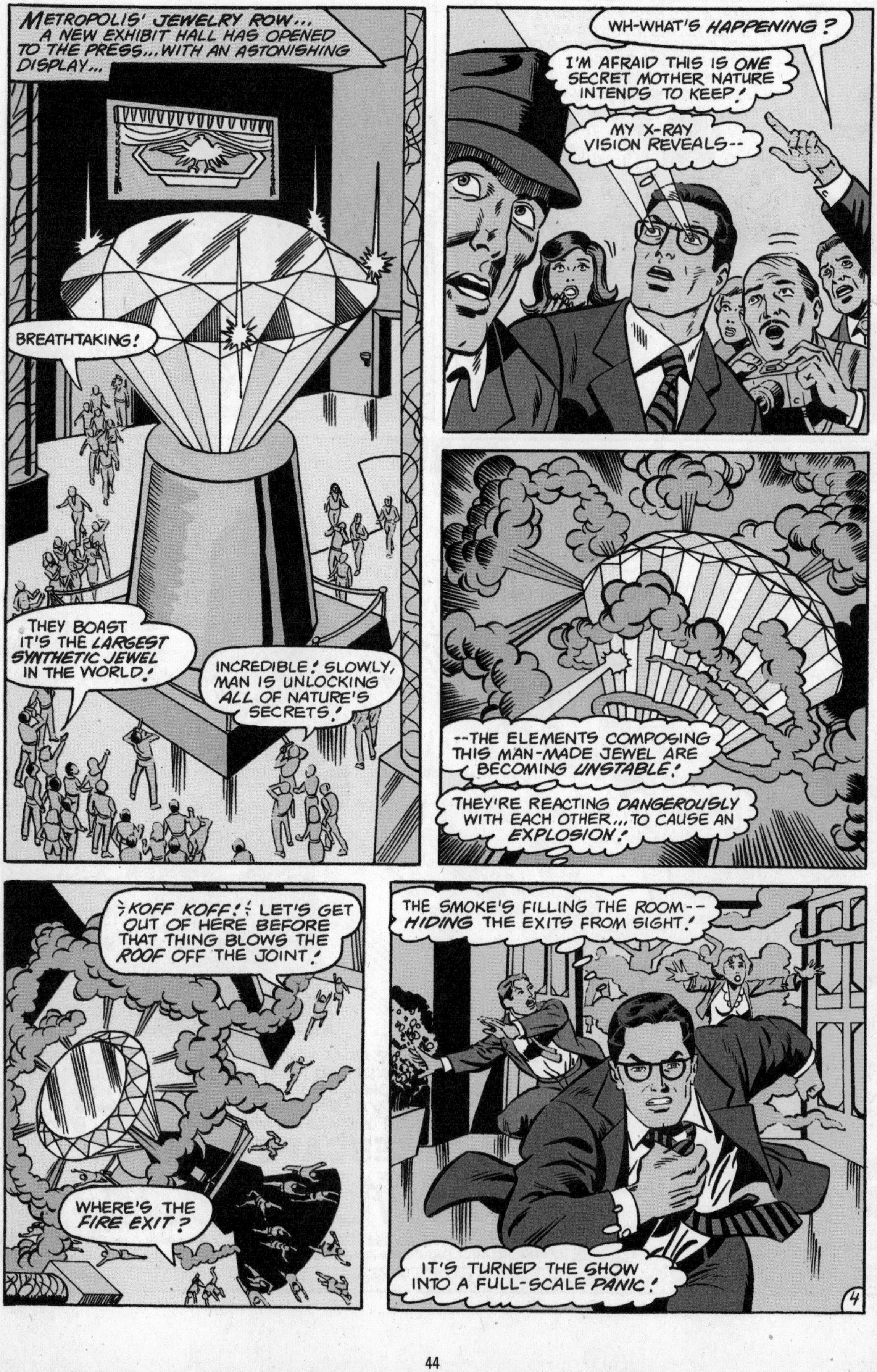
METROPOLIS' JEWELRY ROW... A NEW EXHIBIT HALL HAS OPENED TO THE PRESS...WITH AN ASTONISHING DISPLAY...
BREATHTAKING!
THEY BOAST IT'S THE LARGEST SYNTHETIC JEWEL IN THE WORLD!
INCREDIBLE! SLOWLY, MAN IS UNLOCKING ALL OF NATURE'S SECRETS!
WH-WHAT'S HAPPENING?
I'M AFRAID THIS IS ONE SECRET MOTHER NATURE INTENDS TO KEEP!
MY X-RAY VISION REVEALS--
--THE ELEMENTS COMPOSING THIS MAN-MADE JEWEL ARE BECOMING UNSTABLE!
THEY'RE REACTING DANGEROUSLY WITH EACH OTHER...TO CAUSE AN EXPLOSION!
KOFF KOFF! LET'S GET OUT OF HERE BEFORE THAT THING BLOWS THE ROOF OFF THE JOINT!
WHERE'S THE FIRE EXIT?
THE SMOKE'S FILLING THE ROOM-- HIDING THE EXITS FROM SIGHT!
IT'S TURNED THE SHOW INTO A FULL-SCALE PANIC!
4

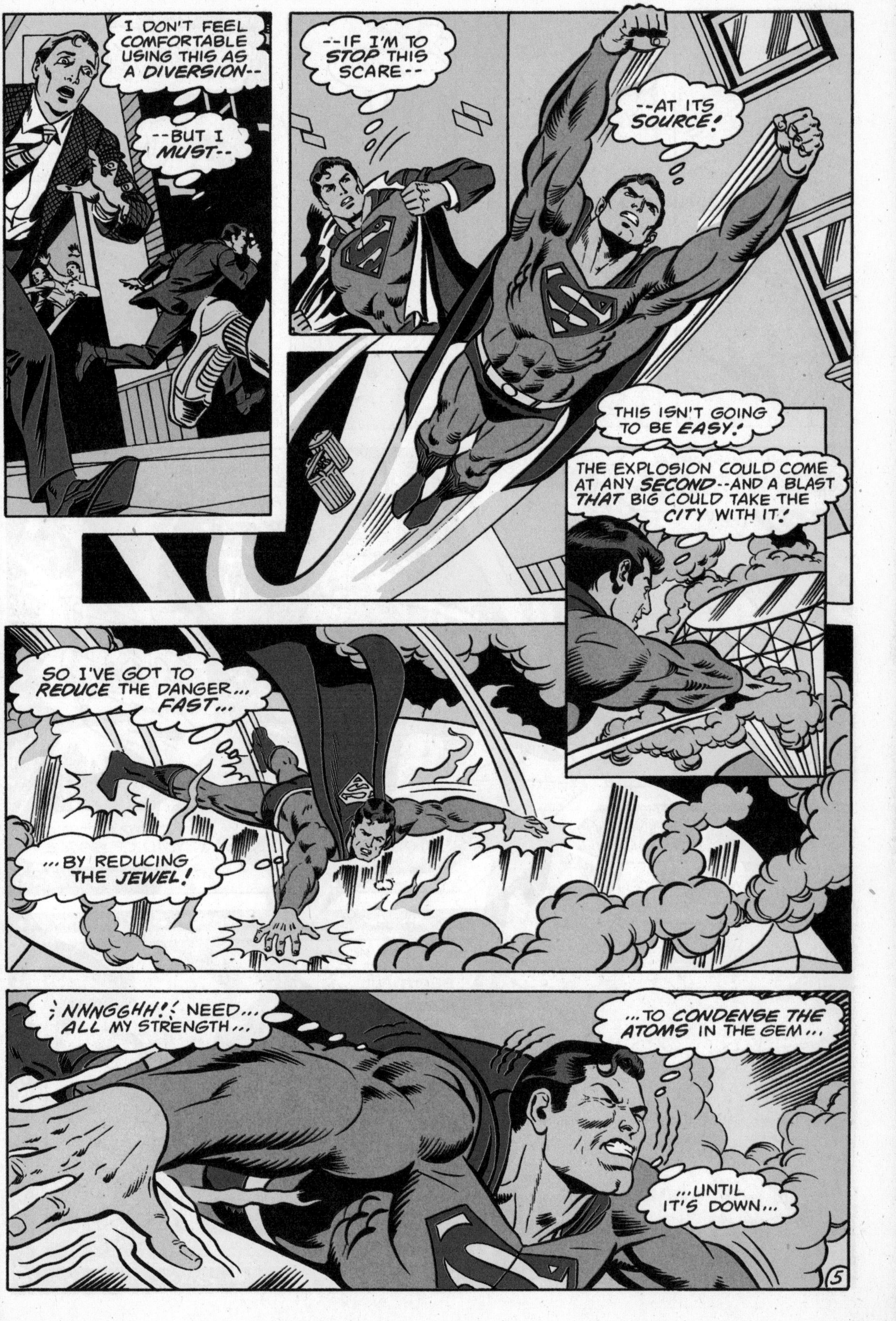

I DON'T FEEL COMFORTABLE USING THIS AS A DIVERSION--
--BUT I MUST--
--IF I'M TO STOP THIS SCARE--
--AT ITS SOURCE!
THIS ISN'T GOING TO BE EASY!
THE EXPLOSION COULD COME AT ANY SECOND--AND A BLAST THAT BIG COULD TAKE THE CITY WITH IT!
SO I'VE GOT TO REDUCE THE DANGER... FAST...
...BY REDUCING THE JEWEL!
¡NNNGGHH!¡ NEED... ALL MY STRENGTH...
...TO CONDENSE THE ATOMS IN THE GEM...
...UNTIL IT'S DOWN...
5

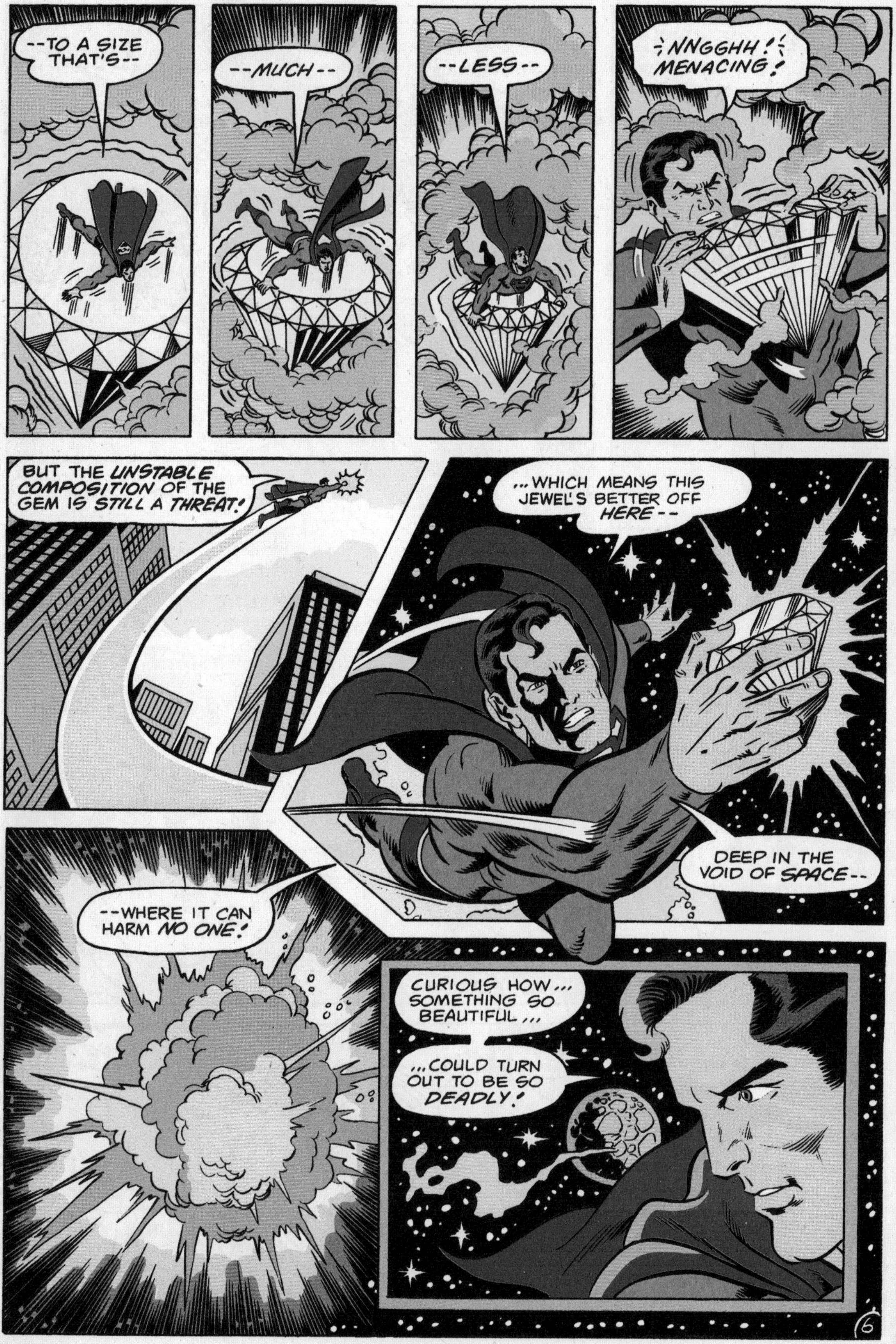
--TO A SIZE THAT'S--
--MUCH--
--LESS--
NNGGHH! MENACING!
BUT THE UNSTABLE COMPOSITION OF THE GEM IS STILL A THREAT!
...WHICH MEANS THIS JEWEL'S BETTER OFF HERE--
DEEP IN THE VOID OF SPACE--
--WHERE IT CAN HARM NO ONE!
CURIOUS HOW... SOMETHING SO BEAUTIFUL...
...COULD TURN OUT TO BE SO DEADLY!
6

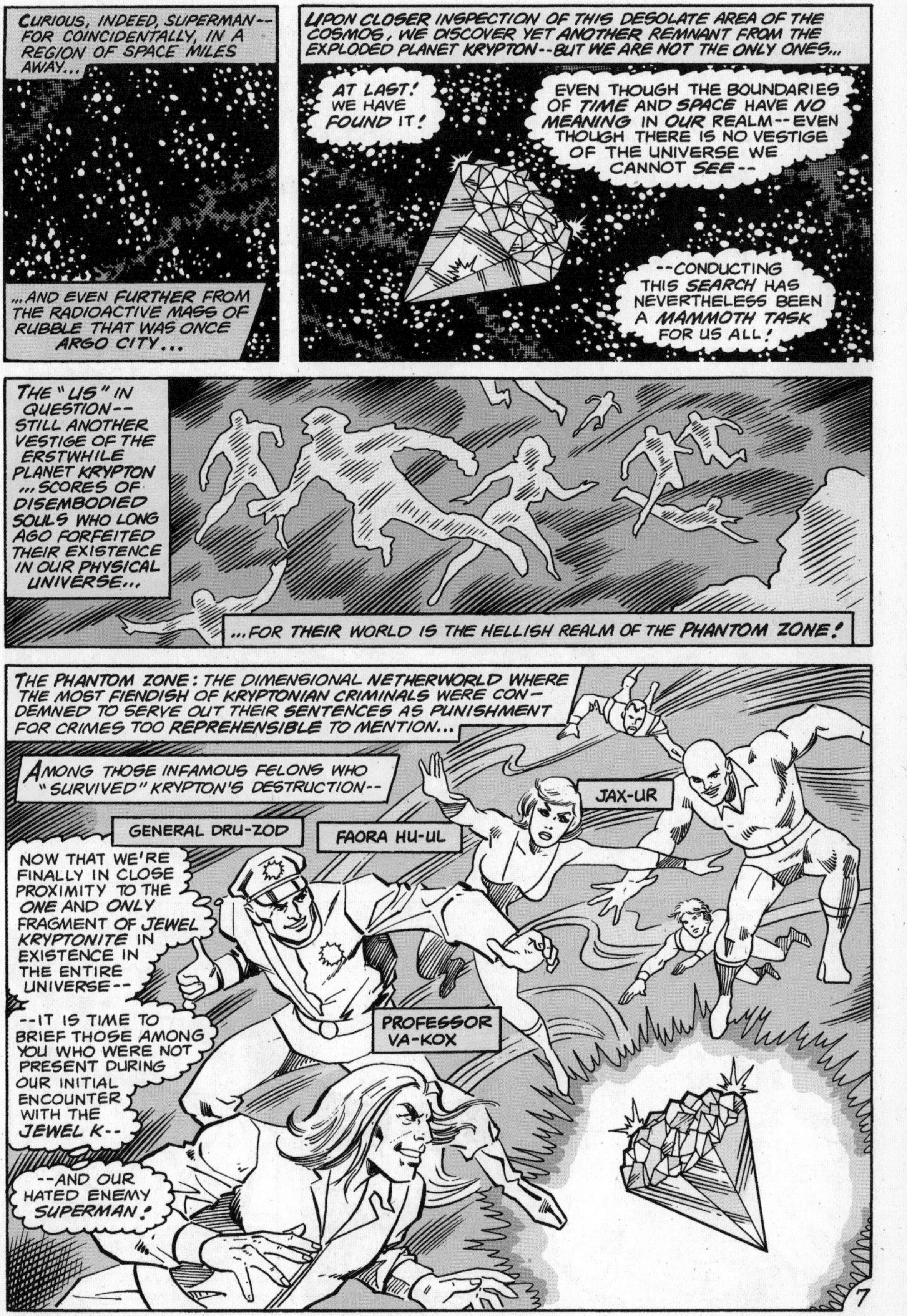
CURIOUS, INDEED, SUPERMAN--FOR COINCIDENTALLY, IN A REGION OF SPACE MILES AWAY...
...AND EVEN FURTHER FROM THE RADIOACTIVE MASS OF RUBBLE THAT WAS ONCE ARGO CITY...
UPON CLOSER INSPECTION OF THIS DESOLATE AREA OF THE COSMOS, WE DISCOVER YET ANOTHER REMNANT FROM THE EXPLODED PLANET KRYPTON--BUT WE ARE NOT THE ONLY ONES...
AT LAST! WE HAVE FOUND IT!
EVEN THOUGH THE BOUNDARIES OF TIME AND SPACE HAVE NO MEANING IN OUR REALM--EVEN THOUGH THERE IS NO VESTIGE OF THE UNIVERSE WE CANNOT SEE--
--CONDUCTING THIS SEARCH HAS NEVERTHELESS BEEN A MAMMOTH TASK FOR US ALL!
THE "US" IN QUESTION--STILL ANOTHER VESTIGE OF THE ERSTWHILE PLANET KRYPTON ...SCORES OF DISEMBODIED SOULS WHO LONG AGO FORFEITED THEIR EXISTENCE IN OUR PHYSICAL UNIVERSE...
...FOR THEIR WORLD IS THE HELLISH REALM OF THE PHANTOM ZONE!
THE PHANTOM ZONE: THE DIMENSIONAL NETHERWORLD WHERE THE MOST FIENDISH OF KRYPTONIAN CRIMINALS WERE CON-DEMNED TO SERVE OUT THEIR SENTENCES AS PUNISHMENT FOR CRIMES TOO REPREHENSIBLE TO MENTION...
AMONG THOSE INFAMOUS FELONS WHO "SURVIVED" KRYPTON'S DESTRUCTION--
JAX-UR
GENERAL DRU-ZOD
FAORA HU-UL
NOW THAT WE'RE FINALLY IN CLOSE PROXIMITY TO THE ONE AND ONLY FRAGMENT OF JEWEL KRYPTONITE IN EXISTENCE IN THE ENTIRE UNIVERSE--
--IT IS TIME TO BRIEF THOSE AMONG YOU WHO WERE NOT PRESENT DURING OUR INITIAL ENCOUNTER WITH THE JEWEL K--
PROFESSOR VA-KOX
--AND OUR HATED ENEMY SUPERMAN!
7

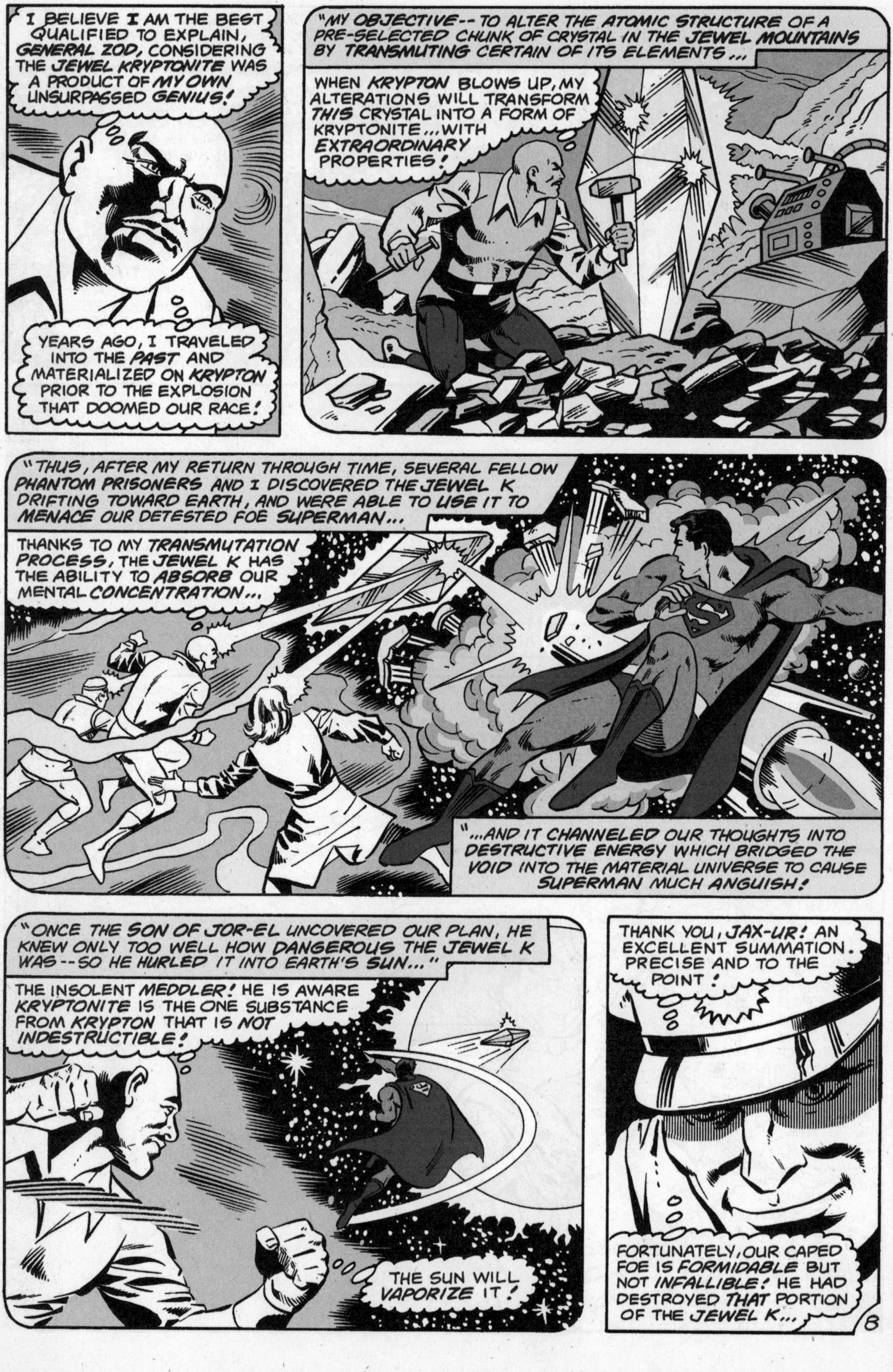
I BELIEVE I AM THE BEST QUALIFIED TO EXPLAIN, GENERAL ZOD, CONSIDERING THE JEWEL KRYPTONITE WAS A PRODUCT OF MY OWN UNSURPASSED GENIUS!
YEARS AGO, I TRAVELED INTO THE PAST AND MATERIALIZED ON KRYPTON PRIOR TO THE EXPLOSION THAT DOOMED OUR RACE!
"MY OBJECTIVE-- TO ALTER THE ATOMIC STRUCTURE OF A PRE-SELECTED CHUNK OF CRYSTAL IN THE JEWEL MOUNTAINS BY TRANSMUTING CERTAIN OF ITS ELEMENTS...
WHEN KRYPTON BLOWS UP, MY ALTERATIONS WILL TRANSFORM THIS CRYSTAL INTO A FORM OF KRYPTONITE... WITH EXTRAORDINARY PROPERTIES!
"THUS, AFTER MY RETURN THROUGH TIME, SEVERAL FELLOW PHANTOM PRISONERS AND I DISCOVERED THE JEWEL K DRIFTING TOWARD EARTH, AND WERE ABLE TO USE IT TO MENACE OUR DETESTED FOE SUPERMAN...
THANKS TO MY TRANSMUTATION PROCESS, THE JEWEL K HAS THE ABILITY TO ABSORB OUR MENTAL CONCENTRATION...
"...AND IT CHANNELED OUR THOUGHTS INTO DESTRUCTIVE ENERGY WHICH BRIDGED THE VOID INTO THE MATERIAL UNIVERSE TO CAUSE SUPERMAN MUCH ANGUISH!
"ONCE THE SON OF JOR-EL UNCOVERED OUR PLAN, HE KNEW ONLY TOO WELL HOW DANGEROUS THE JEWEL K WAS--SO HE HURLED IT INTO EARTH'S SUN..."
THE INSOLENT MEDDLER! HE IS AWARE KRYPTONITE IS THE ONE SUBSTANCE FROM KRYPTON THAT IS NOT INDESTRUCTIBLE!
THE SUN WILL VAPORIZE IT!
THANK YOU, JAX-UR! AN EXCELLENT SUMMATION. PRECISE AND TO THE POINT!
FORTUNATELY, OUR CAPED FOE IS FORMIDABLE BUT NOT INFALLIBLE! HE HAD DESTROYED THAT PORTION OF THE JEWEL K...
8

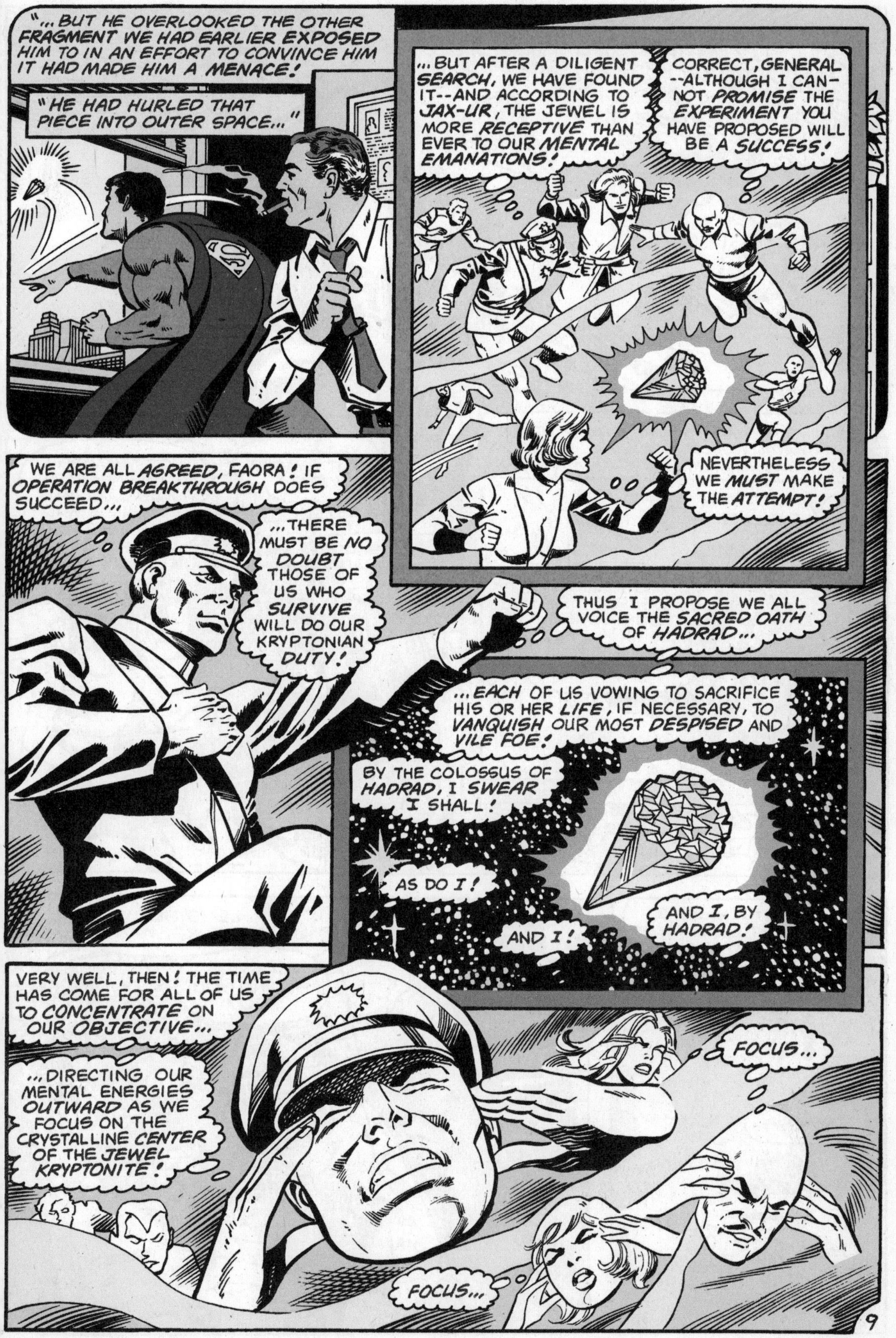
"...BUT HE OVERLOOKED THE OTHER FRAGMENT WE HAD EARLIER EXPOSED HIM TO IN AN EFFORT TO CONVINCE HIM IT HAD MADE HIM A MENACE!
"HE HAD HURLED THAT PIECE INTO OUTER SPACE..."
...BUT AFTER A DILIGENT SEARCH, WE HAVE FOUND IT--AND ACCORDING TO JAX-UR, THE JEWEL IS MORE RECEPTIVE THAN EVER TO OUR MENTAL EMANATIONS!
CORRECT, GENERAL --ALTHOUGH I CANNOT PROMISE THE EXPERIMENT YOU HAVE PROPOSED WILL BE A SUCCESS!
NEVERTHELESS WE MUST MAKE THE ATTEMPT!
WE ARE ALL AGREED, FAORA! IF OPERATION BREAKTHROUGH DOES SUCCEED...
...THERE MUST BE NO DOUBT THOSE OF US WHO SURVIVE WILL DO OUR KRYPTONIAN DUTY!
THUS I PROPOSE WE ALL VOICE THE SACRED OATH OF HADRAD...
...EACH OF US VOWING TO SACRIFICE HIS OR HER LIFE, IF NECESSARY, TO VANQUISH OUR MOST DESPISED AND VILE FOE!
BY THE COLOSSUS OF HADRAD, I SWEAR I SHALL!
AS DO I!
AND I!
AND I, BY HADRAD!
VERY WELL, THEN! THE TIME HAS COME FOR ALL OF US TO CONCENTRATE ON OUR OBJECTIVE...
...DIRECTING OUR MENTAL ENERGIES OUTWARD AS WE FOCUS ON THE CRYSTALLINE CENTER OF THE JEWEL KRYPTONITE!
FOCUS...
FOCUS...
9

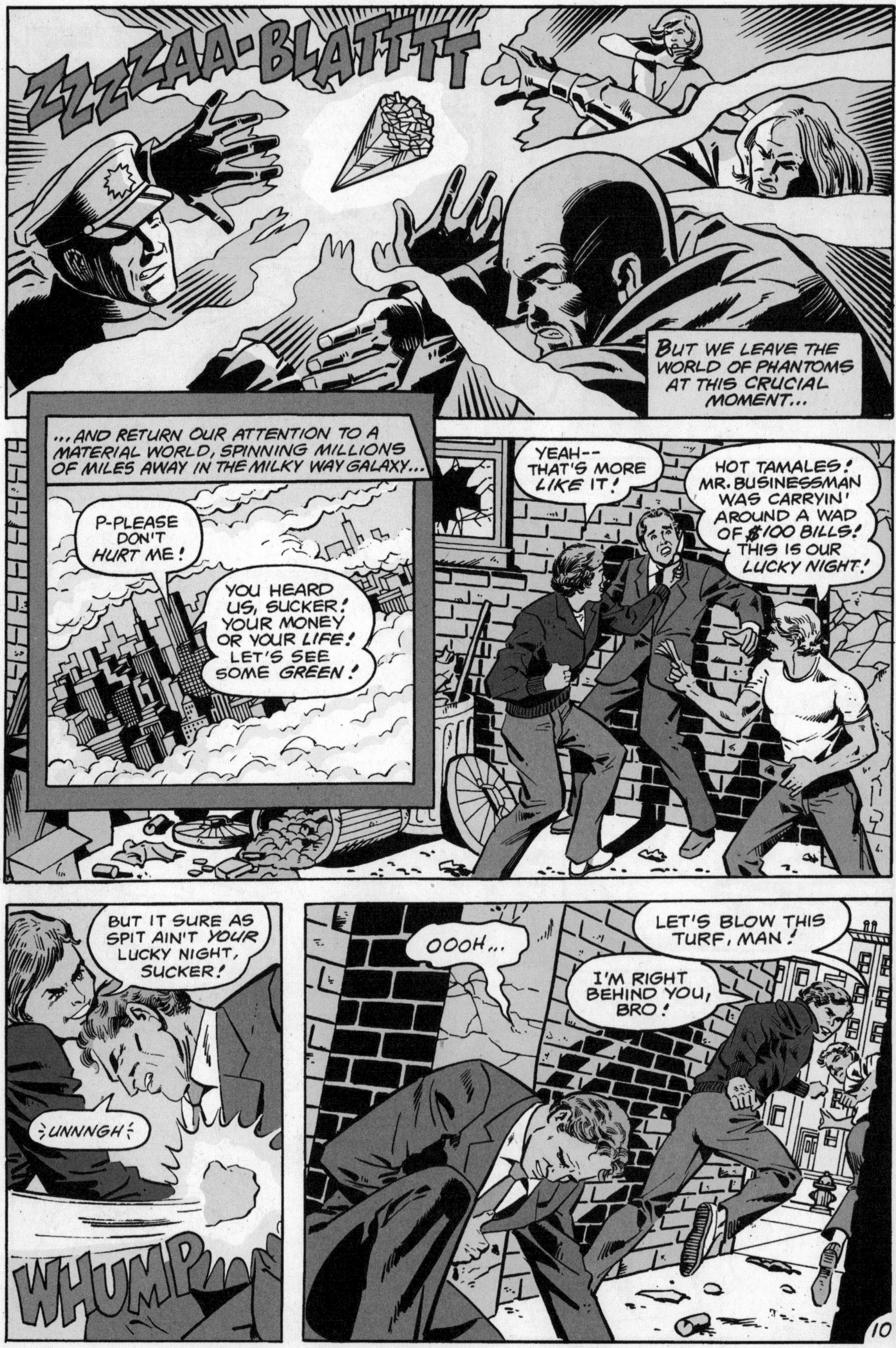
ZZZZAA-BLATTTTT
BUT WE LEAVE THE WORLD OF PHANTOMS AT THIS CRUCIAL MOMENT...
...AND RETURN OUR ATTENTION TO A MATERIAL WORLD, SPINNING MILLIONS OF MILES AWAY IN THE MILKY WAY GALAXY...
P-PLEASE DON'T HURT ME!
YOU HEARD US, SUCKER! YOUR MONEY OR YOUR LIFE! LET'S SEE SOME GREEN!
YEAH-- THAT'S MORE LIKE IT!
HOT TAMALES! MR. BUSINESSMAN WAS CARRYIN' AROUND A WAD OF $100 BILLS! THIS IS OUR LUCKY NIGHT!
BUT IT SURE AS SPIT AIN'T YOUR LUCKY NIGHT, SUCKER!
UNNNGH
WHUMP
OOOH...
LET'S BLOW THIS TURF, MAN!
I'M RIGHT BEHIND YOU, BRO!
10

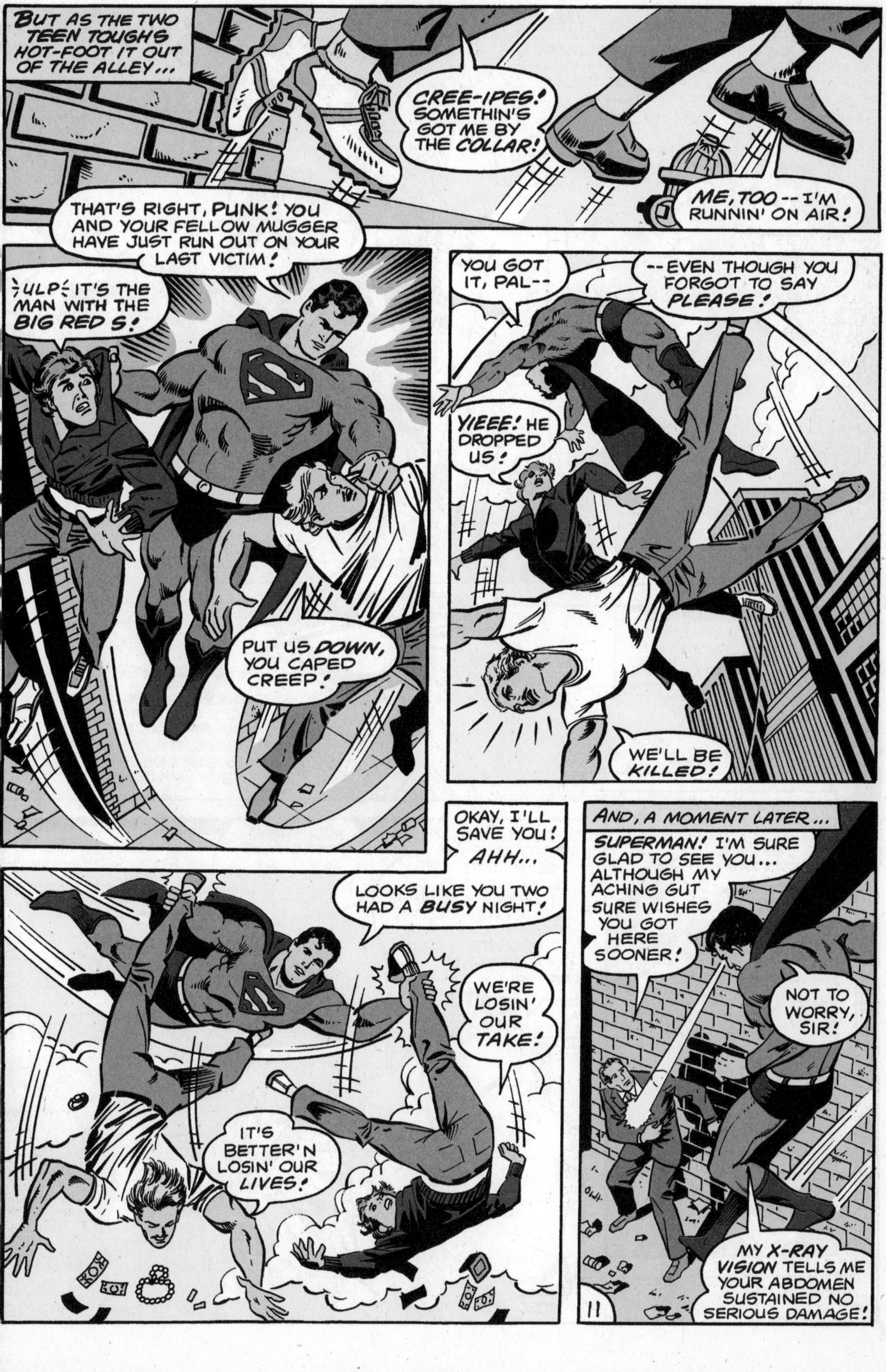
BUT AS THE TWO TEEN TOUGHS HOT-FOOT IT OUT OF THE ALLEY...
CREE-IPES! SOMETHIN'S GOT ME BY THE COLLAR!
ME, TOO -- I'M RUNNIN' ON AIR!
THAT'S RIGHT, PUNK! YOU AND YOUR FELLOW MUGGER HAVE JUST RUN OUT ON YOUR LAST VICTIM!
ULP IT'S THE MAN WITH THE BIG RED S!
PUT US DOWN, YOU CAPED CREEP!
YOU GOT IT, PAL--
--EVEN THOUGH YOU FORGOT TO SAY PLEASE!
YIEEE! HE DROPPED US!
WE'LL BE KILLED!
OKAY, I'LL SAVE YOU! AHH...
LOOKS LIKE YOU TWO HAD A BUSY NIGHT!
WE'RE LOSIN' OUR TAKE!
IT'S BETTER'N LOSIN' OUR LIVES!
AND, A MOMENT LATER...
SUPERMAN! I'M SURE GLAD TO SEE YOU... ALTHOUGH MY ACHING GUT SURE WISHES YOU GOT HERE SOONER!
NOT TO WORRY, SIR!
MY X-RAY VISION TELLS ME YOUR ABDOMEN SUSTAINED NO SERIOUS DAMAGE!
11

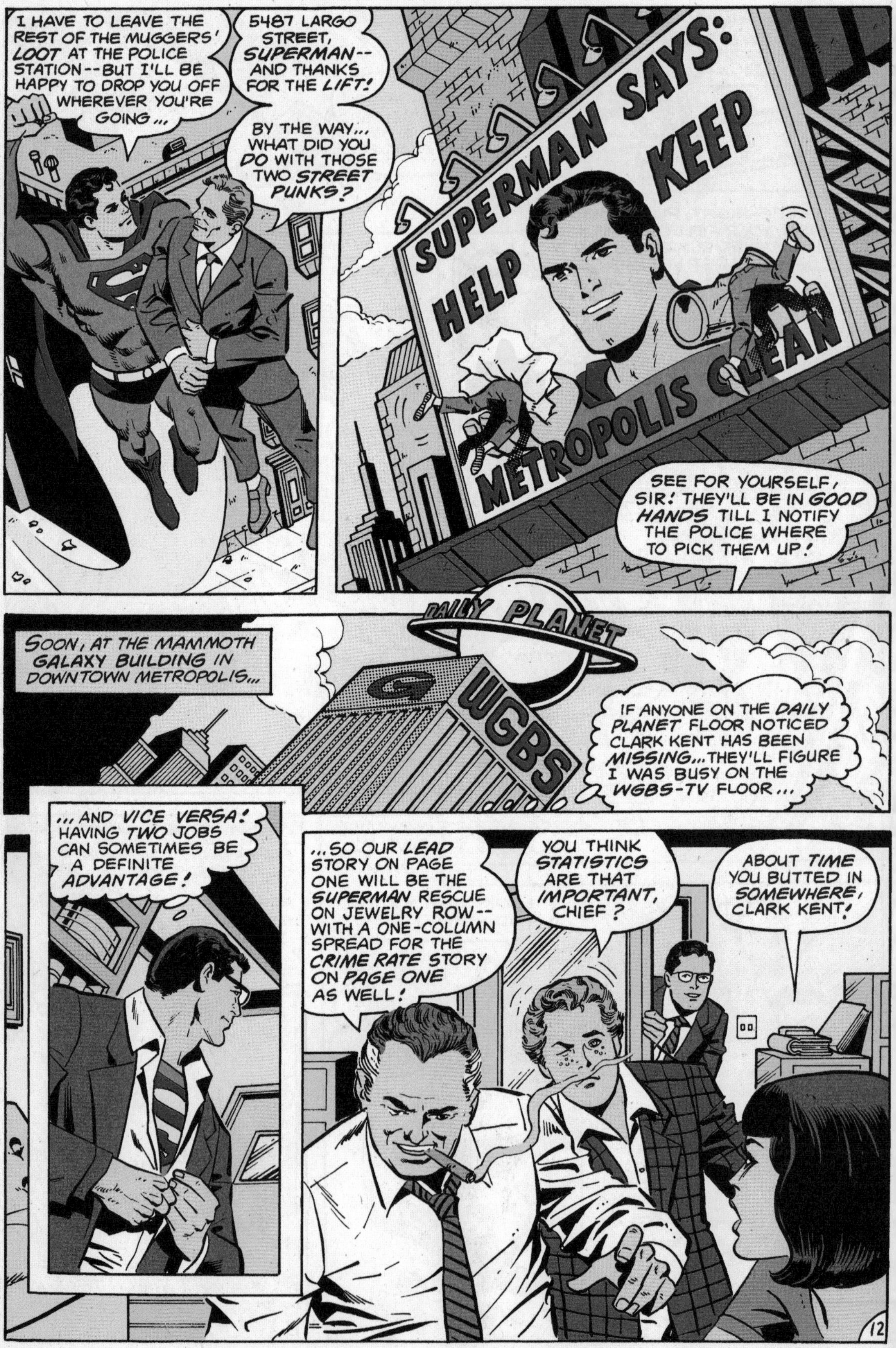
I HAVE TO LEAVE THE REST OF THE MUGGERS' LOOT AT THE POLICE STATION--BUT I'LL BE HAPPY TO DROP YOU OFF WHEREVER YOU'RE GOING...
5487 LARGO STREET, SUPERMAN--AND THANKS FOR THE LIFT!
BY THE WAY... WHAT DID YOU DO WITH THOSE TWO STREET PUNKS?
SUPERMAN SAYS: HELP KEEP METROPOLIS CLEAN
SEE FOR YOURSELF, SIR! THEY'LL BE IN GOOD HANDS TILL I NOTIFY THE POLICE WHERE TO PICK THEM UP!
SOON, AT THE MAMMOTH GALAXY BUILDING IN DOWNTOWN METROPOLIS...
DAILY PLANET
WGBS
IF ANYONE ON THE DAILY PLANET FLOOR NOTICED CLARK KENT HAS BEEN MISSING... THEY'LL FIGURE I WAS BUSY ON THE WGBS-TV FLOOR...
...AND VICE VERSA! HAVING TWO JOBS CAN SOMETIMES BE A DEFINITE ADVANTAGE!
...SO OUR LEAD STORY ON PAGE ONE WILL BE THE SUPERMAN RESCUE ON JEWELRY ROW--WITH A ONE-COLUMN SPREAD FOR THE CRIME RATE STORY ON PAGE ONE AS WELL!
YOU THINK STATISTICS ARE THAT IMPORTANT, CHIEF?
ABOUT TIME YOU BUTTED IN SOMEWHERE, CLARK KENT!
12

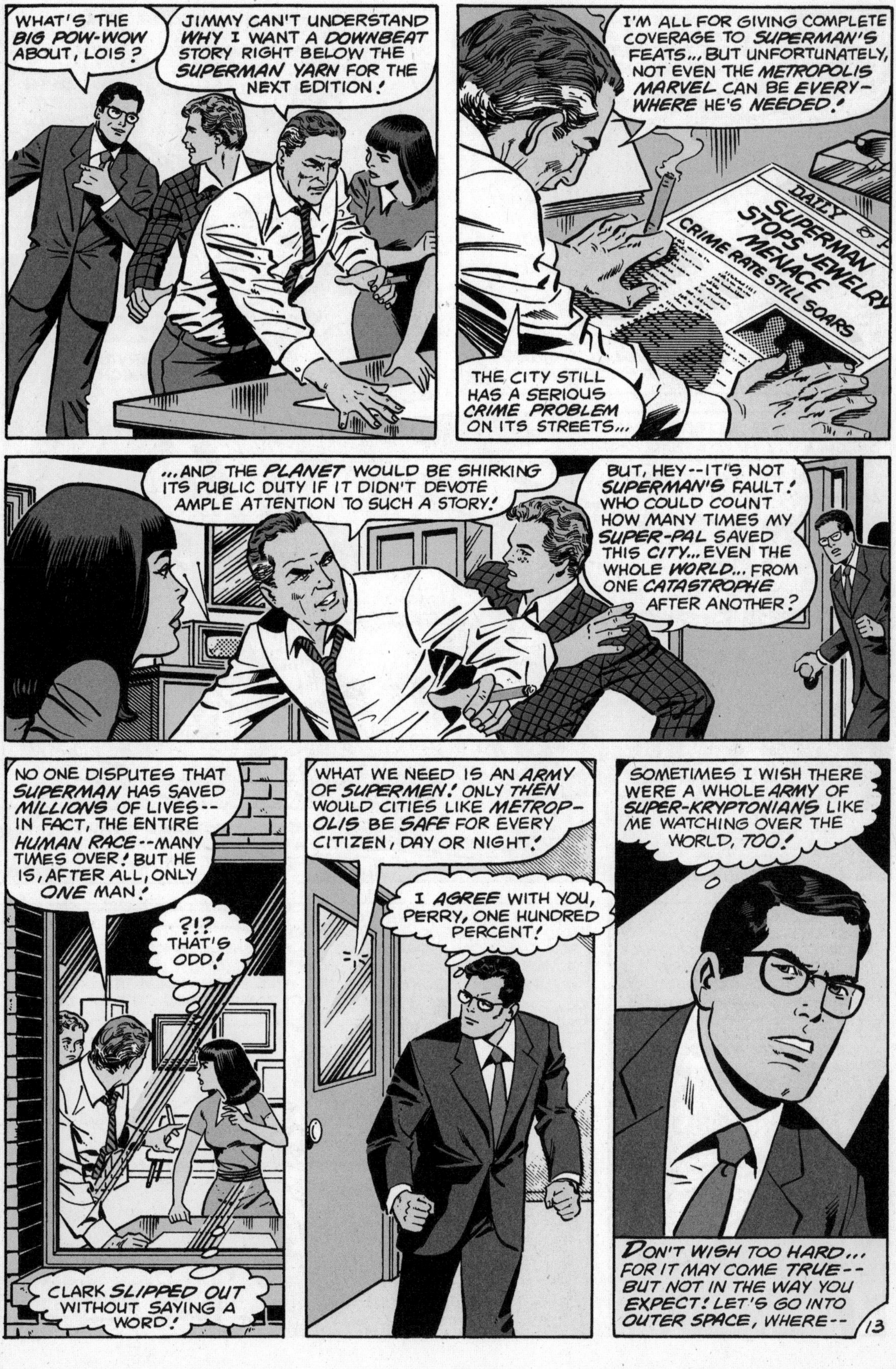
WHAT'S THE BIG POW-WOW ABOUT, LOIS?
JIMMY CAN'T UNDERSTAND WHY I WANT A DOWNBEAT STORY RIGHT BELOW THE SUPERMAN YARN FOR THE NEXT EDITION!
I'M ALL FOR GIVING COMPLETE COVERAGE TO SUPERMAN'S FEATS... BUT UNFORTUNATELY, NOT EVEN THE METROPOLIS MARVEL CAN BE EVERY-WHERE HE'S NEEDED!
DAILY
SUPERMAN STOPS JEWELRY MENACE
CRIME RATE STILL SOARS
THE CITY STILL HAS A SERIOUS CRIME PROBLEM ON ITS STREETS...
...AND THE PLANET WOULD BE SHIRKING ITS PUBLIC DUTY IF IT DIDN'T DEVOTE AMPLE ATTENTION TO SUCH A STORY!
BUT, HEY--IT'S NOT SUPERMAN'S FAULT! WHO COULD COUNT HOW MANY TIMES MY SUPER-PAL SAVED THIS CITY... EVEN THE WHOLE WORLD... FROM ONE CATASTROPHE AFTER ANOTHER?
NO ONE DISPUTES THAT SUPERMAN HAS SAVED MILLIONS OF LIVES--IN FACT, THE ENTIRE HUMAN RACE--MANY TIMES OVER! BUT HE IS, AFTER ALL, ONLY ONE MAN!
?!? THAT'S ODD!
CLARK SLIPPED OUT WITHOUT SAYING A WORD!
WHAT WE NEED IS AN ARMY OF SUPERMEN! ONLY THEN WOULD CITIES LIKE METROP-OLIS BE SAFE FOR EVERY CITIZEN, DAY OR NIGHT!
I AGREE WITH YOU, PERRY, ONE HUNDRED PERCENT!
SOMETIMES I WISH THERE WERE A WHOLE ARMY OF SUPER-KRYPTONIANS LIKE ME WATCHING OVER THE WORLD, TOO!
DON'T WISH TOO HARD... FOR IT MAY COME TRUE--BUT NOT IN THE WAY YOU EXPECT! LET'S GO INTO OUTER SPACE, WHERE--
13

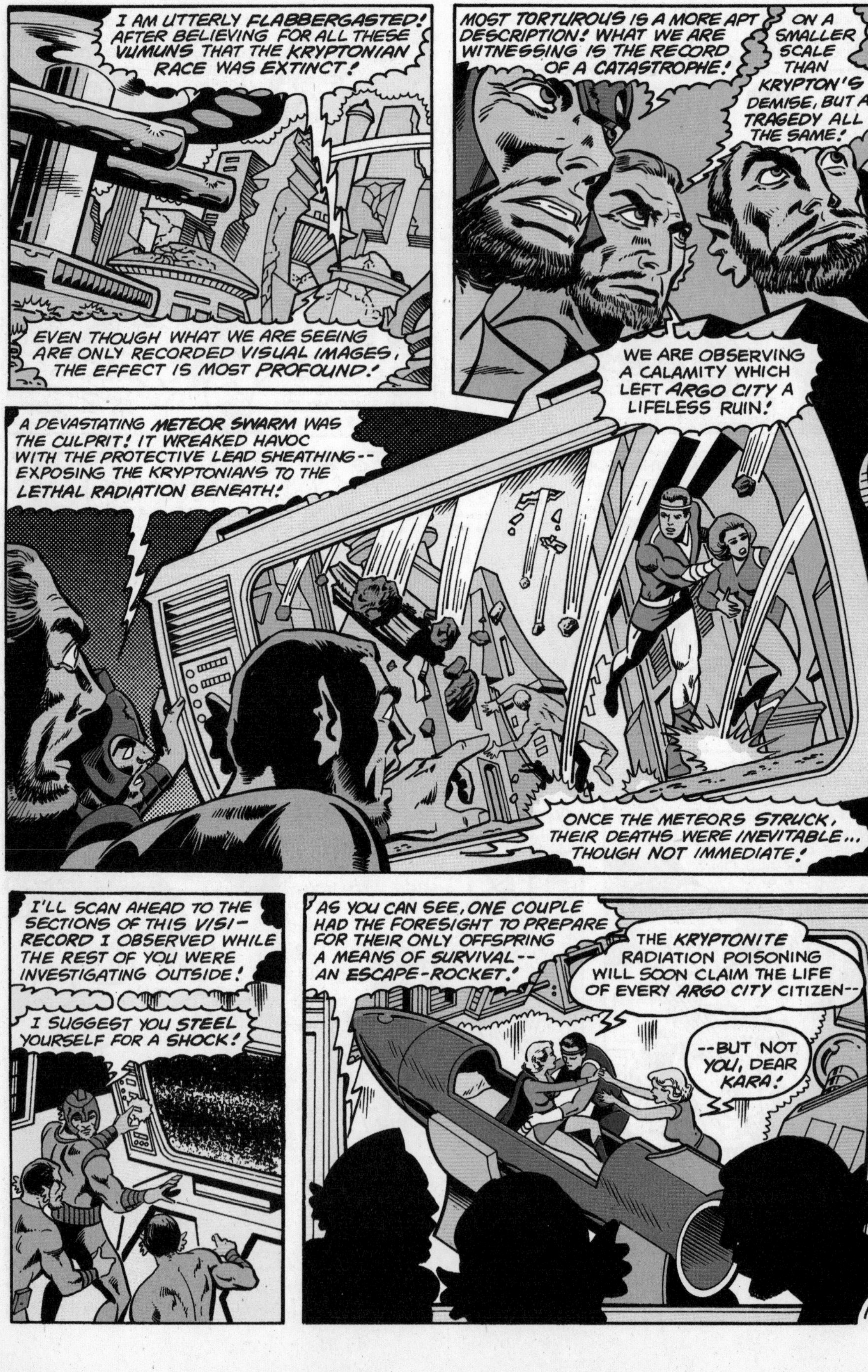
I AM UTTERLY FLABBERGASTED! AFTER BELIEVING FOR ALL THESE VUMUNS THAT THE KRYPTONIAN RACE WAS EXTINCT!
EVEN THOUGH WHAT WE ARE SEEING ARE ONLY RECORDED VISUAL IMAGES, THE EFFECT IS MOST PROFOUND!
MOST TORTUROUS IS A MORE APT DESCRIPTION! WHAT WE ARE WITNESSING IS THE RECORD OF A CATASTROPHE!
ON A SMALLER SCALE THAN KRYPTON'S DEMISE, BUT A TRAGEDY ALL THE SAME!
WE ARE OBSERVING A CALAMITY WHICH LEFT ARGO CITY A LIFELESS RUIN!
A DEVASTATING METEOR SWARM WAS THE CULPRIT! IT WREAKED HAVOC WITH THE PROTECTIVE LEAD SHEATHING-- EXPOSING THE KRYPTONIANS TO THE LETHAL RADIATION BENEATH!
ONCE THE METEORS STRUCK, THEIR DEATHS WERE INEVITABLE... THOUGH NOT IMMEDIATE!
I'LL SCAN AHEAD TO THE SECTIONS OF THIS VISI-RECORD I OBSERVED WHILE THE REST OF YOU WERE INVESTIGATING OUTSIDE!
I SUGGEST YOU STEEL YOURSELF FOR A SHOCK!
AS YOU CAN SEE, ONE COUPLE HAD THE FORESIGHT TO PREPARE FOR THEIR ONLY OFFSPRING A MEANS OF SURVIVAL-- AN ESCAPE-ROCKET!
THE KRYPTONITE RADIATION POISONING WILL SOON CLAIM THE LIFE OF EVERY ARGO CITY CITIZEN--
--BUT NOT YOU, DEAR KARA!
14

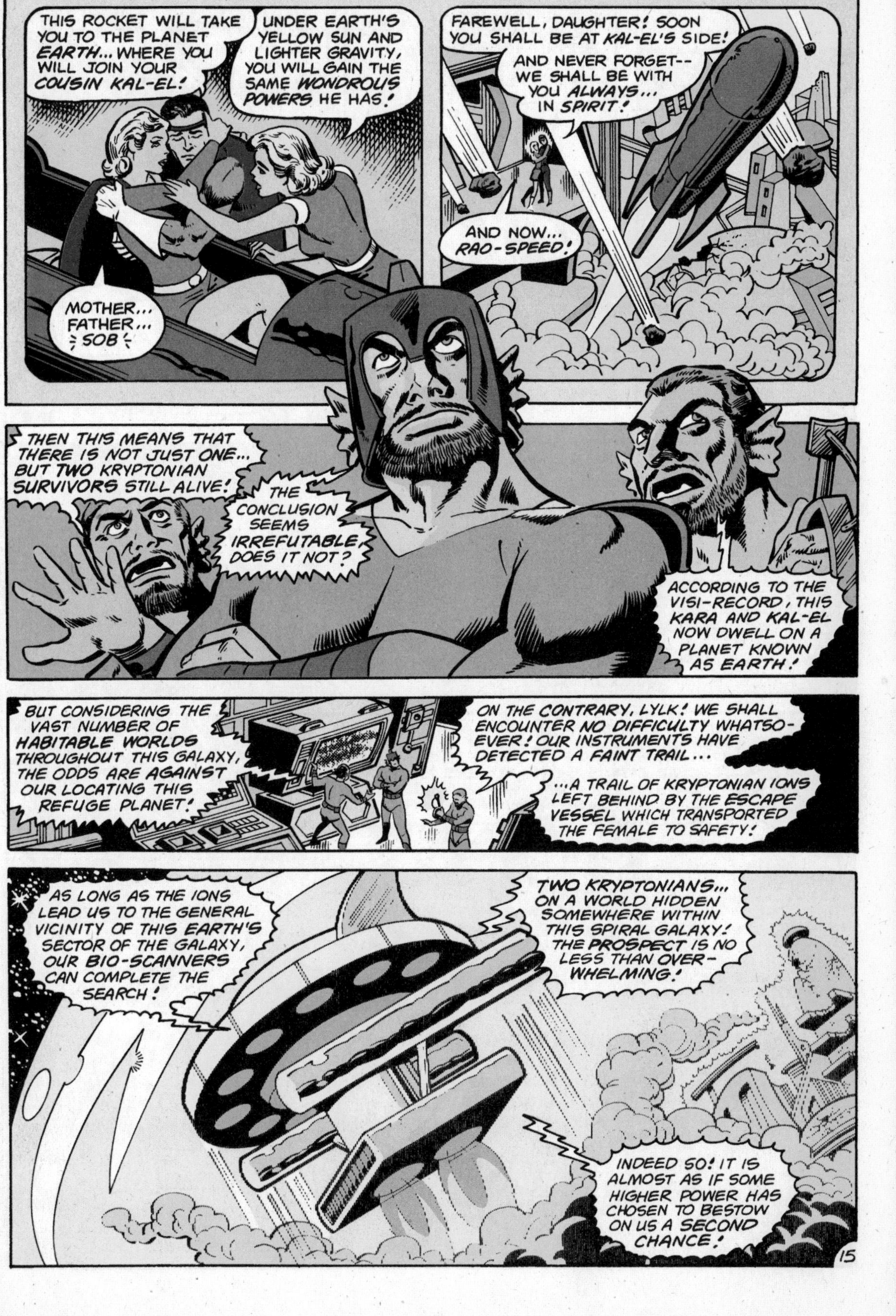
THIS ROCKET WILL TAKE YOU TO THE PLANET EARTH... WHERE YOU WILL JOIN YOUR COUSIN KAL-EL!
UNDER EARTH'S YELLOW SUN AND LIGHTER GRAVITY, YOU WILL GAIN THE SAME WONDROUS POWERS HE HAS!
MOTHER... FATHER... SOB
FAREWELL, DAUGHTER! SOON YOU SHALL BE AT KAL-EL'S SIDE!
AND NEVER FORGET-- WE SHALL BE WITH YOU ALWAYS... IN SPIRIT!
AND NOW... RAO-SPEED!
THEN THIS MEANS THAT THERE IS NOT JUST ONE... BUT TWO KRYPTONIAN SURVIVORS STILL ALIVE!
THE CONCLUSION SEEMS IRREFUTABLE, DOES IT NOT?
ACCORDING TO THE VISI-RECORD, THIS KARA AND KAL-EL NOW DWELL ON A PLANET KNOWN AS EARTH!
BUT CONSIDERING THE VAST NUMBER OF HABITABLE WORLDS THROUGHOUT THIS GALAXY, THE ODDS ARE AGAINST OUR LOCATING THIS REFUGE PLANET!
ON THE CONTRARY, LYLK! WE SHALL ENCOUNTER NO DIFFICULTY WHATSOEVER! OUR INSTRUMENTS HAVE DETECTED A FAINT TRAIL...
...A TRAIL OF KRYPTONIAN IONS LEFT BEHIND BY THE ESCAPE VESSEL WHICH TRANSPORTED THE FEMALE TO SAFETY!
AS LONG AS THE IONS LEAD US TO THE GENERAL VICINITY OF THIS EARTH'S SECTOR OF THE GALAXY, OUR BIO-SCANNERS CAN COMPLETE THE SEARCH!
TWO KRYPTONIANS... ON A WORLD HIDDEN SOMEWHERE WITHIN THIS SPIRAL GALAXY! THE PROSPECT IS NO LESS THAN OVERWHELMING!
INDEED SO! IT IS ALMOST AS IF SOME HIGHER POWER HAS CHOSEN TO BESTOW ON US A SECOND CHANCE!
15

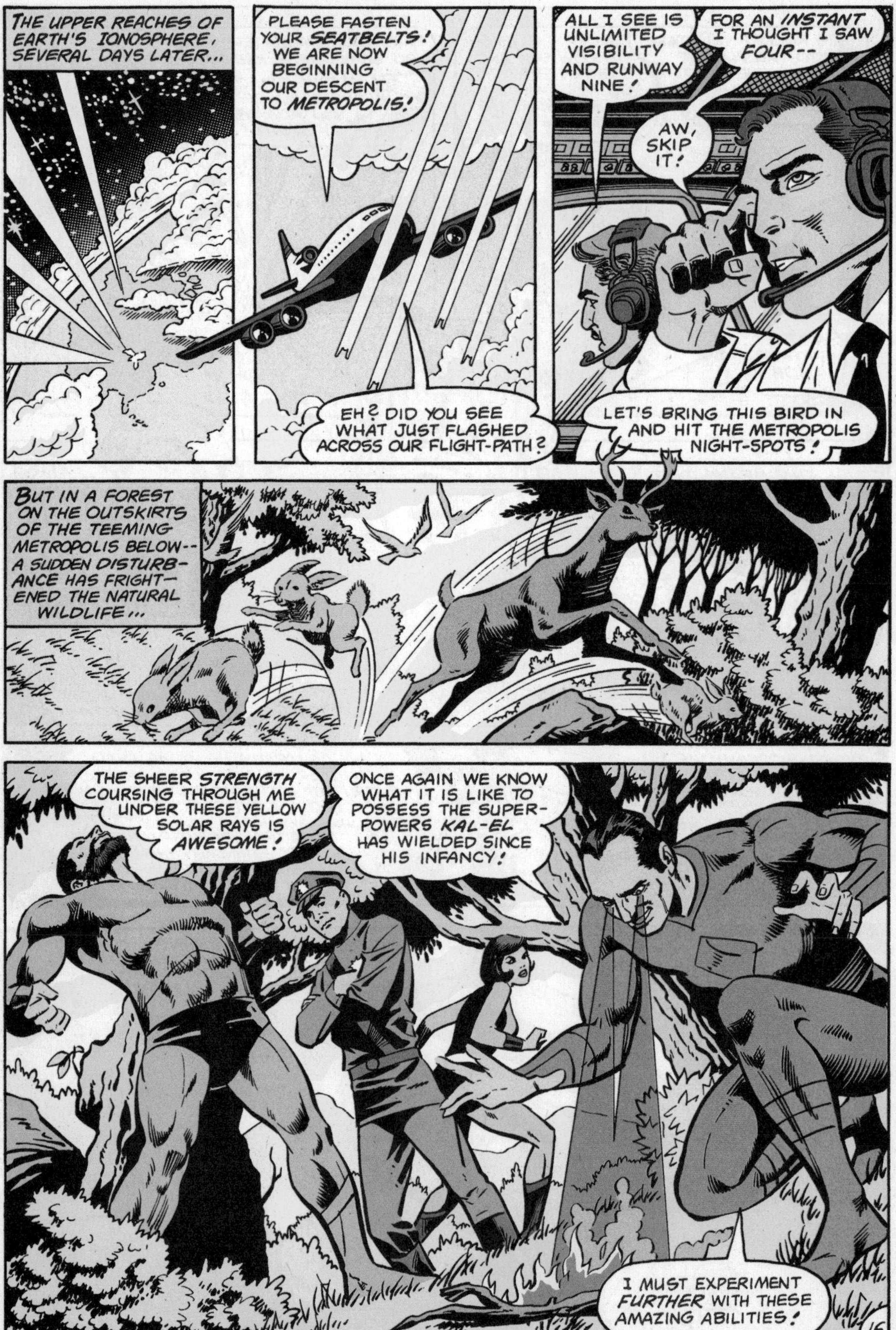
THE UPPER REACHES OF EARTH'S IONOSPHERE, SEVERAL DAYS LATER...
PLEASE FASTEN YOUR SEATBELTS! WE ARE NOW BEGINNING OUR DESCENT TO METROPOLIS!
EH? DID YOU SEE WHAT JUST FLASHED ACROSS OUR FLIGHT-PATH?
ALL I SEE IS UNLIMITED VISIBILITY AND RUNWAY NINE!
FOR AN INSTANT I THOUGHT I SAW FOUR--
AW, SKIP IT!
LET'S BRING THIS BIRD IN AND HIT THE METROPOLIS NIGHT-SPOTS!
BUT IN A FOREST ON THE OUTSKIRTS OF THE TEEMING METROPOLIS BELOW-- A SUDDEN DISTURBANCE HAS FRIGHTENED THE NATURAL WILDLIFE...
THE SHEER STRENGTH COURSING THROUGH ME UNDER THESE YELLOW SOLAR RAYS IS AWESOME!
ONCE AGAIN WE KNOW WHAT IT IS LIKE TO POSSESS THE SUPER-POWERS KAL-EL HAS WIELDED SINCE HIS INFANCY!
I MUST EXPERIMENT FURTHER WITH THESE AMAZING ABILITIES!
16

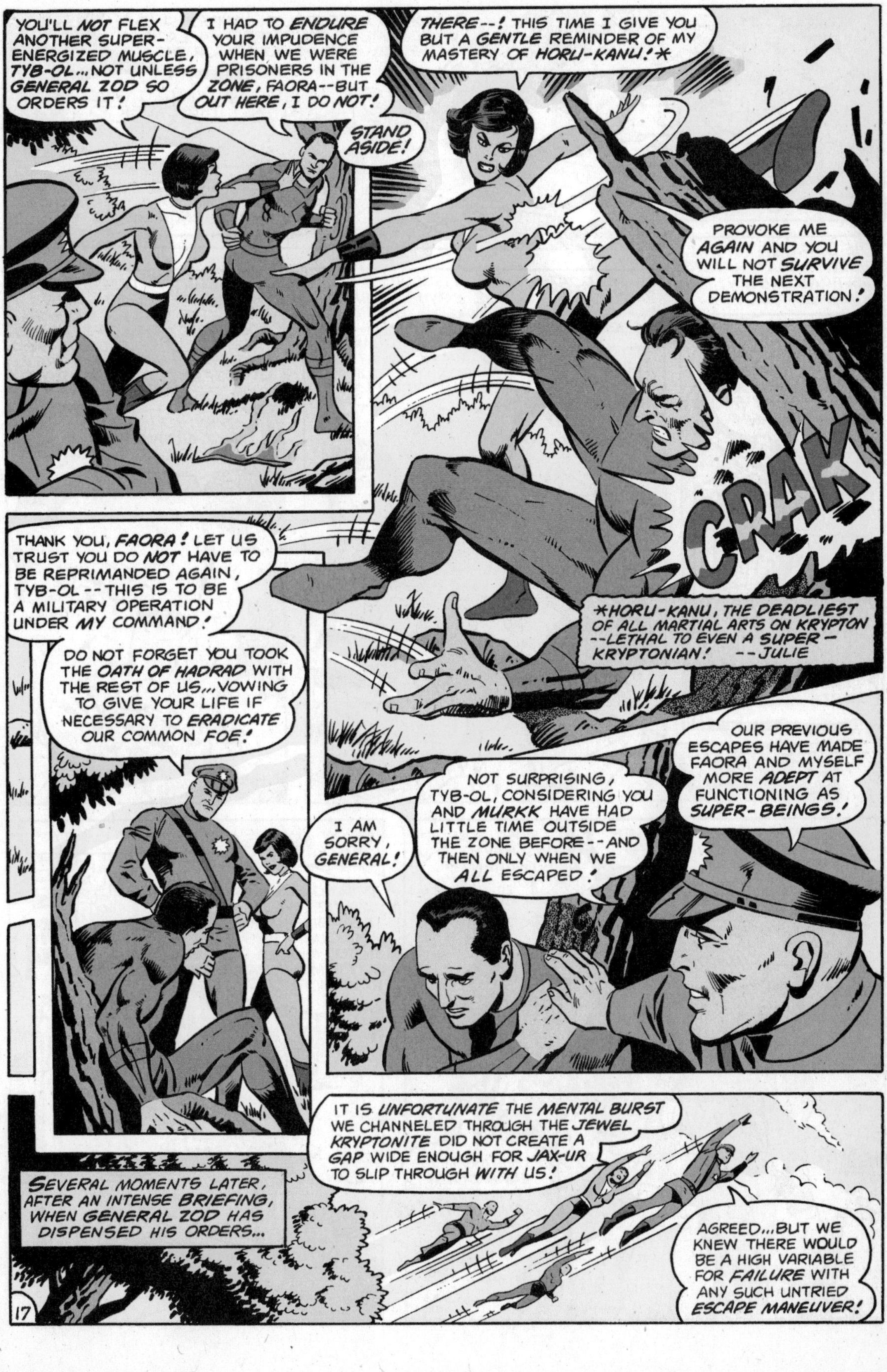
YOU'LL NOT FLEX ANOTHER SUPER-ENERGIZED MUSCLE, TYB-OL... NOT UNLESS GENERAL ZOD SO ORDERS IT!
I HAD TO ENDURE YOUR IMPUDENCE WHEN WE WERE PRISONERS IN THE ZONE, FAORA--BUT OUT HERE, I DO NOT!
STAND ASIDE!
THERE--! THIS TIME I GIVE YOU BUT A GENTLE REMINDER OF MY MASTERY OF HORU-KANU!*
PROVOKE ME AGAIN AND YOU WILL NOT SURVIVE THE NEXT DEMONSTRATION!
CRAK
THANK YOU, FAORA! LET US TRUST YOU DO NOT HAVE TO BE REPRIMANDED AGAIN, TYB-OL--THIS IS TO BE A MILITARY OPERATION UNDER MY COMMAND!
DO NOT FORGET YOU TOOK THE OATH OF HADRAD WITH THE REST OF US... VOWING TO GIVE YOUR LIFE IF NECESSARY TO ERADICATE OUR COMMON FOE!
*HORU-KANU, THE DEADLIEST OF ALL MARTIAL ARTS ON KRYPTON --LETHAL TO EVEN A SUPER-KRYPTONIAN! --JULIE
I AM SORRY, GENERAL!
NOT SURPRISING, TYB-OL, CONSIDERING YOU AND MURKK HAVE HAD LITTLE TIME OUTSIDE THE ZONE BEFORE--AND THEN ONLY WHEN WE ALL ESCAPED!
OUR PREVIOUS ESCAPES HAVE MADE FAORA AND MYSELF MORE ADEPT AT FUNCTIONING AS SUPER-BEINGS!
SEVERAL MOMENTS LATER, AFTER AN INTENSE BRIEFING, WHEN GENERAL ZOD HAS DISPENSED HIS ORDERS...
IT IS UNFORTUNATE THE MENTAL BURST WE CHANNELED THROUGH THE JEWEL KRYPTONITE DID NOT CREATE A GAP WIDE ENOUGH FOR JAX-UR TO SLIP THROUGH WITH US!
AGREED... BUT WE KNEW THERE WOULD BE A HIGH VARIABLE FOR FAILURE WITH ANY SUCH UNTRIED ESCAPE MANEUVER!
17

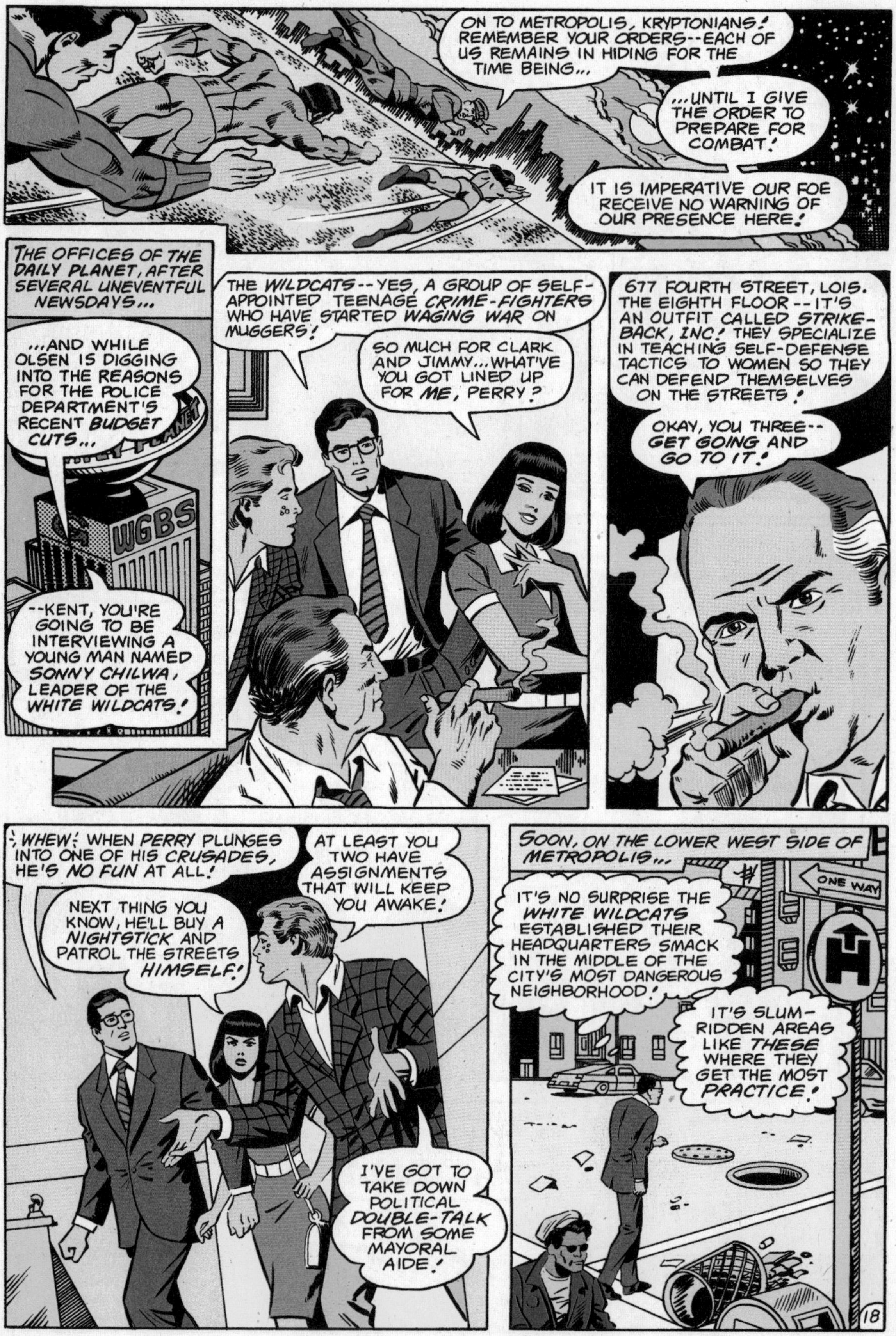
ON TO METROPOLIS, KRYPTONIANS! REMEMBER YOUR ORDERS--EACH OF US REMAINS IN HIDING FOR THE TIME BEING...
...UNTIL I GIVE THE ORDER TO PREPARE FOR COMBAT!
IT IS IMPERATIVE OUR FOE RECEIVE NO WARNING OF OUR PRESENCE HERE!
THE OFFICES OF THE DAILY PLANET, AFTER SEVERAL UNEVENTFUL NEWSDAYS...
...AND WHILE OLSEN IS DIGGING INTO THE REASONS FOR THE POLICE DEPARTMENT'S RECENT BUDGET CUTS...
--KENT, YOU'RE GOING TO BE INTERVIEWING A YOUNG MAN NAMED SONNY CHILWA, LEADER OF THE WHITE WILDCATS!
WGBS
THE WILDCATS--YES, A GROUP OF SELF-APPOINTED TEENAGE CRIME-FIGHTERS WHO HAVE STARTED WAGING WAR ON MUGGERS!
SO MUCH FOR CLARK AND JIMMY...WHAT'VE YOU GOT LINED UP FOR ME, PERRY?
677 FOURTH STREET, LOIS. THE EIGHTH FLOOR--IT'S AN OUTFIT CALLED STRIKE-BACK, INC! THEY SPECIALIZE IN TEACHING SELF-DEFENSE TACTICS TO WOMEN SO THEY CAN DEFEND THEMSELVES ON THE STREETS!
OKAY, YOU THREE--GET GOING AND GO TO IT!
WHEW! WHEN PERRY PLUNGES INTO ONE OF HIS CRUSADES, HE'S NO FUN AT ALL!
NEXT THING YOU KNOW, HE'LL BUY A NIGHTSTICK AND PATROL THE STREETS HIMSELF!
AT LEAST YOU TWO HAVE ASSIGNMENTS THAT WILL KEEP YOU AWAKE!
I'VE GOT TO TAKE DOWN POLITICAL DOUBLE-TALK FROM SOME MAYORAL AIDE!
SOON, ON THE LOWER WEST SIDE OF METROPOLIS...
ONE WAY
IT'S NO SURPRISE THE WHITE WILDCATS ESTABLISHED THEIR HEADQUARTERS SMACK IN THE MIDDLE OF THE CITY'S MOST DANGEROUS NEIGHBORHOOD!
IT'S SLUM-RIDDEN AREAS LIKE THESE WHERE THEY GET THE MOST PRACTICE!
18

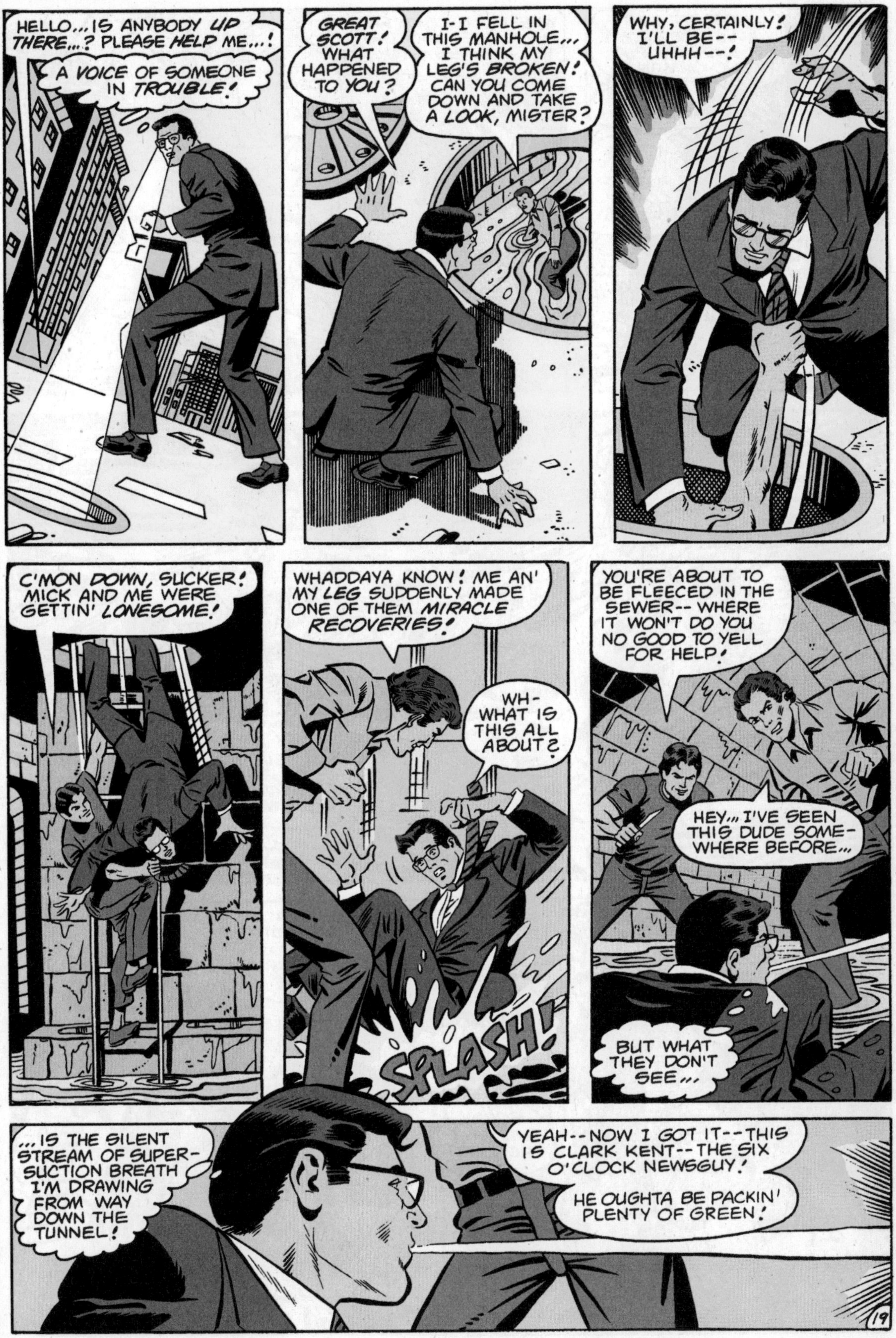
HELLO... IS ANYBODY UP THERE...? PLEASE HELP ME...!
A VOICE OF SOMEONE IN TROUBLE!
GREAT SCOTT! WHAT HAPPENED TO YOU?
I-I FELL IN THIS MANHOLE... I THINK MY LEG'S BROKEN! CAN YOU COME DOWN AND TAKE A LOOK, MISTER?
WHY, CERTAINLY! I'LL BE-- UHHH--!
C'MON DOWN, SUCKER! MICK AND ME WERE GETTIN' LONESOME!
WHADDAYA KNOW! ME AN' MY LEG SUDDENLY MADE ONE OF THEM MIRACLE RECOVERIES!
WH- WHAT IS THIS ALL ABOUT?
SPLASH!
YOU'RE ABOUT TO BE FLEECED IN THE SEWER-- WHERE IT WON'T DO YOU NO GOOD TO YELL FOR HELP!
HEY... I'VE SEEN THIS DUDE SOME-WHERE BEFORE...
BUT WHAT THEY DON'T SEE...
...IS THE SILENT STREAM OF SUPER-SUCTION BREATH I'M DRAWING FROM WAY DOWN THE TUNNEL!
YEAH--NOW I GOT IT--THIS IS CLARK KENT--THE SIX O'CLOCK NEWSGUY!
HE OUGHTA BE PACKIN' PLENTY OF GREEN!
19

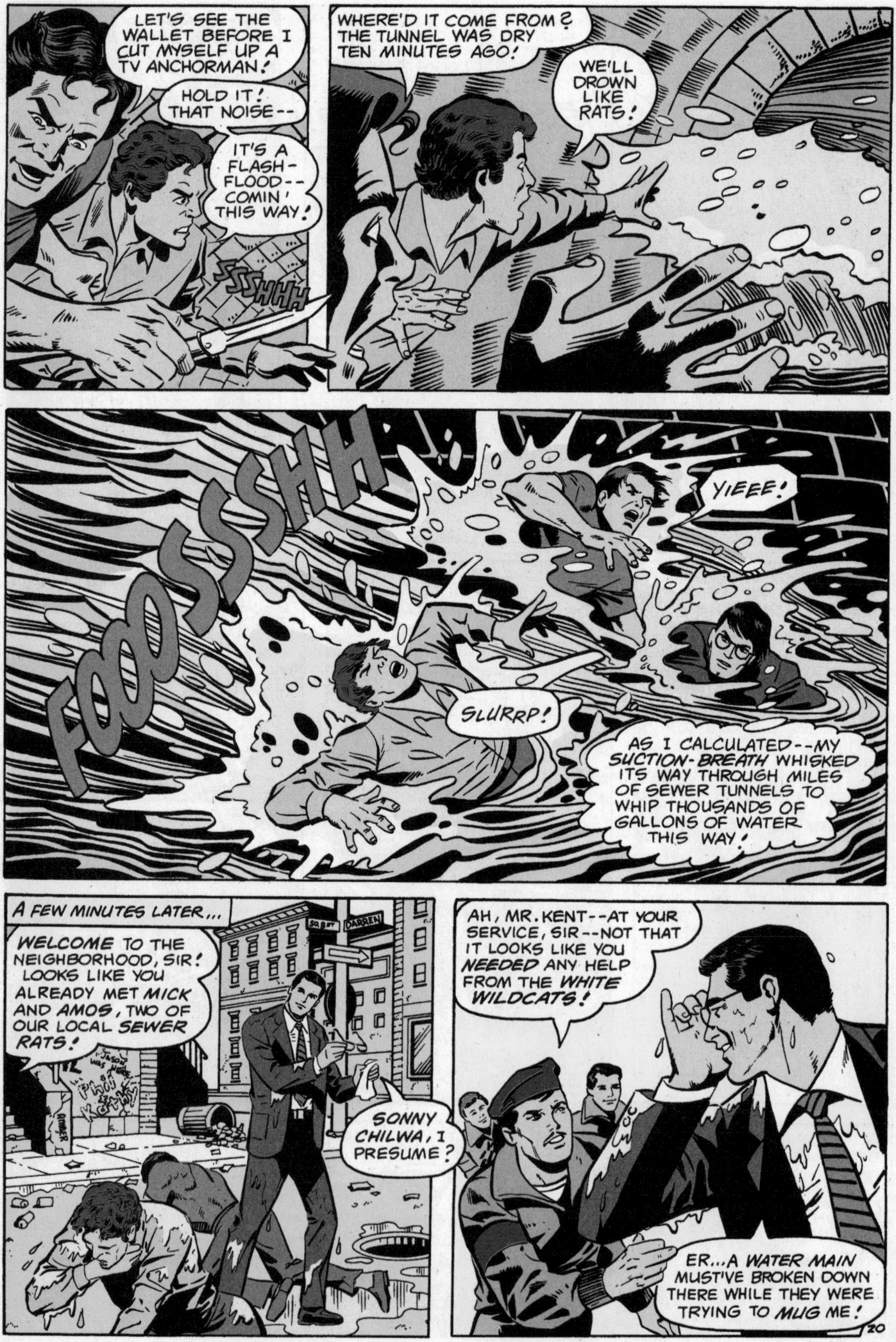
LET'S SEE THE WALLET BEFORE I CUT MYSELF UP A TV ANCHORMAN!
HOLD IT! THAT NOISE--
IT'S A FLASH-FLOOD--COMIN' THIS WAY!
SSSHHH
WHERE'D IT COME FROM? THE TUNNEL WAS DRY TEN MINUTES AGO!
WE'LL DROWN LIKE RATS!
FOOOSSSHH
YIEEE!
SLURRP!
AS I CALCULATED--MY SUCTION-BREATH WHISKED ITS WAY THROUGH MILES OF SEWER TUNNELS TO WHIP THOUSANDS OF GALLONS OF WATER THIS WAY!
A FEW MINUTES LATER...
WELCOME TO THE NEIGHBORHOOD, SIR! LOOKS LIKE YOU ALREADY MET MICK AND AMOS, TWO OF OUR LOCAL SEWER RATS!
DARREN
SONNY CHILWA, I PRESUME?
AH, MR. KENT--AT YOUR SERVICE, SIR--NOT THAT IT LOOKS LIKE YOU NEEDED ANY HELP FROM THE WHITE WILDCATS!
ER...A WATER MAIN MUST'VE BROKEN DOWN THERE WHILE THEY WERE TRYING TO MUG ME!
20

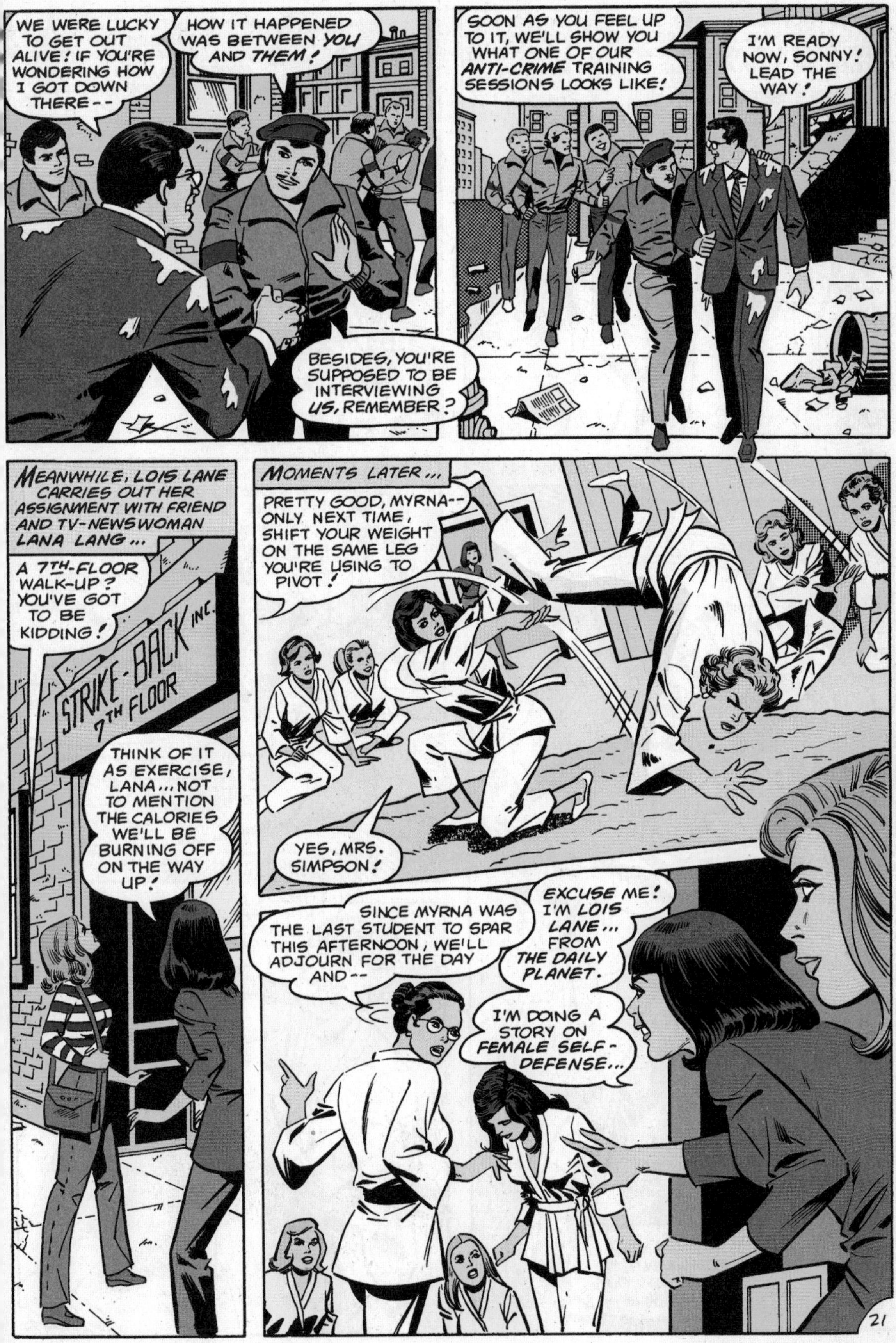
WE WERE LUCKY TO GET OUT ALIVE! IF YOU'RE WONDERING HOW I GOT DOWN THERE--
HOW IT HAPPENED WAS BETWEEN YOU AND THEM!
BESIDES, YOU'RE SUPPOSED TO BE INTERVIEWING US, REMEMBER?
SOON AS YOU FEEL UP TO IT, WE'LL SHOW YOU WHAT ONE OF OUR ANTI-CRIME TRAINING SESSIONS LOOKS LIKE!
I'M READY NOW, SONNY! LEAD THE WAY!
MEANWHILE, LOIS LANE CARRIES OUT HER ASSIGNMENT WITH FRIEND AND TV-NEWSWOMAN LANA LANG...
A 7TH-FLOOR WALK-UP? YOU'VE GOT TO BE KIDDING!
STRIKE-BACK INC. 7TH FLOOR
THINK OF IT AS EXERCISE, LANA... NOT TO MENTION THE CALORIES WE'LL BE BURNING OFF ON THE WAY UP!
MOMENTS LATER...
PRETTY GOOD, MYRNA-- ONLY NEXT TIME, SHIFT YOUR WEIGHT ON THE SAME LEG YOU'RE USING TO PIVOT!
YES, MRS. SIMPSON!
SINCE MYRNA WAS THE LAST STUDENT TO SPAR THIS AFTERNOON, WE'LL ADJOURN FOR THE DAY AND--
EXCUSE ME! I'M LOIS LANE... FROM THE DAILY PLANET.
I'M DOING A STORY ON FEMALE SELF-DEFENSE...
21

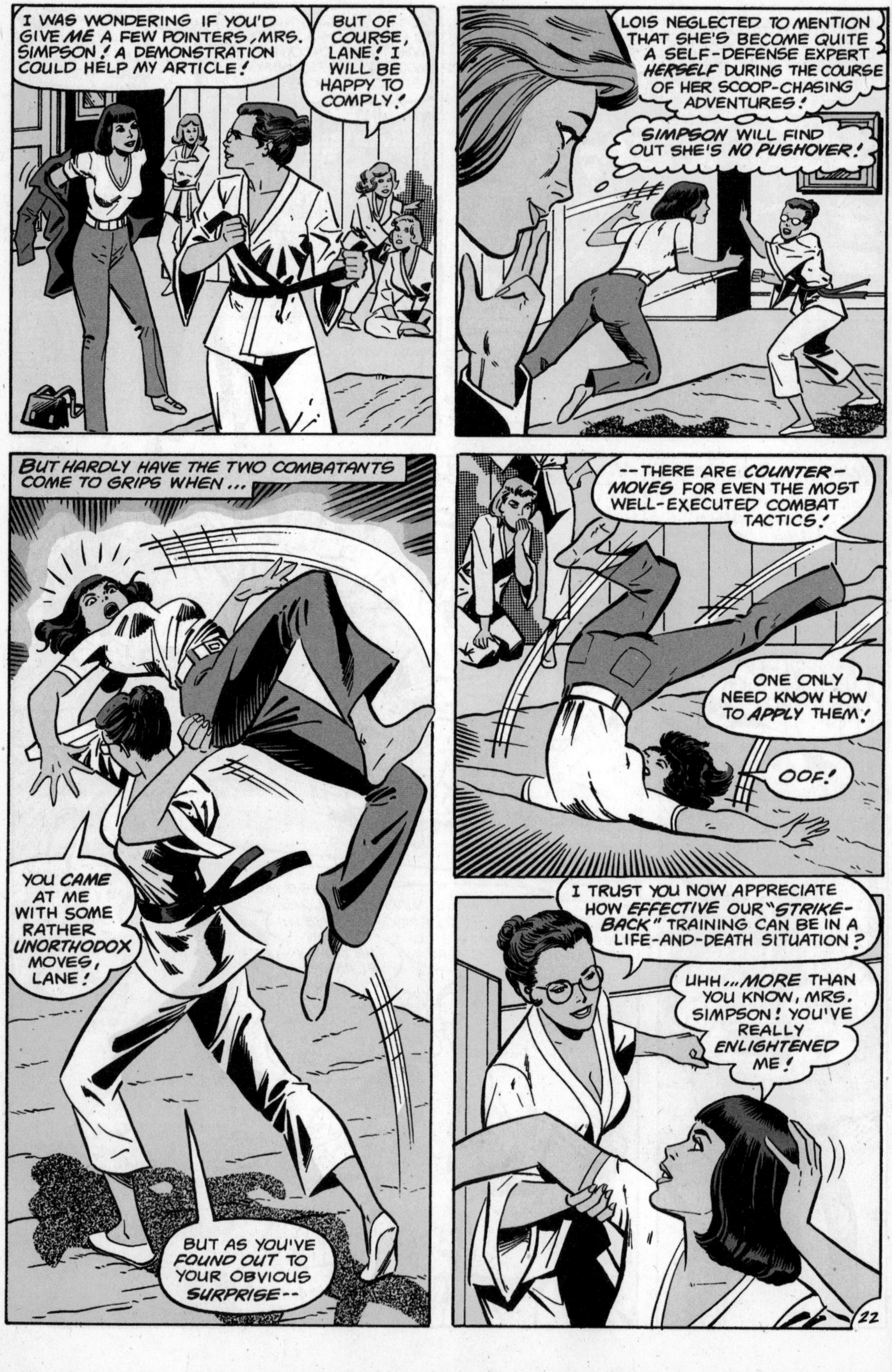
I WAS WONDERING IF YOU'D GIVE ME A FEW POINTERS, MRS. SIMPSON! A DEMONSTRATION COULD HELP MY ARTICLE!
BUT OF COURSE, LANE! I WILL BE HAPPY TO COMPLY!
LOIS NEGLECTED TO MENTION THAT SHE'S BECOME QUITE A SELF-DEFENSE EXPERT HERSELF DURING THE COURSE OF HER SCOOP-CHASING ADVENTURES!
SIMPSON WILL FIND OUT SHE'S NO PUSHOVER!
BUT HARDLY HAVE THE TWO COMBATANTS COME TO GRIPS WHEN...
YOU CAME AT ME WITH SOME RATHER UNORTHODOX MOVES, LANE!
BUT AS YOU'VE FOUND OUT TO YOUR OBVIOUS SURPRISE--
--THERE ARE COUNTER-MOVES FOR EVEN THE MOST WELL-EXECUTED COMBAT TACTICS!
ONE ONLY NEED KNOW HOW TO APPLY THEM!
OOF!
I TRUST YOU NOW APPRECIATE HOW EFFECTIVE OUR "STRIKE-BACK" TRAINING CAN BE IN A LIFE-AND-DEATH SITUATION?
UHH...MORE THAN YOU KNOW, MRS. SIMPSON! YOU'VE REALLY ENLIGHTENED ME!
22

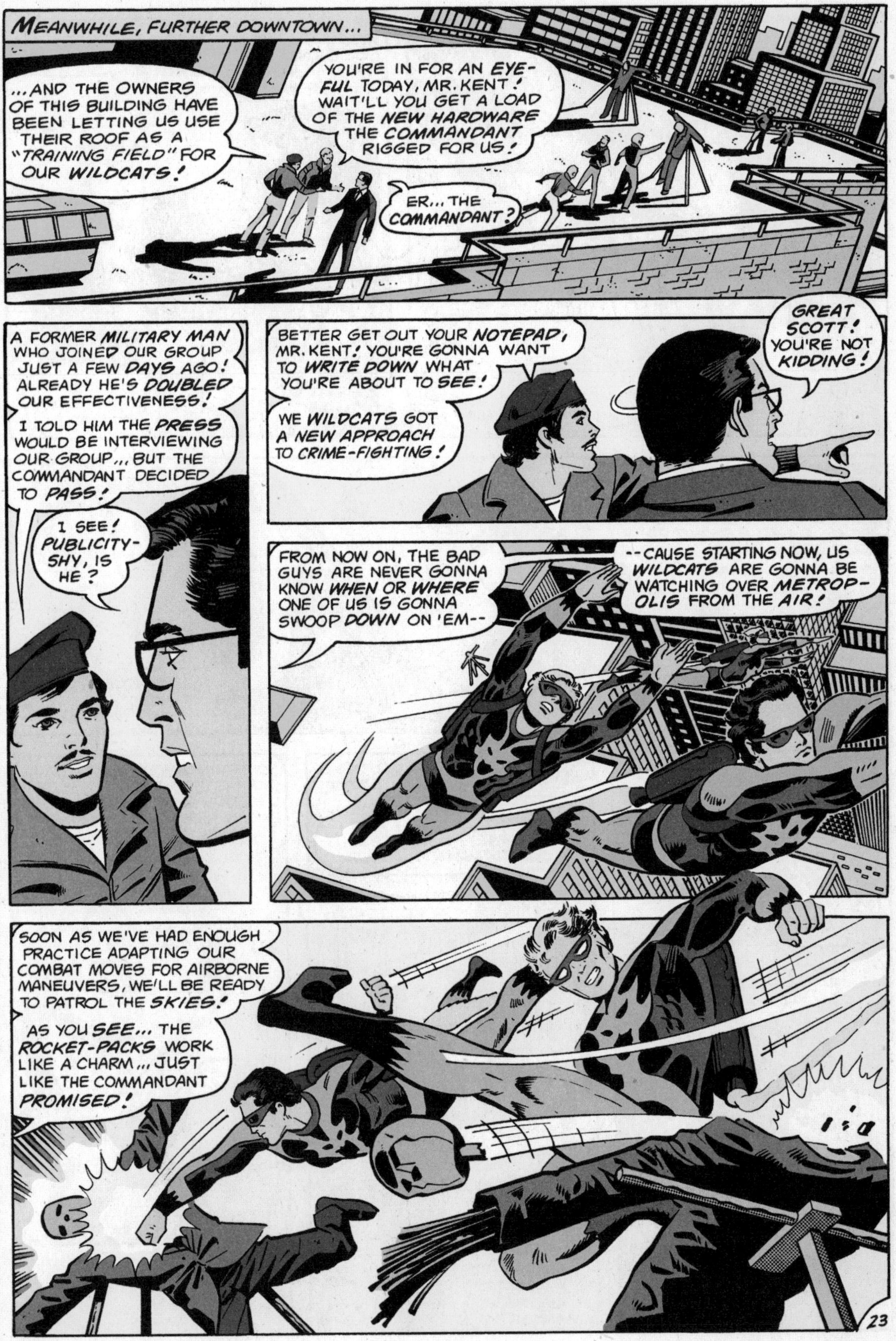
MEANWHILE, FURTHER DOWNTOWN...
...AND THE OWNERS OF THIS BUILDING HAVE BEEN LETTING US USE THEIR ROOF AS A "TRAINING FIELD" FOR OUR WILDCATS!
YOU'RE IN FOR AN EYE-FUL TODAY, MR. KENT! WAIT'LL YOU GET A LOAD OF THE NEW HARDWARE THE COMMANDANT RIGGED FOR US!
ER... THE COMMANDANT?
A FORMER MILITARY MAN WHO JOINED OUR GROUP JUST A FEW DAYS AGO! ALREADY HE'S DOUBLED OUR EFFECTIVENESS!
I TOLD HIM THE PRESS WOULD BE INTERVIEWING OUR GROUP... BUT THE COMMANDANT DECIDED TO PASS!
I SEE! PUBLICITY-SHY, IS HE?
BETTER GET OUT YOUR NOTEPAD, MR. KENT! YOU'RE GONNA WANT TO WRITE DOWN WHAT YOU'RE ABOUT TO SEE!
WE WILDCATS GOT A NEW APPROACH TO CRIME-FIGHTING!
GREAT SCOTT! YOU'RE NOT KIDDING!
FROM NOW ON, THE BAD GUYS ARE NEVER GONNA KNOW WHEN OR WHERE ONE OF US IS GONNA SWOOP DOWN ON 'EM--
--CAUSE STARTING NOW, US WILDCATS ARE GONNA BE WATCHING OVER METROP-OLIS FROM THE AIR!
SOON AS WE'VE HAD ENOUGH PRACTICE ADAPTING OUR COMBAT MOVES FOR AIRBORNE MANEUVERS, WE'LL BE READY TO PATROL THE SKIES!
AS YOU SEE... THE ROCKET-PACKS WORK LIKE A CHARM... JUST LIKE THE COMMANDANT PROMISED!
23

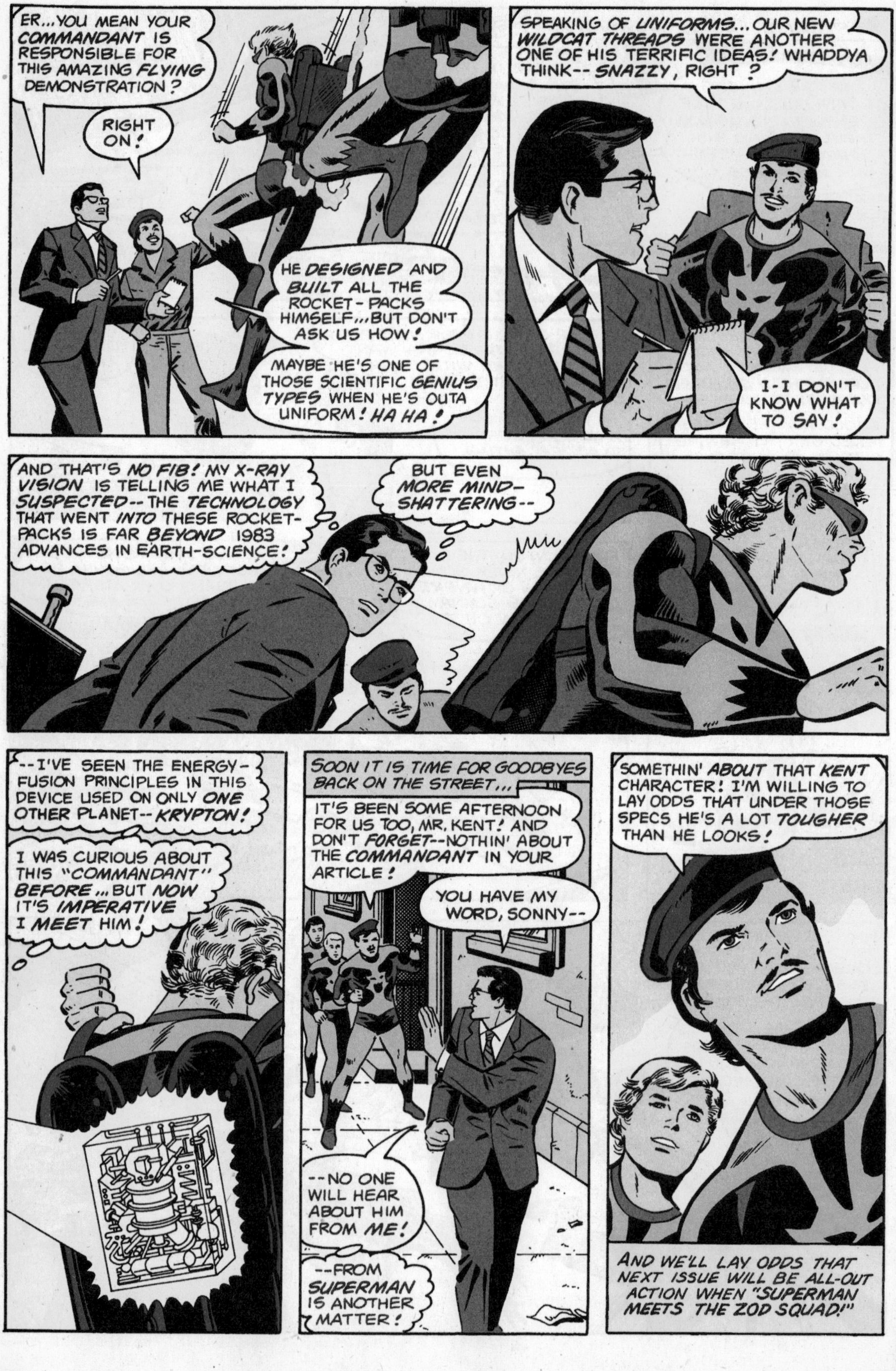
ER...YOU MEAN YOUR COMMANDANT IS RESPONSIBLE FOR THIS AMAZING FLYING DEMONSTRATION?
RIGHT ON!
HE DESIGNED AND BUILT ALL THE ROCKET-PACKS HIMSELF... BUT DON'T ASK US HOW!
MAYBE HE'S ONE OF THOSE SCIENTIFIC GENIUS TYPES WHEN HE'S OUTA UNIFORM! HA HA!
SPEAKING OF UNIFORMS... OUR NEW WILDCAT THREADS WERE ANOTHER ONE OF HIS TERRIFIC IDEAS! WHADDYA THINK-- SNAZZY, RIGHT?
I-I DON'T KNOW WHAT TO SAY!
AND THAT'S NO FIB! MY X-RAY VISION IS TELLING ME WHAT I SUSPECTED-- THE TECHNOLOGY THAT WENT INTO THESE ROCKET-PACKS IS FAR BEYOND 1983 ADVANCES IN EARTH-SCIENCE!
BUT EVEN MORE MIND-SHATTERING--
--I'VE SEEN THE ENERGY-FUSION PRINCIPLES IN THIS DEVICE USED ON ONLY ONE OTHER PLANET-- KRYPTON!
I WAS CURIOUS ABOUT THIS "COMMANDANT" BEFORE... BUT NOW IT'S IMPERATIVE I MEET HIM!
SOON IT IS TIME FOR GOODBYES BACK ON THE STREET...
IT'S BEEN SOME AFTERNOON FOR US TOO, MR. KENT! AND DON'T FORGET--NOTHIN' ABOUT THE COMMANDANT IN YOUR ARTICLE!
YOU HAVE MY WORD, SONNY--
--NO ONE WILL HEAR ABOUT HIM FROM ME!
--FROM SUPERMAN IS ANOTHER MATTER!
SOMETHIN' ABOUT THAT KENT CHARACTER! I'M WILLING TO LAY ODDS THAT UNDER THOSE SPECS HE'S A LOT TOUGHER THAN HE LOOKS!
AND WE'LL LAY ODDS THAT NEXT ISSUE WILL BE ALL-OUT ACTION WHEN "SUPERMAN MEETS THE ZOD SQUAD!"

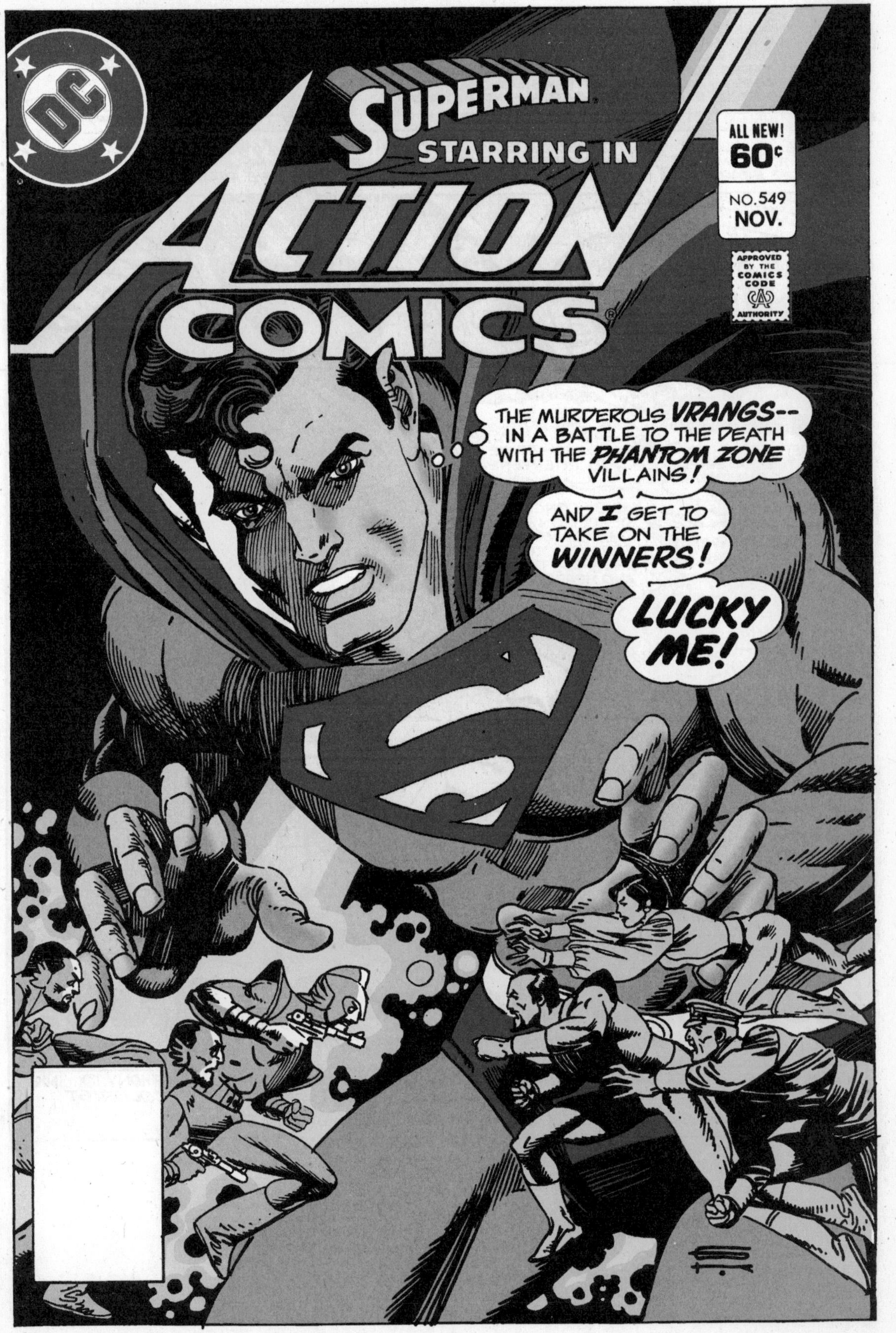
SUPERMAN
STARRING IN
ACTION COMICS
ALL NEW! 60¢
NO. 549
NOV.
APPROVED BY THE COMICS CODE AUTHORITY
THE MURDEROUS VRANGS-- IN A BATTLE TO THE DEATH WITH THE PHANTOM ZONE VILLAINS!
AND I GET TO TAKE ON THE WINNERS!
LUCKY ME!

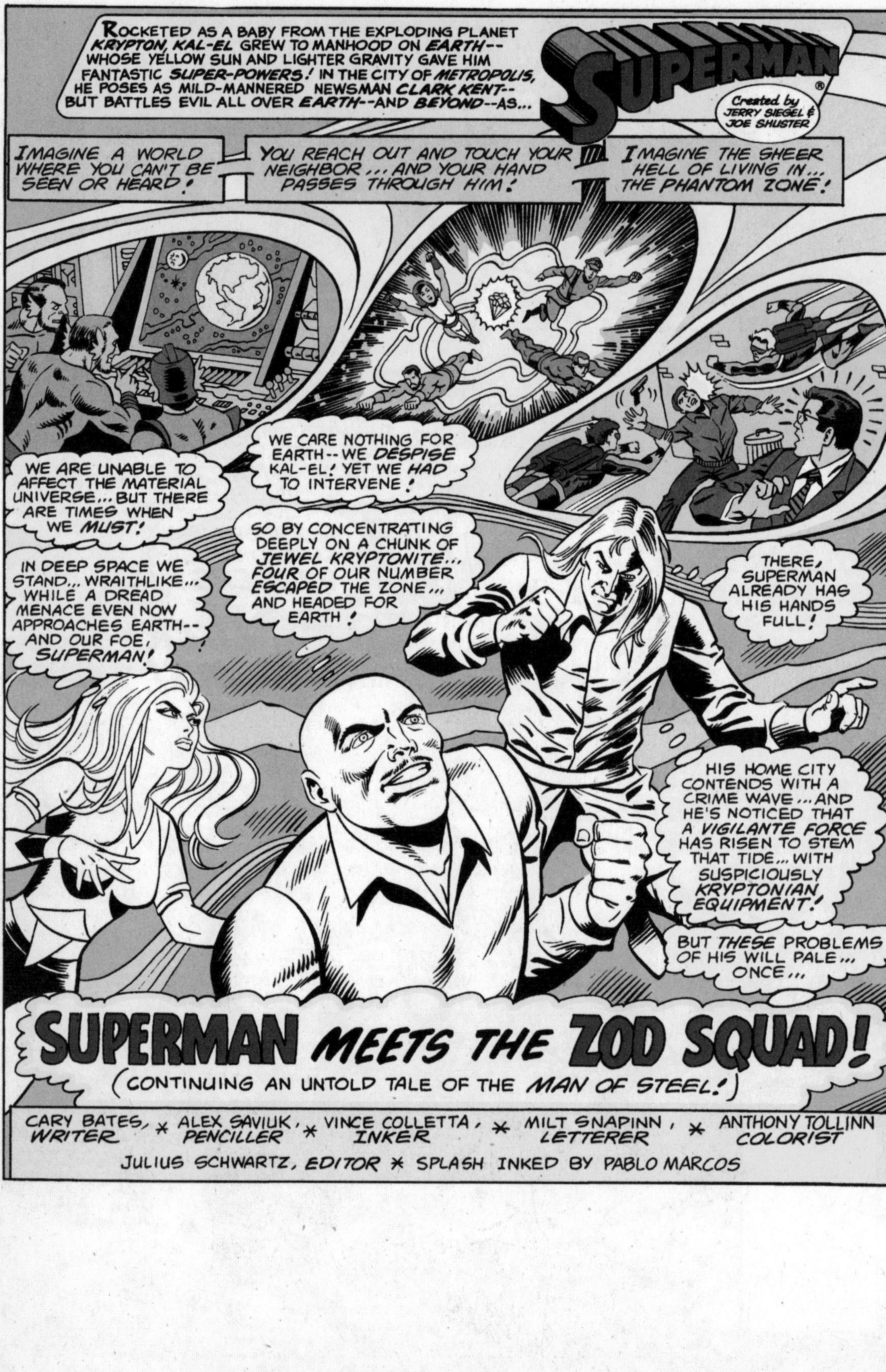

ROCKETED AS A BABY FROM THE EXPLODING PLANET KRYPTON, KAL-EL GREW TO MANHOOD ON EARTH-- WHOSE YELLOW SUN AND LIGHTER GRAVITY GAVE HIM FANTASTIC SUPER-POWERS! IN THE CITY OF METROPOLIS, HE POSES AS MILD-MANNERED NEWSMAN CLARK KENT-- BUT BATTLES EVIL ALL OVER EARTH--AND BEYOND--AS...
SUPERMAN®
Created by JERRY SIEGEL & JOE SHUSTER
IMAGINE A WORLD WHERE YOU CAN'T BE SEEN OR HEARD!
YOU REACH OUT AND TOUCH YOUR NEIGHBOR... AND YOUR HAND PASSES THROUGH HIM!
IMAGINE THE SHEER HELL OF LIVING IN... THE PHANTOM ZONE!
WE ARE UNABLE TO AFFECT THE MATERIAL UNIVERSE... BUT THERE ARE TIMES WHEN WE MUST!
WE CARE NOTHING FOR EARTH--WE DESPISE KAL-EL! YET WE HAD TO INTERVENE!
IN DEEP SPACE WE STAND... WRAITHLIKE... WHILE A DREAD MENACE EVEN NOW APPROACHES EARTH-- AND OUR FOE, SUPERMAN!
SO BY CONCENTRATING DEEPLY ON A CHUNK OF JEWEL KRYPTONITE... FOUR OF OUR NUMBER ESCAPED THE ZONE... AND HEADED FOR EARTH!
THERE, SUPERMAN ALREADY HAS HIS HANDS FULL!
HIS HOME CITY CONTENDS WITH A CRIME WAVE... AND HE'S NOTICED THAT A VIGILANTE FORCE HAS RISEN TO STEM THAT TIDE... WITH SUSPICIOUSLY KRYPTONIAN EQUIPMENT!
BUT THESE PROBLEMS OF HIS WILL PALE... ONCE...
SUPERMAN MEETS THE ZOD SQUAD!
(CONTINUING AN UNTOLD TALE OF THE MAN OF STEEL!)
CARY BATES, WRITER * ALEX SAVIUK, PENCILLER * VINCE COLLETTA, INKER * MILT SNAPINN, LETTERER * ANTHONY TOLLINN COLORIST
JULIUS SCHWARTZ, EDITOR * SPLASH INKED BY PABLO MARCOS

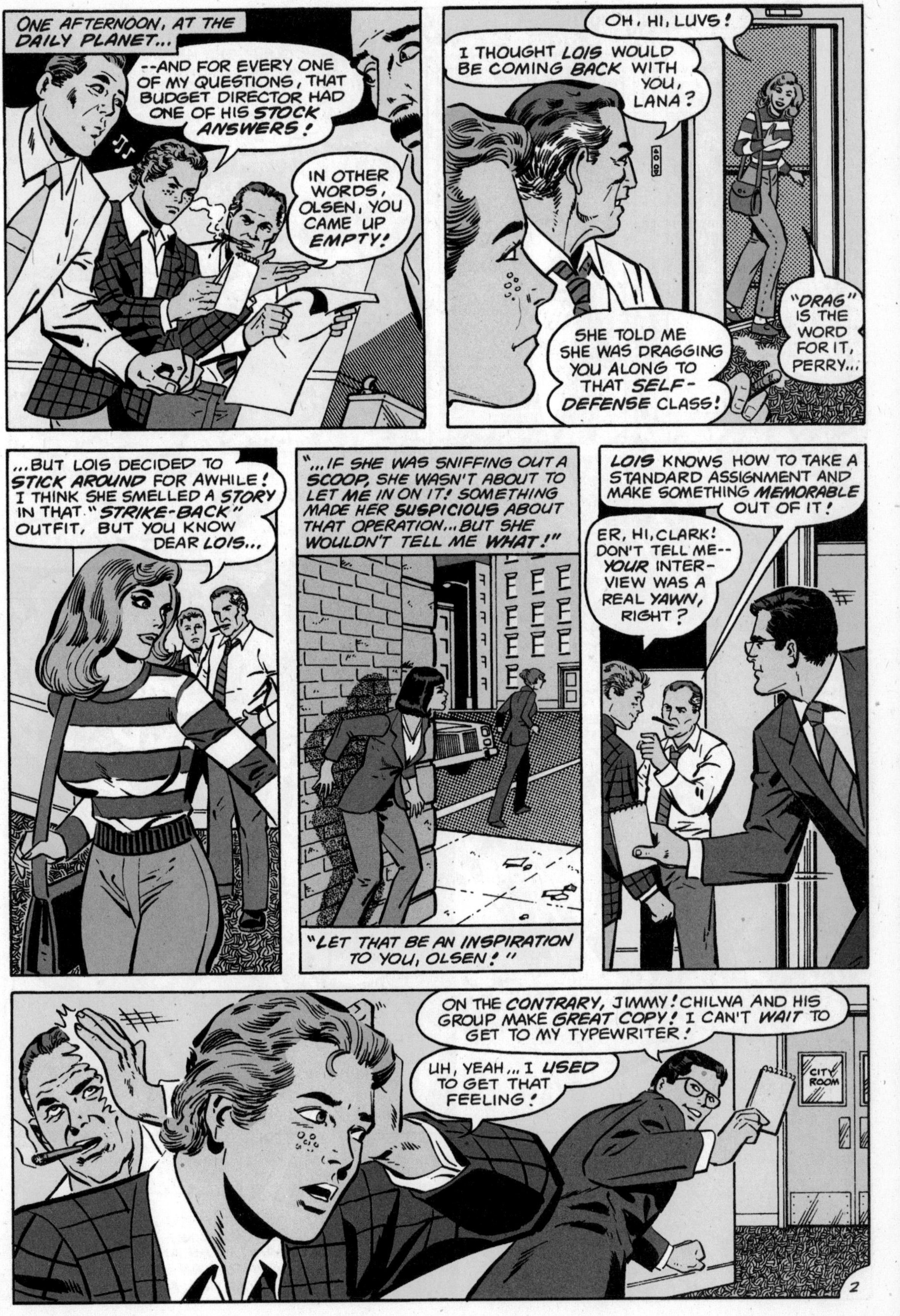
ONE AFTERNOON, AT THE DAILY PLANET...
--AND FOR EVERY ONE OF MY QUESTIONS, THAT BUDGET DIRECTOR HAD ONE OF HIS STOCK ANSWERS!
IN OTHER WORDS, OLSEN, YOU CAME UP EMPTY!
OH, HI, LUVS!
I THOUGHT LOIS WOULD BE COMING BACK WITH YOU, LANA?
SHE TOLD ME SHE WAS DRAGGING YOU ALONG TO THAT SELF-DEFENSE CLASS!
"DRAG" IS THE WORD FOR IT, PERRY...
...BUT LOIS DECIDED TO STICK AROUND FOR AWHILE! I THINK SHE SMELLED A STORY IN THAT "STRIKE-BACK" OUTFIT, BUT YOU KNOW DEAR LOIS...
"...IF SHE WAS SNIFFING OUT A SCOOP, SHE WASN'T ABOUT TO LET ME IN ON IT! SOMETHING MADE HER SUSPICIOUS ABOUT THAT OPERATION...BUT SHE WOULDN'T TELL ME WHAT!"
"LET THAT BE AN INSPIRATION TO YOU, OLSEN!"
LOIS KNOWS HOW TO TAKE A STANDARD ASSIGNMENT AND MAKE SOMETHING MEMORABLE OUT OF IT!
ER, HI, CLARK! DON'T TELL ME--YOUR INTER-VIEW WAS A REAL YAWN, RIGHT?
ON THE CONTRARY, JIMMY! CHILWA AND HIS GROUP MAKE GREAT COPY! I CAN'T WAIT TO GET TO MY TYPEWRITER!
UH, YEAH... I USED TO GET THAT FEELING!
CITY ROOM
2

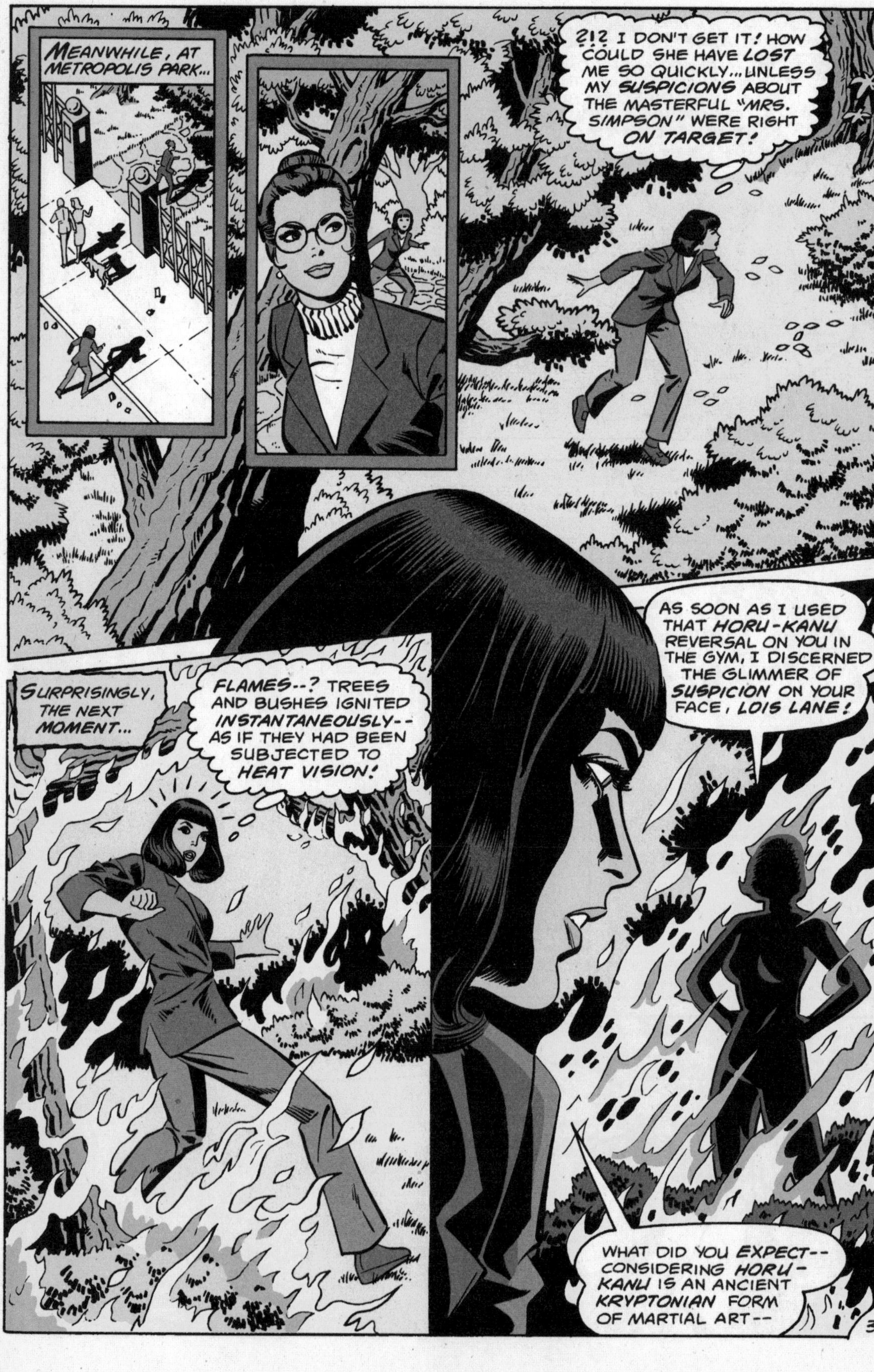
MEANWHILE, AT METROPOLIS PARK...
?!? I DON'T GET IT! HOW COULD SHE HAVE LOST ME SO QUICKLY... UNLESS MY SUSPICIONS ABOUT THE MASTERFUL "MRS. SIMPSON" WERE RIGHT ON TARGET!
SURPRISINGLY, THE NEXT MOMENT...
FLAMES--? TREES AND BUSHES IGNITED INSTANTANEOUSLY--AS IF THEY HAD BEEN SUBJECTED TO HEAT VISION!
AS SOON AS I USED THAT HORU-KANU REVERSAL ON YOU IN THE GYM, I DISCERNED THE GLIMMER OF SUSPICION ON YOUR FACE, LOIS LANE!
WHAT DID YOU EXPECT--CONSIDERING HORU-KANU IS AN ANCIENT KRYPTONIAN FORM OF MARTIAL ART--
3

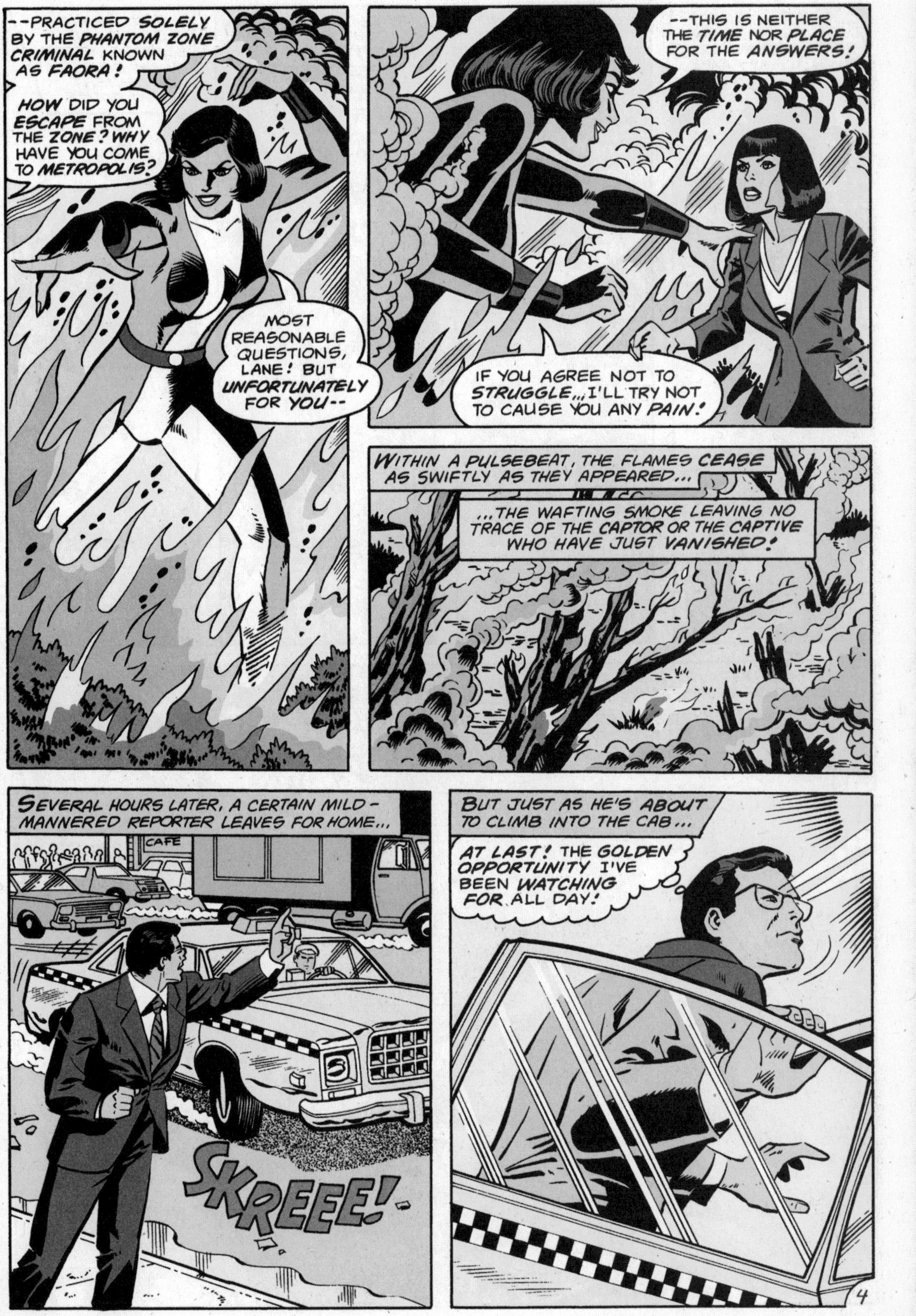
--PRACTICED SOLELY BY THE PHANTOM ZONE CRIMINAL KNOWN AS FAORA!
HOW DID YOU ESCAPE FROM THE ZONE? WHY HAVE YOU COME TO METROPOLIS?
MOST REASONABLE QUESTIONS, LANE! BUT UNFORTUNATELY FOR YOU--
--THIS IS NEITHER THE TIME NOR PLACE FOR THE ANSWERS!
IF YOU AGREE NOT TO STRUGGLE... I'LL TRY NOT TO CAUSE YOU ANY PAIN!
WITHIN A PULSEBEAT, THE FLAMES CEASE AS SWIFTLY AS THEY APPEARED...
...THE WAFTING SMOKE LEAVING NO TRACE OF THE CAPTOR OR THE CAPTIVE WHO HAVE JUST VANISHED!
SEVERAL HOURS LATER, A CERTAIN MILD-MANNERED REPORTER LEAVES FOR HOME...
CAFE
SKREEEE!
BUT JUST AS HE'S ABOUT TO CLIMB INTO THE CAB...
AT LAST! THE GOLDEN OPPORTUNITY I'VE BEEN WATCHING FOR ALL DAY!
4

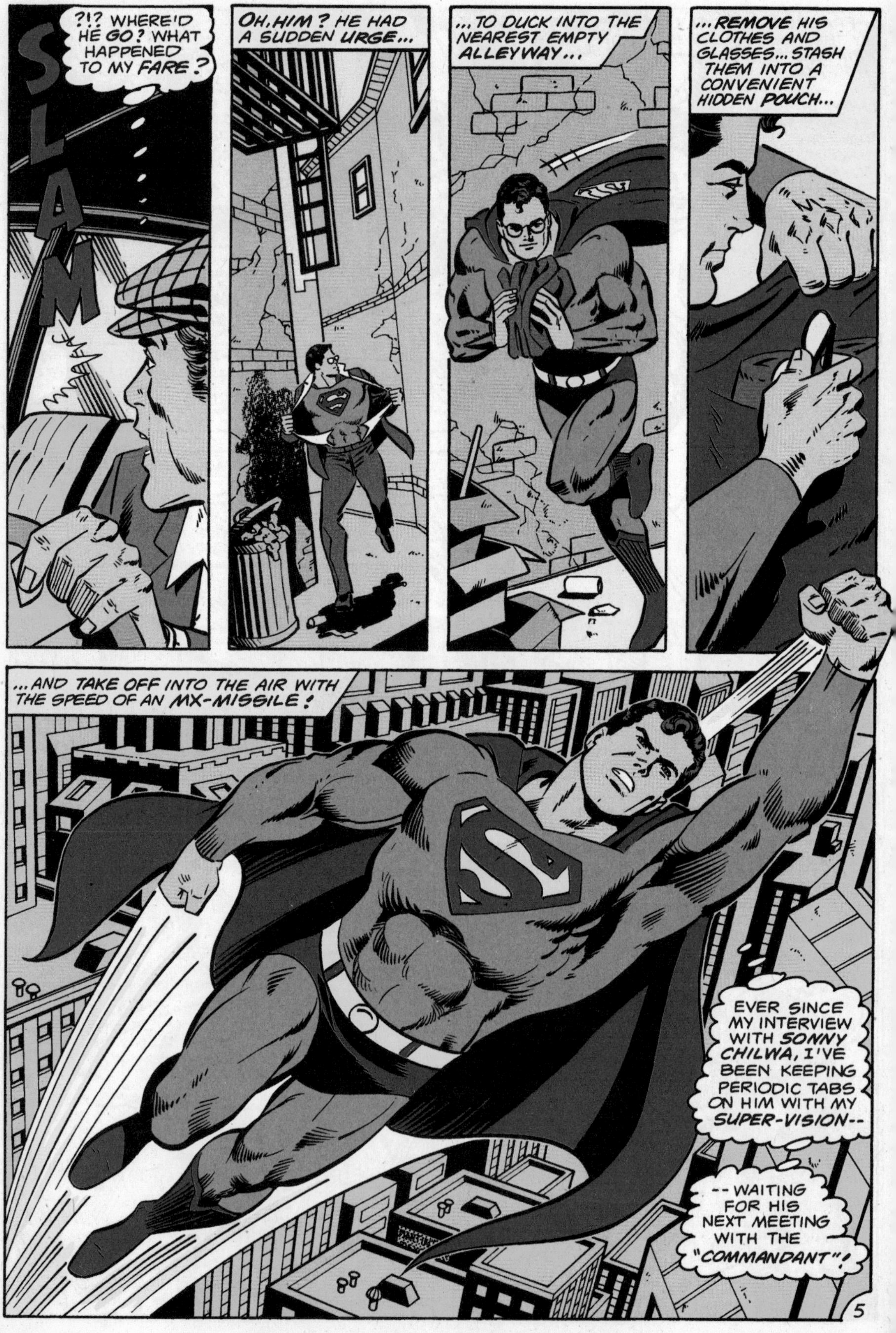
?!? WHERE'D HE GO? WHAT HAPPENED TO MY FARE?
SLAM
OH, HIM? HE HAD A SUDDEN URGE...
...TO DUCK INTO THE NEAREST EMPTY ALLEYWAY...
...REMOVE HIS CLOTHES AND GLASSES... STASH THEM INTO A CONVENIENT HIDDEN POUCH...
...AND TAKE OFF INTO THE AIR WITH THE SPEED OF AN MX-MISSILE!
EVER SINCE MY INTERVIEW WITH SONNY CHILWA, I'VE BEEN KEEPING PERIODIC TABS ON HIM WITH MY SUPER-VISION--
--WAITING FOR HIS NEXT MEETING WITH THE "COMMANDANT"!
5

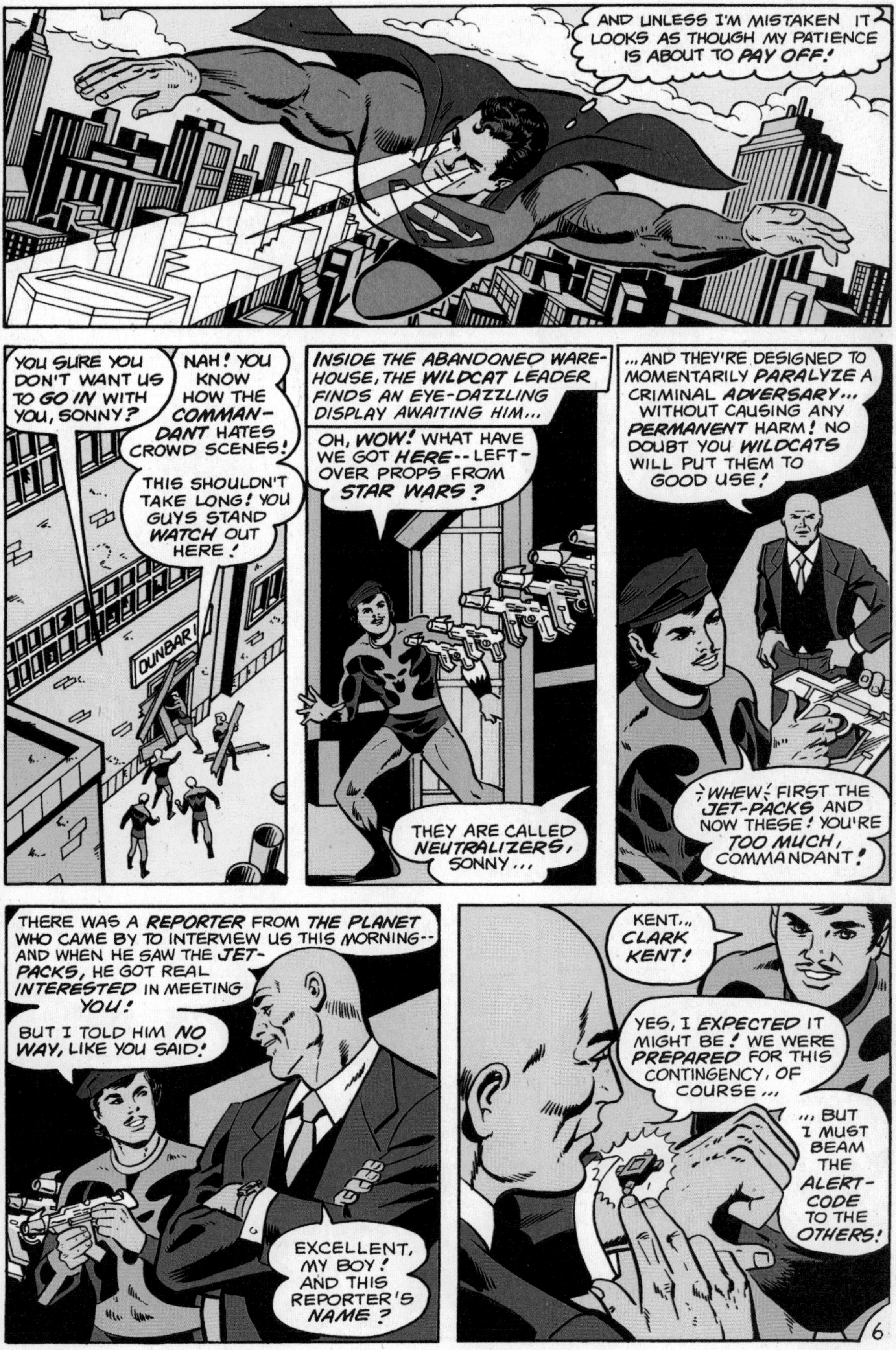
AND UNLESS I'M MISTAKEN IT LOOKS AS THOUGH MY PATIENCE IS ABOUT TO PAY OFF!
YOU SURE YOU DON'T WANT US TO GO IN WITH YOU, SONNY?
NAH! YOU KNOW HOW THE COMMAN-DANT HATES CROWD SCENES!
THIS SHOULDN'T TAKE LONG! YOU GUYS STAND WATCH OUT HERE!
DUNBAR
INSIDE THE ABANDONED WARE-HOUSE, THE WILDCAT LEADER FINDS AN EYE-DAZZLING DISPLAY AWAITING HIM...
OH, WOW! WHAT HAVE WE GOT HERE-- LEFT-OVER PROPS FROM STAR WARS?
THEY ARE CALLED NEUTRALIZERS, SONNY...
...AND THEY'RE DESIGNED TO MOMENTARILY PARALYZE A CRIMINAL ADVERSARY... WITHOUT CAUSING ANY PERMANENT HARM! NO DOUBT YOU WILDCATS WILL PUT THEM TO GOOD USE!
WHEW! FIRST THE JET-PACKS AND NOW THESE! YOU'RE TOO MUCH, COMMANDANT!
THERE WAS A REPORTER FROM THE PLANET WHO CAME BY TO INTERVIEW US THIS MORNING-- AND WHEN HE SAW THE JET-PACKS, HE GOT REAL INTERESTED IN MEETING YOU!
BUT I TOLD HIM NO WAY, LIKE YOU SAID!
EXCELLENT, MY BOY! AND THIS REPORTER'S NAME?
KENT... CLARK KENT!
YES, I EXPECTED IT MIGHT BE! WE WERE PREPARED FOR THIS CONTINGENCY, OF COURSE...
...BUT I MUST BEAM THE ALERT-CODE TO THE OTHERS!
6

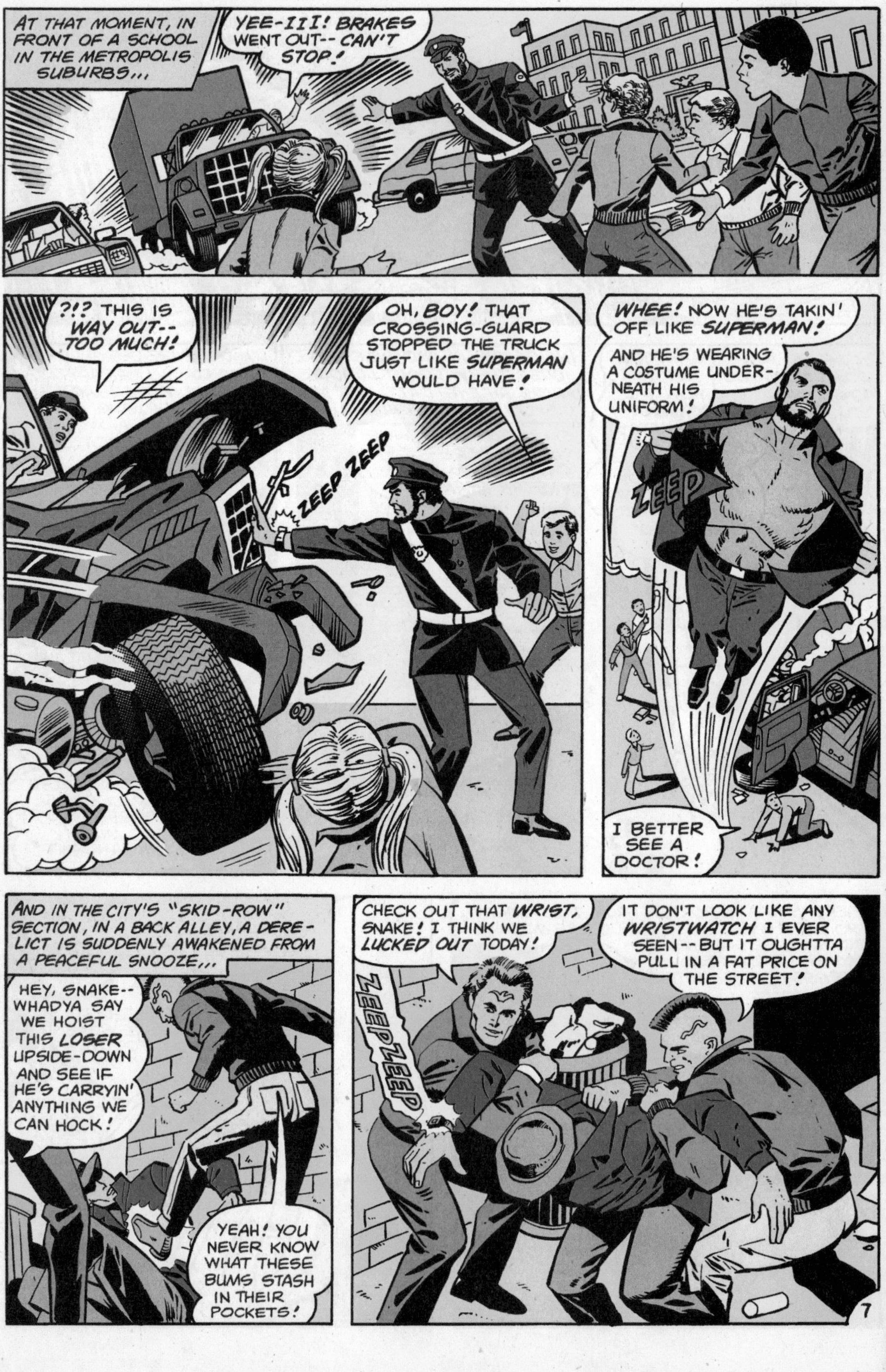
AT THAT MOMENT, IN FRONT OF A SCHOOL IN THE METROPOLIS SUBURBS...
YEE-III! BRAKES WENT OUT-- CAN'T STOP!
?!? THIS IS WAY OUT-- TOO MUCH!
OH, BOY! THAT CROSSING-GUARD STOPPED THE TRUCK JUST LIKE SUPERMAN WOULD HAVE!
ZEEP ZEEP
WHEE! NOW HE'S TAKIN' OFF LIKE SUPERMAN!
AND HE'S WEARING A COSTUME UNDERNEATH HIS UNIFORM!
ZEEP
I BETTER SEE A DOCTOR!
AND IN THE CITY'S "SKID-ROW" SECTION, IN A BACK ALLEY, A DERELICT IS SUDDENLY AWAKENED FROM A PEACEFUL SNOOZE...
HEY, SNAKE-- WHADYA SAY WE HOIST THIS LOSER UPSIDE-DOWN AND SEE IF HE'S CARRYIN' ANYTHING WE CAN HOCK!
YEAH! YOU NEVER KNOW WHAT THESE BUMS STASH IN THEIR POCKETS!
CHECK OUT THAT WRIST, SNAKE! I THINK WE LUCKED OUT TODAY!
IT DON'T LOOK LIKE ANY WRISTWATCH I EVER SEEN-- BUT IT OUGHTTA PULL IN A FAT PRICE ON THE STREET!
ZEEP ZEEP
7

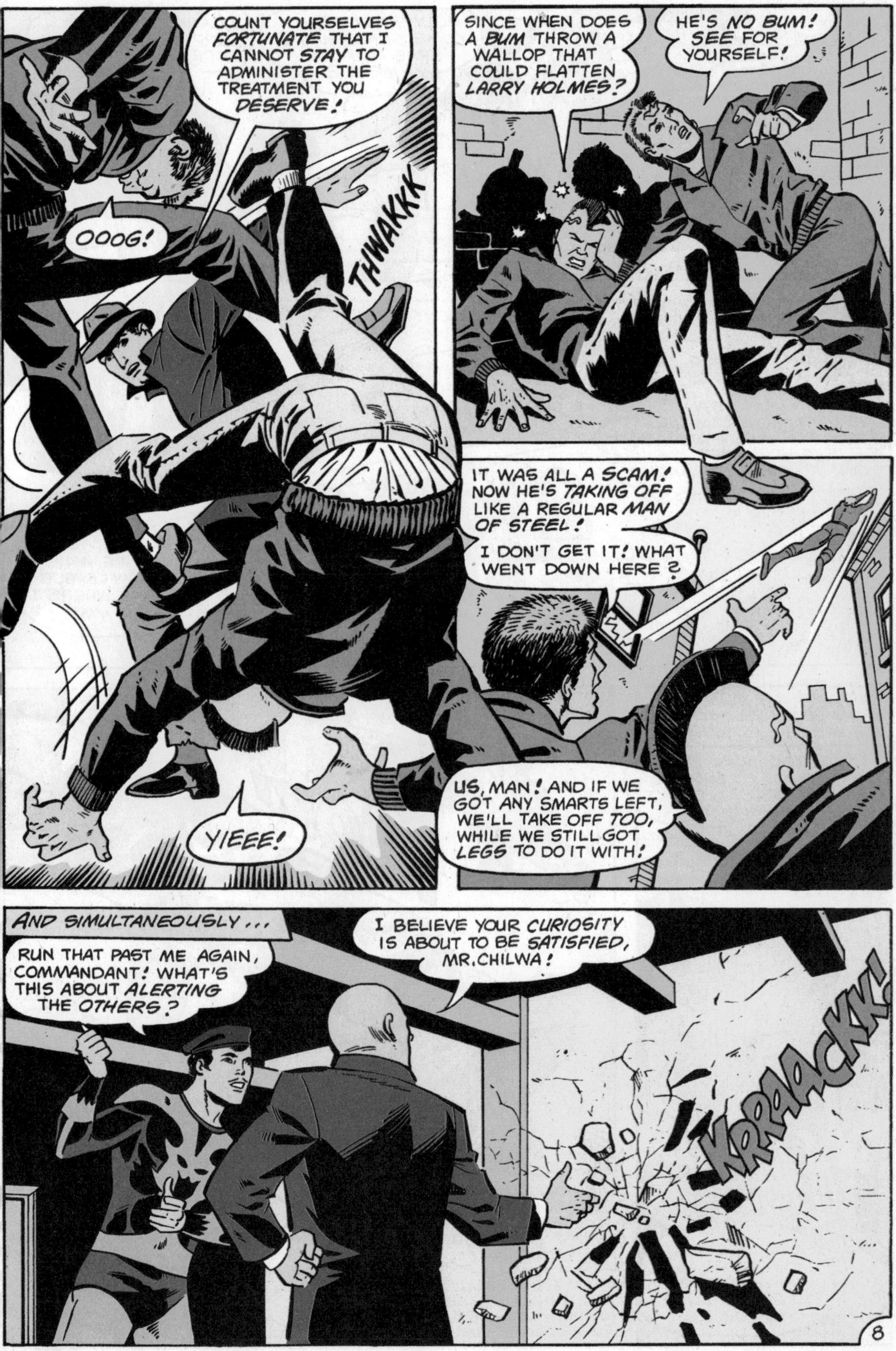
COUNT YOURSELVES FORTUNATE THAT I CANNOT STAY TO ADMINISTER THE TREATMENT YOU DESERVE!
OOOG!
THWAKKK
YIEEE!
SINCE WHEN DOES A BUM THROW A WALLOP THAT COULD FLATTEN LARRY HOLMES?
HE'S NO BUM! SEE FOR YOURSELF!
IT WAS ALL A SCAM! NOW HE'S TAKING OFF LIKE A REGULAR MAN OF STEEL!
I DON'T GET IT! WHAT WENT DOWN HERE?
US, MAN! AND IF WE GOT ANY SMARTS LEFT, WE'LL TAKE OFF TOO, WHILE WE STILL GOT LEGS TO DO IT WITH!
AND SIMULTANEOUSLY...
RUN THAT PAST ME AGAIN, COMMANDANT! WHAT'S THIS ABOUT ALERTING THE OTHERS?
I BELIEVE YOUR CURIOSITY IS ABOUT TO BE SATISFIED, MR. CHILWA!
KRRAACKK!
8

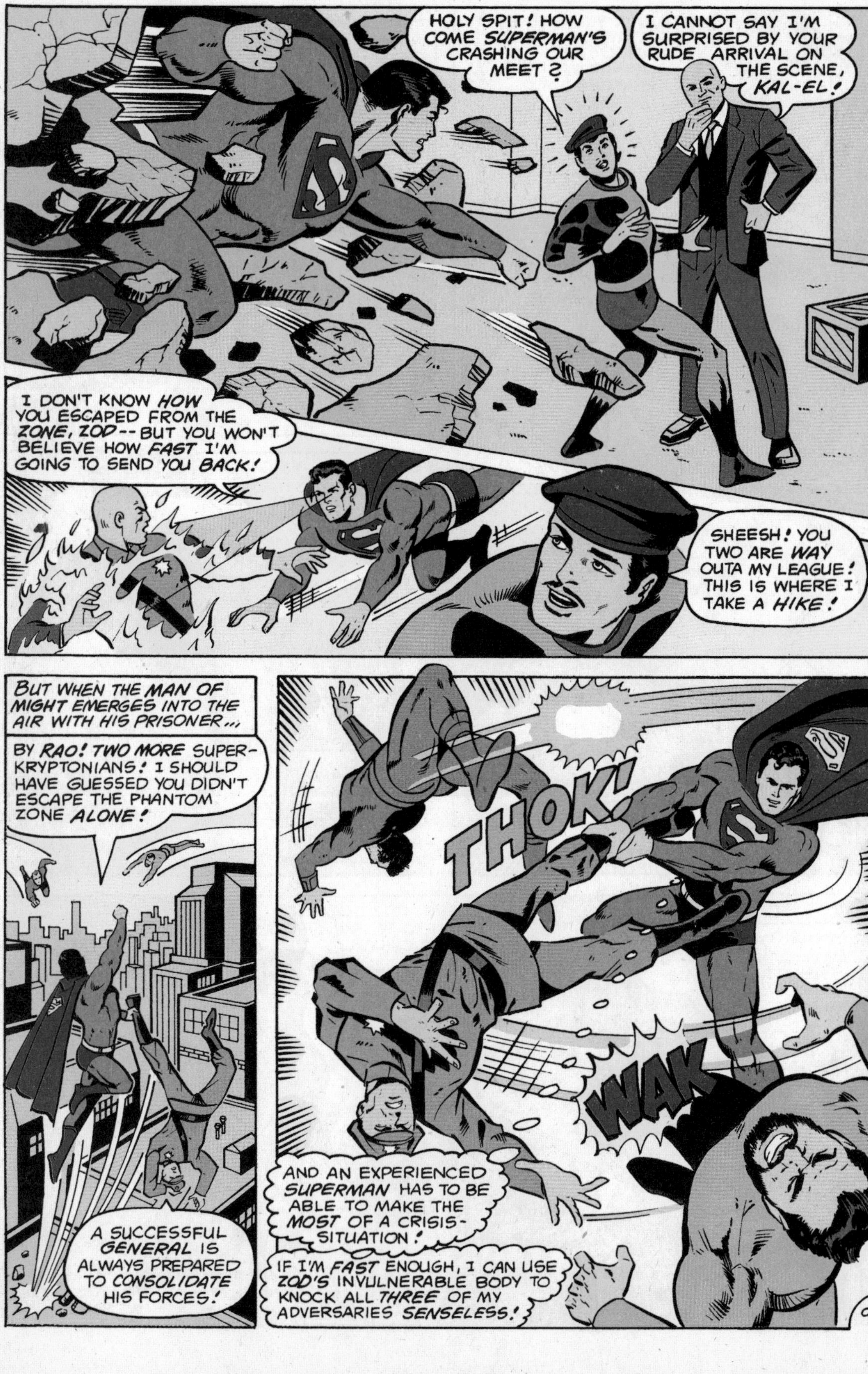
HOLY SPIT! HOW COME SUPERMAN'S CRASHING OUR MEET?
I CANNOT SAY I'M SURPRISED BY YOUR RUDE ARRIVAL ON THE SCENE, KAL-EL!
I DON'T KNOW HOW YOU ESCAPED FROM THE ZONE, ZOD--BUT YOU WON'T BELIEVE HOW FAST I'M GOING TO SEND YOU BACK!
SHEESH! YOU TWO ARE WAY OUTA MY LEAGUE! THIS IS WHERE I TAKE A HIKE!
BUT WHEN THE MAN OF MIGHT EMERGES INTO THE AIR WITH HIS PRISONER...
BY RAO! TWO MORE SUPER-KRYPTONIANS! I SHOULD HAVE GUESSED YOU DIDN'T ESCAPE THE PHANTOM ZONE ALONE!
A SUCCESSFUL GENERAL IS ALWAYS PREPARED TO CONSOLIDATE HIS FORCES!
THOK!
WAK
AND AN EXPERIENCED SUPERMAN HAS TO BE ABLE TO MAKE THE MOST OF A CRISIS-SITUATION!
IF I'M FAST ENOUGH, I CAN USE ZOD'S INVULNERABLE BODY TO KNOCK ALL THREE OF MY ADVERSARIES SENSELESS!
9

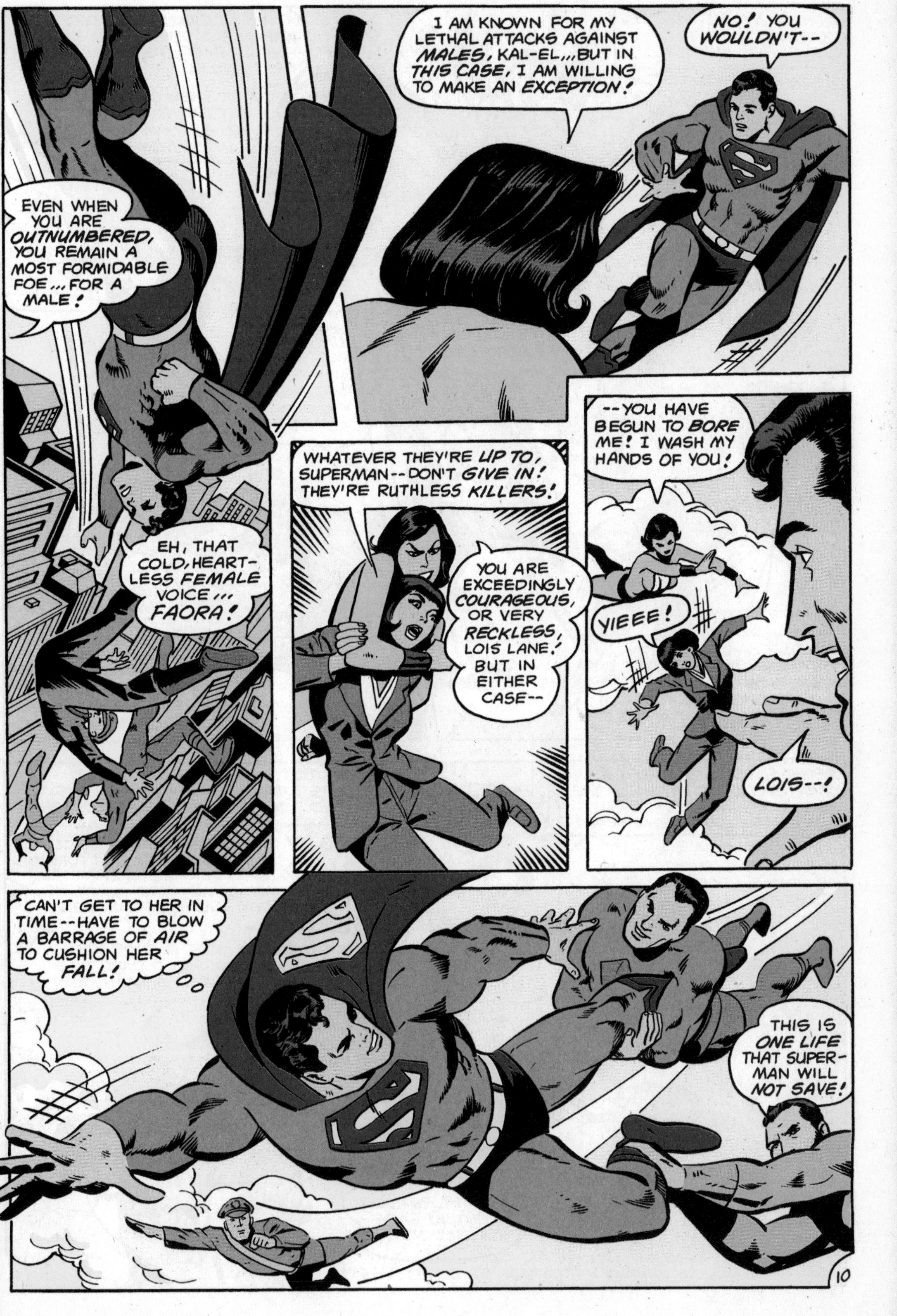
EVEN WHEN YOU ARE OUTNUMBERED, YOU REMAIN A MOST FORMIDABLE FOE... FOR A MALE!
EH, THAT COLD, HEARTLESS FEMALE VOICE... FAORA!
I AM KNOWN FOR MY LETHAL ATTACKS AGAINST MALES, KAL-EL... BUT IN THIS CASE, I AM WILLING TO MAKE AN EXCEPTION!
NO! YOU WOULDN'T--
WHATEVER THEY'RE UP TO, SUPERMAN--DON'T GIVE IN! THEY'RE RUTHLESS KILLERS!
YOU ARE EXCEEDINGLY COURAGEOUS, OR VERY RECKLESS, LOIS LANE! BUT IN EITHER CASE--
--YOU HAVE BEGUN TO BORE ME! I WASH MY HANDS OF YOU!
YIEEE!
LOIS--!
CAN'T GET TO HER IN TIME--HAVE TO BLOW A BARRAGE OF AIR TO CUSHION HER FALL!
THIS IS ONE LIFE THAT SUPERMAN WILL NOT SAVE!
10

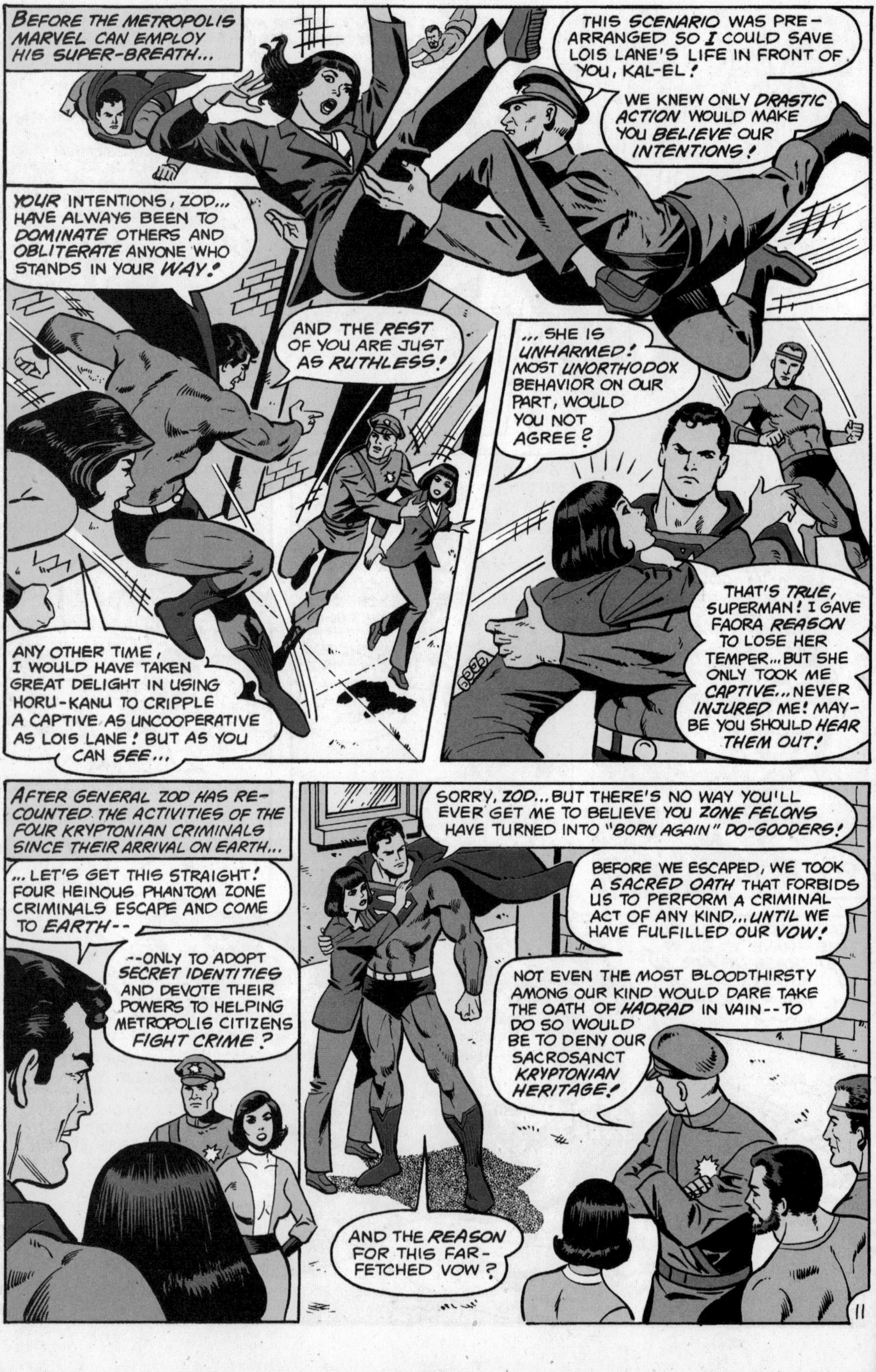

BEFORE THE METROPOLIS MARVEL CAN EMPLOY HIS SUPER-BREATH...
THIS SCENARIO WAS PRE-ARRANGED SO I COULD SAVE LOIS LANE'S LIFE IN FRONT OF YOU, KAL-EL!
WE KNEW ONLY DRASTIC ACTION WOULD MAKE YOU BELIEVE OUR INTENTIONS!
YOUR INTENTIONS, ZOD... HAVE ALWAYS BEEN TO DOMINATE OTHERS AND OBLITERATE ANYONE WHO STANDS IN YOUR WAY!
AND THE REST OF YOU ARE JUST AS RUTHLESS!
ANY OTHER TIME, I WOULD HAVE TAKEN GREAT DELIGHT IN USING HORU-KANU TO CRIPPLE A CAPTIVE AS UNCOOPERATIVE AS LOIS LANE! BUT AS YOU CAN SEE...
...SHE IS UNHARMED! MOST UNORTHODOX BEHAVIOR ON OUR PART, WOULD YOU NOT AGREE?
THAT'S TRUE, SUPERMAN! I GAVE FAORA REASON TO LOSE HER TEMPER...BUT SHE ONLY TOOK ME CAPTIVE...NEVER INJURED ME! MAY-BE YOU SHOULD HEAR THEM OUT!
AFTER GENERAL ZOD HAS RE-COUNTED THE ACTIVITIES OF THE FOUR KRYPTONIAN CRIMINALS SINCE THEIR ARRIVAL ON EARTH...
...LET'S GET THIS STRAIGHT! FOUR HEINOUS PHANTOM ZONE CRIMINALS ESCAPE AND COME TO EARTH--
--ONLY TO ADOPT SECRET IDENTITIES AND DEVOTE THEIR POWERS TO HELPING METROPOLIS CITIZENS FIGHT CRIME?
SORRY, ZOD...BUT THERE'S NO WAY YOU'LL EVER GET ME TO BELIEVE YOU ZONE FELONS HAVE TURNED INTO "BORN AGAIN" DO-GOODERS!
BEFORE WE ESCAPED, WE TOOK A SACRED OATH THAT FORBIDS US TO PERFORM A CRIMINAL ACT OF ANY KIND... UNTIL WE HAVE FULFILLED OUR VOW!
NOT EVEN THE MOST BLOODTHIRSTY AMONG OUR KIND WOULD DARE TAKE THE OATH OF HADRAD IN VAIN--TO DO SO WOULD BE TO DENY OUR SACROSANCT KRYPTONIAN HERITAGE!
AND THE REASON FOR THIS FAR-FETCHED VOW?
11

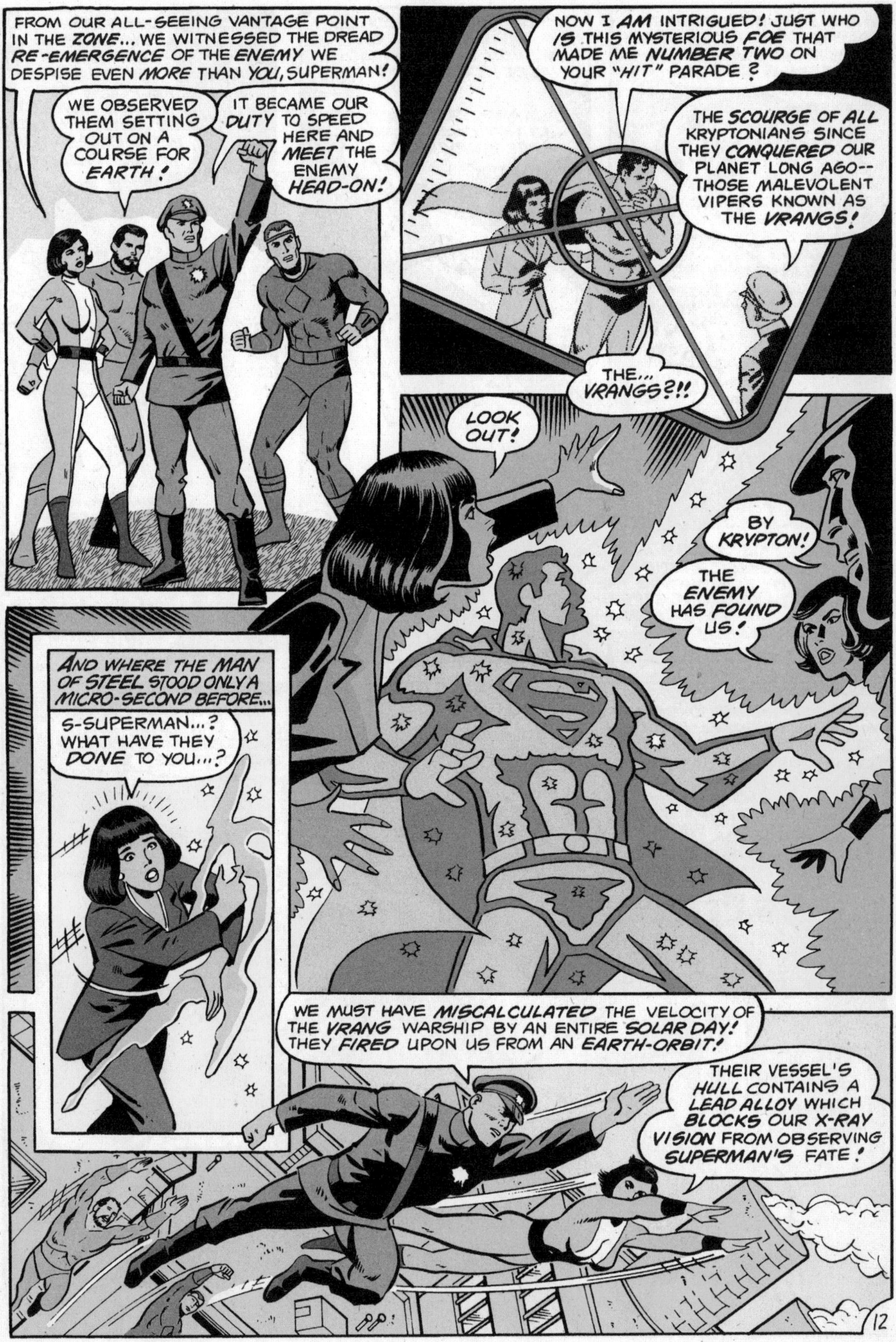
FROM OUR ALL-SEEING VANTAGE POINT IN THE ZONE... WE WITNESSED THE DREAD RE-EMERGENCE OF THE ENEMY WE DESPISE EVEN MORE THAN YOU, SUPERMAN!
WE OBSERVED THEM SETTING OUT ON A COURSE FOR EARTH!
IT BECAME OUR DUTY TO SPEED HERE AND MEET THE ENEMY HEAD-ON!
NOW I AM INTRIGUED! JUST WHO IS THIS MYSTERIOUS FOE THAT MADE ME NUMBER TWO ON YOUR "HIT" PARADE?
THE SCOURGE OF ALL KRYPTONIANS SINCE THEY CONQUERED OUR PLANET LONG AGO-- THOSE MALEVOLENT VIPERS KNOWN AS THE VRANGS!
THE... VRANGS?!!
LOOK OUT!
BY KRYPTON!
THE ENEMY HAS FOUND US!
AND WHERE THE MAN OF STEEL STOOD ONLY A MICRO-SECOND BEFORE...
S-SUPERMAN...? WHAT HAVE THEY DONE TO YOU...?
WE MUST HAVE MISCALCULATED THE VELOCITY OF THE VRANG WARSHIP BY AN ENTIRE SOLAR DAY! THEY FIRED UPON US FROM AN EARTH-ORBIT!
THEIR VESSEL'S HULL CONTAINS A LEAD ALLOY WHICH BLOCKS OUR X-RAY VISION FROM OBSERVING SUPERMAN'S FATE!
12

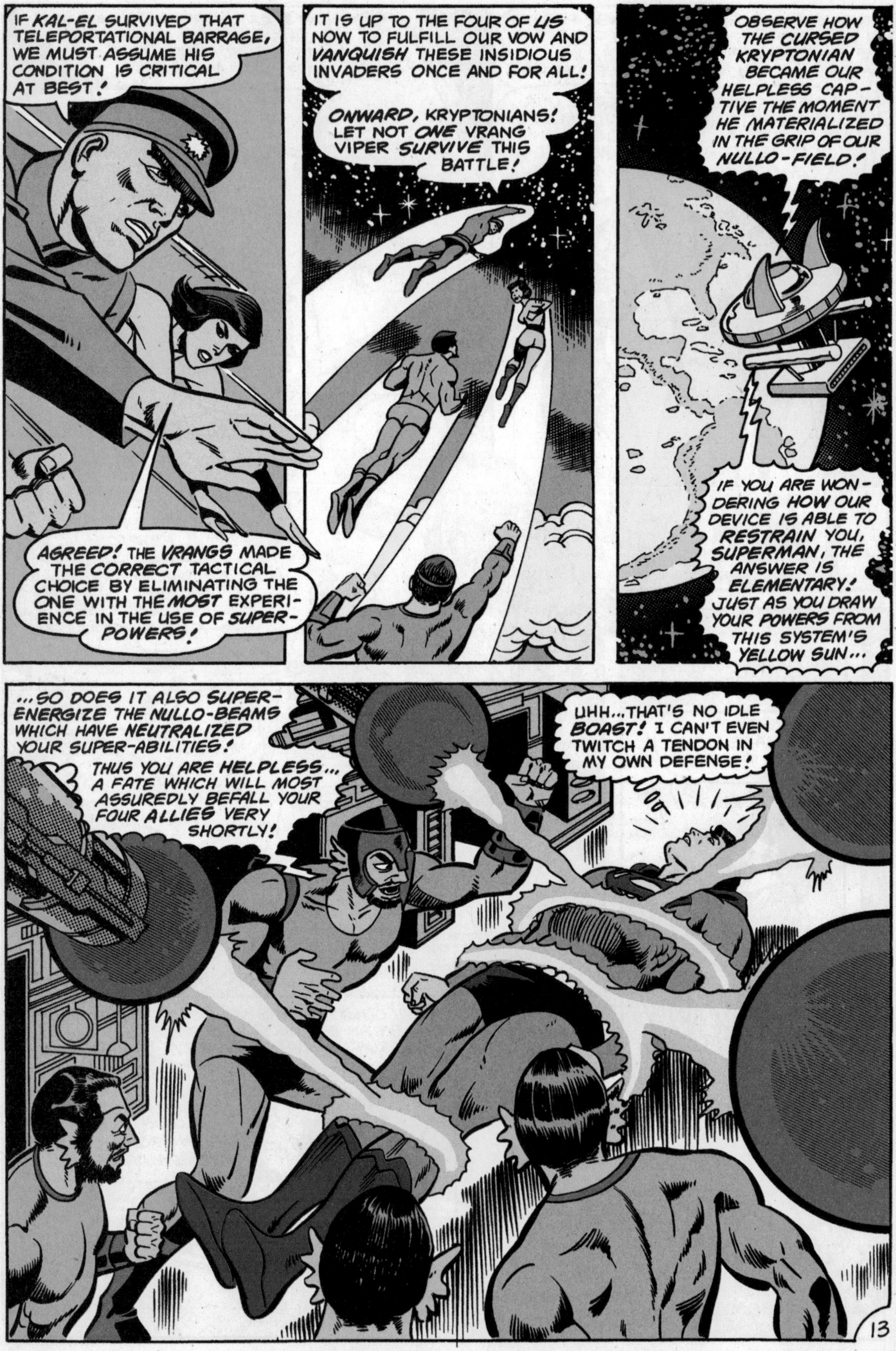
IF KAL-EL SURVIVED THAT TELEPORTATIONAL BARRAGE, WE MUST ASSUME HIS CONDITION IS CRITICAL AT BEST!
AGREED! THE VRANGS MADE THE CORRECT TACTICAL CHOICE BY ELIMINATING THE ONE WITH THE MOST EXPERIENCE IN THE USE OF SUPER-POWERS!
IT IS UP TO THE FOUR OF US NOW TO FULFILL OUR VOW AND VANQUISH THESE INSIDIOUS INVADERS ONCE AND FOR ALL!
ONWARD, KRYPTONIANS! LET NOT ONE VRANG VIPER SURVIVE THIS BATTLE!
OBSERVE HOW THE CURSED KRYPTONIAN BECAME OUR HELPLESS CAPTIVE THE MOMENT HE MATERIALIZED IN THE GRIP OF OUR NULLO-FIELD!
IF YOU ARE WONDERING HOW OUR DEVICE IS ABLE TO RESTRAIN YOU, SUPERMAN, THE ANSWER IS ELEMENTARY! JUST AS YOU DRAW YOUR POWERS FROM THIS SYSTEM'S YELLOW SUN...
...SO DOES IT ALSO SUPER-ENERGIZE THE NULLO-BEAMS WHICH HAVE NEUTRALIZED YOUR SUPER-ABILITIES!
THUS YOU ARE HELPLESS... A FATE WHICH WILL MOST ASSUREDLY BEFALL YOUR FOUR ALLIES VERY SHORTLY!
UHH...THAT'S NO IDLE BOAST! I CAN'T EVEN TWITCH A TENDON IN MY OWN DEFENSE!
13

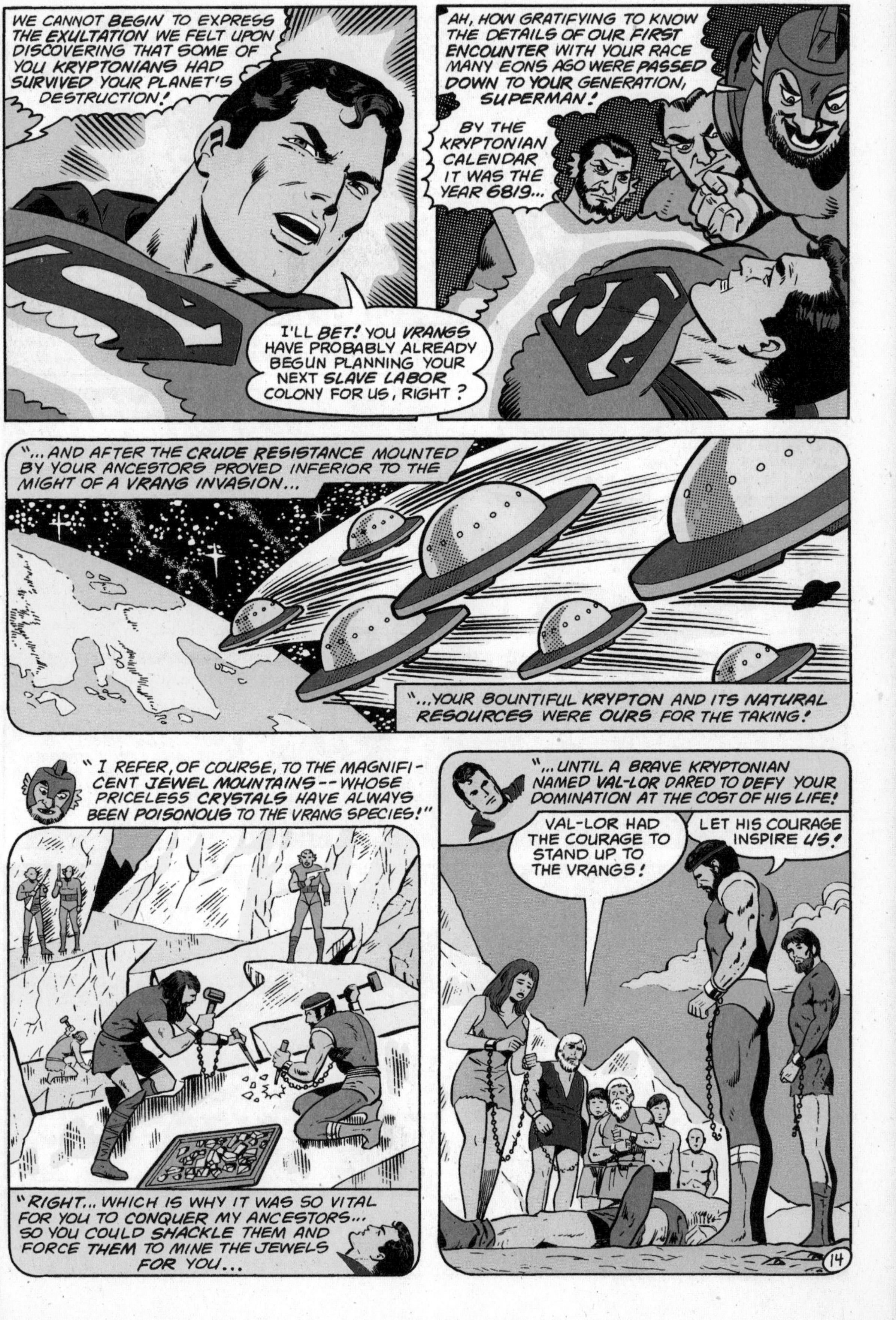
WE CANNOT BEGIN TO EXPRESS THE EXULTATION WE FELT UPON DISCOVERING THAT SOME OF YOU KRYPTONIANS HAD SURVIVED YOUR PLANET'S DESTRUCTION!
I'LL BET! YOU VRANGS HAVE PROBABLY ALREADY BEGUN PLANNING YOUR NEXT SLAVE LABOR COLONY FOR US, RIGHT?
AH, HOW GRATIFYING TO KNOW THE DETAILS OF OUR FIRST ENCOUNTER WITH YOUR RACE MANY EONS AGO WERE PASSED DOWN TO YOUR GENERATION, SUPERMAN!
BY THE KRYPTONIAN CALENDAR IT WAS THE YEAR 6819...
"...AND AFTER THE CRUDE RESISTANCE MOUNTED BY YOUR ANCESTORS PROVED INFERIOR TO THE MIGHT OF A VRANG INVASION...
"...YOUR BOUNTIFUL KRYPTON AND ITS NATURAL RESOURCES WERE OURS FOR THE TAKING!
"I REFER, OF COURSE, TO THE MAGNIFICENT JEWEL MOUNTAINS--WHOSE PRICELESS CRYSTALS HAVE ALWAYS BEEN POISONOUS TO THE VRANG SPECIES!"
"RIGHT... WHICH IS WHY IT WAS SO VITAL FOR YOU TO CONQUER MY ANCESTORS... SO YOU COULD SHACKLE THEM AND FORCE THEM TO MINE THE JEWELS FOR YOU...
"...UNTIL A BRAVE KRYPTONIAN NAMED VAL-LOR DARED TO DEFY YOUR DOMINATION AT THE COST OF HIS LIFE!
VAL-LOR HAD THE COURAGE TO STAND UP TO THE VRANGS!
LET HIS COURAGE INSPIRE US!
14

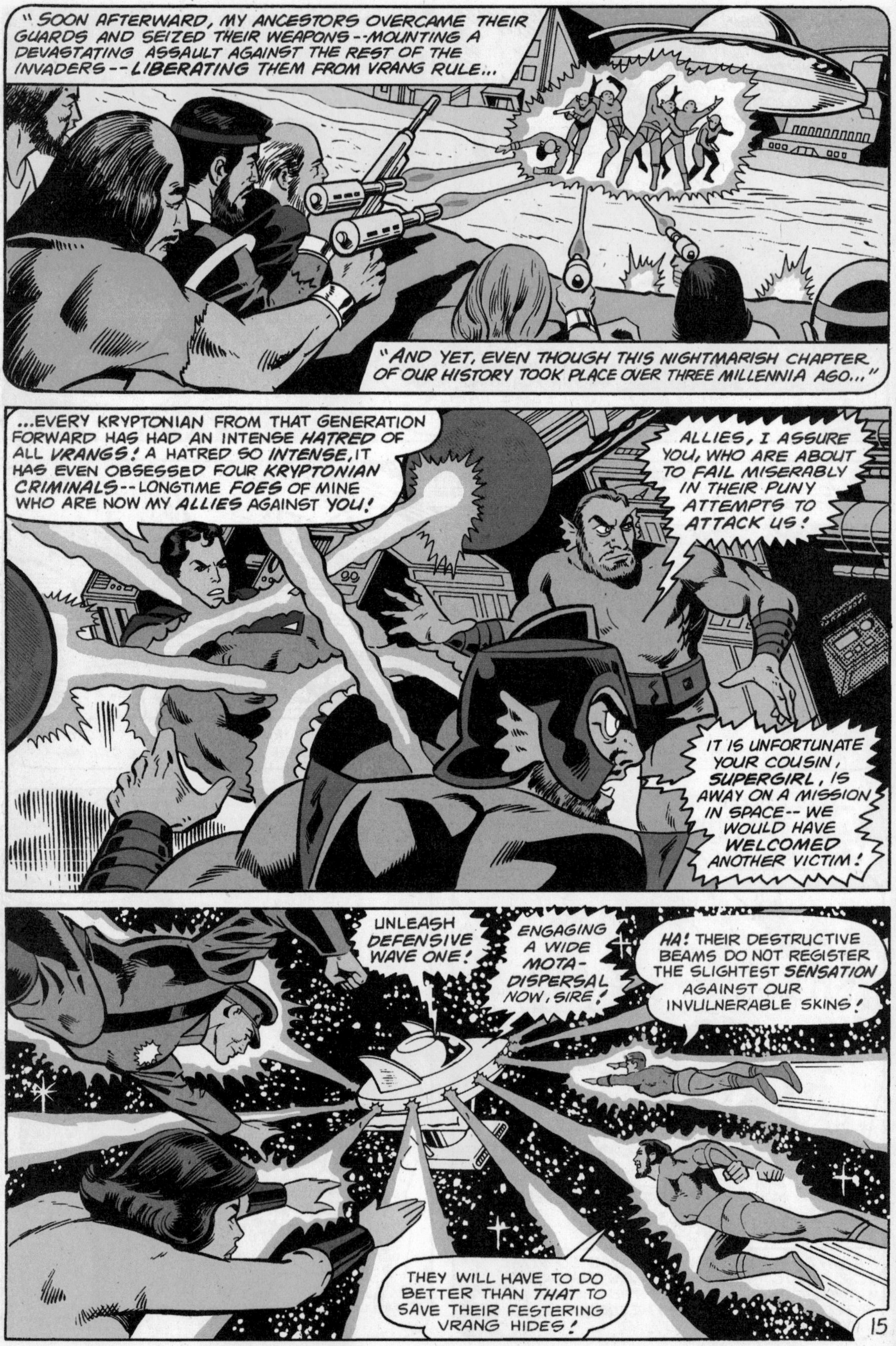
"SOON AFTERWARD, MY ANCESTORS OVERCAME THEIR GUARDS AND SEIZED THEIR WEAPONS--MOUNTING A DEVASTATING ASSAULT AGAINST THE REST OF THE INVADERS--LIBERATING THEM FROM VRANG RULE...
"AND YET, EVEN THOUGH THIS NIGHTMARISH CHAPTER OF OUR HISTORY TOOK PLACE OVER THREE MILLENNIA AGO..."
...EVERY KRYPTONIAN FROM THAT GENERATION FORWARD HAS HAD AN INTENSE HATRED OF ALL VRANGS! A HATRED SO INTENSE, IT HAS EVEN OBSESSED FOUR KRYPTONIAN CRIMINALS--LONGTIME FOES OF MINE WHO ARE NOW MY ALLIES AGAINST YOU!
ALLIES, I ASSURE YOU, WHO ARE ABOUT TO FAIL MISERABLY IN THEIR PUNY ATTEMPTS TO ATTACK US!
IT IS UNFORTUNATE YOUR COUSIN, SUPERGIRL, IS AWAY ON A MISSION IN SPACE--WE WOULD HAVE WELCOMED ANOTHER VICTIM!
UNLEASH DEFENSIVE WAVE ONE!
ENGAGING A WIDE MOTA-DISPERSAL NOW, SIRE!
HA! THEIR DESTRUCTIVE BEAMS DO NOT REGISTER THE SLIGHTEST SENSATION AGAINST OUR INVULNERABLE SKINS!
THEY WILL HAVE TO DO BETTER THAN THAT TO SAVE THEIR FESTERING VRANG HIDES!
15

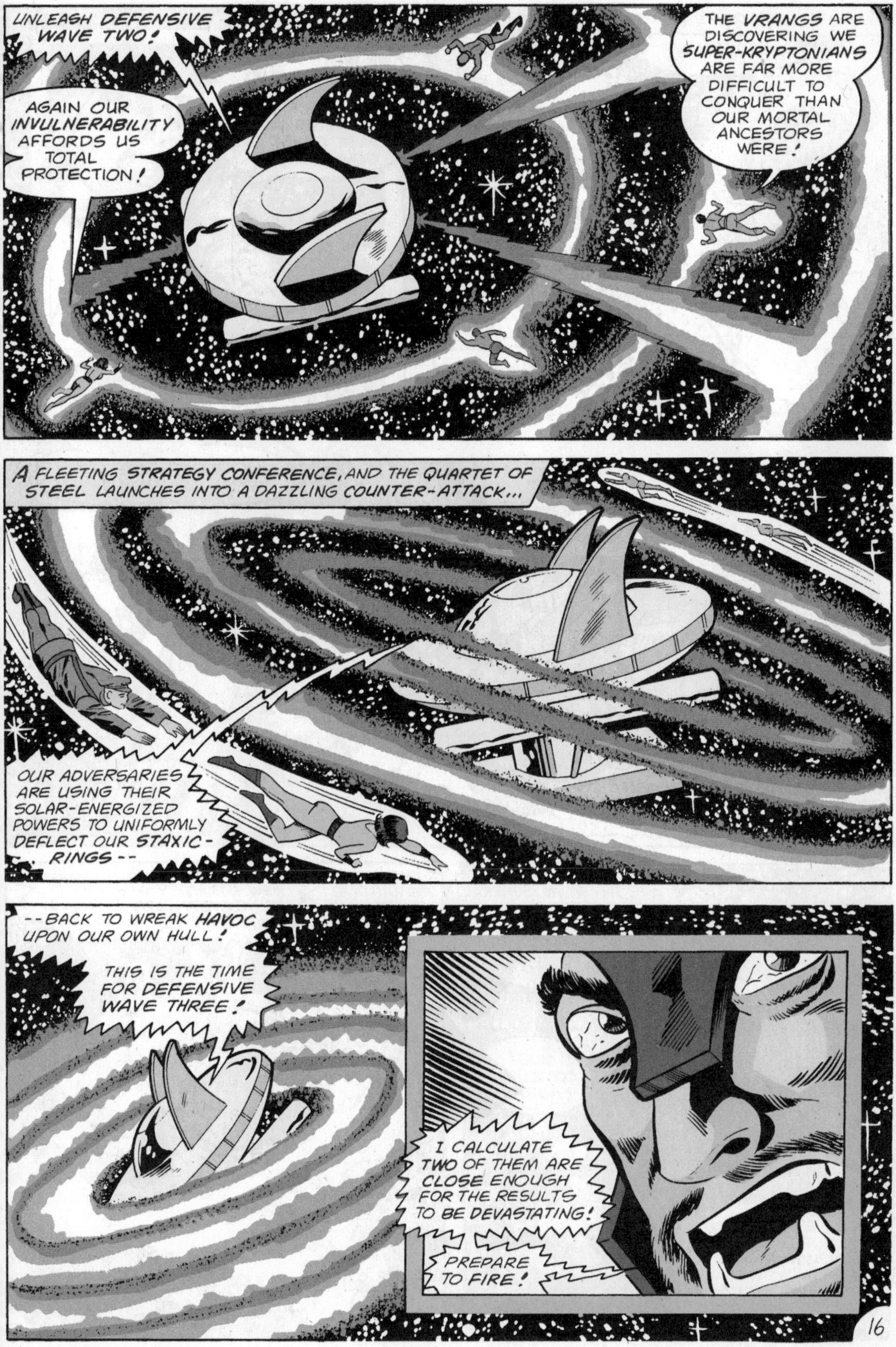

UNLEASH DEFENSIVE WAVE TWO!
AGAIN OUR INVULNERABILITY AFFORDS US TOTAL PROTECTION!
THE VRANGS ARE DISCOVERING WE SUPER-KRYPTONIANS ARE FAR MORE DIFFICULT TO CONQUER THAN OUR MORTAL ANCESTORS WERE!
A FLEETING STRATEGY CONFERENCE, AND THE QUARTET OF STEEL LAUNCHES INTO A DAZZLING COUNTER-ATTACK...
OUR ADVERSARIES ARE USING THEIR SOLAR-ENERGIZED POWERS TO UNIFORMLY DEFLECT OUR STAXIC-RINGS--
--BACK TO WREAK HAVOC UPON OUR OWN HULL!
THIS IS THE TIME FOR DEFENSIVE WAVE THREE!
I CALCULATE TWO OF THEM ARE CLOSE ENOUGH FOR THE RESULTS TO BE DEVASTATING!
PREPARE TO FIRE!
16

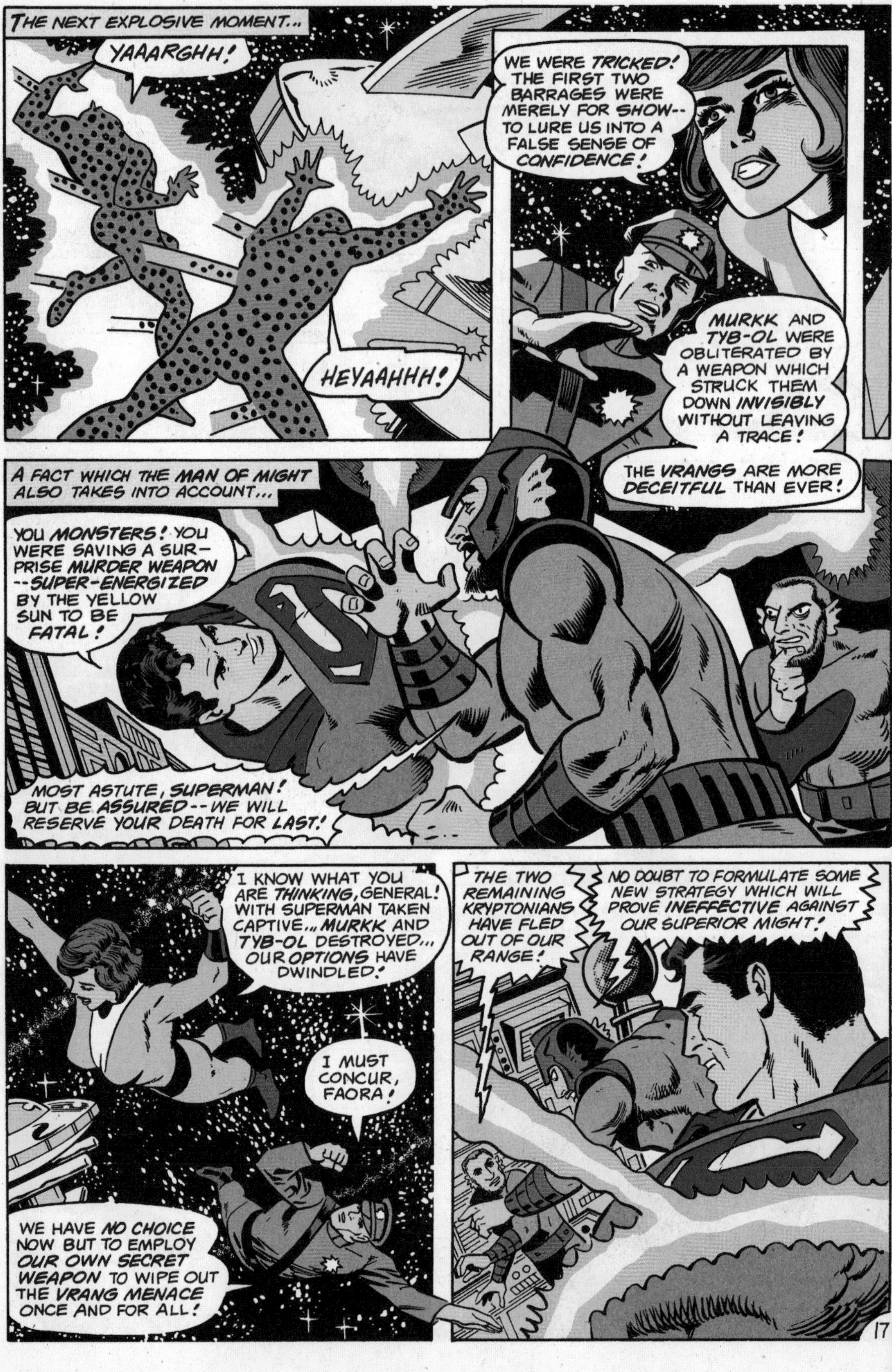
THE NEXT EXPLOSIVE MOMENT...
YAAARGHH!
HEYAAHHH!
WE WERE TRICKED! THE FIRST TWO BARRAGES WERE MERELY FOR SHOW-- TO LURE US INTO A FALSE SENSE OF CONFIDENCE!
MURKK AND TYB-OL WERE OBLITERATED BY A WEAPON WHICH STRUCK THEM DOWN INVISIBLY WITHOUT LEAVING A TRACE!
THE VRANGS ARE MORE DECEITFUL THAN EVER!
A FACT WHICH THE MAN OF MIGHT ALSO TAKES INTO ACCOUNT...
YOU MONSTERS! YOU WERE SAVING A SURPRISE MURDER WEAPON --SUPER-ENERGIZED BY THE YELLOW SUN TO BE FATAL!
MOST ASTUTE, SUPERMAN! BUT BE ASSURED--WE WILL RESERVE YOUR DEATH FOR LAST!
I KNOW WHAT YOU ARE THINKING, GENERAL! WITH SUPERMAN TAKEN CAPTIVE... MURKK AND TYB-OL DESTROYED... OUR OPTIONS HAVE DWINDLED!
I MUST CONCUR, FAORA!
WE HAVE NO CHOICE NOW BUT TO EMPLOY OUR OWN SECRET WEAPON TO WIPE OUT THE VRANG MENACE ONCE AND FOR ALL!
THE TWO REMAINING KRYPTONIANS HAVE FLED OUT OF OUR RANGE!
NO DOUBT TO FORMULATE SOME NEW STRATEGY WHICH WILL PROVE INEFFECTIVE AGAINST OUR SUPERIOR MIGHT!
17

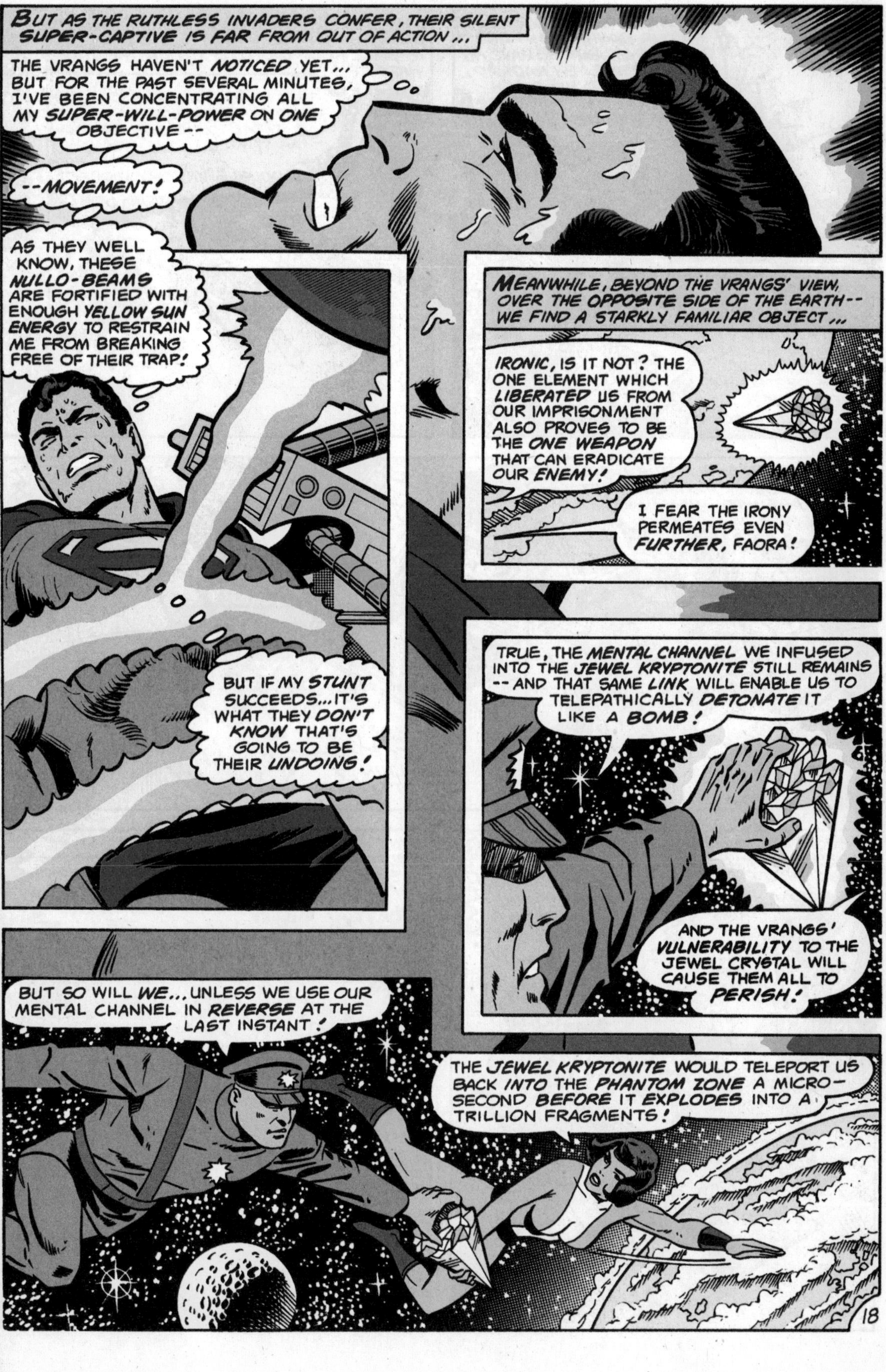
BUT AS THE RUTHLESS INVADERS CONFER, THEIR SILENT SUPER-CAPTIVE IS FAR FROM OUT OF ACTION...
THE VRANGS HAVEN'T NOTICED YET... BUT FOR THE PAST SEVERAL MINUTES, I'VE BEEN CONCENTRATING ALL MY SUPER-WILL-POWER ON ONE OBJECTIVE --
--MOVEMENT!
AS THEY WELL KNOW, THESE NULLO-BEAMS ARE FORTIFIED WITH ENOUGH YELLOW SUN ENERGY TO RESTRAIN ME FROM BREAKING FREE OF THEIR TRAP!
BUT IF MY STUNT SUCCEEDS... IT'S WHAT THEY DON'T KNOW THAT'S GOING TO BE THEIR UNDOING!
MEANWHILE, BEYOND THE VRANGS' VIEW, OVER THE OPPOSITE SIDE OF THE EARTH-- WE FIND A STARKLY FAMILIAR OBJECT...
IRONIC, IS IT NOT? THE ONE ELEMENT WHICH LIBERATED US FROM OUR IMPRISONMENT ALSO PROVES TO BE THE ONE WEAPON THAT CAN ERADICATE OUR ENEMY!
I FEAR THE IRONY PERMEATES EVEN FURTHER, FAORA!
TRUE, THE MENTAL CHANNEL WE INFUSED INTO THE JEWEL KRYPTONITE STILL REMAINS -- AND THAT SAME LINK WILL ENABLE US TO TELEPATHICALLY DETONATE IT LIKE A BOMB!
AND THE VRANGS' VULNERABILITY TO THE JEWEL CRYSTAL WILL CAUSE THEM ALL TO PERISH!
BUT SO WILL WE... UNLESS WE USE OUR MENTAL CHANNEL IN REVERSE AT THE LAST INSTANT!
THE JEWEL KRYPTONITE WOULD TELEPORT US BACK INTO THE PHANTOM ZONE A MICRO-SECOND BEFORE IT EXPLODES INTO A TRILLION FRAGMENTS!
18

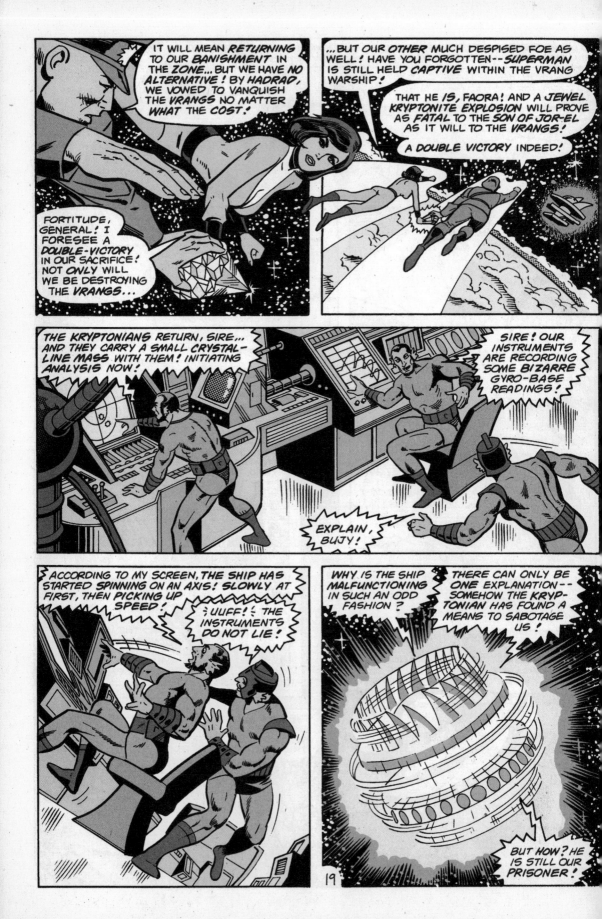

IT WILL MEAN *RETURNING* TO OUR *BANISHMENT* IN THE *ZONE*... BUT WE HAVE *NO ALTERNATIVE!* BY HADRAD, WE VOWED TO VANQUISH THE *VRANGS* NO MATTER WHAT THE *COST!*

...BUT OUR *OTHER* MUCH DESPISED FOE AS WELL! HAVE YOU FORGOTTEN-- *SUPERMAN* IS STILL HELD *CAPTIVE* WITHIN THE *VRANG* WARSHIP!

THAT HE *IS*, FAORA! AND A *JEWEL KRYPTONITE EXPLOSION* WILL PROVE AS *FATAL* TO THE *SON OF JOR-EL* AS IT WILL TO THE *VRANGS!* A *DOUBLE VICTORY* INDEED!

FORTITUDE, GENERAL! I FORESEE A *DOUBLE-VICTORY* IN OUR SACRIFICE! NOT *ONLY* WILL WE BE DESTROYING THE *VRANGS*...

THE KRYPTONIANS RETURN, SIRE... AND THEY CARRY A SMALL *CRYSTAL-LINE MASS* WITH THEM! INITIATING ANALYSIS NOW!

SIRE! OUR INSTRUMENTS ARE RECORDING SOME BIZARRE GYRO-BASE READINGS!

EXPLAIN, BUJY!

ACCORDING TO MY SCREEN, THE SHIP HAS STARTED SPINNING ON AN AXIS! SLOWLY AT FIRST, THEN PICKING UP SPEED!

§UUFF!§ THE INSTRUMENTS DO NOT LIE!

WHY IS THE SHIP MALFUNCTIONING IN SUCH AN ODD FASHION?

THERE CAN ONLY BE ONE EXPLANATION-- SOMEHOW THE KRYPTONIAN HAS FOUND A MEANS TO SABOTAGE US!

BUT HOW? HE IS STILL OUR PRISONER!

19

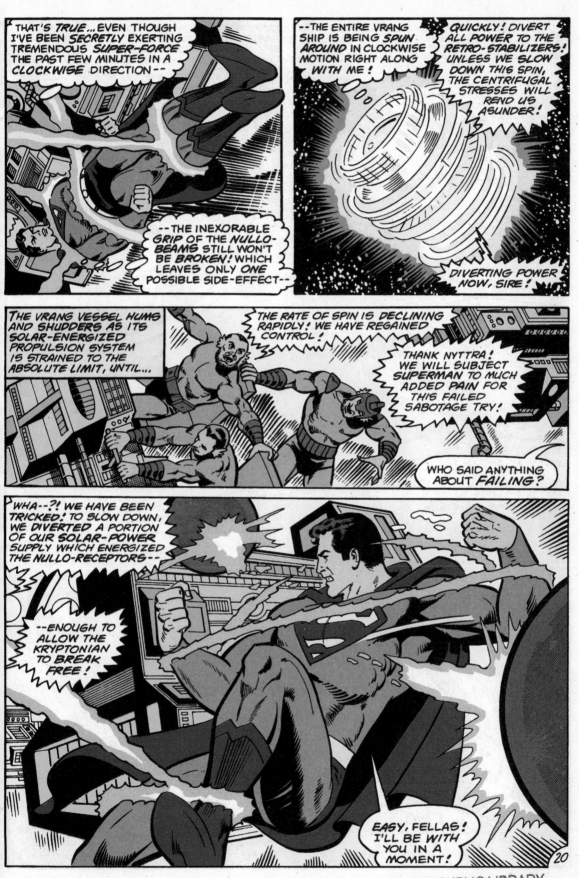

THAT'S *TRUE*... EVEN THOUGH I'VE BEEN *SECRETLY* EXERTING TREMENDOUS *SUPER-FORCE* THE PAST FEW MINUTES IN A *CLOCKWISE* DIRECTION--

--THE INEXORABLE *GRIP* OF THE *NULLO-BEAMS* STILL WON'T BE BROKEN! WHICH LEAVES ONLY *ONE* POSSIBLE SIDE-EFFECT--

--THE ENTIRE VRANG SHIP IS BEING *SPUN* AROUND IN CLOCKWISE MOTION RIGHT ALONG WITH ME!

QUICKLY! DIVERT *ALL* POWER TO THE *RETRO-STABILIZERS!* UNLESS WE SLOW DOWN THIS SPIN, THE *CENTRIFUGAL* STRESSES WILL REND US *ASUNDER!*

DIVERTING POWER NOW, SIRE!

THE VRANG VESSEL HUMS AND SHUDDERS AS ITS SOLAR-ENERGIZED PROPULSION SYSTEM IS STRAINED TO THE ABSOLUTE LIMIT, UNTIL...

THE RATE OF SPIN IS DECLINING RAPIDLY! WE HAVE REGAINED CONTROL!

THANK NYTTRA! WE WILL SUBJECT SUPERMAN TO MUCH ADDED PAIN FOR THIS FAILED SABOTAGE TRY!

WHO SAID ANYTHING ABOUT *FAILING?*

WHA--?! WE HAVE BEEN *TRICKED!* TO SLOW DOWN, WE DIVERTED A PORTION OF OUR SOLAR-POWER SUPPLY WHICH *ENERGIZED* THE NULLO-RECEPTORS--

--ENOUGH TO ALLOW THE KRYPTONIAN TO BREAK *FREE!*

EASY, FELLAS! I'LL BE *WITH* YOU IN A MOMENT!

20

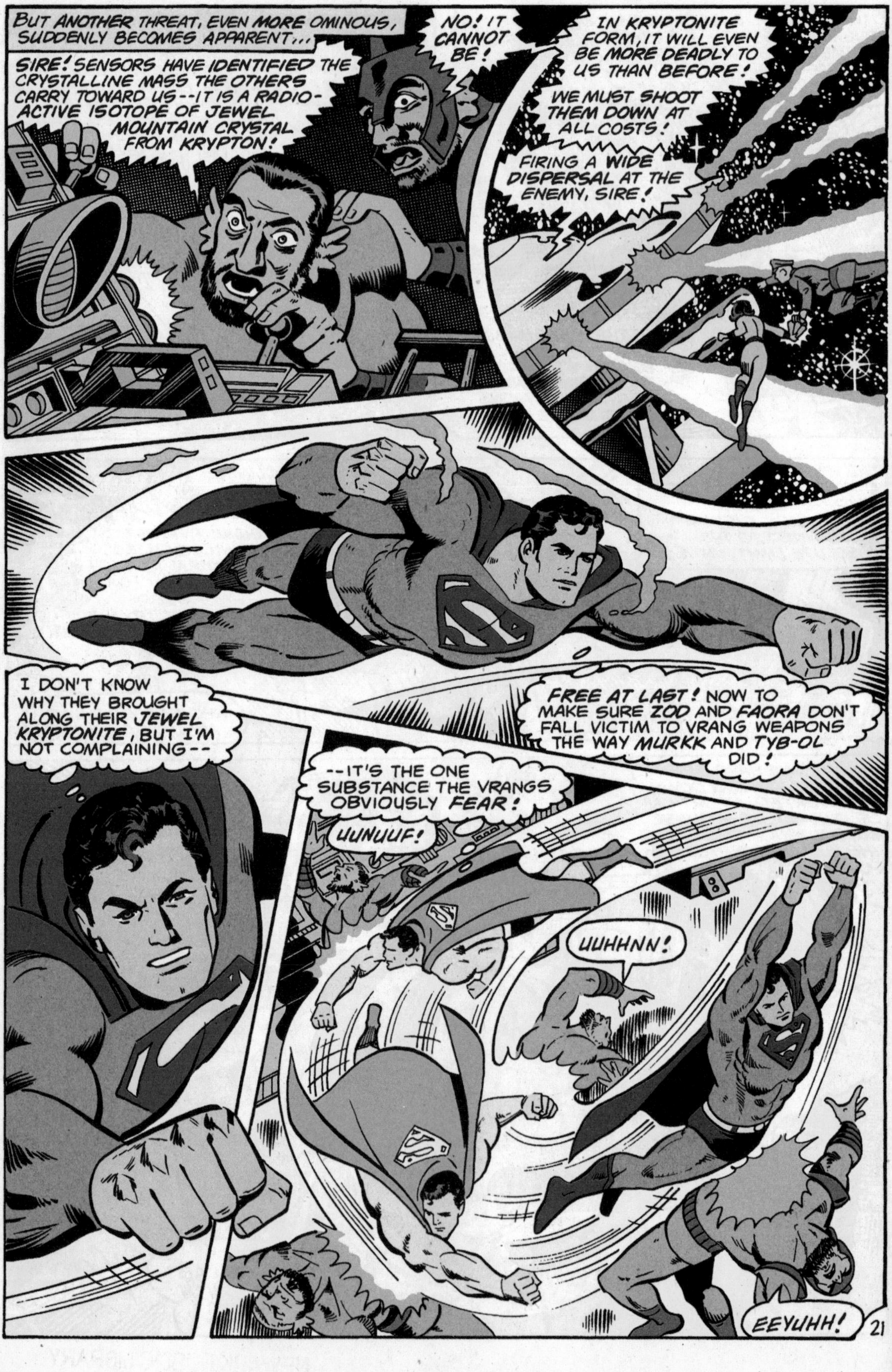
BUT ANOTHER THREAT, EVEN MORE OMINOUS, SUDDENLY BECOMES APPARENT...
SIRE! SENSORS HAVE IDENTIFIED THE CRYSTALLINE MASS THE OTHERS CARRY TOWARD US--IT IS A RADIO-ACTIVE ISOTOPE OF JEWEL MOUNTAIN CRYSTAL FROM KRYPTON!
NO! IT CANNOT BE!
IN KRYPTONITE FORM, IT WILL EVEN BE MORE DEADLY TO US THAN BEFORE!
WE MUST SHOOT THEM DOWN AT ALL COSTS!
FIRING A WIDE DISPERSAL AT THE ENEMY, SIRE!
I DON'T KNOW WHY THEY BROUGHT ALONG THEIR JEWEL KRYPTONITE, BUT I'M NOT COMPLAINING--
FREE AT LAST! NOW TO MAKE SURE ZOD AND FAORA DON'T FALL VICTIM TO VRANG WEAPONS THE WAY MURKK AND TYB-OL DID!
--IT'S THE ONE SUBSTANCE THE VRANGS OBVIOUSLY FEAR!
UUNUUF!
UUHHNN!
EEYUHH!
21

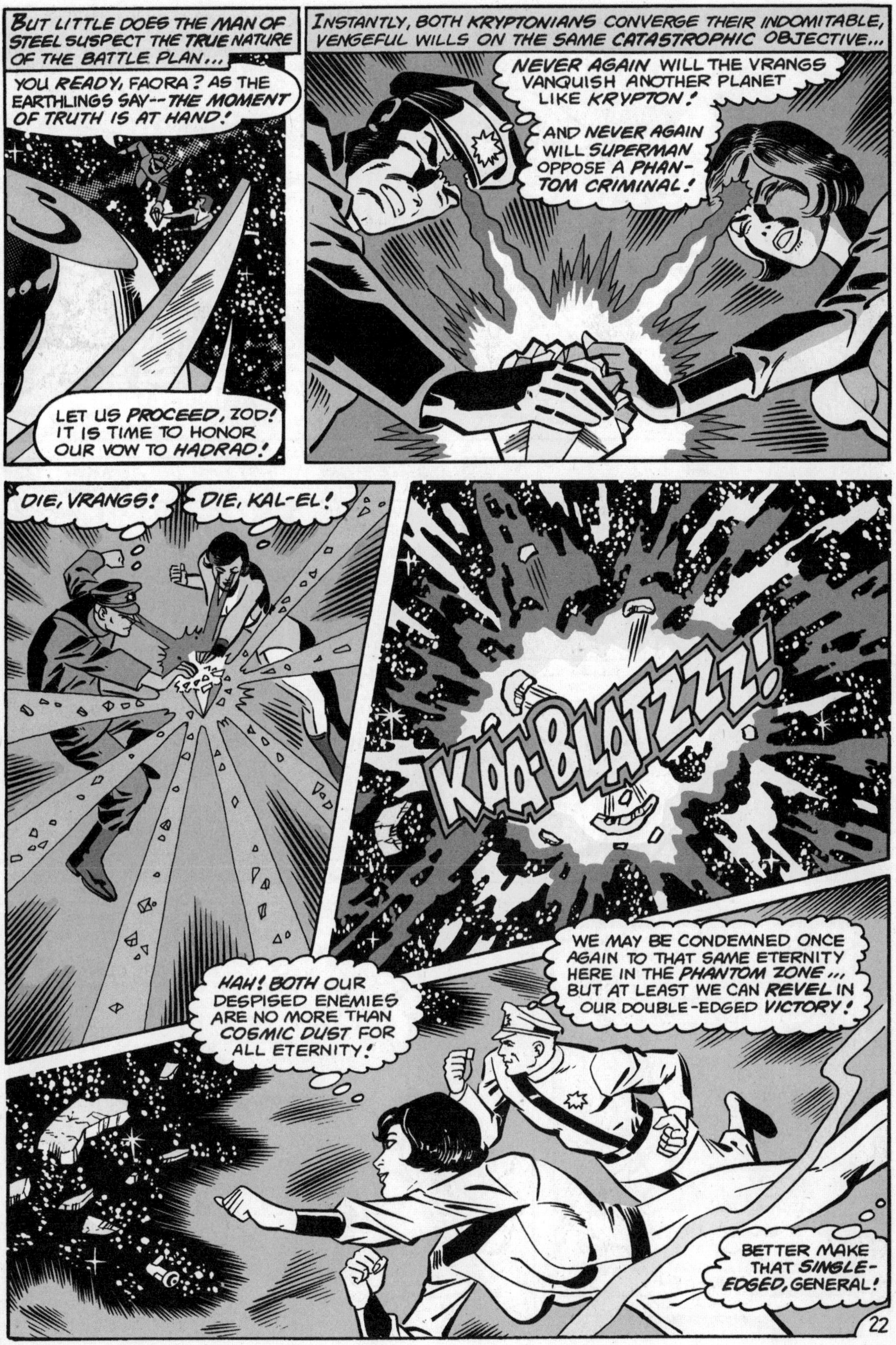

BUT LITTLE DOES THE MAN OF STEEL SUSPECT THE TRUE NATURE OF THE BATTLE PLAN...
YOU READY, FAORA? AS THE EARTHLINGS SAY--THE MOMENT OF TRUTH IS AT HAND!
LET US PROCEED, ZOD! IT IS TIME TO HONOR OUR VOW TO HADRAD!
INSTANTLY, BOTH KRYPTONIANS CONVERGE THEIR INDOMITABLE, VENGEFUL WILLS ON THE SAME CATASTROPHIC OBJECTIVE...
NEVER AGAIN WILL THE VRANGS VANQUISH ANOTHER PLANET LIKE KRYPTON!
AND NEVER AGAIN WILL SUPERMAN OPPOSE A PHANTOM CRIMINAL!
DIE, VRANGS!
DIE, KAL-EL!
KAA-BLATZZZ!
HAH! BOTH OUR DESPISED ENEMIES ARE NO MORE THAN COSMIC DUST FOR ALL ETERNITY!
WE MAY BE CONDEMNED ONCE AGAIN TO THAT SAME ETERNITY HERE IN THE PHANTOM ZONE... BUT AT LEAST WE CAN REVEL IN OUR DOUBLE-EDGED VICTORY!
BETTER MAKE THAT SINGLE-EDGED, GENERAL!
22

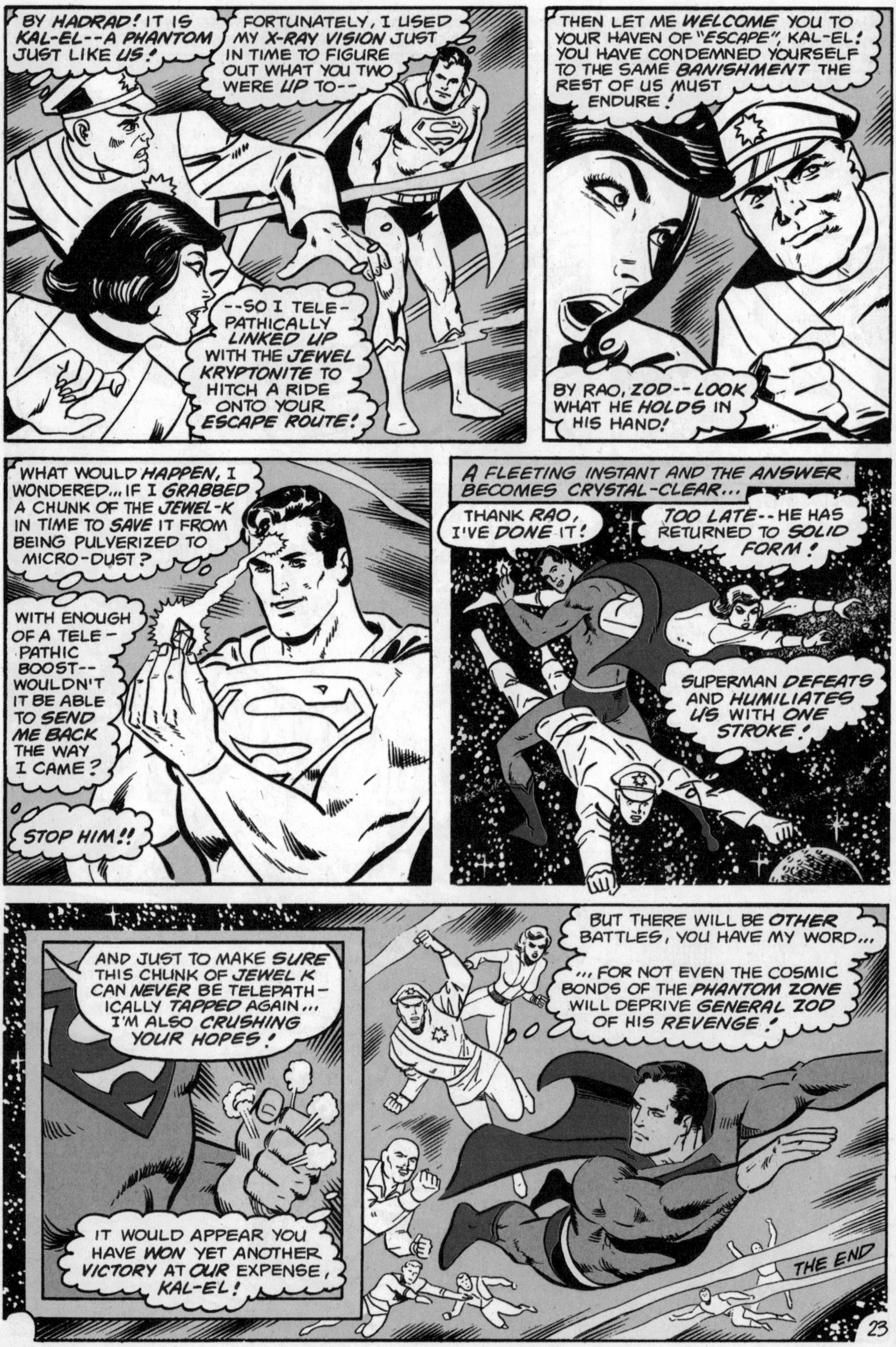
BY HADRAD! IT IS KAL-EL--A PHANTOM JUST LIKE US!
FORTUNATELY, I USED MY X-RAY VISION JUST IN TIME TO FIGURE OUT WHAT YOU TWO WERE UP TO--
--SO I TELE-PATHICALLY LINKED UP WITH THE JEWEL KRYPTONITE TO HITCH A RIDE ONTO YOUR ESCAPE ROUTE!
THEN LET ME WELCOME YOU TO YOUR HAVEN OF "ESCAPE", KAL-EL! YOU HAVE CONDEMNED YOURSELF TO THE SAME BANISHMENT THE REST OF US MUST ENDURE!
BY RAO, ZOD--LOOK WHAT HE HOLDS IN HIS HAND!
WHAT WOULD HAPPEN, I WONDERED... IF I GRABBED A CHUNK OF THE JEWEL-K IN TIME TO SAVE IT FROM BEING PULVERIZED TO MICRO-DUST?
WITH ENOUGH OF A TELE-PATHIC BOOST--WOULDN'T IT BE ABLE TO SEND ME BACK THE WAY I CAME?
STOP HIM!!
A FLEETING INSTANT AND THE ANSWER BECOMES CRYSTAL-CLEAR...
THANK RAO, I'VE DONE IT!
TOO LATE--HE HAS RETURNED TO SOLID FORM!
SUPERMAN DEFEATS AND HUMILIATES US WITH ONE STROKE!
AND JUST TO MAKE SURE THIS CHUNK OF JEWEL K CAN NEVER BE TELEPATH-ICALLY TAPPED AGAIN... I'M ALSO CRUSHING YOUR HOPES!
IT WOULD APPEAR YOU HAVE WON YET ANOTHER VICTORY AT OUR EXPENSE, KAL-EL!
BUT THERE WILL BE OTHER BATTLES, YOU HAVE MY WORD...
...FOR NOT EVEN THE COSMIC BONDS OF THE PHANTOM ZONE WILL DEPRIVE GENERAL ZOD OF HIS REVENGE!
THE END
23

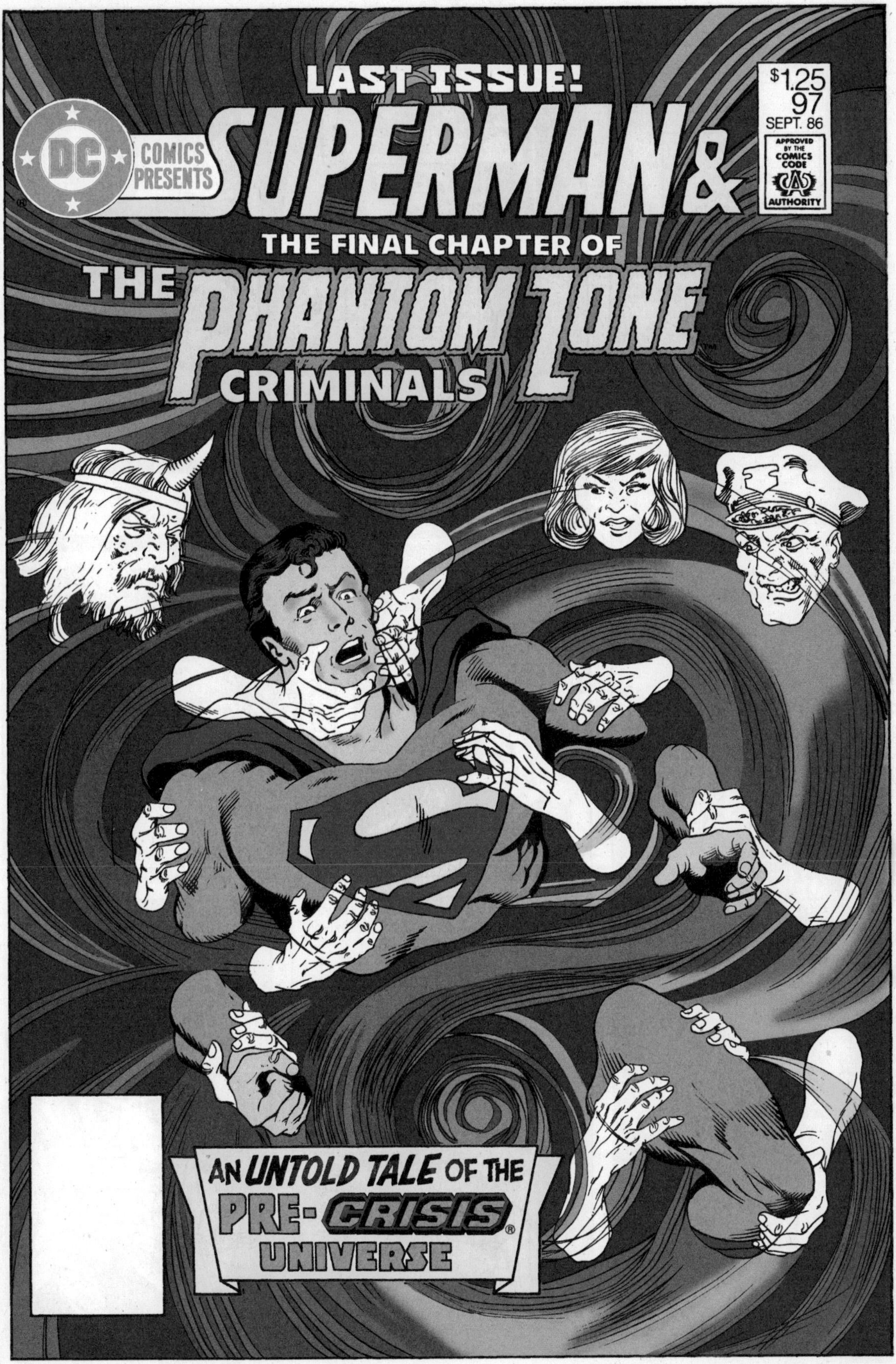
LAST ISSUE!
$1.25
97
SEPT. 86
APPROVED BY THE COMICS CODE AUTHORITY
DC COMICS PRESENTS
SUPERMAN &
THE FINAL CHAPTER OF
THE PHANTOM ZONE CRIMINALS
AN UNTOLD TALE OF THE
PRE-CRISIS
UNIVERSE

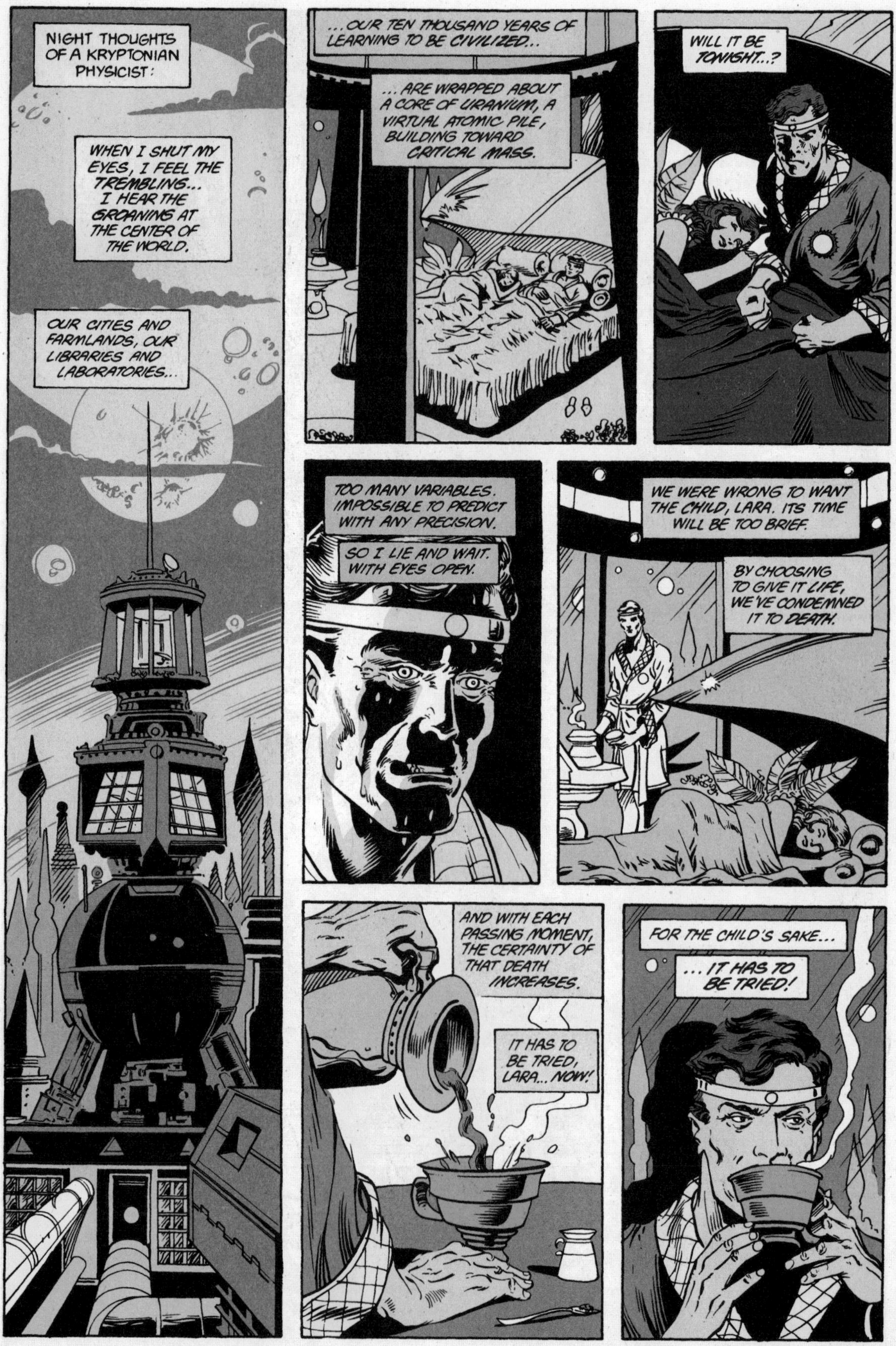
NIGHT THOUGHTS OF A KRYPTONIAN PHYSICIST:
WHEN I SHUT MY EYES, I FEEL THE TREMBLING... I HEAR THE GROANING AT THE CENTER OF THE WORLD.
OUR CITIES AND FARMLANDS, OUR LIBRARIES AND LABORATORIES...
...OUR TEN THOUSAND YEARS OF LEARNING TO BE CIVILIZED...
...ARE WRAPPED ABOUT A CORE OF URANIUM, A VIRTUAL ATOMIC PILE, BUILDING TOWARD CRITICAL MASS.
WILL IT BE TONIGHT...?
TOO MANY VARIABLES. IMPOSSIBLE TO PREDICT WITH ANY PRECISION.
SO I LIE AND WAIT. WITH EYES OPEN.
WE WERE WRONG TO WANT THE CHILD, LARA. ITS TIME WILL BE TOO BRIEF.
BY CHOOSING TO GIVE IT LIFE, WE'VE CONDEMNED IT TO DEATH.
AND WITH EACH PASSING MOMENT, THE CERTAINTY OF THAT DEATH INCREASES.
IT HAS TO BE TRIED, LARA... NOW!
FOR THE CHILD'S SAKE...
...IT HAS TO BE TRIED!

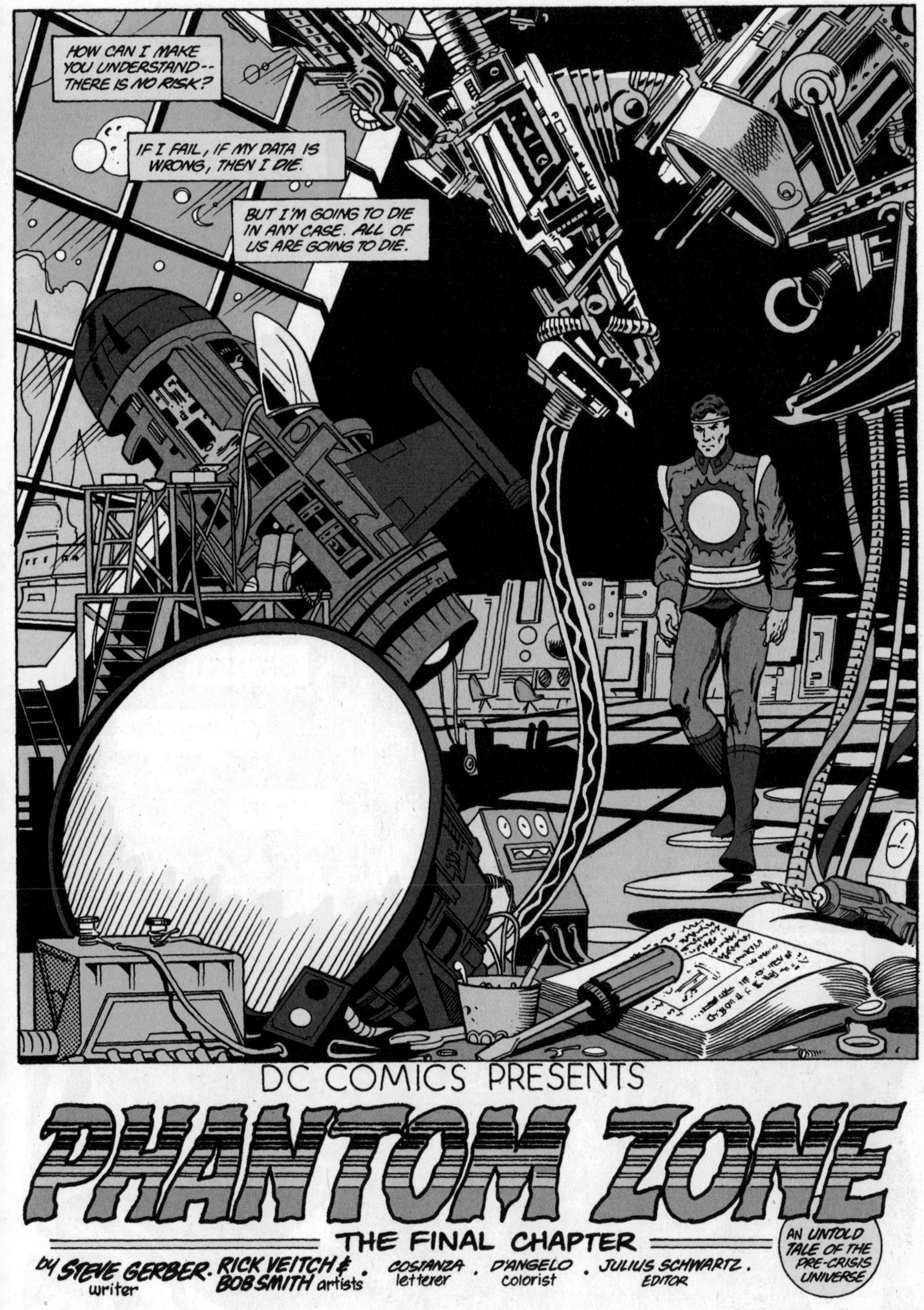
HOW CAN I MAKE YOU UNDERSTAND-- THERE IS NO RISK?
IF I FAIL, IF MY DATA IS WRONG, THEN I DIE.
BUT I'M GOING TO DIE IN ANY CASE. ALL OF US ARE GOING TO DIE.

DC COMICS PRESENTS

PHANTOM ZONE

THE FINAL CHAPTER

by STEVE GERBER writer . RICK VEITCH & BOB SMITH artists . COSTANZA letterer . D'ANGELO colorist . JULIUS SCHWARTZ . EDITOR

AN UNTOLD TALE OF THE PRE-CRISIS UNIVERSE

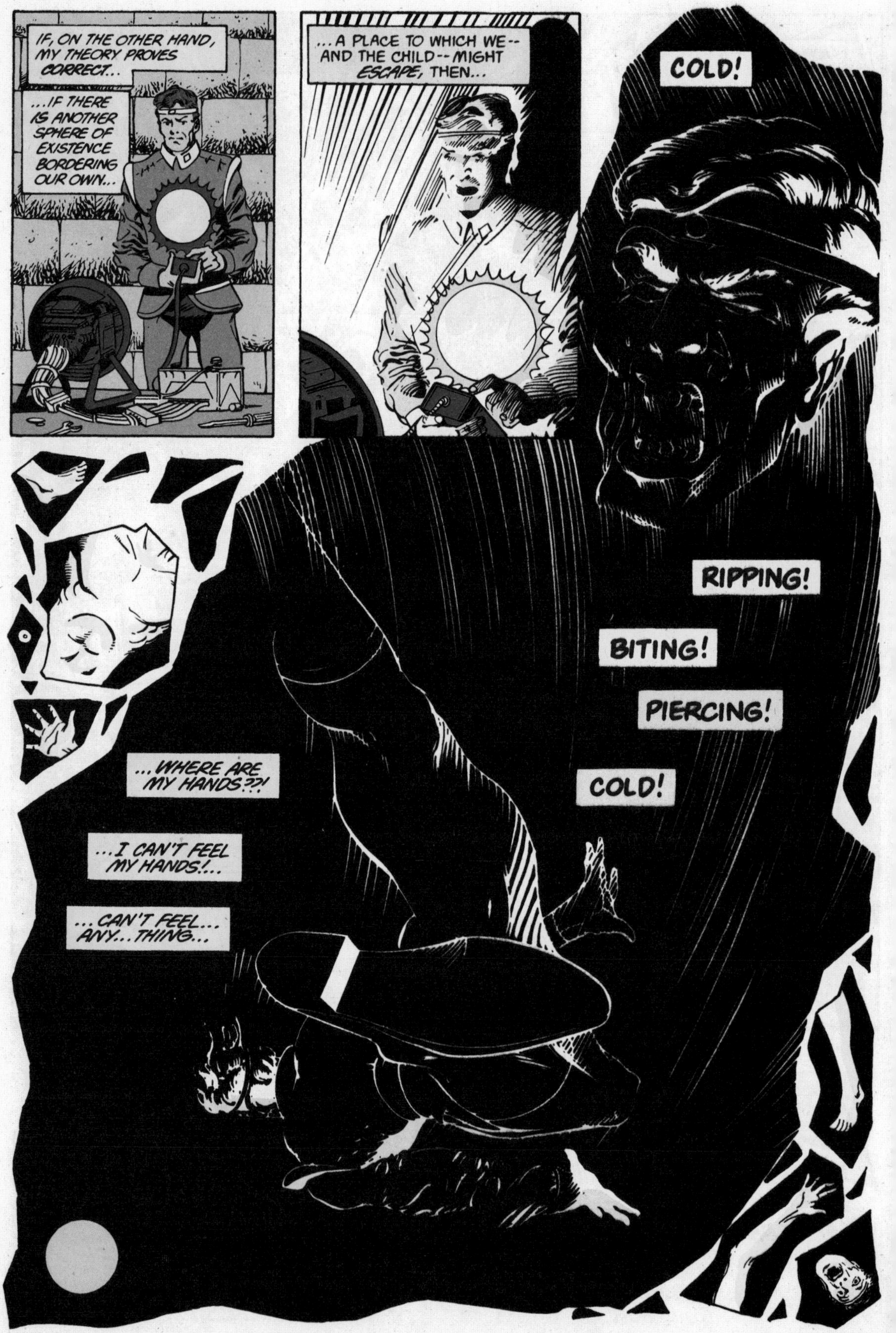
IF, ON THE OTHER HAND, MY THEORY PROVES CORRECT...
...IF THERE IS ANOTHER SPHERE OF EXISTENCE BORDERING OUR OWN...
...A PLACE TO WHICH WE--AND THE CHILD--MIGHT ESCAPE, THEN...
COLD!
RIPPING!
BITING!
PIERCING!
COLD!
...WHERE ARE MY HANDS??!
...I CAN'T FEEL MY HANDS!...
...CAN'T FEEL... ANY...THING...

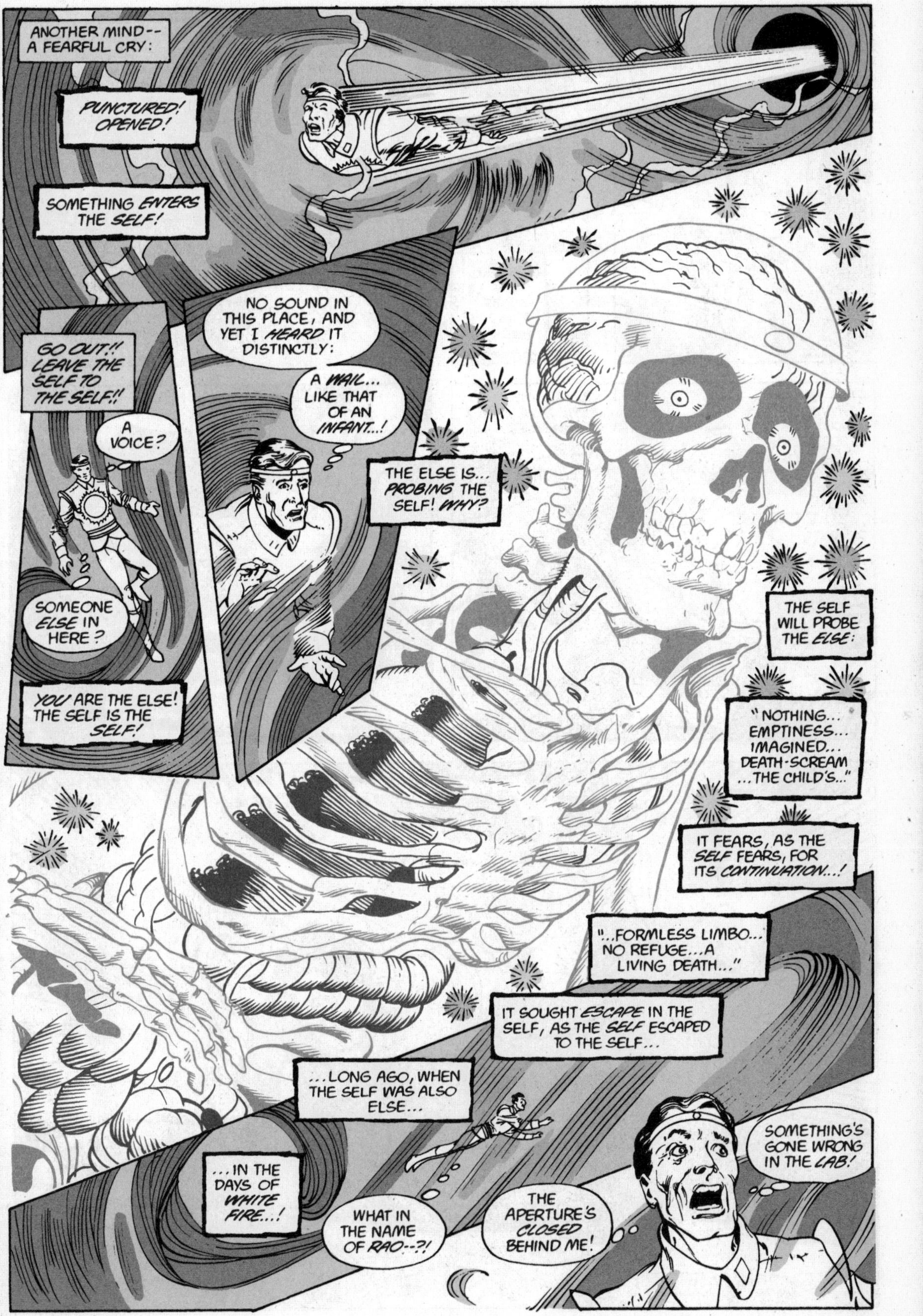
ANOTHER MIND-- A FEARFUL CRY:
PUNCTURED! OPENED!
SOMETHING ENTERS THE SELF!
GO OUT!! LEAVE THE SELF TO THE SELF!!
A VOICE?
SOMEONE ELSE IN HERE?
YOU ARE THE ELSE! THE SELF IS THE SELF!
NO SOUND IN THIS PLACE, AND YET I HEARD IT DISTINCTLY:
A WAIL... LIKE THAT OF AN INFANT...!
THE ELSE IS... PROBING THE SELF! WHY?
THE SELF WILL PROBE THE ELSE:
"NOTHING... EMPTINESS... IMAGINED... DEATH-SCREAM ...THE CHILD'S..."
IT FEARS, AS THE SELF FEARS, FOR ITS CONTINUATION...!
"...FORMLESS LIMBO... NO REFUGE...A LIVING DEATH..."
IT SOUGHT ESCAPE IN THE SELF, AS THE SELF ESCAPED TO THE SELF...
...LONG AGO, WHEN THE SELF WAS ALSO ELSE...
...IN THE DAYS OF WHITE FIRE...!
WHAT IN THE NAME OF RAO--?!
THE APERTURE'S CLOSED BEHIND ME!
SOMETHING'S GONE WRONG IN THE LAB!

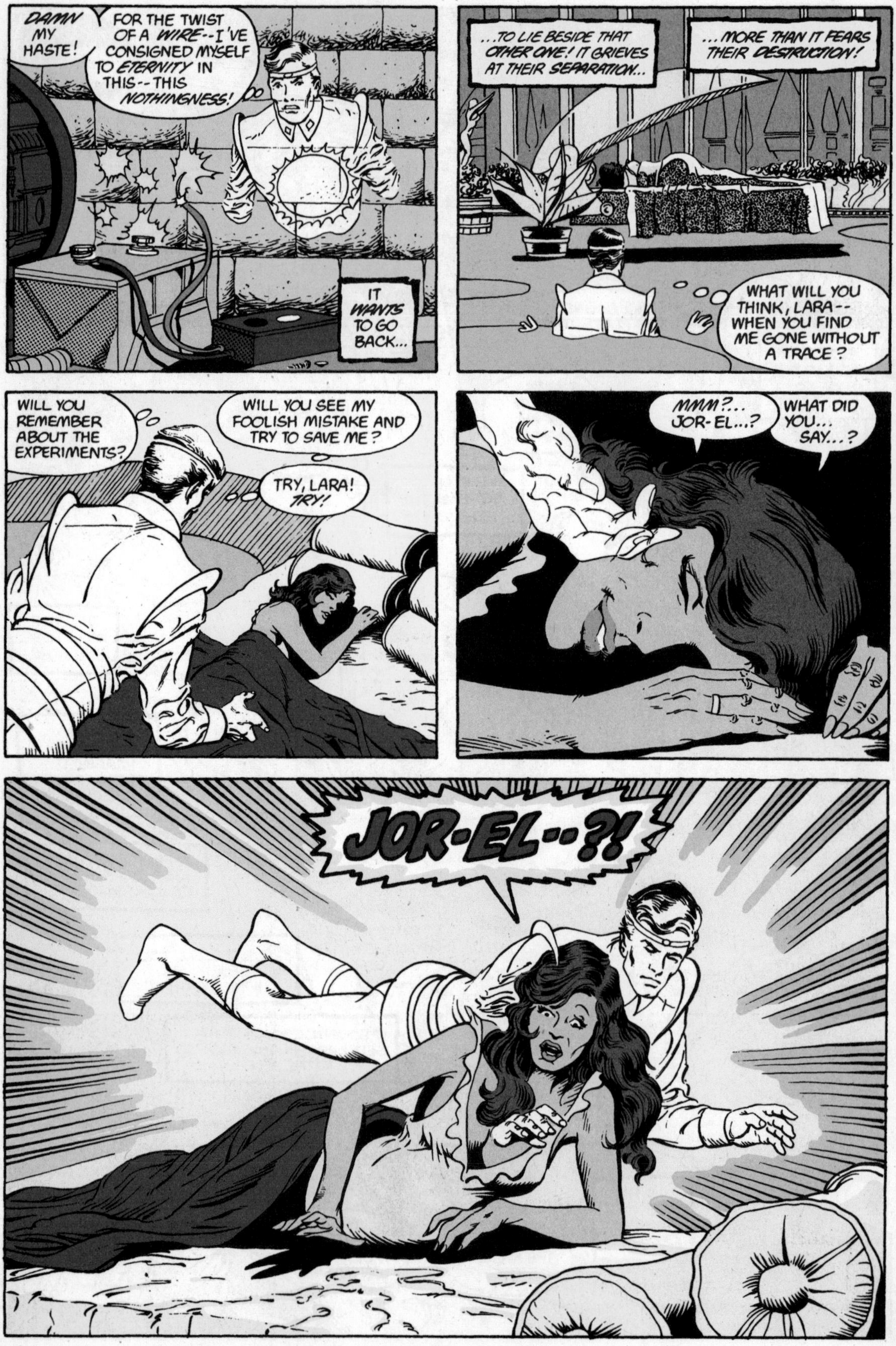
DAMN MY HASTE!
FOR THE TWIST OF A WIRE--I'VE CONSIGNED MYSELF TO ETERNITY IN THIS--THIS NOTHINGNESS!
IT WANTS TO GO BACK...
...TO LIE BESIDE THAT OTHER ONE! IT GRIEVES AT THEIR SEPARATION...
...MORE THAN IT FEARS THEIR DESTRUCTION!
WHAT WILL YOU THINK, LARA-- WHEN YOU FIND ME GONE WITHOUT A TRACE?
WILL YOU REMEMBER ABOUT THE EXPERIMENTS?
WILL YOU SEE MY FOOLISH MISTAKE AND TRY TO SAVE ME?
TRY, LARA! TRY!
MMM?... JOR-EL...?
WHAT DID YOU... SAY...?
JOR-EL--?!

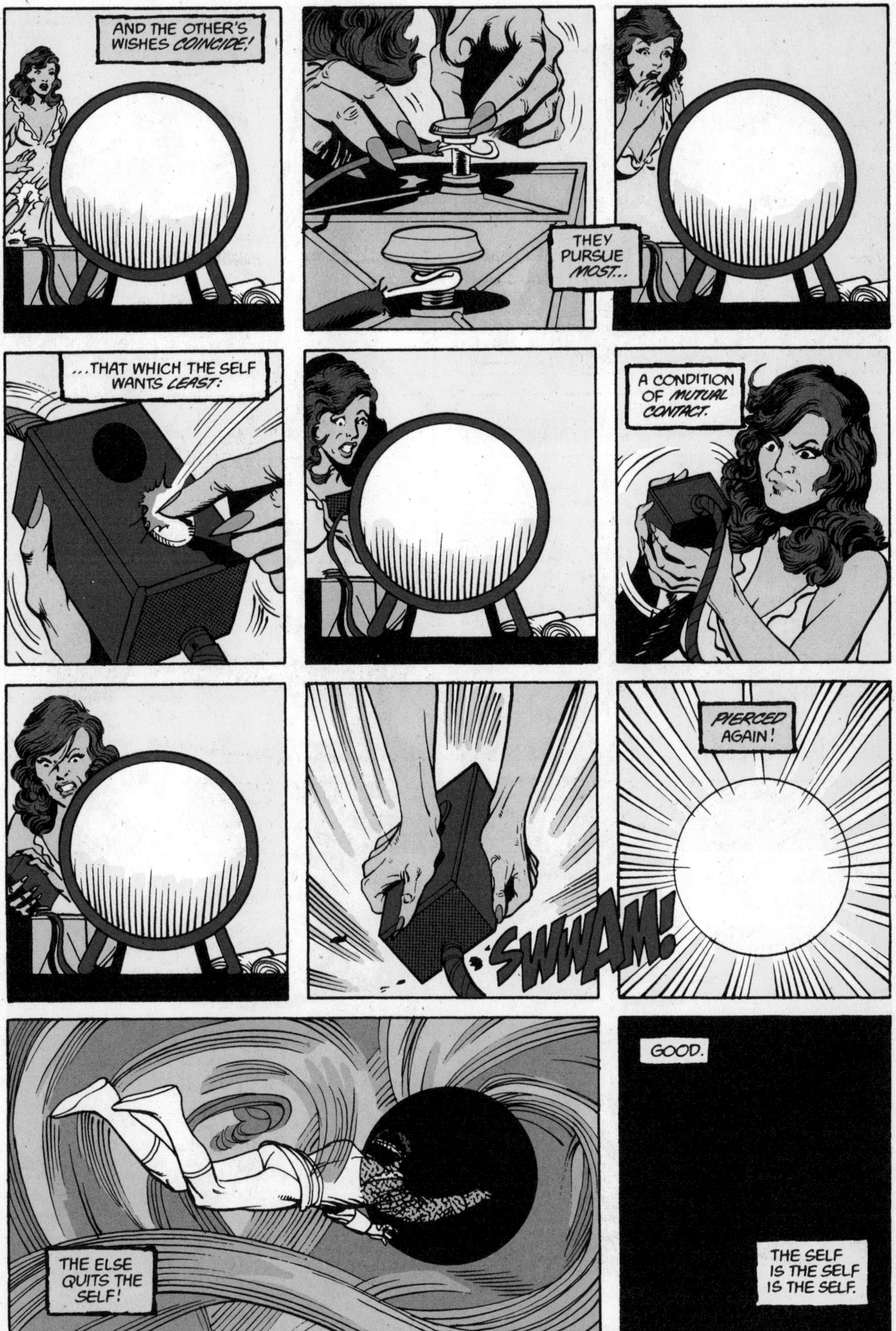
AND THE OTHER'S WISHES COINCIDE!
THEY PURSUE MOST...
...THAT WHICH THE SELF WANTS LEAST:
A CONDITION OF MUTUAL CONTACT.
SWWAM!
PIERCED AGAIN!
THE ELSE QUITS THE SELF!
GOOD.
THE SELF IS THE SELF IS THE SELF.

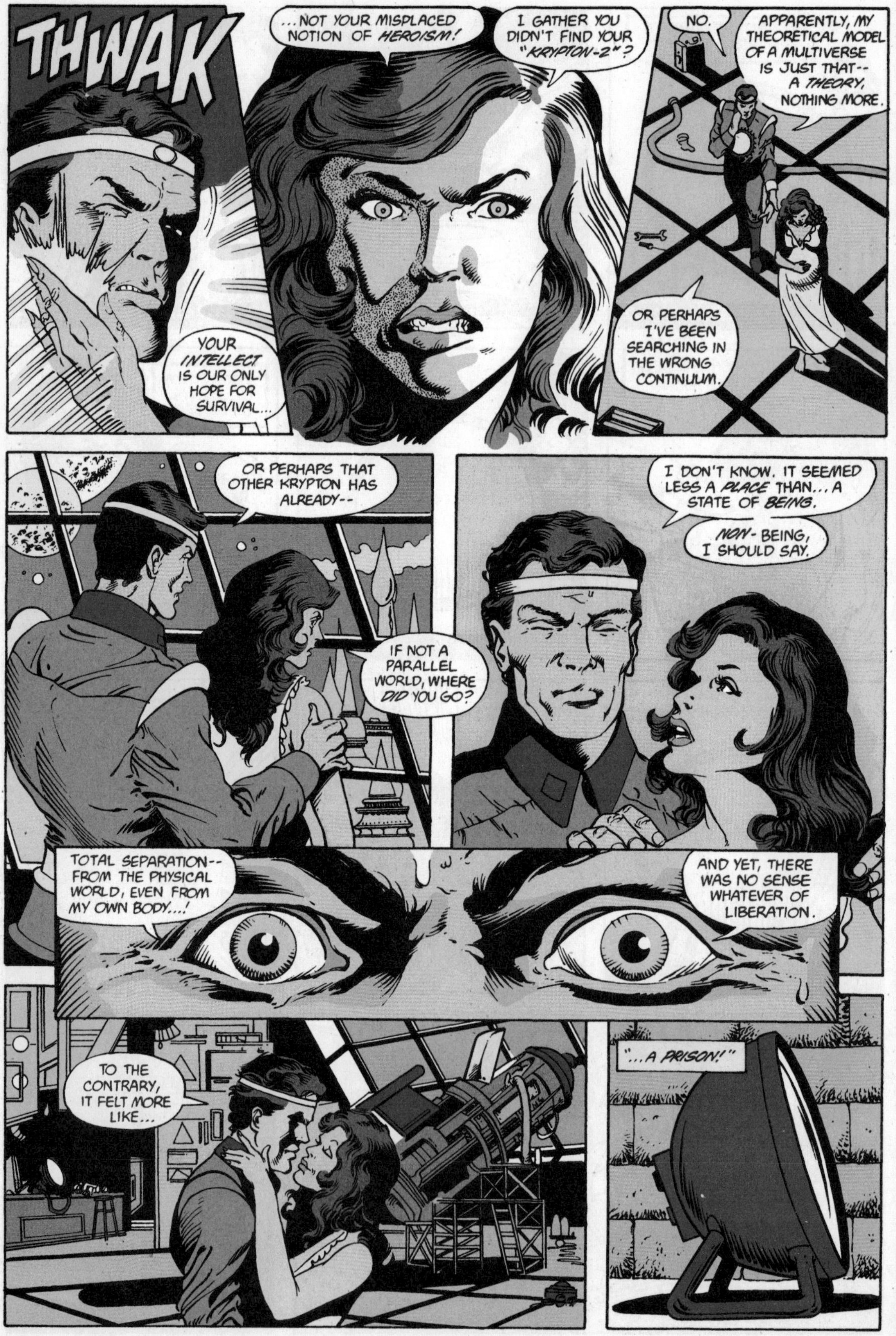
THWAK
YOUR INTELLECT IS OUR ONLY HOPE FOR SURVIVAL...
...NOT YOUR MISPLACED NOTION OF HEROISM!
I GATHER YOU DIDN'T FIND YOUR "KRYPTON-2"?
NO.
APPARENTLY, MY THEORETICAL MODEL OF A MULTIVERSE IS JUST THAT-- A THEORY, NOTHING MORE.
OR PERHAPS I'VE BEEN SEARCHING IN THE WRONG CONTINUUM.
OR PERHAPS THAT OTHER KRYPTON HAS ALREADY--
IF NOT A PARALLEL WORLD, WHERE DID YOU GO?
I DON'T KNOW. IT SEEMED LESS A PLACE THAN... A STATE OF BEING.
NON- BEING, I SHOULD SAY.
TOTAL SEPARATION-- FROM THE PHYSICAL WORLD, EVEN FROM MY OWN BODY...!
AND YET, THERE WAS NO SENSE WHATEVER OF LIBERATION.
TO THE CONTRARY, IT FELT MORE LIKE...
"...A PRISON!"

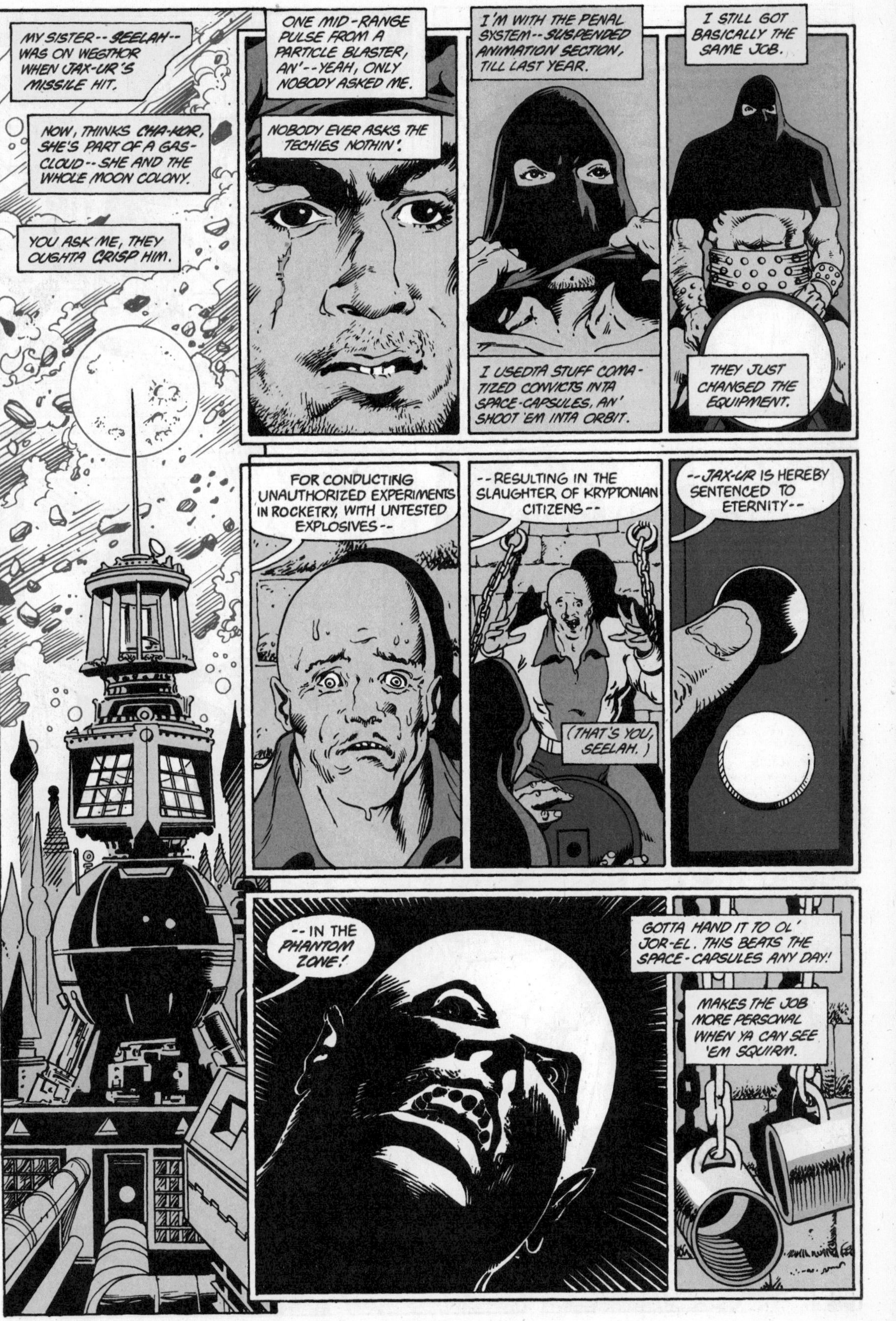
MY SISTER--SEELAH--WAS ON WEGTHOR WHEN JAX-UR'S MISSILE HIT.
NOW, THINKS CHA-KOR, SHE'S PART OF A GAS-CLOUD--SHE AND THE WHOLE MOON COLONY.
YOU ASK ME, THEY OUGHTA CRISP HIM.
ONE MID-RANGE PULSE FROM A PARTICLE BLASTER, AN'--YEAH, ONLY NOBODY ASKED ME.
NOBODY EVER ASKS THE TECHIES NOTHIN'.
I'M WITH THE PENAL SYSTEM--SUSPENDED ANIMATION SECTION, TILL LAST YEAR.
I USEDTA STUFF COMA-TIZED CONVICTS INTA SPACE-CAPSULES, AN' SHOOT 'EM INTA ORBIT.
I STILL GOT BASICALLY THE SAME JOB.
THEY JUST CHANGED THE EQUIPMENT.
FOR CONDUCTING UNAUTHORIZED EXPERIMENTS IN ROCKETRY, WITH UNTESTED EXPLOSIVES--
--RESULTING IN THE SLAUGHTER OF KRYPTONIAN CITIZENS--
(THAT'S YOU, SEELAH.)
--JAX-UR IS HEREBY SENTENCED TO ETERNITY--
--IN THE PHANTOM ZONE!
GOTTA HAND IT TO OL' JOR-EL. THIS BEATS THE SPACE-CAPSULES ANY DAY!
MAKES THE JOB MORE PERSONAL WHEN YA CAN SEE 'EM SQUIRM.

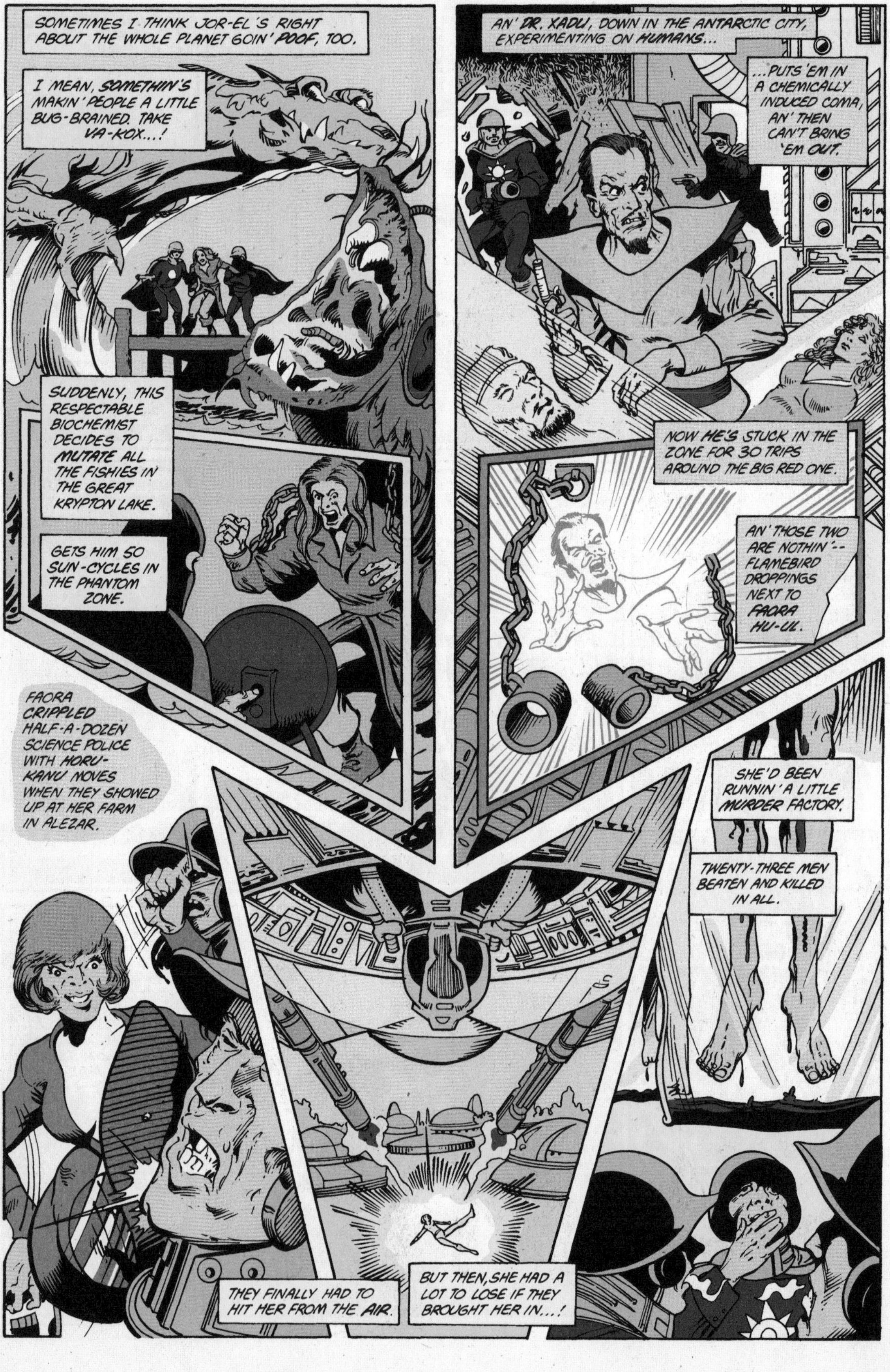
SOMETIMES I THINK JOR-EL'S RIGHT ABOUT THE WHOLE PLANET GOIN' POOF, TOO.
I MEAN, SOMETHIN'S MAKIN' PEOPLE A LITTLE BUG-BRAINED. TAKE VA-KOX...!
SUDDENLY, THIS RESPECTABLE BIOCHEMIST DECIDES TO MUTATE ALL THE FISHIES IN THE GREAT KRYPTON LAKE.
GETS HIM 50 SUN-CYCLES IN THE PHANTOM ZONE.
AN' DR. XADU, DOWN IN THE ANTARCTIC CITY, EXPERIMENTING ON HUMANS...
...PUTS 'EM IN A CHEMICALLY INDUCED COMA, AN' THEN CAN'T BRING 'EM OUT.
NOW HE'S STUCK IN THE ZONE FOR 30 TRIPS AROUND THE BIG RED ONE.
AN' THOSE TWO ARE NOTHIN'-- FLAMEBIRD DROPPINGS NEXT TO FAORA HU-UL.
FAORA CRIPPLED HALF-A-DOZEN SCIENCE POLICE WITH HORU-KANU MOVES WHEN THEY SHOWED UP AT HER FARM IN ALEZAR.
THEY FINALLY HAD TO HIT HER FROM THE AIR.
BUT THEN, SHE HAD A LOT TO LOSE IF THEY BROUGHT HER IN...!
SHE'D BEEN RUNNIN' A LITTLE MURDER FACTORY.
TWENTY-THREE MEN BEATEN AND KILLED IN ALL.

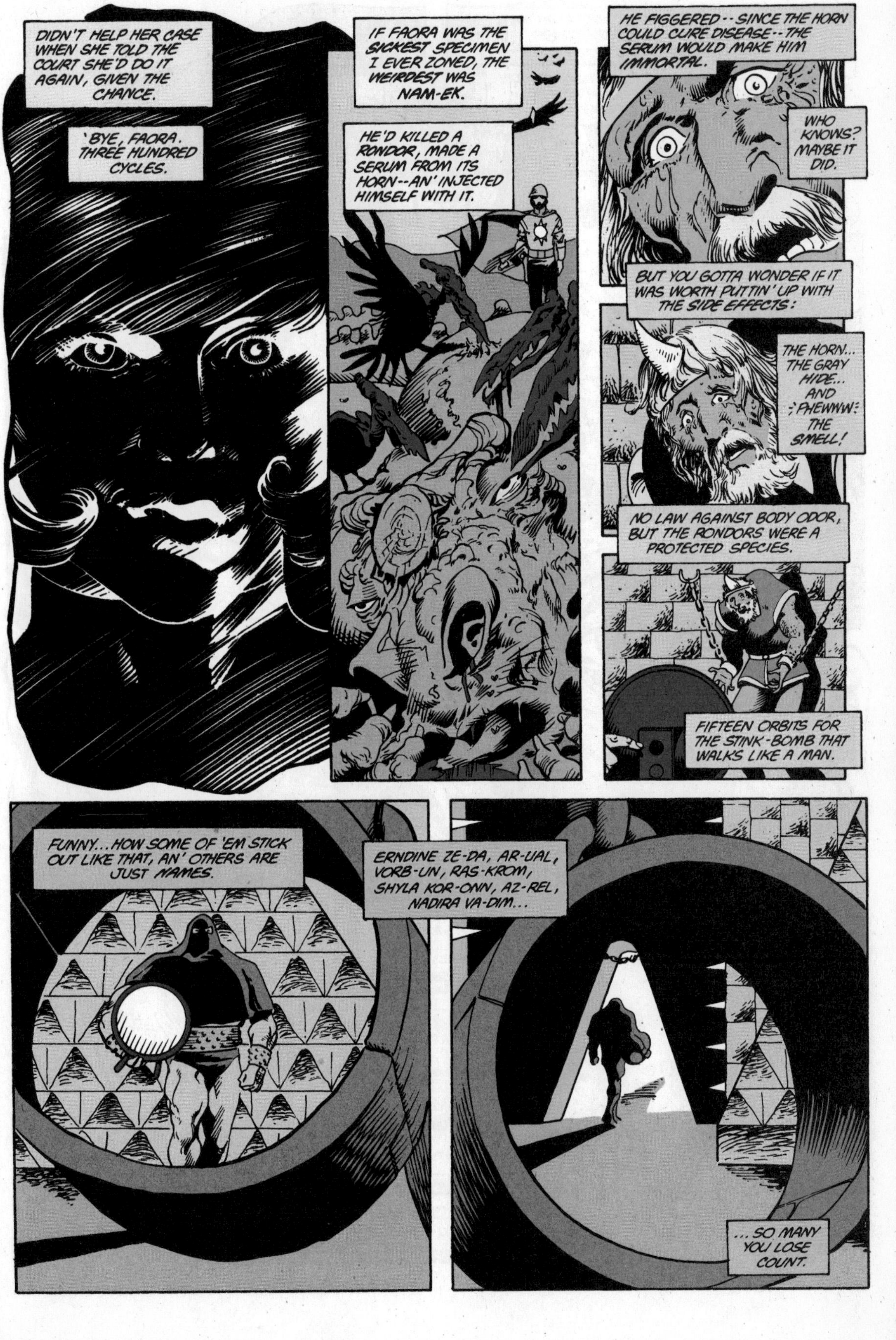
DIDN'T HELP HER CASE WHEN SHE TOLD THE COURT SHE'D DO IT AGAIN, GIVEN THE CHANCE.
'BYE, FAORA. THREE HUNDRED CYCLES.
IF FAORA WAS THE SICKEST SPECIMEN I EVER ZONED, THE WEIRDEST WAS NAM-EK.
HE'D KILLED A RONDOR, MADE A SERUM FROM ITS HORN--AN' INJECTED HIMSELF WITH IT.
HE FIGGERED--SINCE THE HORN COULD CURE DISEASE--THE SERUM WOULD MAKE HIM IMMORTAL.
WHO KNOWS? MAYBE IT DID.
BUT YOU GOTTA WONDER IF IT WAS WORTH PUTTIN' UP WITH THE SIDE EFFECTS:
THE HORN... THE GRAY HIDE... AND PHEWWW: THE SMELL!
NO LAW AGAINST BODY ODOR, BUT THE RONDORS WERE A PROTECTED SPECIES.
FIFTEEN ORBITS FOR THE STINK-BOMB THAT WALKS LIKE A MAN.
FUNNY... HOW SOME OF 'EM STICK OUT LIKE THAT, AN' OTHERS ARE JUST NAMES.
ERNDINE ZE-DA, AR-UAL, VORB-UN, RAS-KROM, SHYLA KOR-ONN, AZ-REL, NADIRA VA-DIM...
...SO MANY YOU LOSE COUNT.

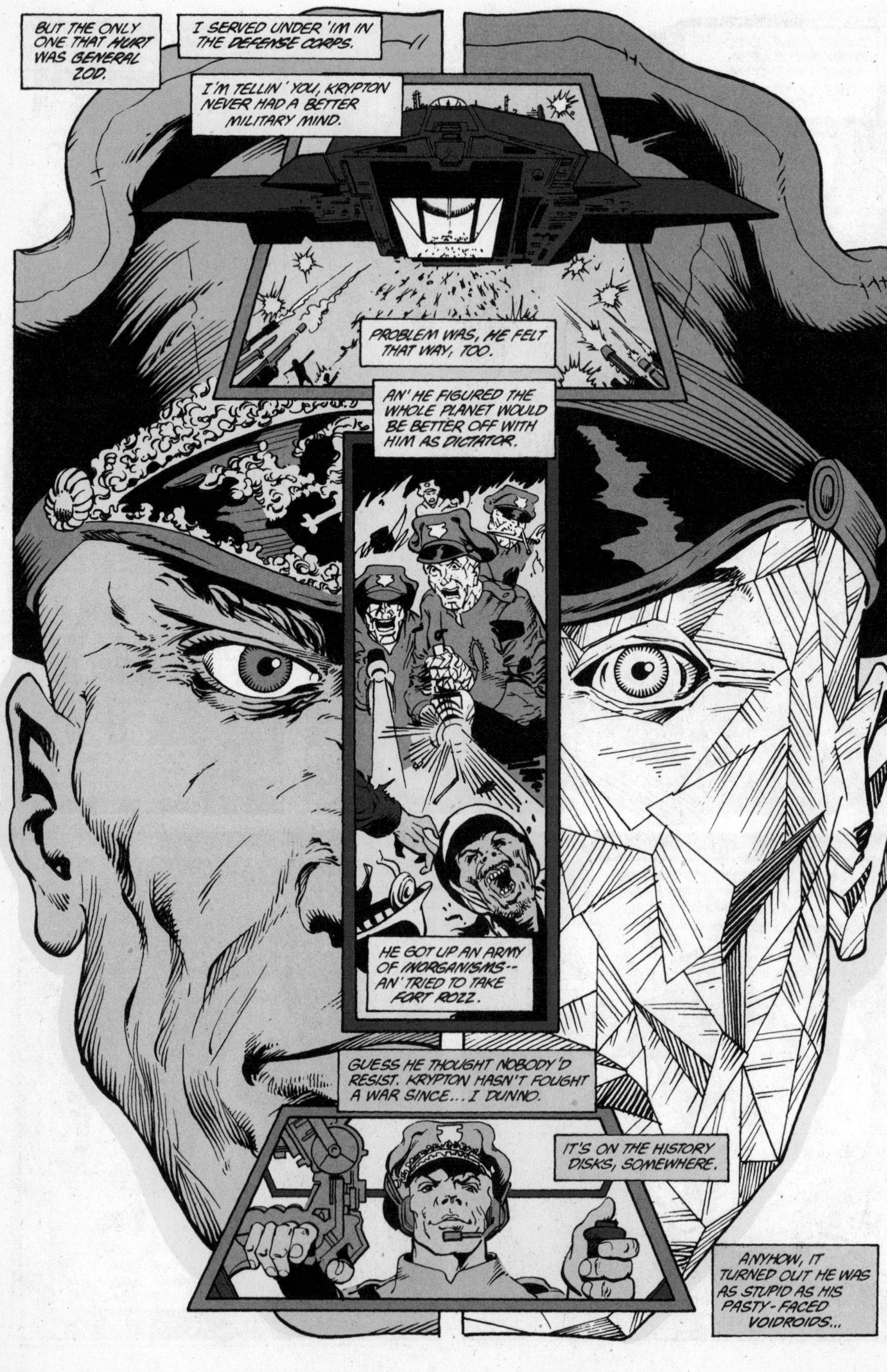
BUT THE ONLY ONE THAT HURT WAS GENERAL ZOD.
I SERVED UNDER 'IM IN THE DEFENSE CORPS.
I'M TELLIN' YOU, KRYPTON NEVER HAD A BETTER MILITARY MIND.
PROBLEM WAS, HE FELT THAT WAY, TOO.
AN' HE FIGURED THE WHOLE PLANET WOULD BE BETTER OFF WITH HIM AS DICTATOR.
HE GOT UP AN ARMY OF INORGANISMS-- AN' TRIED TO TAKE FORT ROZZ.
GUESS HE THOUGHT NOBODY'D RESIST. KRYPTON HASN'T FOUGHT A WAR SINCE... I DUNNO.
IT'S ON THE HISTORY DISKS, SOMEWHERE.
ANYHOW, IT TURNED OUT HE WAS AS STUPID AS HIS PASTY-FACED VOIDROIDS...

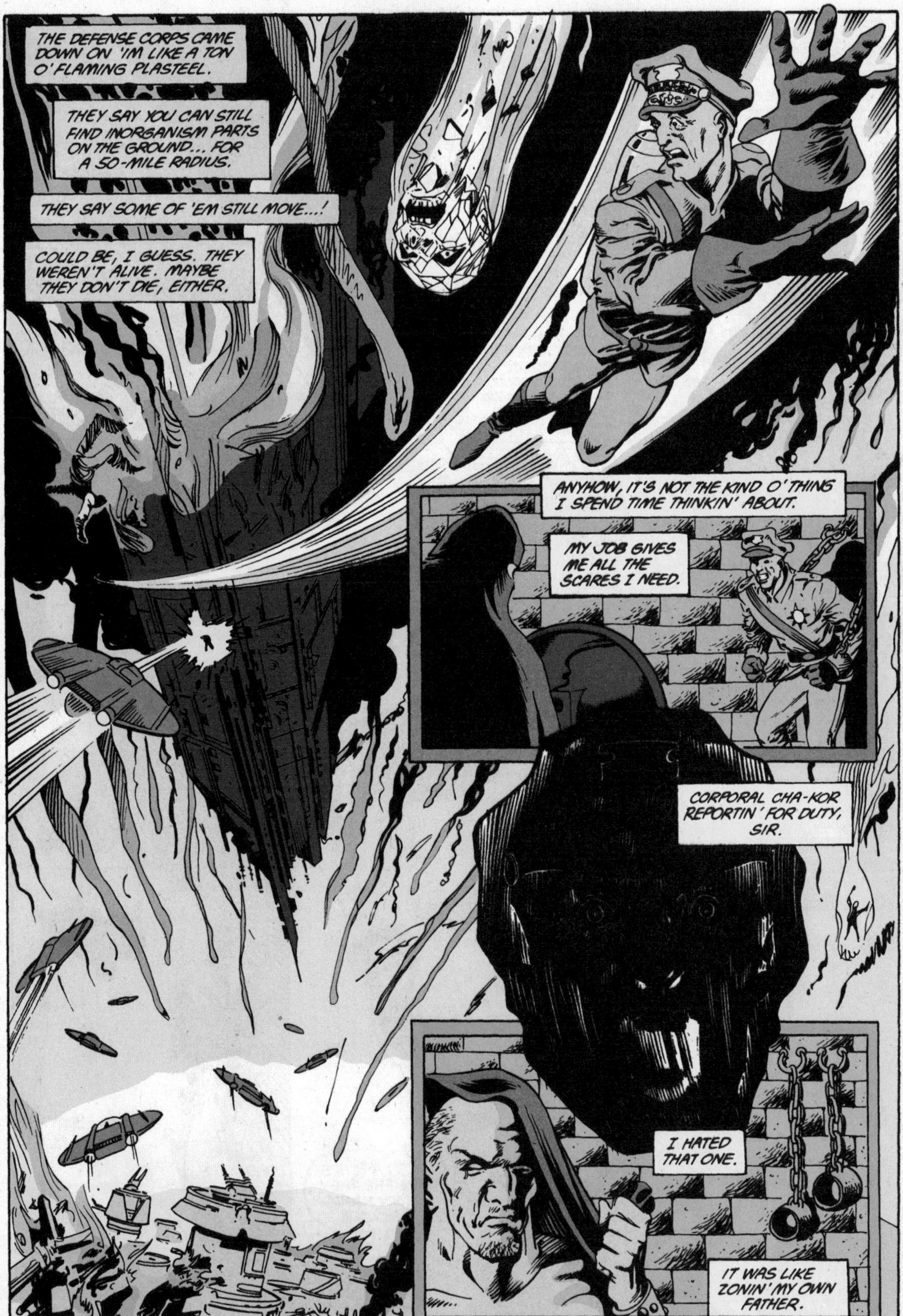
THE DEFENSE CORPS CAME DOWN ON 'IM LIKE A TON O' FLAMING PLASTEEL.
THEY SAY YOU CAN STILL FIND INORGANISM PARTS ON THE GROUND... FOR A 50-MILE RADIUS.
THEY SAY SOME OF 'EM STILL MOVE...!
COULD BE, I GUESS. THEY WEREN'T ALIVE. MAYBE THEY DON'T DIE, EITHER.
ANYHOW, IT'S NOT THE KIND O' THING I SPEND TIME THINKIN' ABOUT.
MY JOB GIVES ME ALL THE SCARES I NEED.
CORPORAL CHA-KOR REPORTIN' FOR DUTY, SIR.
I HATED THAT ONE.
IT WAS LIKE ZONIN' MY OWN FATHER.

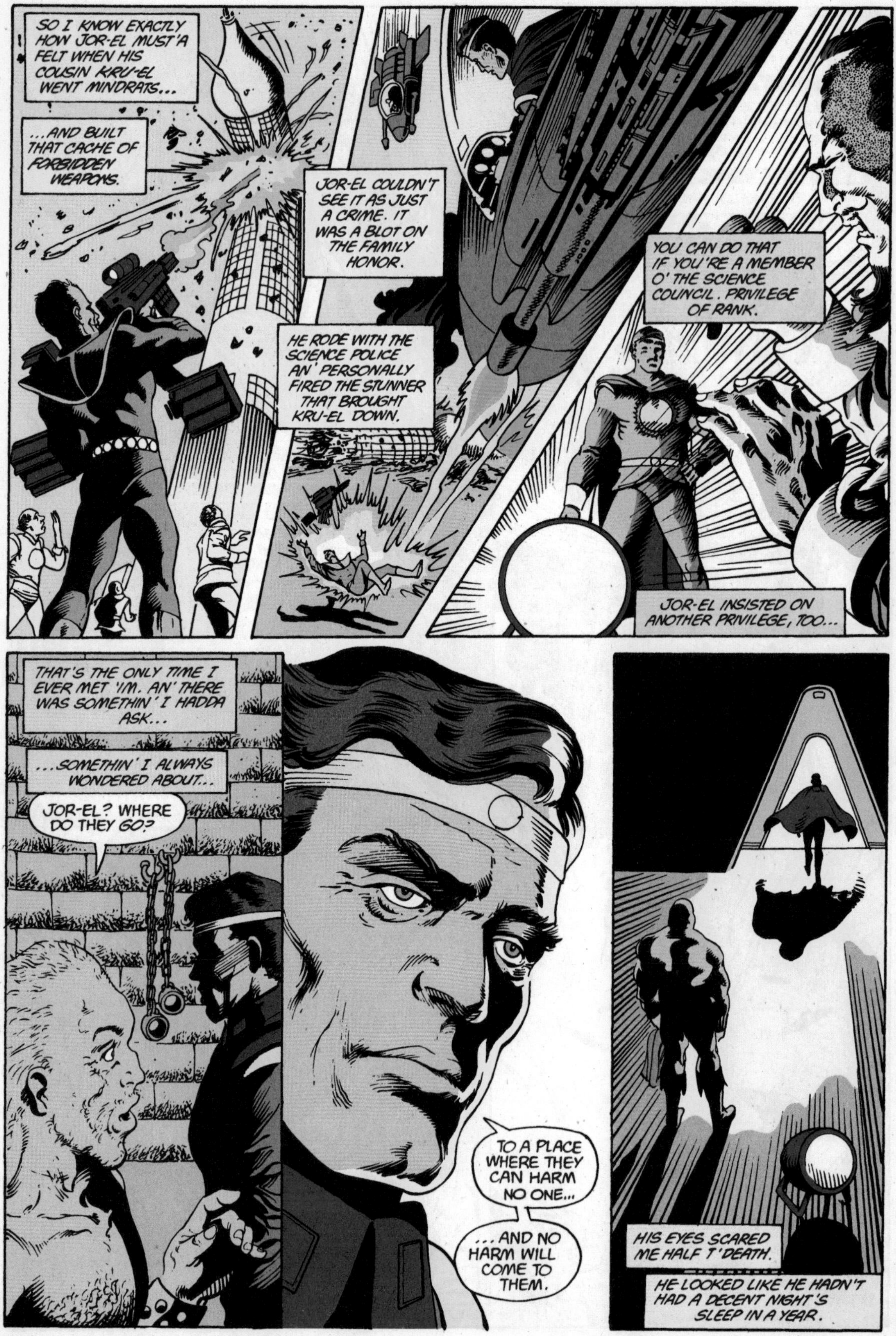
SO I KNOW EXACTLY HOW JOR-EL MUST'A FELT WHEN HIS COUSIN KRU-EL WENT MINDRATS...
...AND BUILT THAT CACHE OF FORBIDDEN WEAPONS.
JOR-EL COULDN'T SEE IT AS JUST A CRIME. IT WAS A BLOT ON THE FAMILY HONOR.
HE RODE WITH THE SCIENCE POLICE AN' PERSONALLY FIRED THE STUNNER THAT BROUGHT KRU-EL DOWN.
YOU CAN DO THAT IF YOU'RE A MEMBER O' THE SCIENCE COUNCIL. PRIVILEGE OF RANK.
JOR-EL INSISTED ON ANOTHER PRIVILEGE, TOO...
THAT'S THE ONLY TIME I EVER MET 'IM. AN' THERE WAS SOMETHIN' I HADDA ASK...
...SOMETHIN' I ALWAYS WONDERED ABOUT...
JOR-EL? WHERE DO THEY GO?
TO A PLACE WHERE THEY CAN HARM NO ONE...
...AND NO HARM WILL COME TO THEM.
HIS EYES SCARED ME HALF T'DEATH.
HE LOOKED LIKE HE HADN'T HAD A DECENT NIGHT'S SLEEP IN A YEAR.

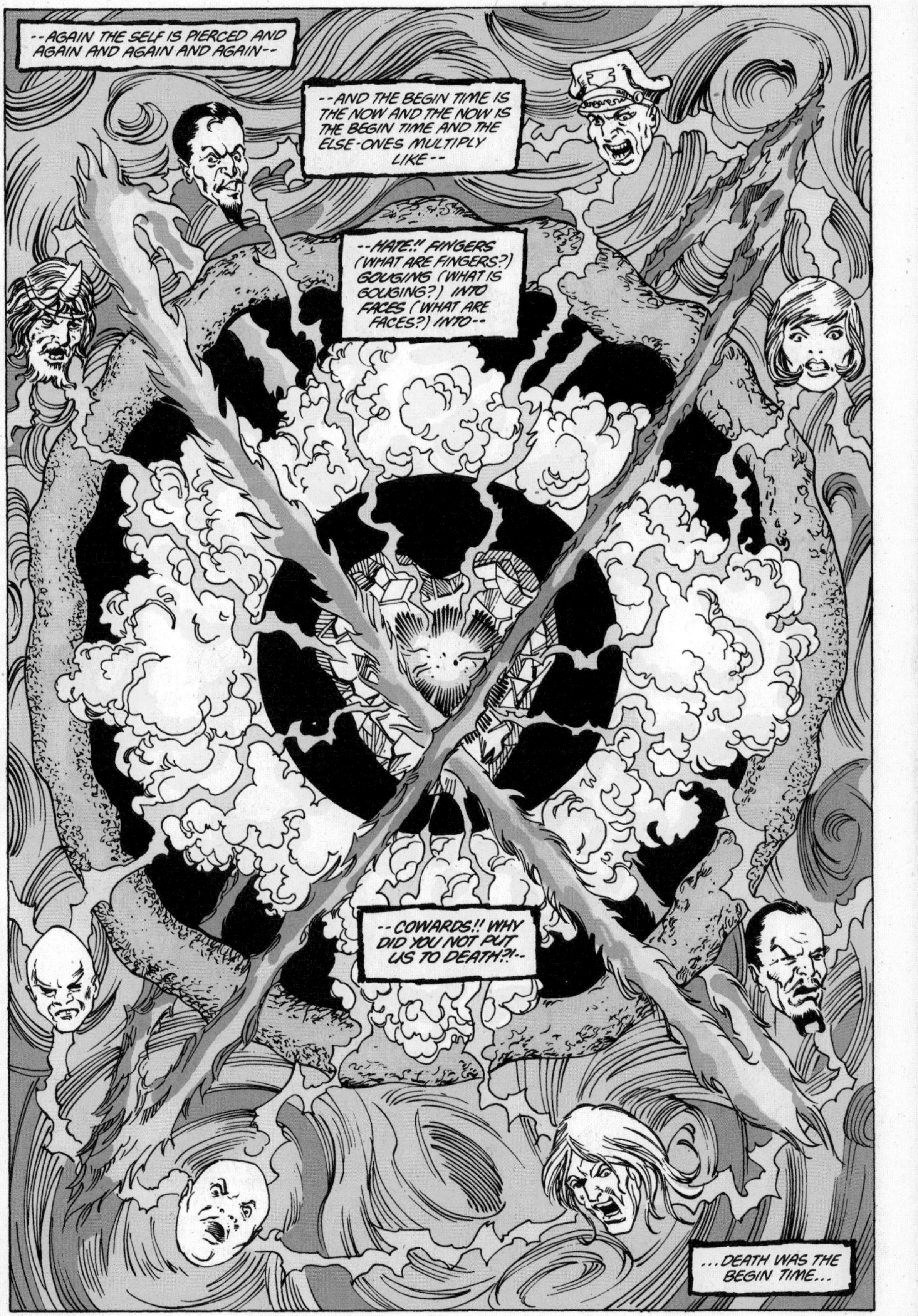
--AGAIN THE SELF IS PIERCED AND AGAIN AND AGAIN AND AGAIN--
--AND THE BEGIN TIME IS THE NOW AND THE NOW IS THE BEGIN TIME AND THE ELSE-ONES MULTIPLY LIKE--
--HATE!" FINGERS (WHAT ARE FINGERS?) GOUGING (WHAT IS GOUGING?) INTO FACES (WHAT ARE FACES?) INTO--
--COWARDS!! WHY DID YOU NOT PUT US TO DEATH?!--
...DEATH WAS THE BEGIN TIME...

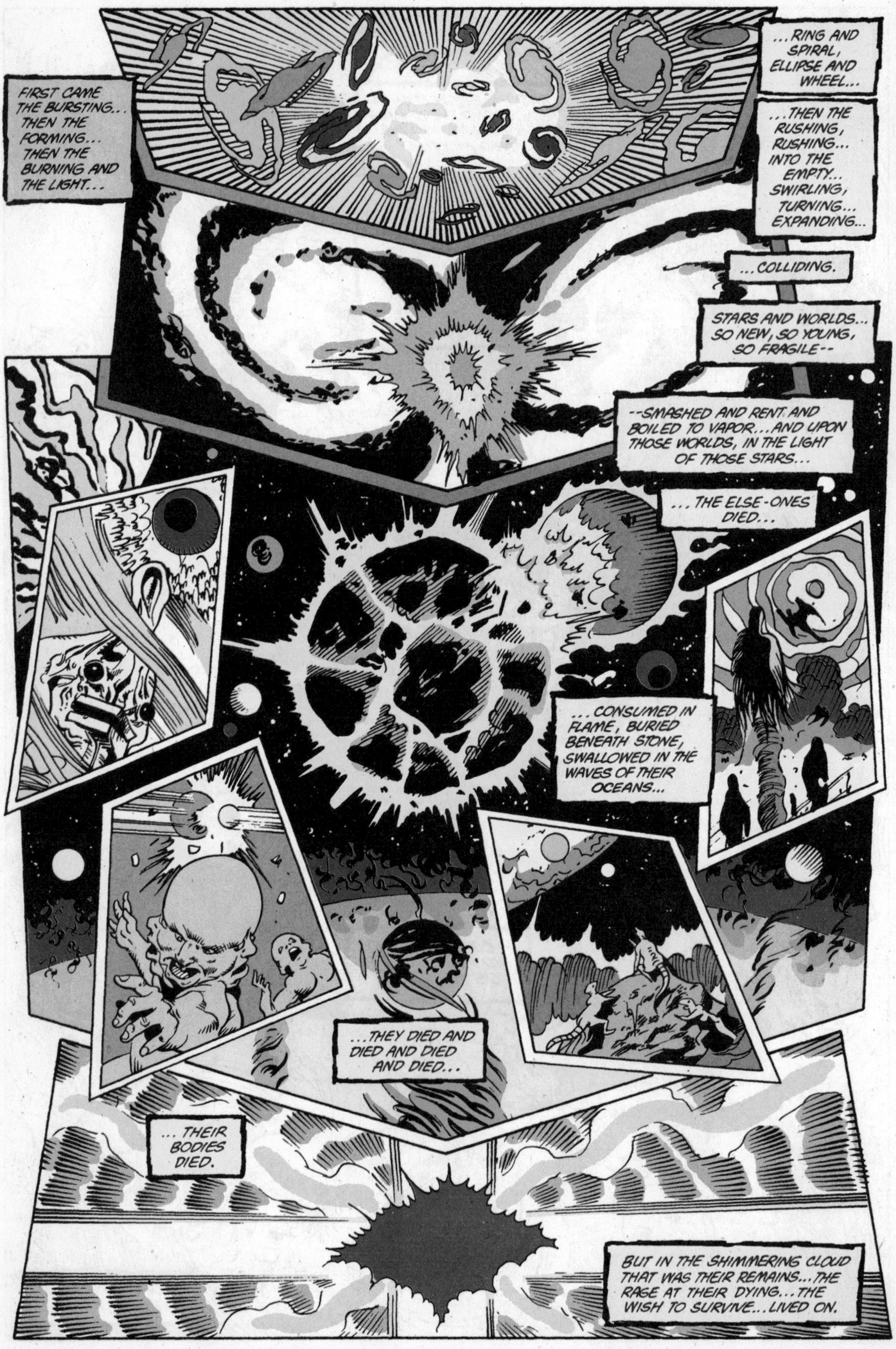
FIRST CAME THE BURSTING... THEN THE FORMING... THEN THE BURNING AND THE LIGHT...
...RING AND SPIRAL, ELLIPSE AND WHEEL...
...THEN THE RUSHING, RUSHING... INTO THE EMPTY... SWIRLING, TURNING... EXPANDING...
...COLLIDING.
STARS AND WORLDS... SO NEW, SO YOUNG, SO FRAGILE--
--SMASHED AND RENT AND BOILED TO VAPOR... AND UPON THOSE WORLDS, IN THE LIGHT OF THOSE STARS...
...THE ELSE-ONES DIED...
...CONSUMED IN FLAME, BURIED BENEATH STONE, SWALLOWED IN THE WAVES OF THEIR OCEANS...
...THEY DIED AND DIED AND DIED AND DIED...
...THEIR BODIES DIED.
BUT IN THE SHIMMERING CLOUD THAT WAS THEIR REMAINS... THE RAGE AT THEIR DYING... THE WISH TO SURVIVE... LIVED ON.

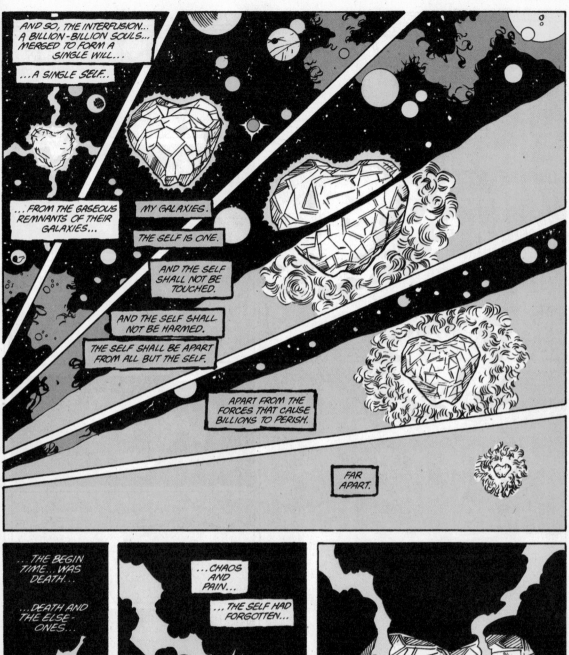

AND SO, THE INTERFUSION... A BILLION-BILLION SOULS... MERGED TO FORM A SINGLE WILL...

...A SINGLE SELF...

...FROM THE GASEOUS REMNANTS OF THEIR GALAXIES...

MY GALAXIES.

THE SELF IS ONE.

AND THE SELF SHALL NOT BE TOUCHED.

AND THE SELF SHALL NOT BE HARMED.

THE SELF SHALL BE APART FROM ALL BUT THE SELF.

APART FROM THE FORCES THAT CAUSE BILLIONS TO PERISH.

FAR APART.

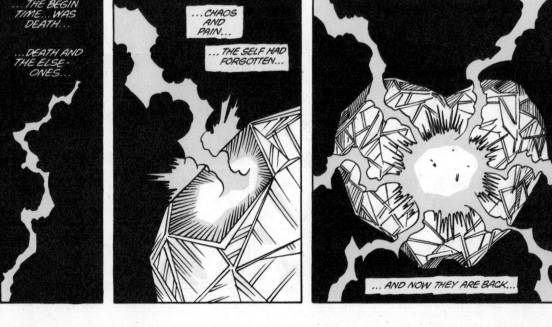

...THE BEGIN TIME...WAS DEATH...

...DEATH AND THE ELSE-ONES...

...CHAOS AND PAIN...

...THE SELF HAD FORGOTTEN...

...AND NOW THEY ARE BACK...

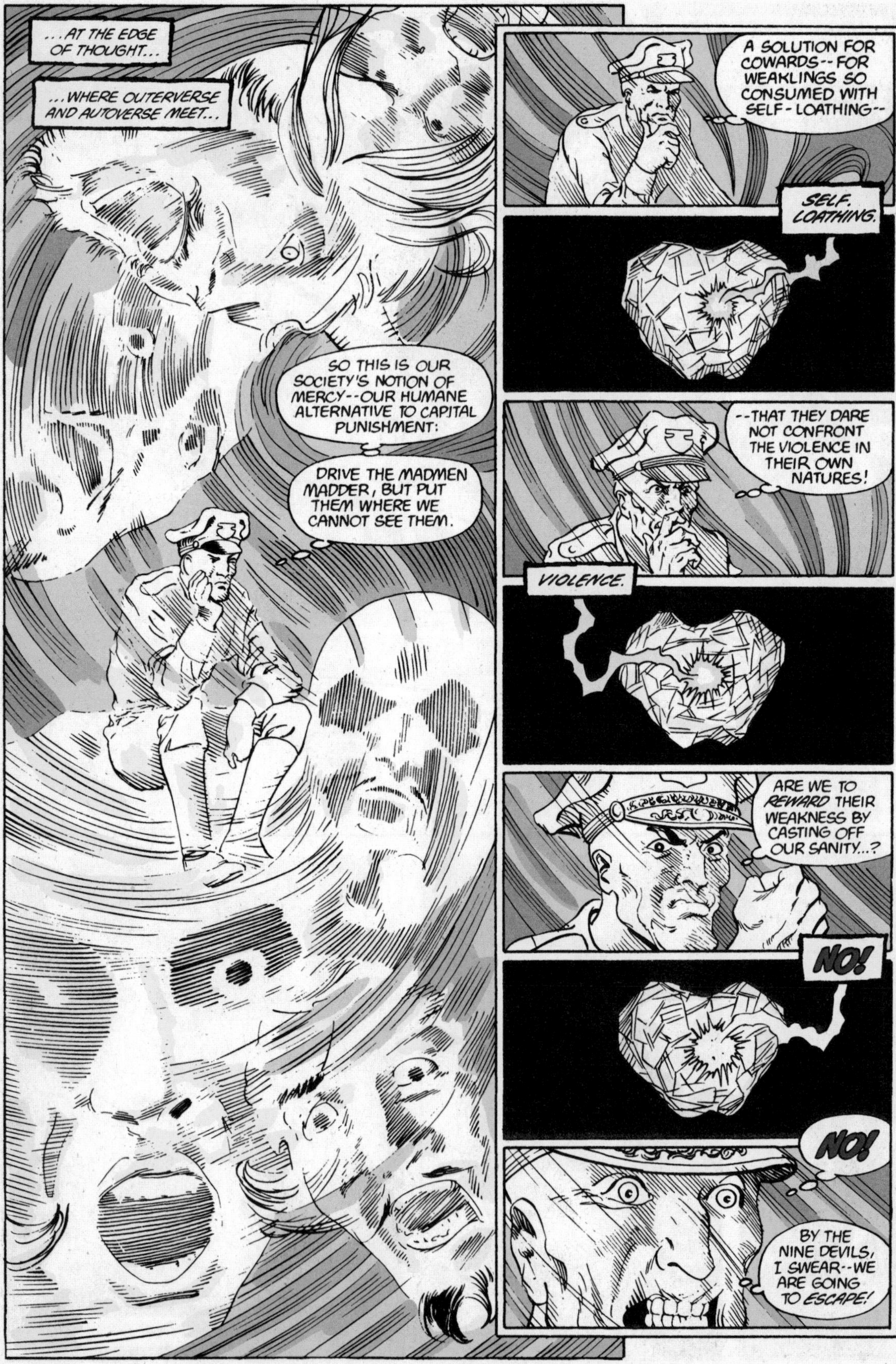
...AT THE EDGE OF THOUGHT...
...WHERE OUTERVERSE AND AUTOVERSE MEET...
SO THIS IS OUR SOCIETY'S NOTION OF MERCY--OUR HUMANE ALTERNATIVE TO CAPITAL PUNISHMENT:
DRIVE THE MADMEN MADDER, BUT PUT THEM WHERE WE CANNOT SEE THEM.
A SOLUTION FOR COWARDS--FOR WEAKLINGS SO CONSUMED WITH SELF-LOATHING--
SELF. LOATHING.
--THAT THEY DARE NOT CONFRONT THE VIOLENCE IN THEIR OWN NATURES!
VIOLENCE.
ARE WE TO REWARD THEIR WEAKNESS BY CASTING OFF OUR SANITY...?
NO!
NO!
BY THE NINE DEVILS, I SWEAR--WE ARE GOING TO ESCAPE!

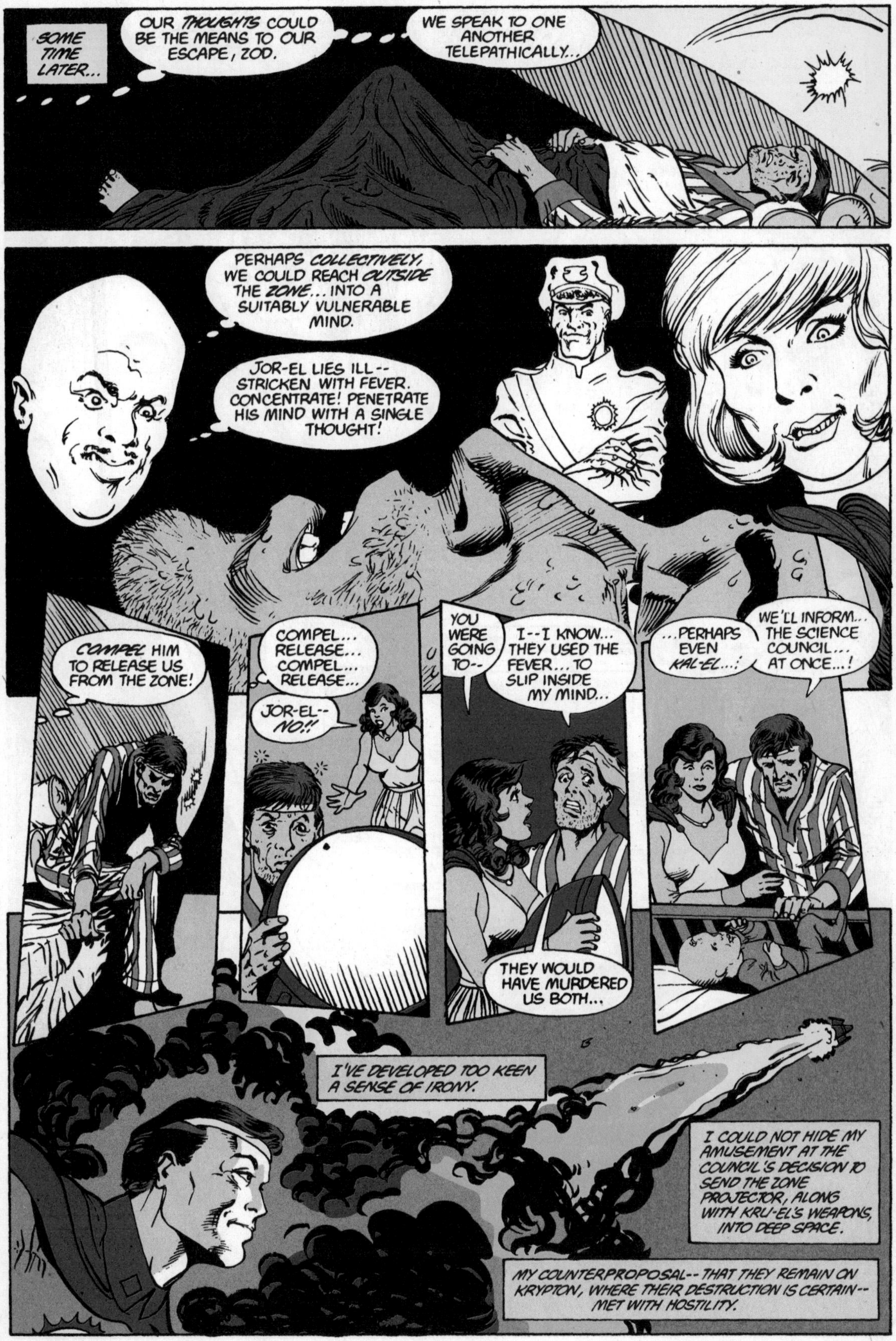
SOME TIME LATER...
OUR THOUGHTS COULD BE THE MEANS TO OUR ESCAPE, ZOD.
WE SPEAK TO ONE ANOTHER TELEPATHICALLY...
PERHAPS COLLECTIVELY, WE COULD REACH OUTSIDE THE ZONE... INTO A SUITABLY VULNERABLE MIND.
JOR-EL LIES ILL-- STRICKEN WITH FEVER. CONCENTRATE! PENETRATE HIS MIND WITH A SINGLE THOUGHT!
COMPEL HIM TO RELEASE US FROM THE ZONE!
COMPEL... RELEASE... COMPEL... RELEASE...
JOR-EL-- NO!!
YOU WERE GOING TO--
I--I KNOW... THEY USED THE FEVER... TO SLIP INSIDE MY MIND...
THEY WOULD HAVE MURDERED US BOTH...
...PERHAPS EVEN KAL-EL...!
WE'LL INFORM... THE SCIENCE COUNCIL... AT ONCE...!
I'VE DEVELOPED TOO KEEN A SENSE OF IRONY.
I COULD NOT HIDE MY AMUSEMENT AT THE COUNCIL'S DECISION TO SEND THE ZONE PROJECTOR, ALONG WITH KRU-EL'S WEAPONS, INTO DEEP SPACE.
MY COUNTERPROPOSAL-- THAT THEY REMAIN ON KRYPTON, WHERE THEIR DESTRUCTION IS CERTAIN-- MET WITH HOSTILITY.

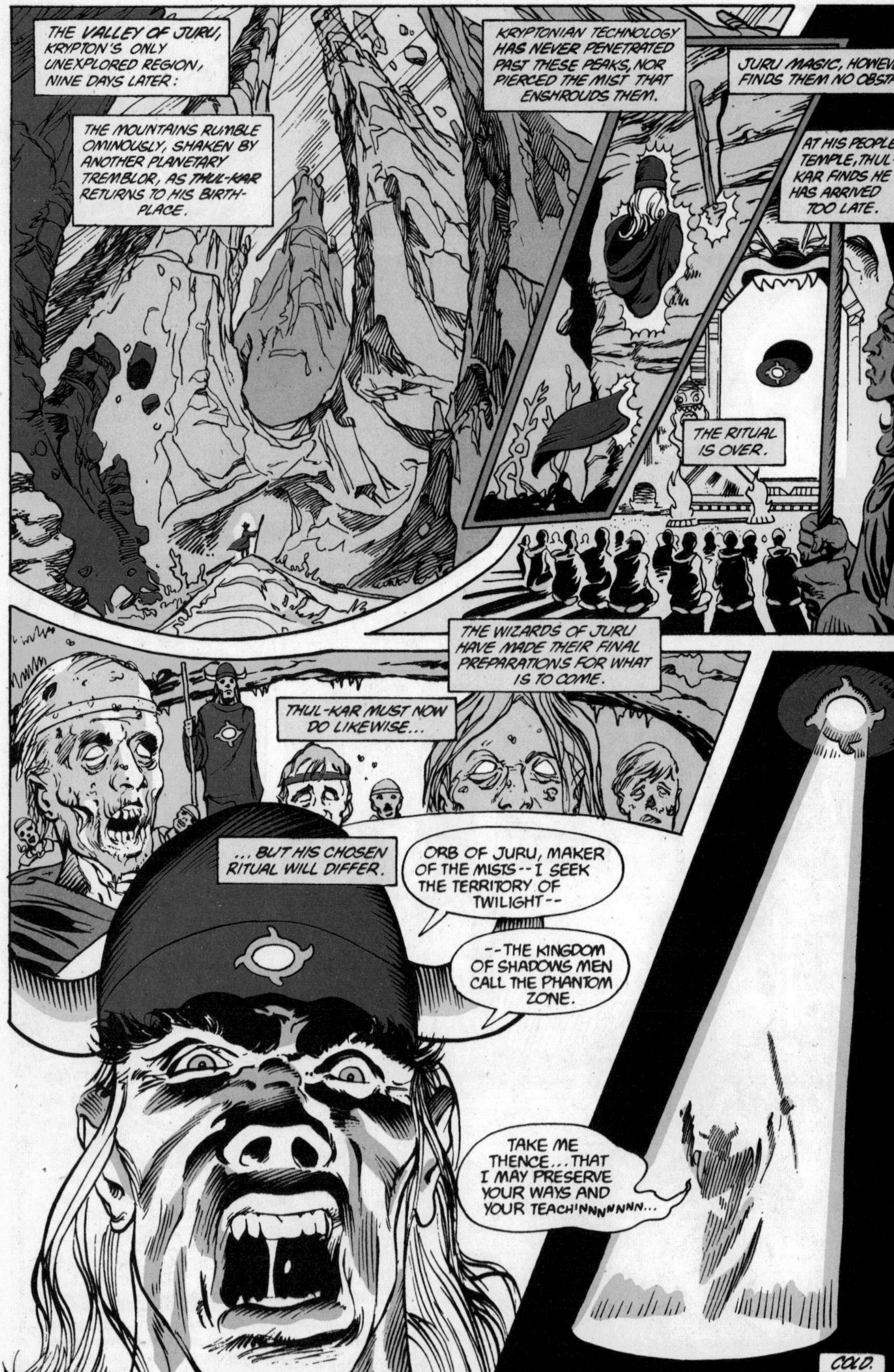
THE VALLEY OF JURU, KRYPTON'S ONLY UNEXPLORED REGION, NINE DAYS LATER:
THE MOUNTAINS RUMBLE OMINOUSLY, SHAKEN BY ANOTHER PLANETARY TREMBLOR, AS THUL-KAR RETURNS TO HIS BIRTH-PLACE.
KRYPTONIAN TECHNOLOGY HAS NEVER PENETRATED PAST THESE PEAKS, NOR PIERCED THE MIST THAT ENSHROUDS THEM.
JURU MAGIC, HOWEVER, FINDS THEM NO OBSTACLE.
AT HIS PEOPLE'S TEMPLE, THUL-KAR FINDS HE HAS ARRIVED TOO LATE.
THE RITUAL IS OVER.
THE WIZARDS OF JURU HAVE MADE THEIR FINAL PREPARATIONS FOR WHAT IS TO COME.
THUL-KAR MUST NOW DO LIKEWISE...
... BUT HIS CHOSEN RITUAL WILL DIFFER.
ORB OF JURU, MAKER OF THE MISTS -- I SEEK THE TERRITORY OF TWILIGHT --
-- THE KINGDOM OF SHADOWS MEN CALL THE PHANTOM ZONE.
TAKE ME THENCE... THAT I MAY PRESERVE YOUR WAYS AND YOUR TEACH'NNNNNNN...
COLD.

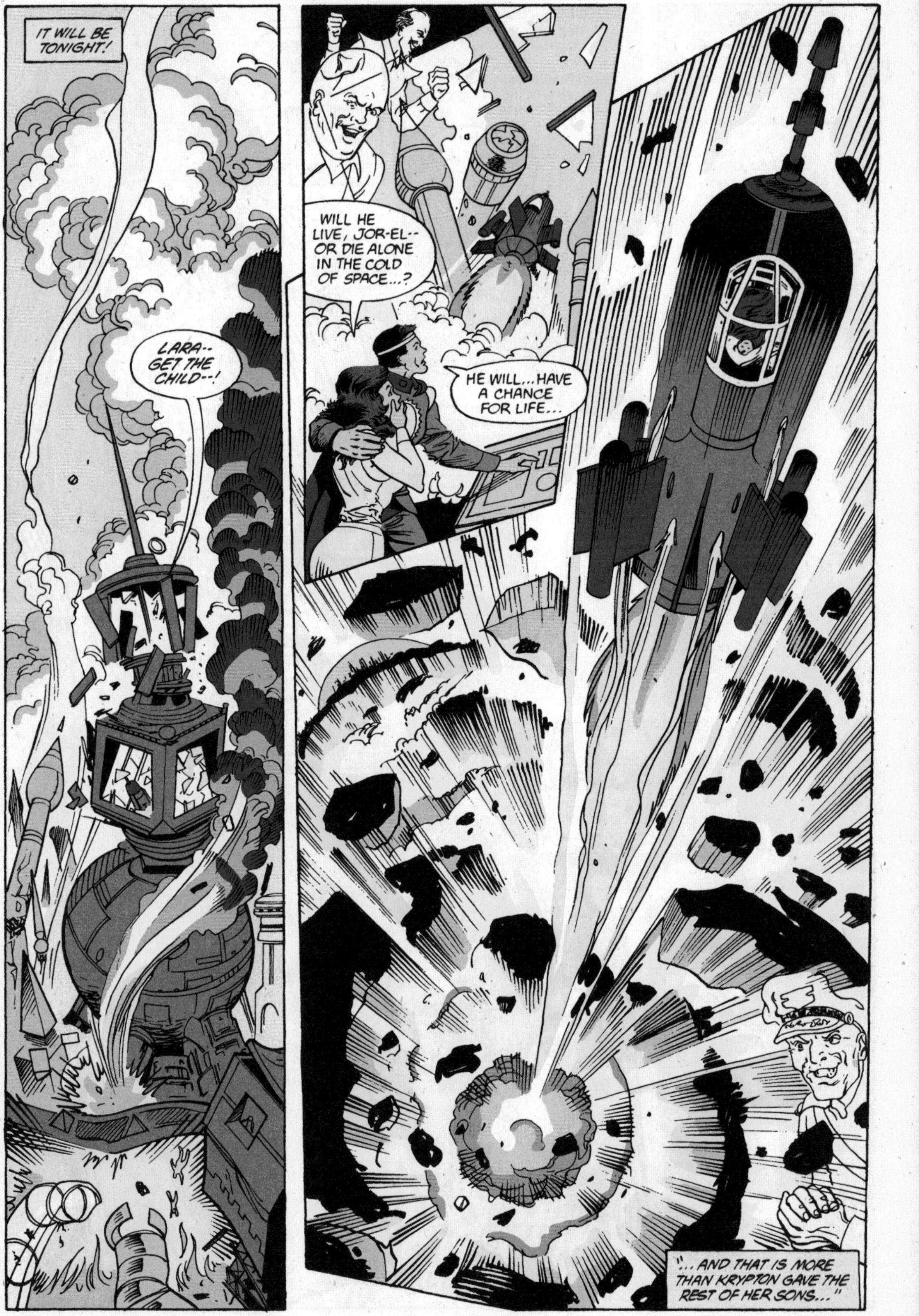
IT WILL BE TONIGHT!
LARA-- GET THE CHILD--!
WILL HE LIVE, JOR-EL-- OR DIE ALONE IN THE COLD OF SPACE...?
HE WILL... HAVE A CHANCE FOR LIFE...
"... AND THAT IS MORE THAN KRYPTON GAVE THE REST OF HER SONS..."

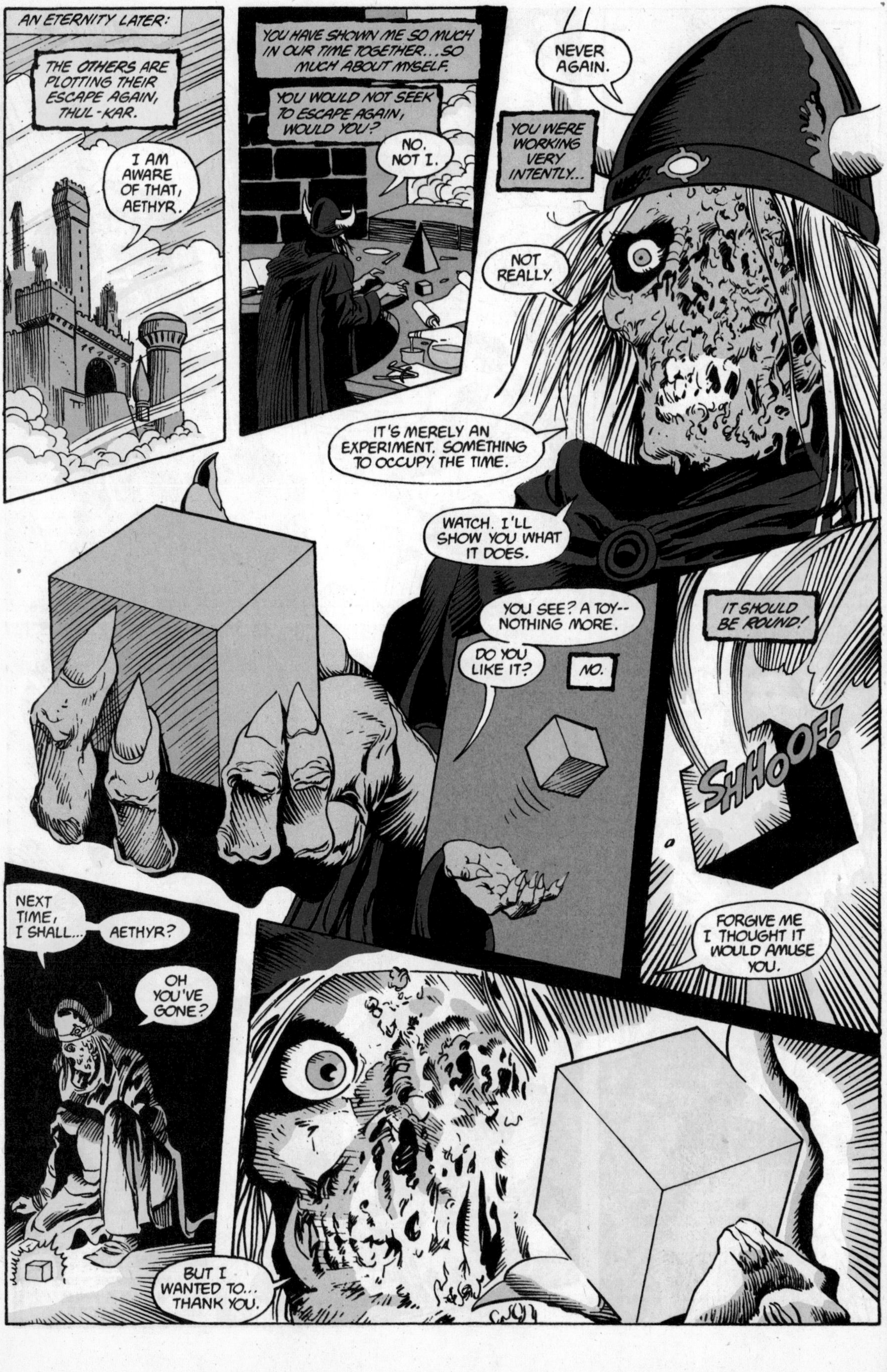
AN ETERNITY LATER:
THE OTHERS ARE PLOTTING THEIR ESCAPE AGAIN, THUL-KAR.
I AM AWARE OF THAT, AETHYR.
YOU HAVE SHOWN ME SO MUCH IN OUR TIME TOGETHER... SO MUCH ABOUT MYSELF.
YOU WOULD NOT SEEK TO ESCAPE AGAIN, WOULD YOU?
NO. NOT I.
NEVER AGAIN.
YOU WERE WORKING VERY INTENTLY...
NOT REALLY.
IT'S MERELY AN EXPERIMENT. SOMETHING TO OCCUPY THE TIME.
WATCH. I'LL SHOW YOU WHAT IT DOES.
YOU SEE? A TOY-- NOTHING MORE.
DO YOU LIKE IT?
NO.
IT SHOULD BE ROUND!
SHHOOF!
FORGIVE ME I THOUGHT IT WOULD AMUSE YOU.
NEXT TIME, I SHALL...
AETHYR?
OH YOU'VE GONE?
BUT I WANTED TO... THANK YOU.

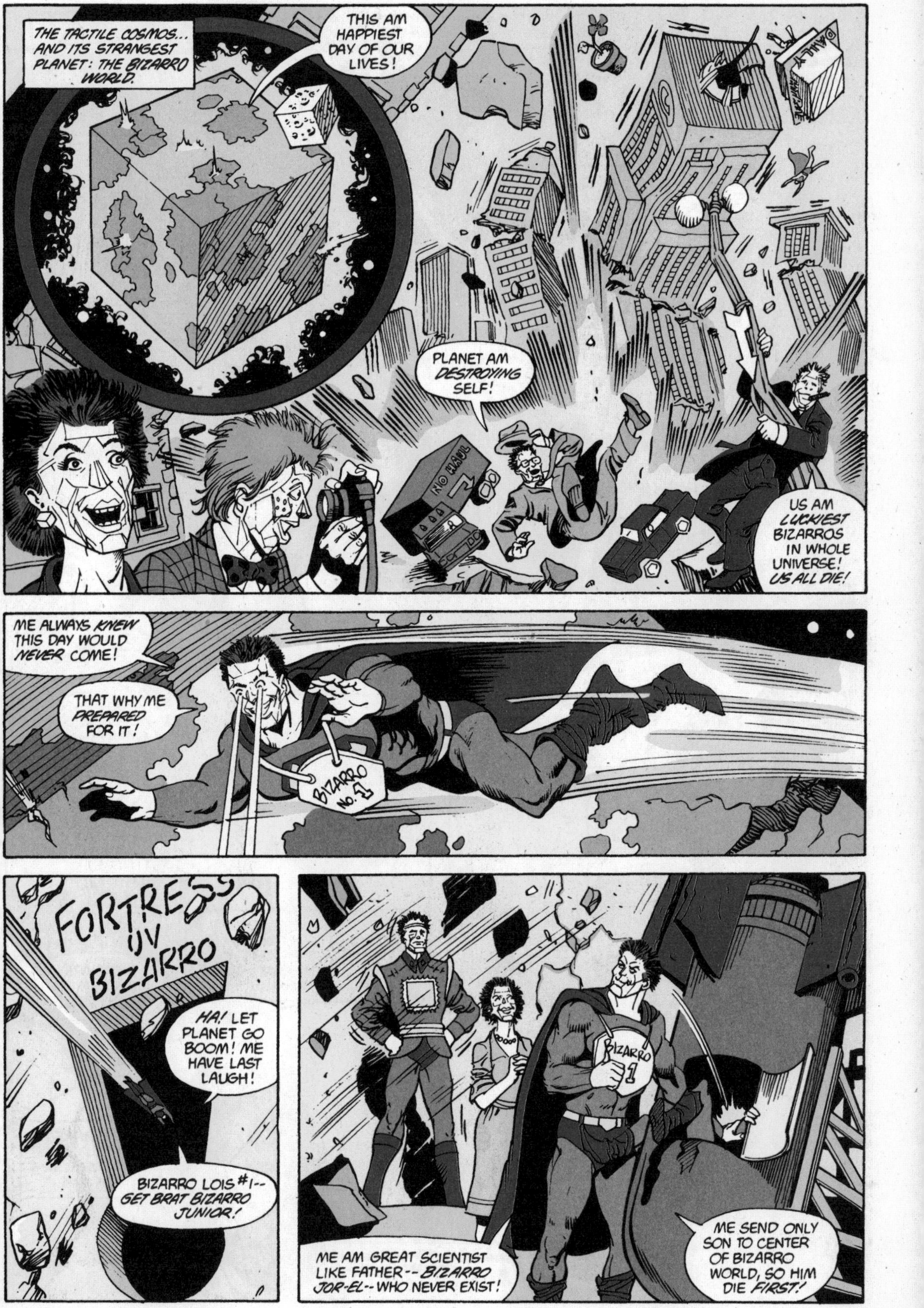
THE TACTILE COSMOS... AND ITS STRANGEST PLANET: THE BIZARRO WORLD.
THIS AM HAPPIEST DAY OF OUR LIVES!
PLANET AM DESTROYING SELF!
US AM LUCKIEST BIZARROS IN WHOLE UNIVERSE! US ALL DIE!
ME ALWAYS KNEW THIS DAY WOULD NEVER COME!
THAT WHY ME PREPARED FOR IT!
BIZARRO NO. 1
FORTRESS UV BIZARRO
HA! LET PLANET GO BOOM! ME HAVE LAST LAUGH!
BIZARRO LOIS #1-- GET BRAT BIZARRO JUNIOR!
BIZARRO 1
ME AM GREAT SCIENTIST LIKE FATHER-- BIZARRO JOR-EL-- WHO NEVER EXIST!
ME SEND ONLY SON TO CENTER OF BIZARRO WORLD, SO HIM DIE FIRST!

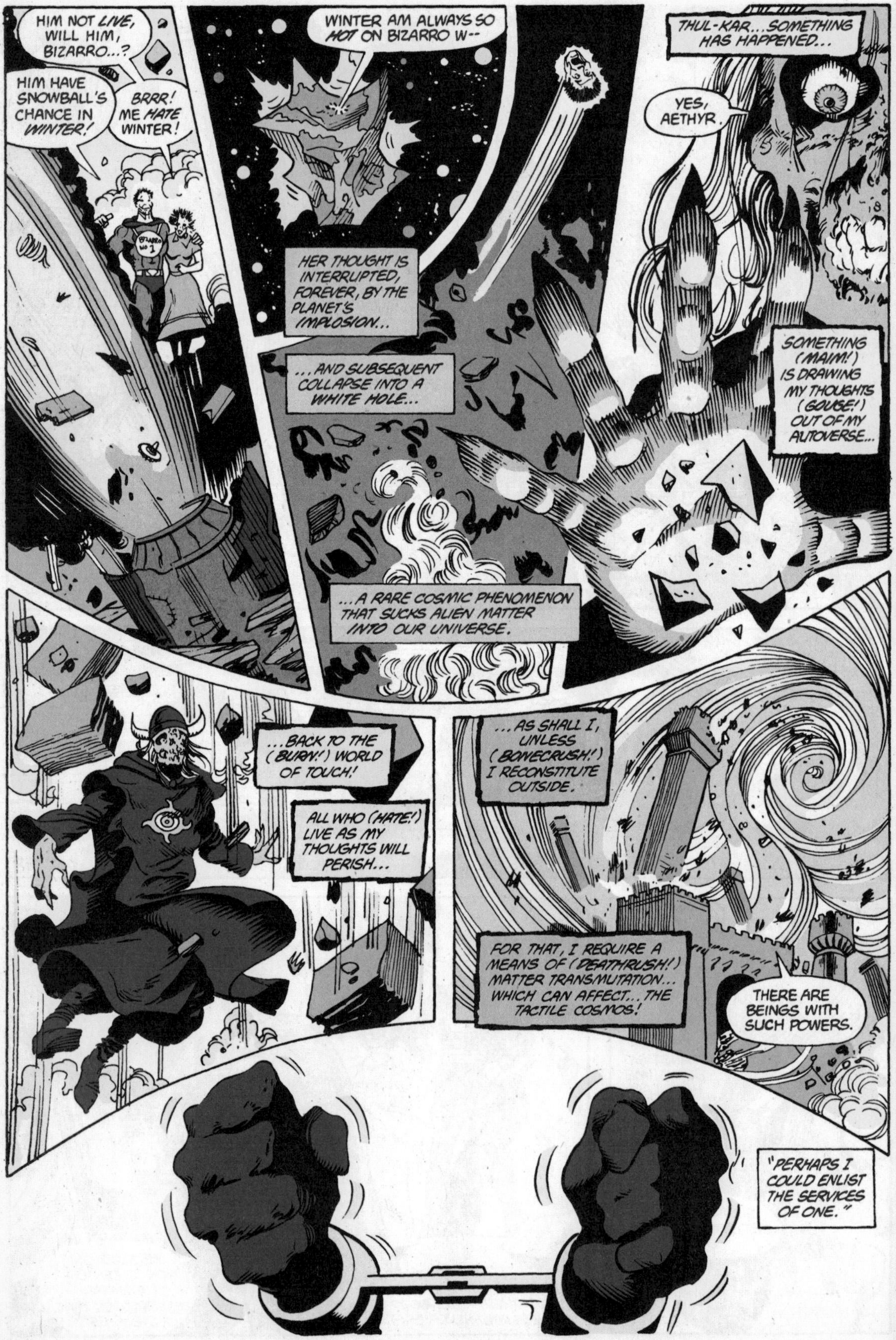
HIM NOT LIVE, WILL HIM, BIZARRO...?
HIM HAVE SNOWBALL'S CHANCE IN WINTER!
BRRR! ME HATE WINTER!
BIZARRO NO 1
WINTER AM ALWAYS SO HOT ON BIZARRO W--
HER THOUGHT IS INTERRUPTED, FOREVER, BY THE PLANET'S IMPLOSION...
...AND SUBSEQUENT COLLAPSE INTO A WHITE HOLE...
...A RARE COSMIC PHENOMENON THAT SUCKS ALIEN MATTER INTO OUR UNIVERSE.
THUL-KAR...SOMETHING HAS HAPPENED...
YES, AETHYR.
SOMETHING (MAIM!) IS DRAWING MY THOUGHTS (GOUGE!) OUT OF MY AUTOVERSE...
...BACK TO THE (BURY!) WORLD OF TOUCH!
ALL WHO (HATE!) LIVE AS MY THOUGHTS WILL PERISH...
...AS SHALL I, UNLESS (BONECRUSH!) I RECONSTITUTE OUTSIDE.
FOR THAT, I REQUIRE A MEANS OF (DEATHRUSH!) MATTER TRANSMUTATION... WHICH CAN AFFECT...THE TACTILE COSMOS!
THERE ARE BEINGS WITH SUCH POWERS.
"PERHAPS I COULD ENLIST THE SERVICES OF ONE."

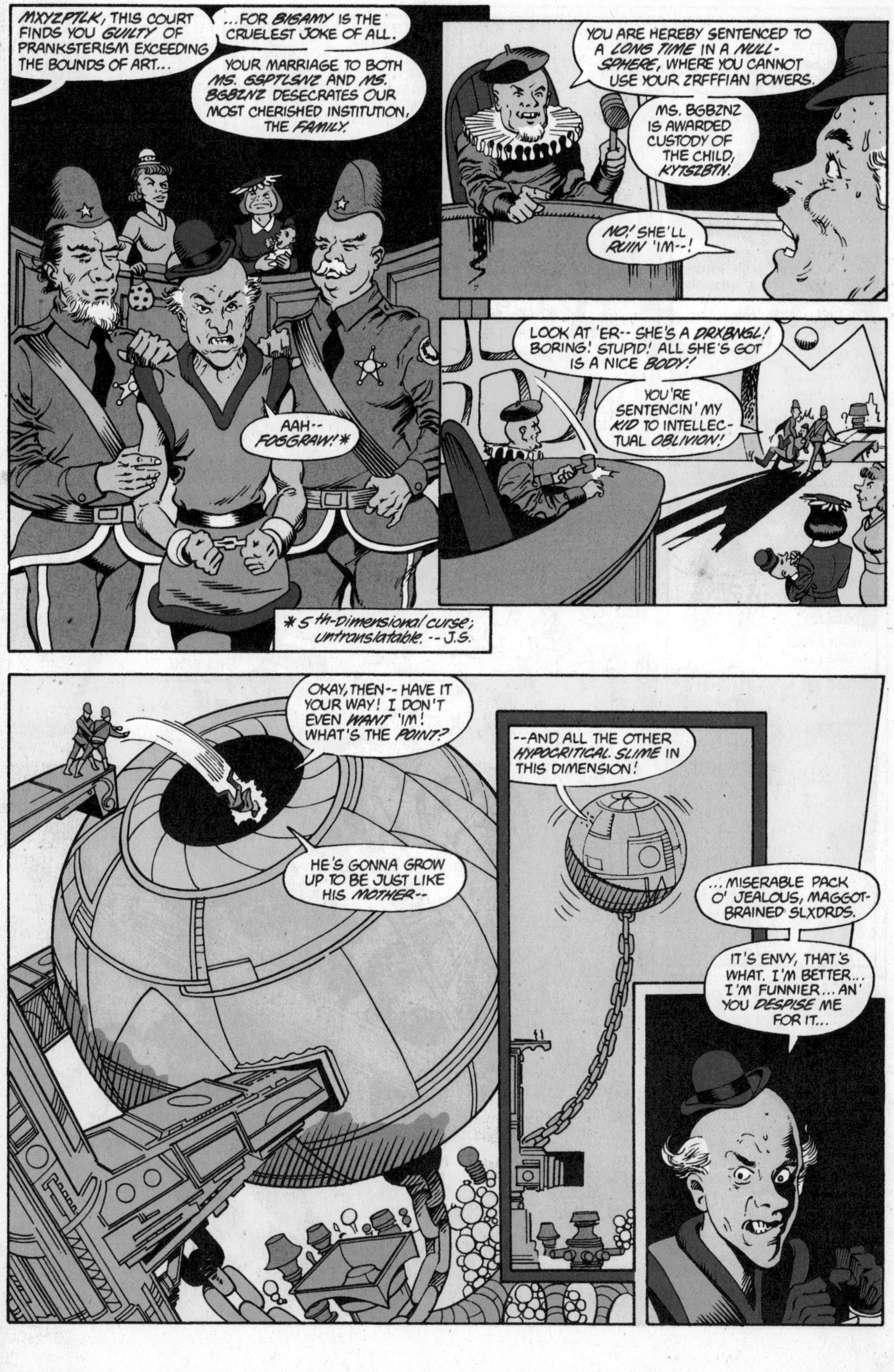
MXYZPTLK, THIS COURT FINDS YOU GUILTY OF PRANKSTERISM EXCEEDING THE BOUNDS OF ART...
...FOR BIGAMY IS THE CRUELEST JOKE OF ALL.
YOUR MARRIAGE TO BOTH MS. GSPTLSNZ AND MS. BGBZNZ DESECRATES OUR MOST CHERISHED INSTITUTION, THE FAMILY.
AAH-- FOSGRAW!*
* 5th-Dimensional curse; untranslatable. --J.S.
YOU ARE HEREBY SENTENCED TO A LONG TIME IN A NULL-SPHERE, WHERE YOU CANNOT USE YOUR ZRFFIAN POWERS.
MS. BGBZNZ IS AWARDED CUSTODY OF THE CHILD, KYTSZBTN.
NO! SHE'LL RUIN 'IM--!
LOOK AT 'ER-- SHE'S A DRXBNGL! BORING! STUPID! ALL SHE'S GOT IS A NICE BODY!
YOU'RE SENTENCIN' MY KID TO INTELLECTUAL OBLIVION!
OKAY, THEN-- HAVE IT YOUR WAY! I DON'T EVEN WANT 'IM! WHAT'S THE POINT?
HE'S GONNA GROW UP TO BE JUST LIKE HIS MOTHER--
--AND ALL THE OTHER HYPOCRITICAL SLIME IN THIS DIMENSION!
...MISERABLE PACK O' JEALOUS, MAGGOT-BRAINED SLXDRDS.
IT'S ENVY, THAT'S WHAT. I'M BETTER... I'M FUNNIER... AN' YOU DESPISE ME FOR IT...

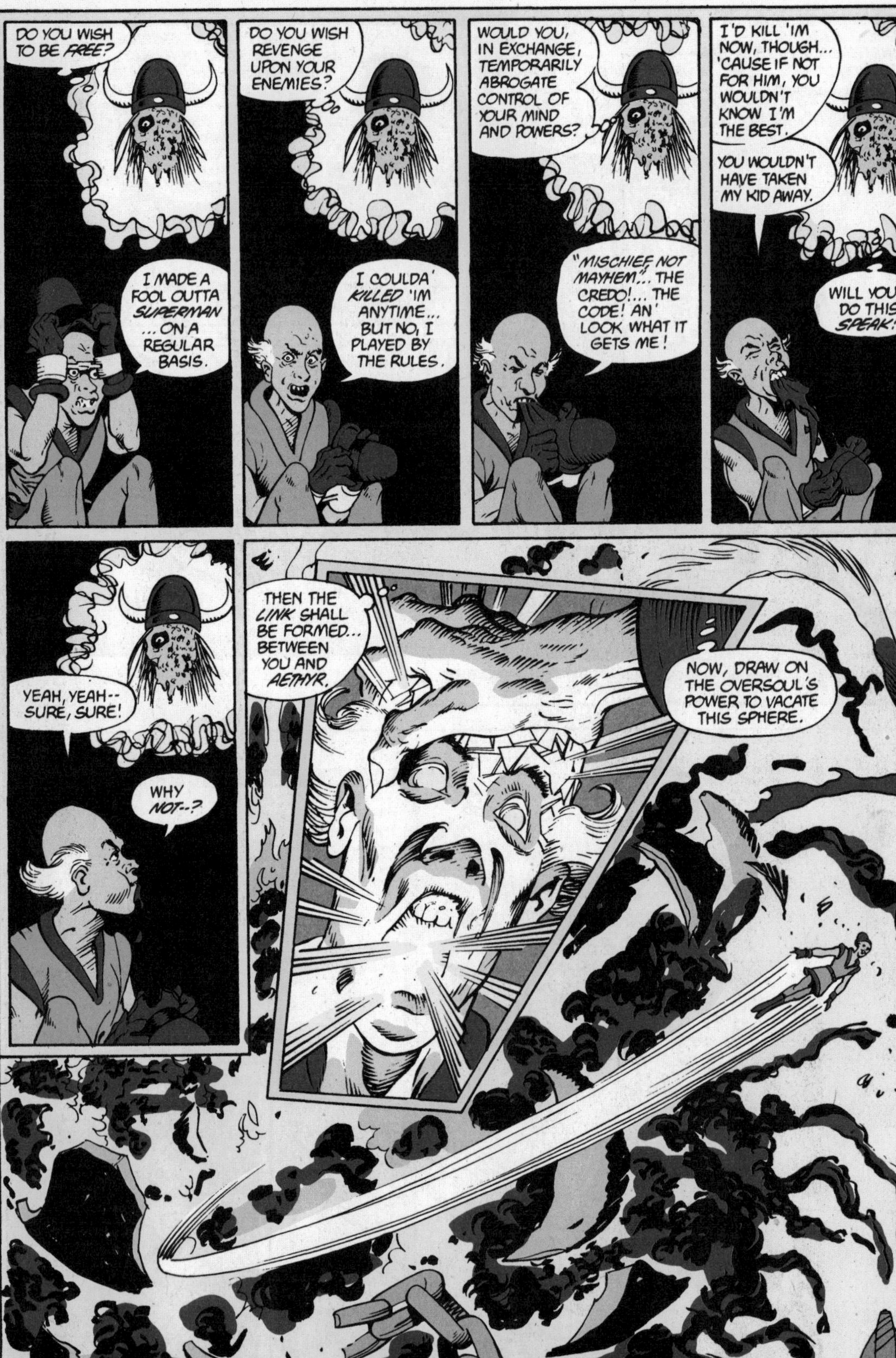
DO YOU WISH TO BE FREE?
I MADE A FOOL OUTTA SUPERMAN ...ON A REGULAR BASIS.
DO YOU WISH REVENGE UPON YOUR ENEMIES?
I COULDA' KILLED 'IM ANYTIME... BUT NO, I PLAYED BY THE RULES.
WOULD YOU, IN EXCHANGE, TEMPORARILY ABROGATE CONTROL OF YOUR MIND AND POWERS?
"MISCHIEF, NOT MAYHEM."... THE CREDO!... THE CODE! AN' LOOK WHAT IT GETS ME!
I'D KILL 'IM NOW, THOUGH... 'CAUSE IF NOT FOR HIM, YOU WOULDN'T KNOW I'M THE BEST.
YOU WOULDN'T HAVE TAKEN MY KID AWAY.
WILL YOU DO THIS? SPEAK!
YEAH, YEAH-- SURE, SURE!
WHY NOT--?
THEN THE LINK SHALL BE FORMED... BETWEEN YOU AND AETHYR.
NOW, DRAW ON THE OVERSOUL'S POWER TO VACATE THIS SPHERE.

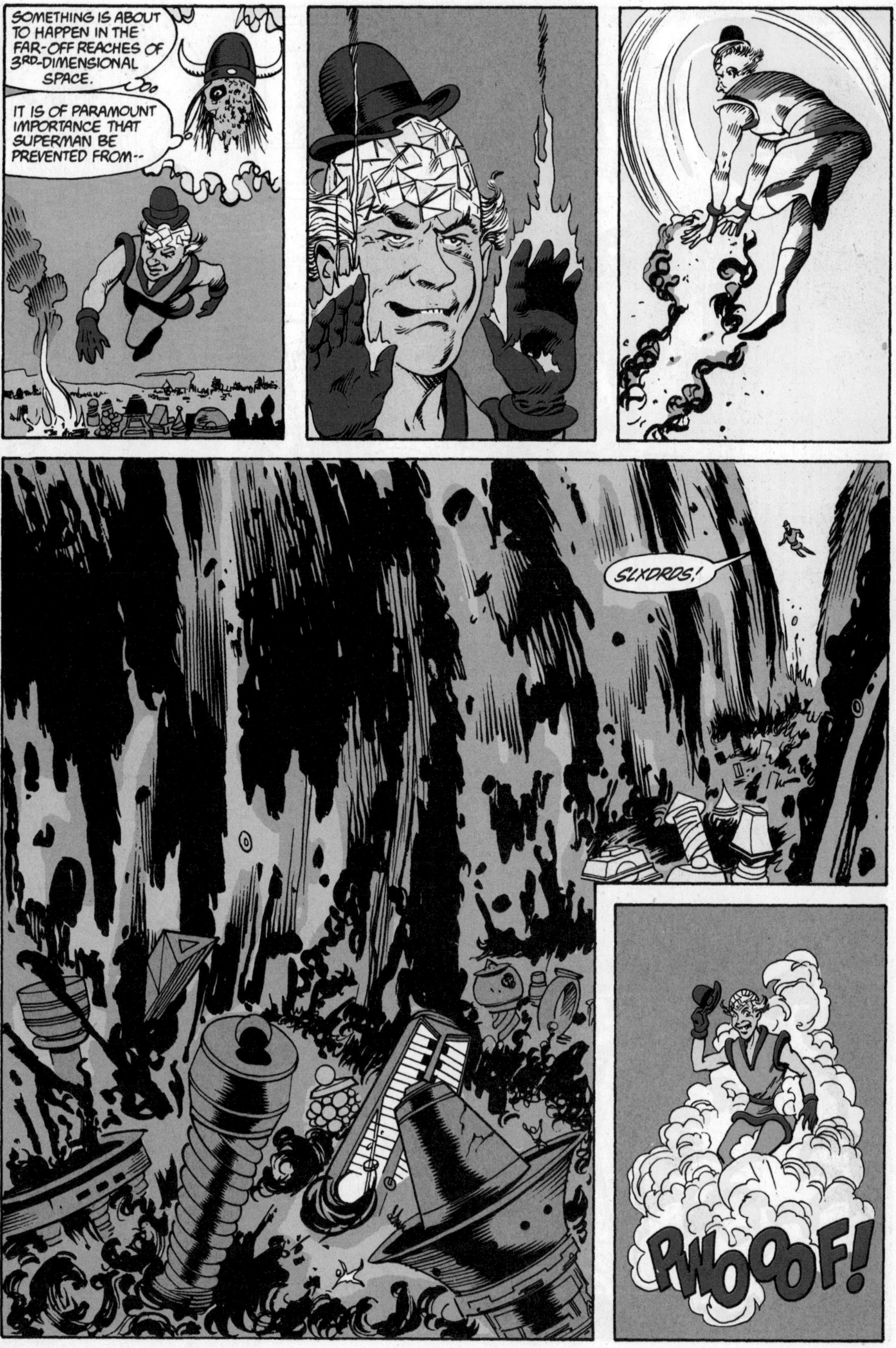
SOMETHING IS ABOUT TO HAPPEN IN THE FAR-OFF REACHES OF 3RD-DIMENSIONAL SPACE.
IT IS OF PARAMOUNT IMPORTANCE THAT SUPERMAN BE PREVENTED FROM--
SLXDRDS!
PWOOOOF!

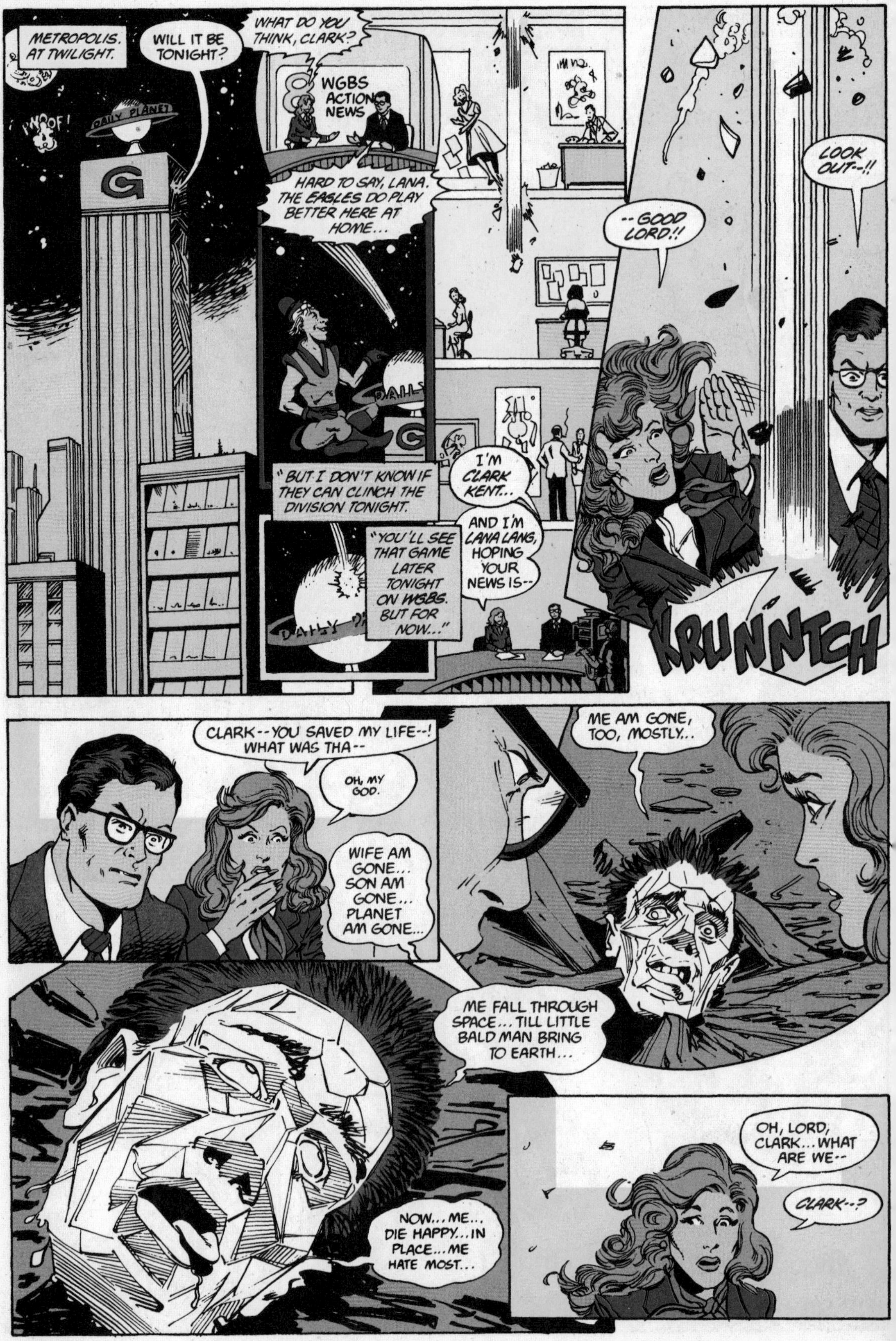

METROPOLIS. AT TWILIGHT.
WILL IT BE TONIGHT?
WHAT DO YOU THINK, CLARK?
WGBS ACTION NEWS
WOOF!
DAILY PLANET
HARD TO SAY, LANA. THE EAGLES DO PLAY BETTER HERE AT HOME...
"BUT I DON'T KNOW IF THEY CAN CLINCH THE DIVISION TONIGHT.
"YOU'LL SEE THAT GAME LATER TONIGHT ON WGBS. BUT FOR NOW..."
I'M CLARK KENT...
AND I'M LANA LANG, HOPING YOUR NEWS IS--
--GOOD LORD!!
LOOK OUT--!!
KRUNNTCH
CLARK--YOU SAVED MY LIFE--! WHAT WAS THA--
OH, MY GOD.
WIFE AM GONE... SON AM GONE... PLANET AM GONE...
ME AM GONE, TOO, MOSTLY...
ME FALL THROUGH SPACE... TILL LITTLE BALD MAN BRING TO EARTH...
NOW... ME... DIE HAPPY... IN PLACE... ME HATE MOST...
OH, LORD, CLARK... WHAT ARE WE--
CLARK--?

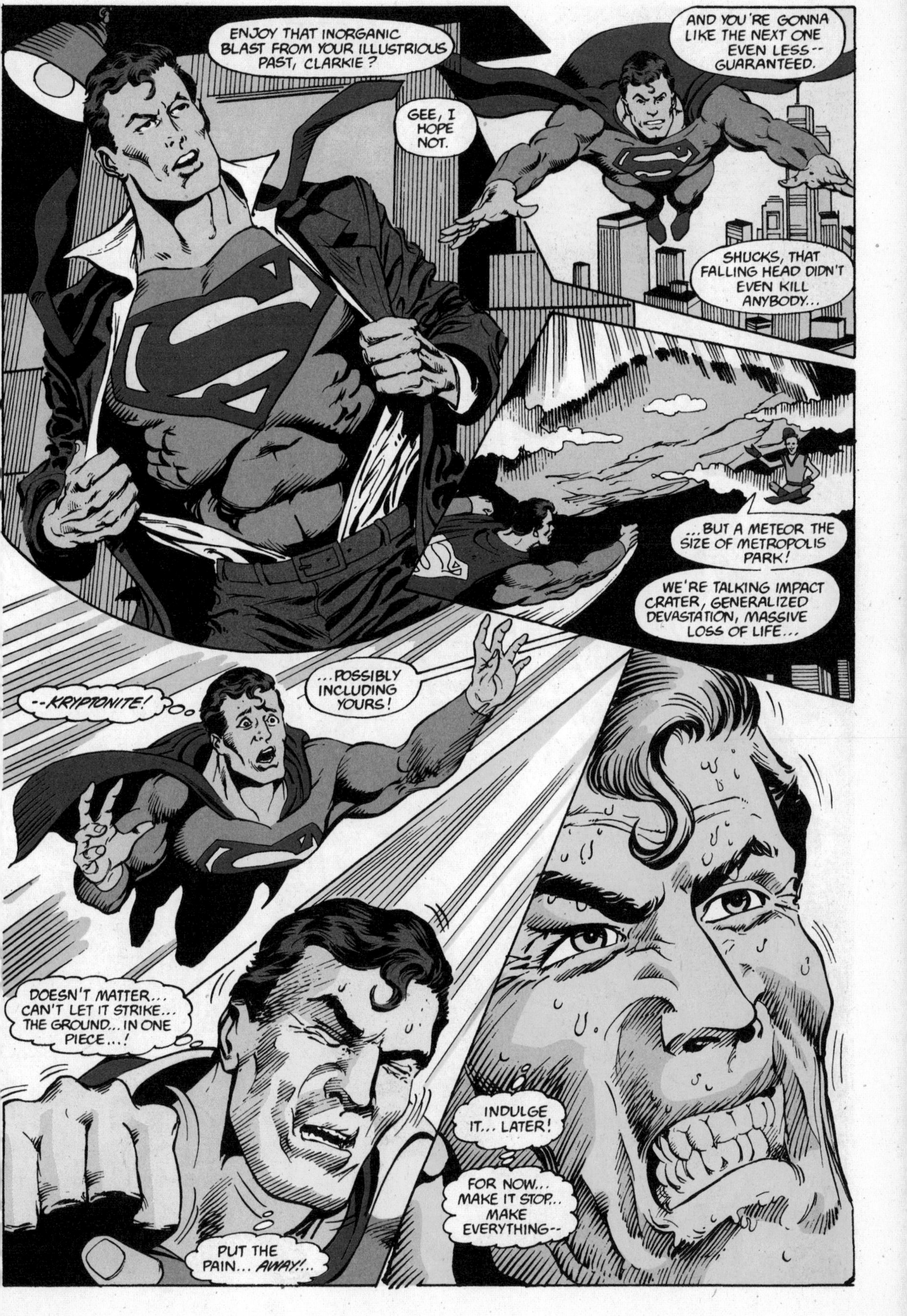
ENJOY THAT INORGANIC BLAST FROM YOUR ILLUSTRIOUS PAST, CLARKIE?
GEE, I HOPE NOT.
AND YOU'RE GONNA LIKE THE NEXT ONE EVEN LESS-- GUARANTEED.
SHUCKS, THAT FALLING HEAD DIDN'T EVEN KILL ANYBODY...
...BUT A METEOR THE SIZE OF METROPOLIS PARK!
WE'RE TALKING IMPACT CRATER, GENERALIZED DEVASTATION, MASSIVE LOSS OF LIFE...
--KRYPTONITE!
...POSSIBLY INCLUDING YOURS!
DOESN'T MATTER... CAN'T LET IT STRIKE... THE GROUND... IN ONE PIECE...!
INDULGE IT... LATER!
FOR NOW... MAKE IT STOP... MAKE EVERYTHING--
PUT THE PAIN... AWAY!...

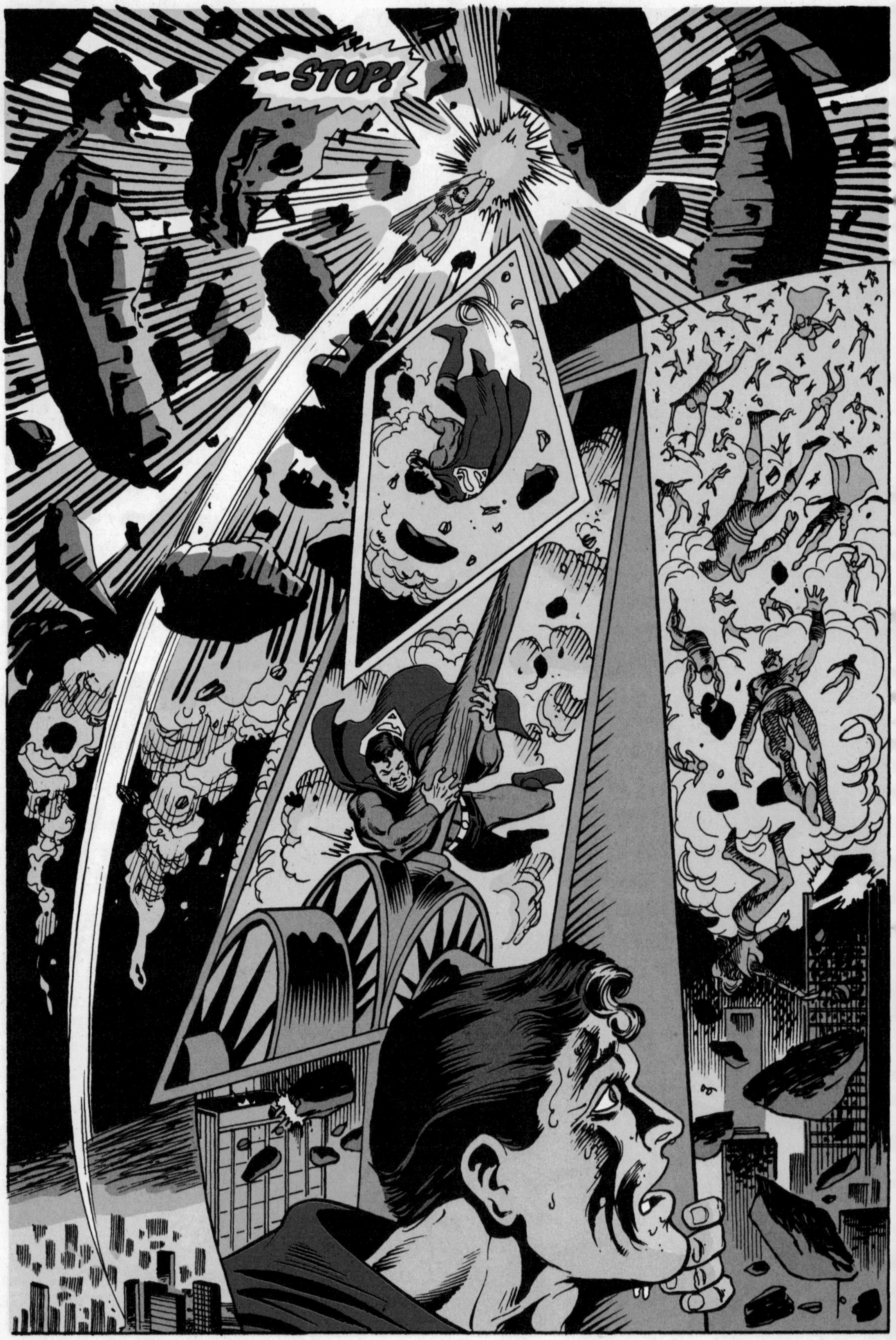
--STOP!

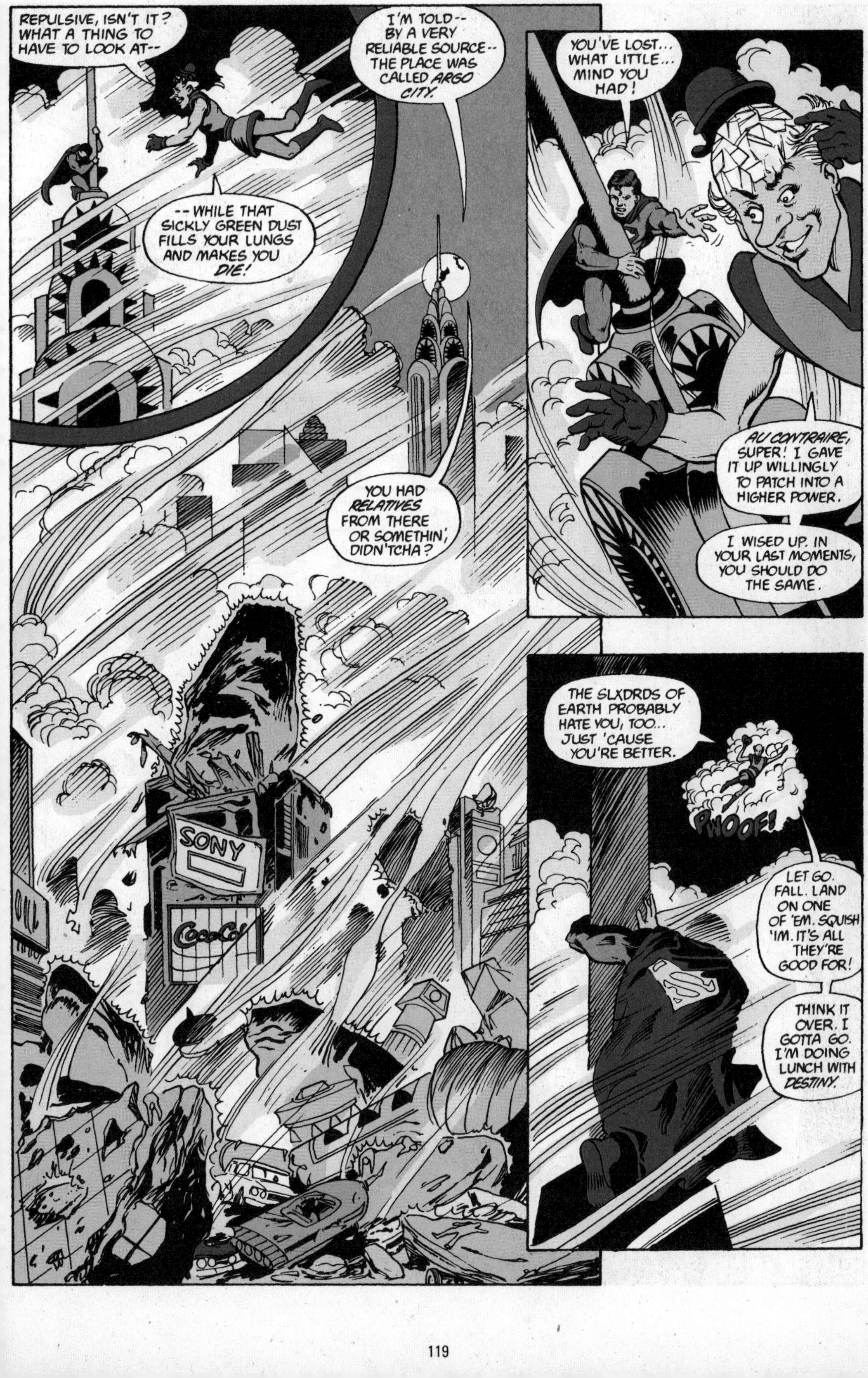
REPULSIVE, ISN'T IT? WHAT A THING TO HAVE TO LOOK AT--
I'M TOLD-- BY A VERY RELIABLE SOURCE-- THE PLACE WAS CALLED ARGO CITY.
-- WHILE THAT SICKLY GREEN DUST FILLS YOUR LUNGS AND MAKES YOU DIE!
YOU HAD RELATIVES FROM THERE OR SOMETHIN', DIDN'TCHA?
SONY
YOU'VE LOST... WHAT LITTLE... MIND YOU HAD!
AU CONTRAIRE, SUPER! I GAVE IT UP WILLINGLY TO PATCH INTO A HIGHER POWER.
I WISED UP. IN YOUR LAST MOMENTS, YOU SHOULD DO THE SAME.
THE SLXDRDS OF EARTH PROBABLY HATE YOU, TOO... JUST 'CAUSE YOU'RE BETTER.
PWOOF!
LET GO. FALL. LAND ON ONE OF 'EM. SQUISH 'IM. IT'S ALL THEY'RE GOOD FOR!
THINK IT OVER. I GOTTA GO. I'M DOING LUNCH WITH DESTINY.

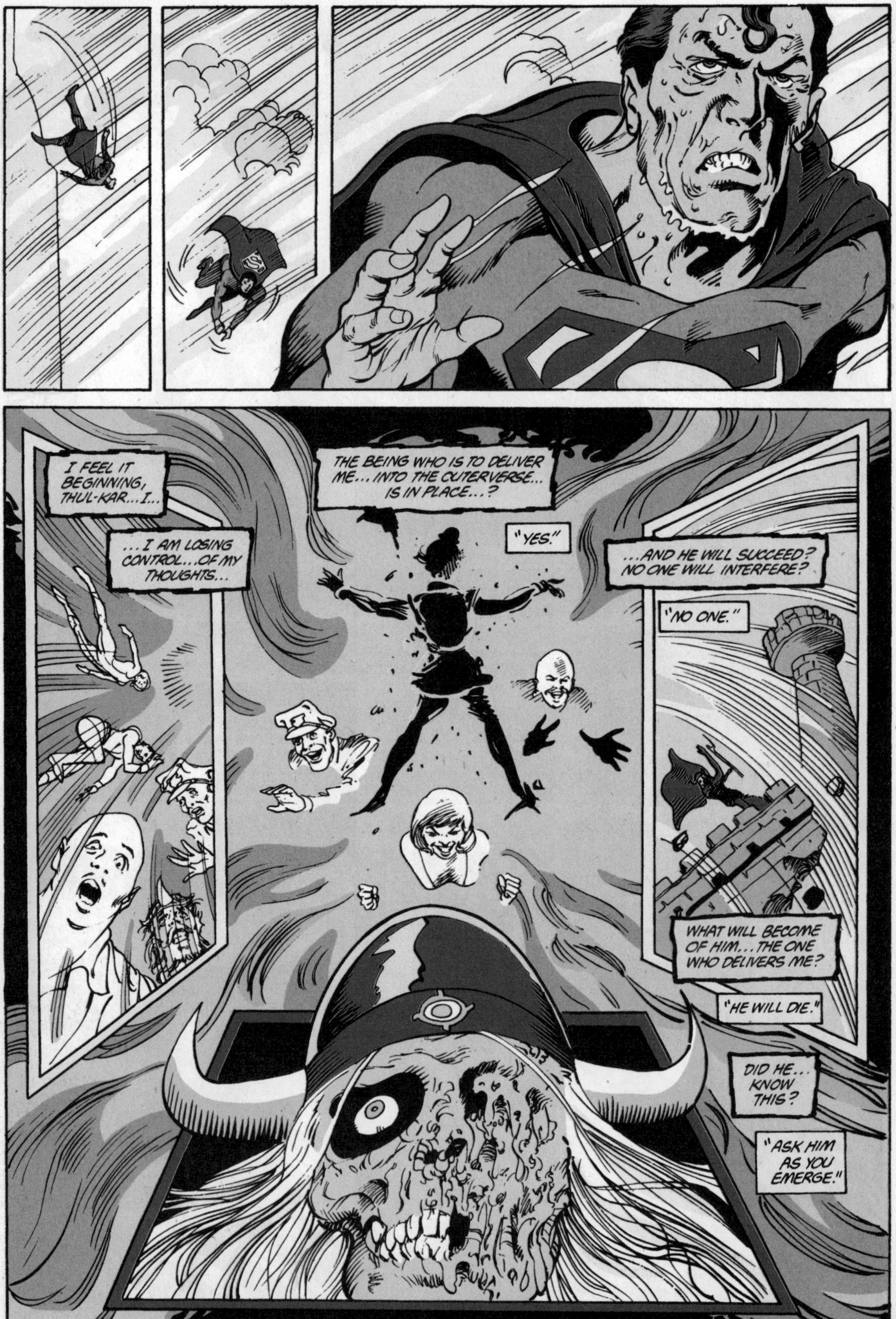
I FEEL IT BEGINNING, THUL-KAR... I...
...I AM LOSING CONTROL... OF MY THOUGHTS...
THE BEING WHO IS TO DELIVER ME... INTO THE OUTERVERSE... IS IN PLACE...?
"YES."
...AND HE WILL SUCCEED? NO ONE WILL INTERFERE?
"NO ONE."
WHAT WILL BECOME OF HIM... THE ONE WHO DELIVERS ME?
"HE WILL DIE."
DID HE... KNOW THIS?
"ASK HIM AS YOU EMERGE."

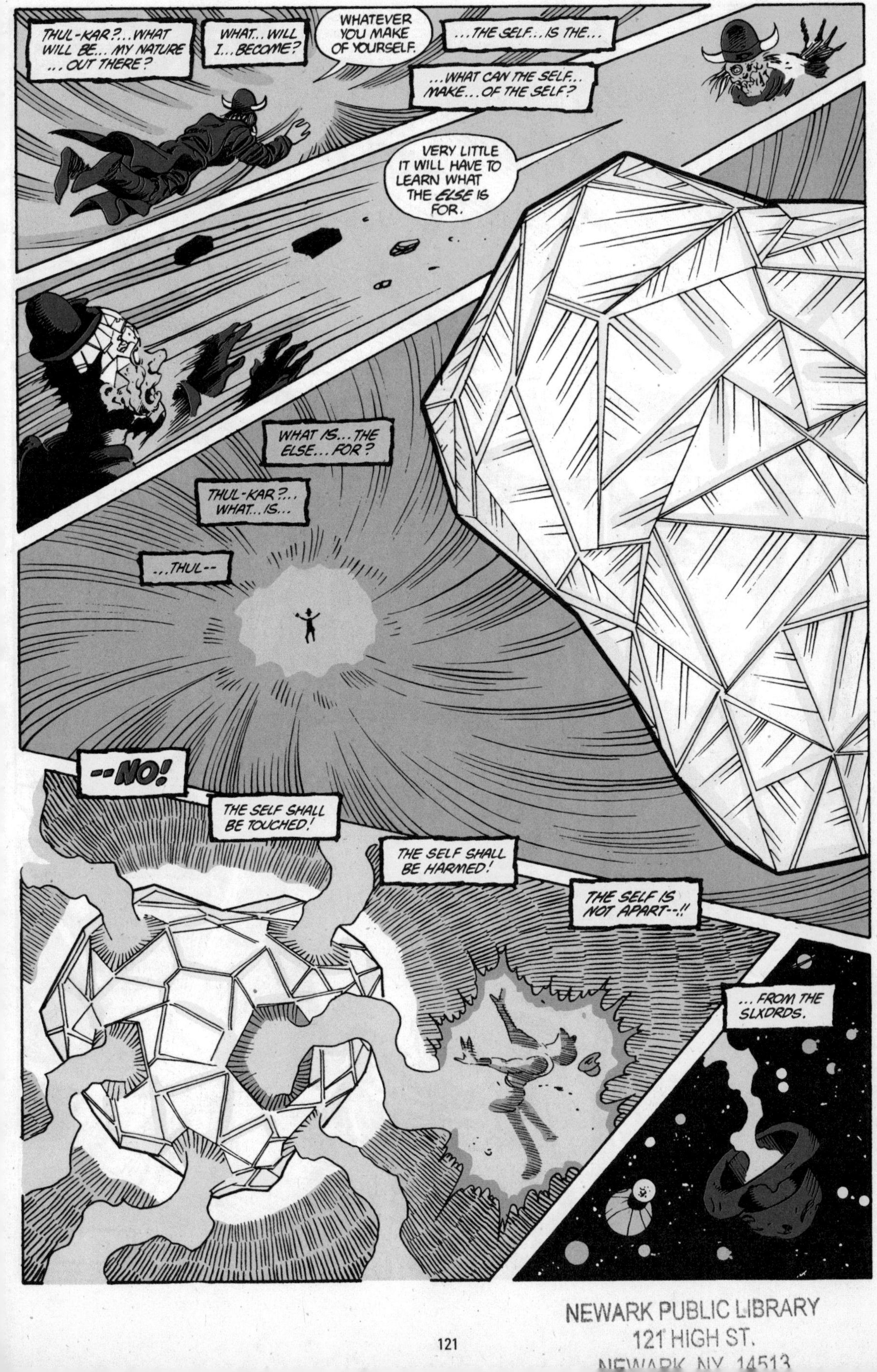
THUL-KAR?...WHAT WILL BE... MY NATURE ...OUT THERE?
WHAT... WILL I...BECOME?
WHATEVER YOU MAKE OF YOURSELF.
...THE SELF... IS THE...
...WHAT CAN THE SELF... MAKE... OF THE SELF?
VERY LITTLE IT WILL HAVE TO LEARN WHAT THE ELSE IS FOR.
WHAT IS... THE ELSE... FOR?
THUL-KAR?... WHAT... IS...
...THUL--
--NO!
THE SELF SHALL BE TOUCHED!
THE SELF SHALL BE HARMED!
THE SELF IS NOT APART--!!
...FROM THE SLXDRDS.

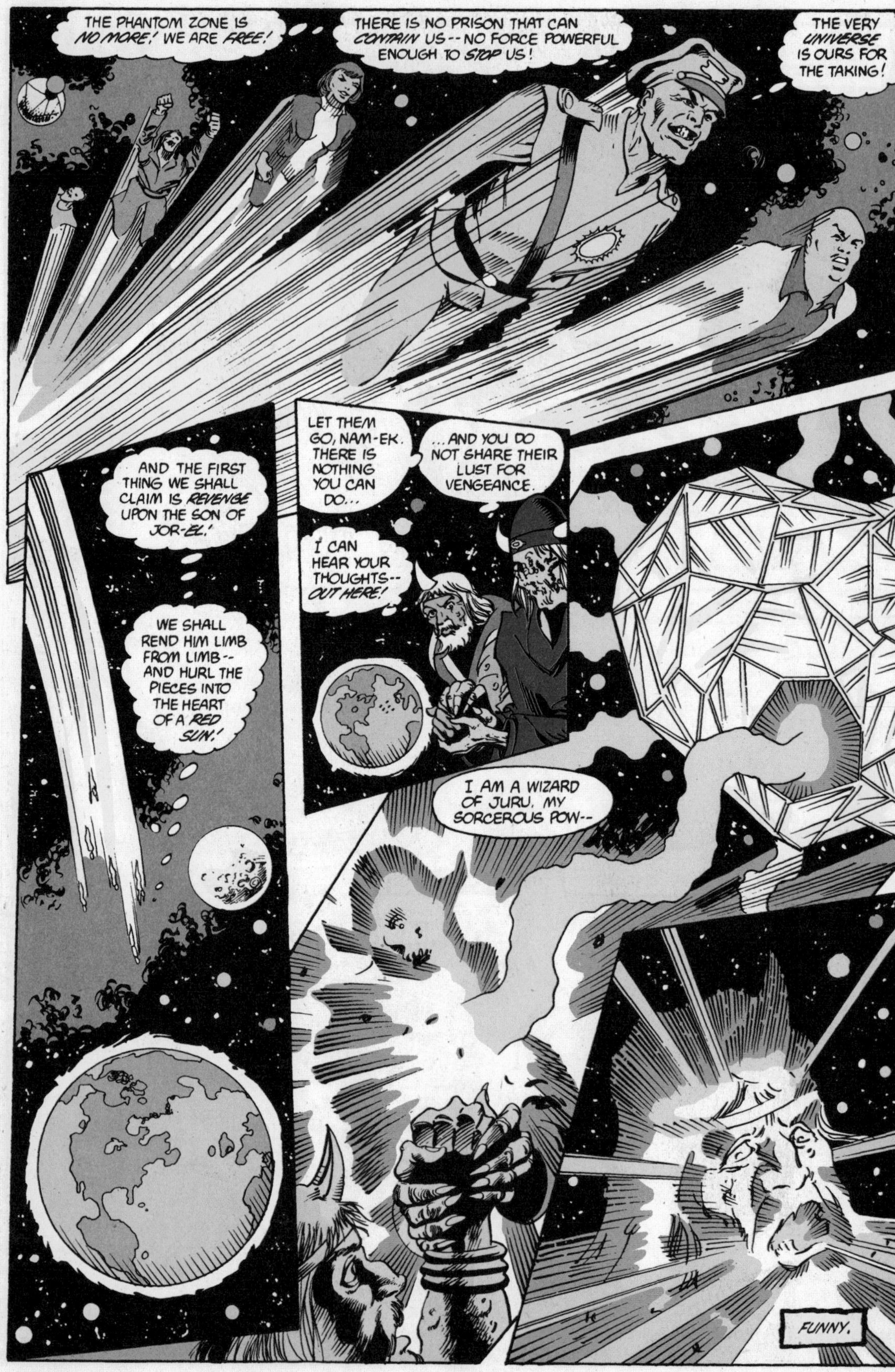

THE PHANTOM ZONE IS NO MORE! WE ARE FREE!
THERE IS NO PRISON THAT CAN CONTAIN US -- NO FORCE POWERFUL ENOUGH TO STOP US!
THE VERY UNIVERSE IS OURS FOR THE TAKING!
AND THE FIRST THING WE SHALL CLAIM IS REVENGE UPON THE SON OF JOR-EL!
WE SHALL REND HIM LIMB FROM LIMB -- AND HURL THE PIECES INTO THE HEART OF A RED SUN!
LET THEM GO, NAM-EK. THERE IS NOTHING YOU CAN DO...
...AND YOU DO NOT SHARE THEIR LUST FOR VENGEANCE.
I CAN HEAR YOUR THOUGHTS-- OUT HERE!
I AM A WIZARD OF JURU. MY SORCEROUS POW--
FUNNY.

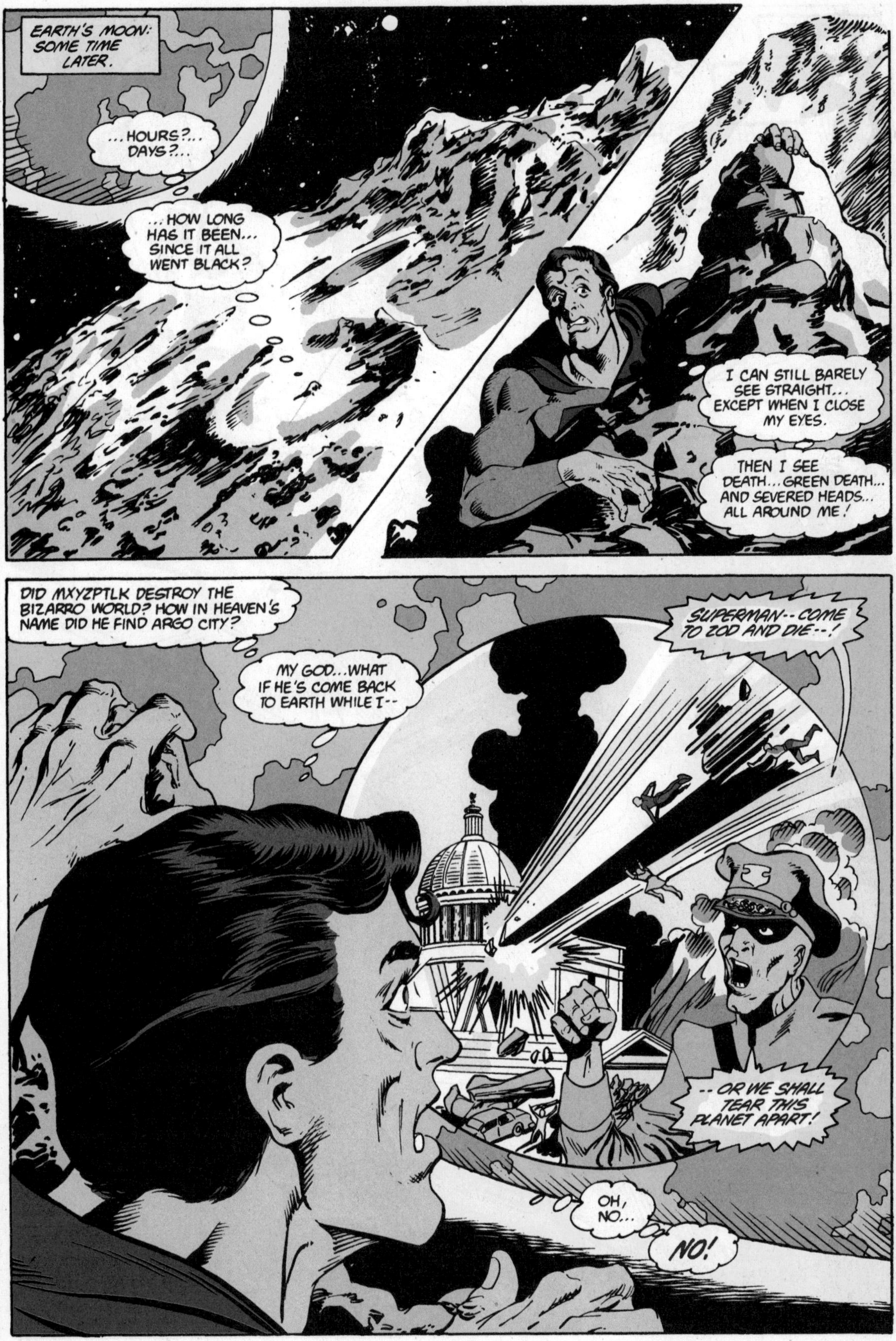
EARTH'S MOON: SOME TIME LATER.
...HOURS?... DAYS?...
...HOW LONG HAS IT BEEN... SINCE IT ALL WENT BLACK?
I CAN STILL BARELY SEE STRAIGHT... EXCEPT WHEN I CLOSE MY EYES.
THEN I SEE DEATH...GREEN DEATH... AND SEVERED HEADS... ALL AROUND ME!
DID MXYZPTLK DESTROY THE BIZARRO WORLD? HOW IN HEAVEN'S NAME DID HE FIND ARGO CITY?
MY GOD...WHAT IF HE'S COME BACK TO EARTH WHILE I--
SUPERMAN--COME TO ZOD AND DIE--!
--OR WE SHALL TEAR THIS PLANET APART!
OH, NO...
NO!

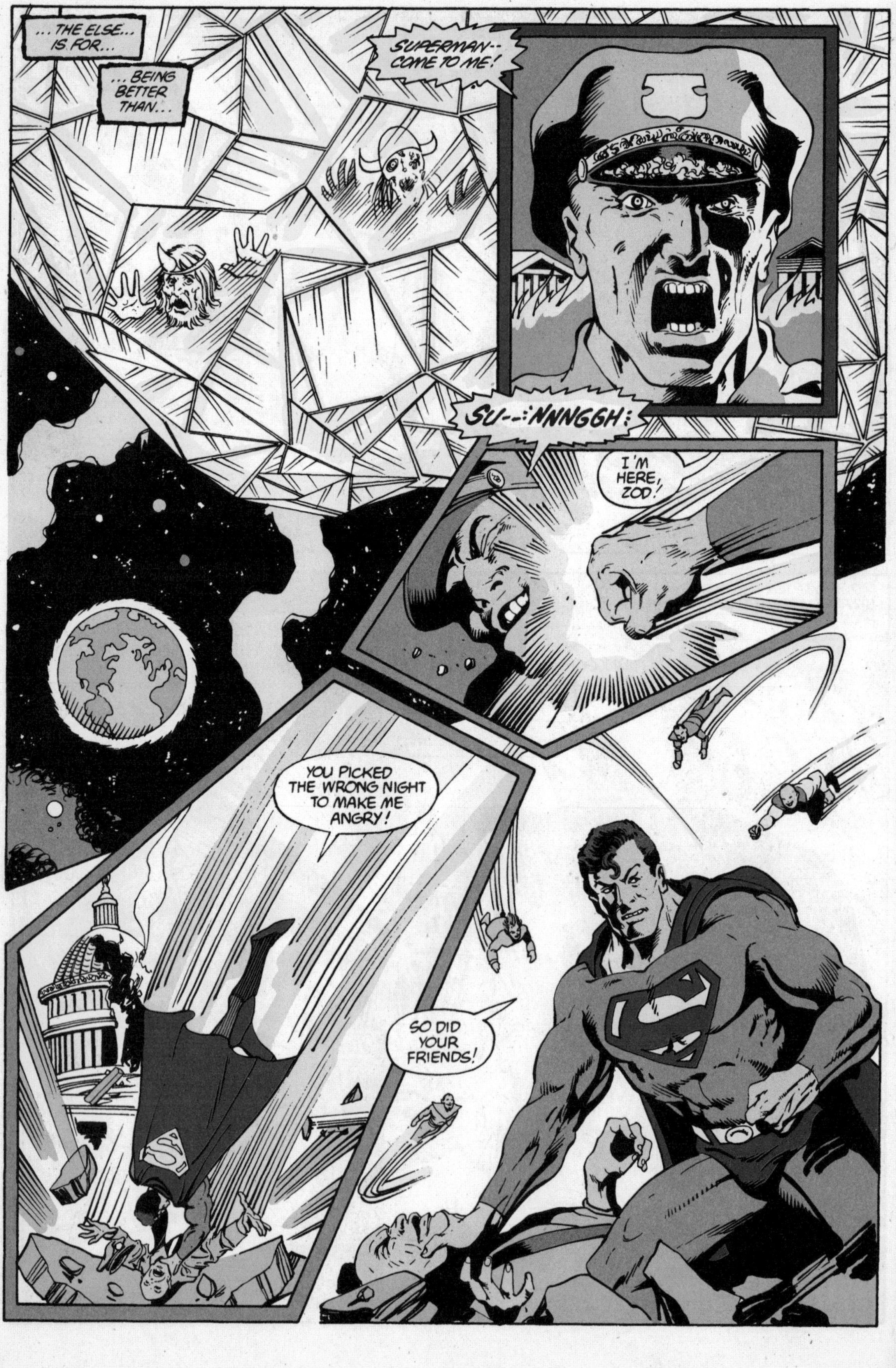
...THE ELSE... IS FOR...
...BEING BETTER THAN...
SUPERMAN-- COME TO ME!
SU--!NNNGGH!
I'M HERE, ZOD!
YOU PICKED THE WRONG NIGHT TO MAKE ME ANGRY!
SO DID YOUR FRIENDS!

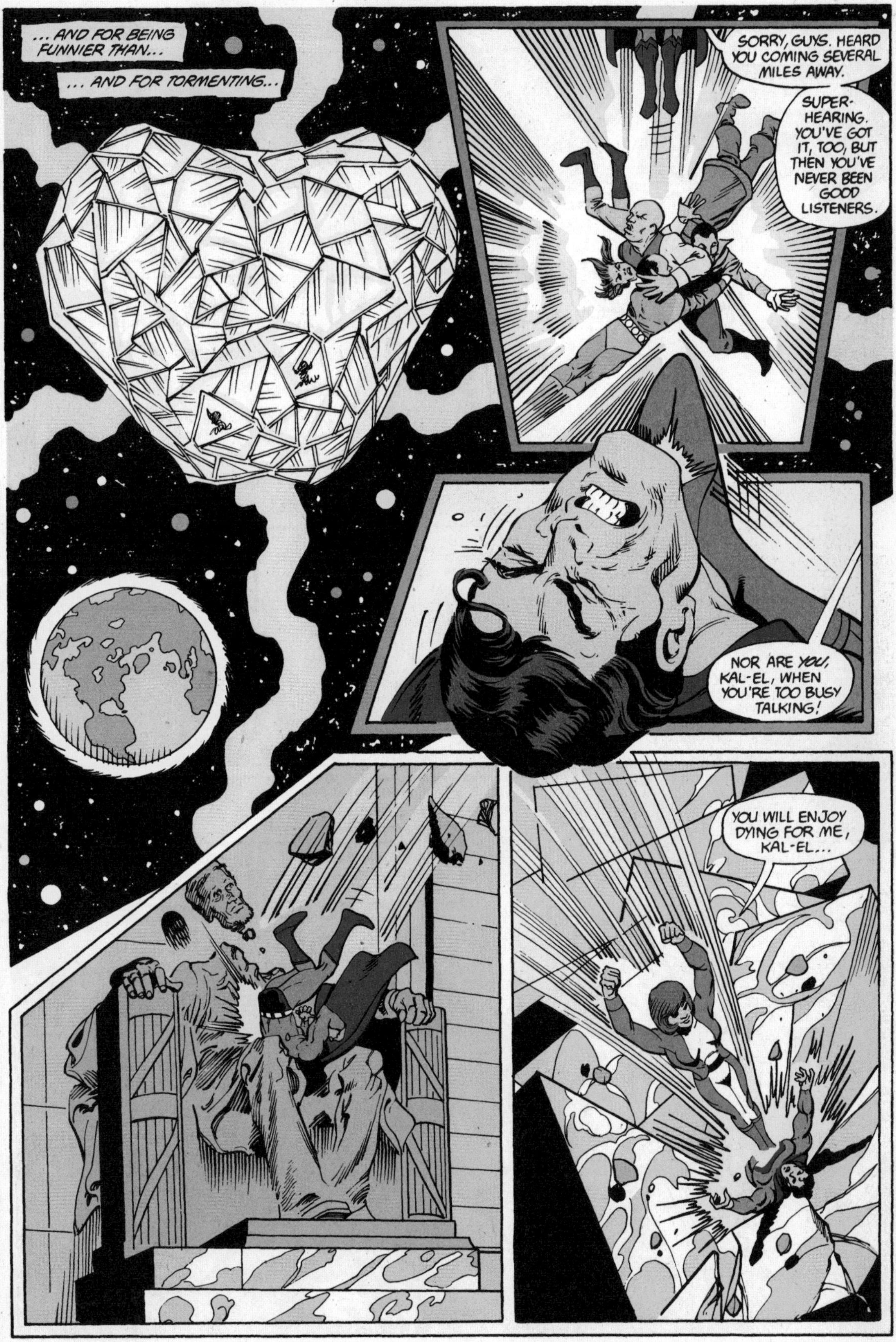
...AND FOR BEING FUNNIER THAN...
...AND FOR TORMENTING...
SORRY, GUYS. HEARD YOU COMING SEVERAL MILES AWAY.
SUPER-HEARING. YOU'VE GOT IT, TOO, BUT THEN YOU'VE NEVER BEEN GOOD LISTENERS.
NOR ARE YOU, KAL-EL, WHEN YOU'RE TOO BUSY TALKING!
YOU WILL ENJOY DYING FOR ME, KAL-EL...

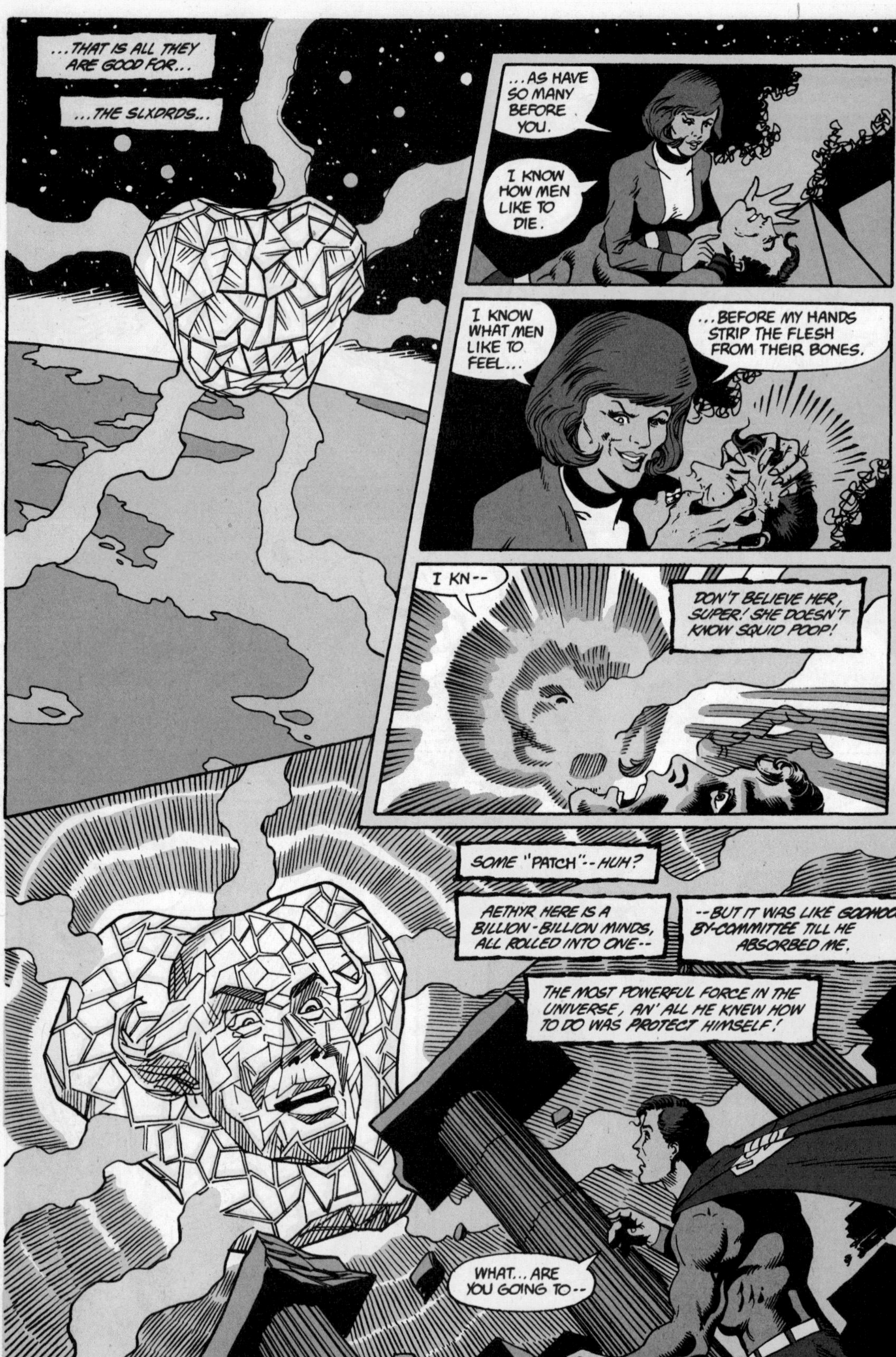
...THAT IS ALL THEY ARE GOOD FOR...
...THE SLXDRDS...
...AS HAVE SO MANY BEFORE YOU.
I KNOW HOW MEN LIKE TO DIE.
I KNOW WHAT MEN LIKE TO FEEL...
...BEFORE MY HANDS STRIP THE FLESH FROM THEIR BONES.
I KN--
DON'T BELIEVE HER, SUPER! SHE DOESN'T KNOW SQUID POOP!
SOME "PATCH"--HUH?
AETHYR HERE IS A BILLION-BILLION MINDS, ALL ROLLED INTO ONE--
--BUT IT WAS LIKE GODHOOD-BY-COMMITTEE TILL HE ABSORBED ME.
THE MOST POWERFUL FORCE IN THE UNIVERSE, AN' ALL HE KNEW HOW TO DO WAS PROTECT HIMSELF!
WHAT...ARE YOU GOING TO--

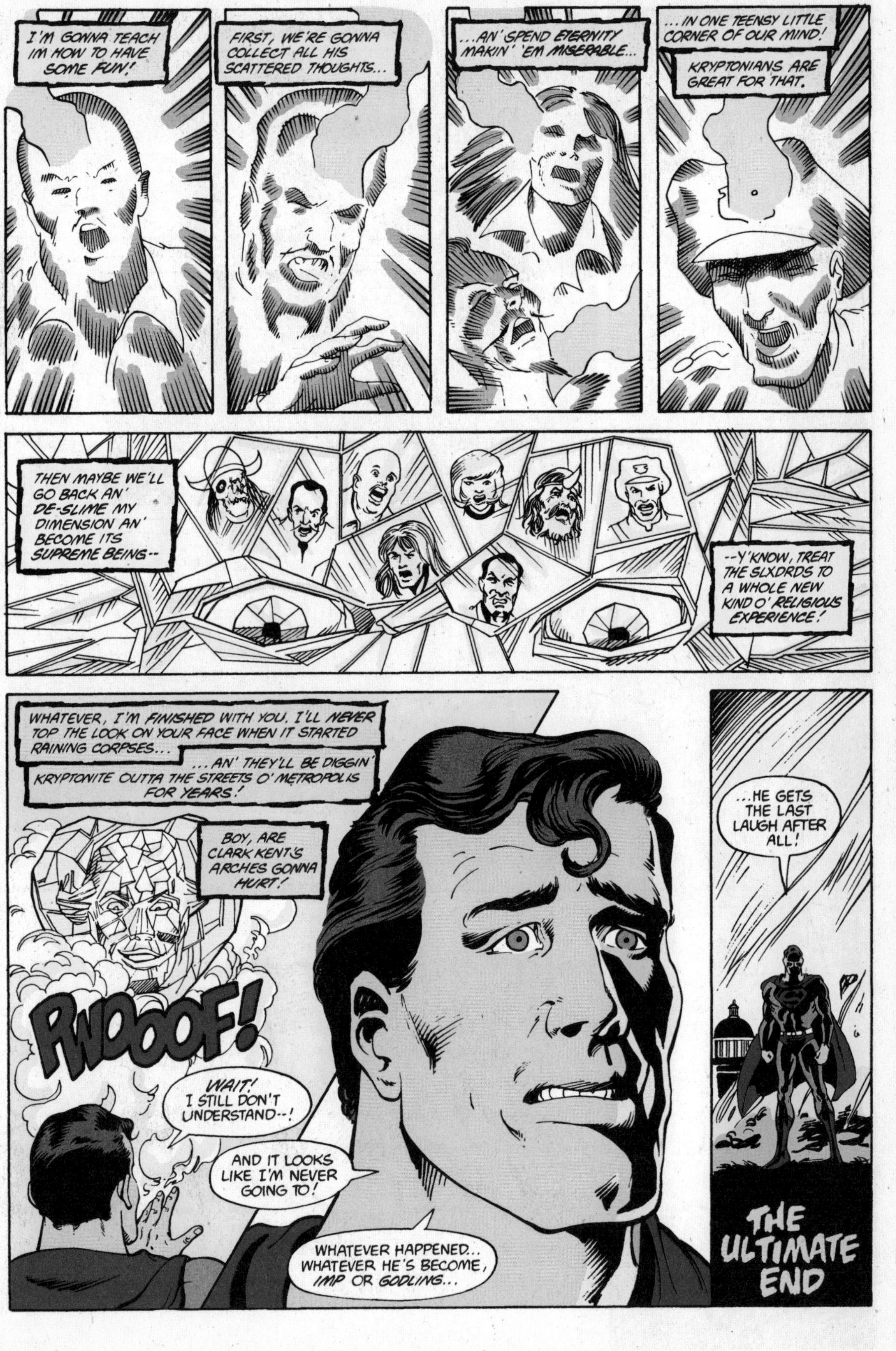
I'M GONNA TEACH IM HOW TO HAVE SOME FUN!
FIRST, WE'RE GONNA COLLECT ALL HIS SCATTERED THOUGHTS...
...AN' SPEND ETERNITY MAKIN' 'EM MISERABLE...
...IN ONE TEENSY LITTLE CORNER OF OUR MIND!
KRYPTONIANS ARE GREAT FOR THAT.
THEN MAYBE WE'LL GO BACK AN' DE-SLIME MY DIMENSION AN' BECOME ITS SUPREME BEING--
--Y'KNOW, TREAT THE SLXDRDS TO A WHOLE NEW KIND O' RELIGIOUS EXPERIENCE!
WHATEVER, I'M FINISHED WITH YOU. I'LL NEVER TOP THE LOOK ON YOUR FACE WHEN IT STARTED RAINING CORPSES...
...AN' THEY'LL BE DIGGIN' KRYPTONITE OUTTA THE STREETS O' METROPOLIS FOR YEARS!
BOY, ARE CLARK KENT'S ARCHES GONNA HURT!
PWOOOF!
WAIT! I STILL DON'T UNDERSTAND--!
AND IT LOOKS LIKE I'M NEVER GOING TO!
WHATEVER HAPPENED... WHATEVER HE'S BECOME, IMP OR GODLING...
...HE GETS THE LAST LAUGH AFTER ALL!
THE ULTIMATE END

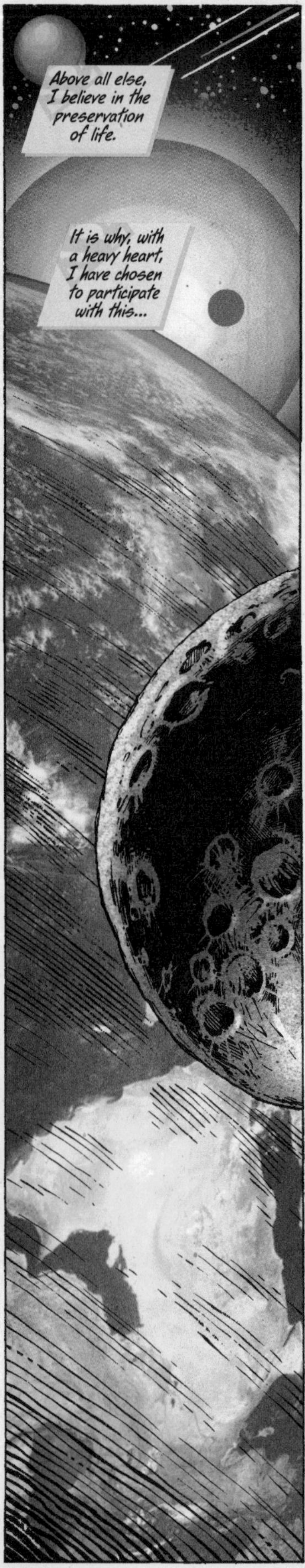
Above all else, I believe in the preservation of life.
It is why, with a heavy heart, I have chosen to participate with this...

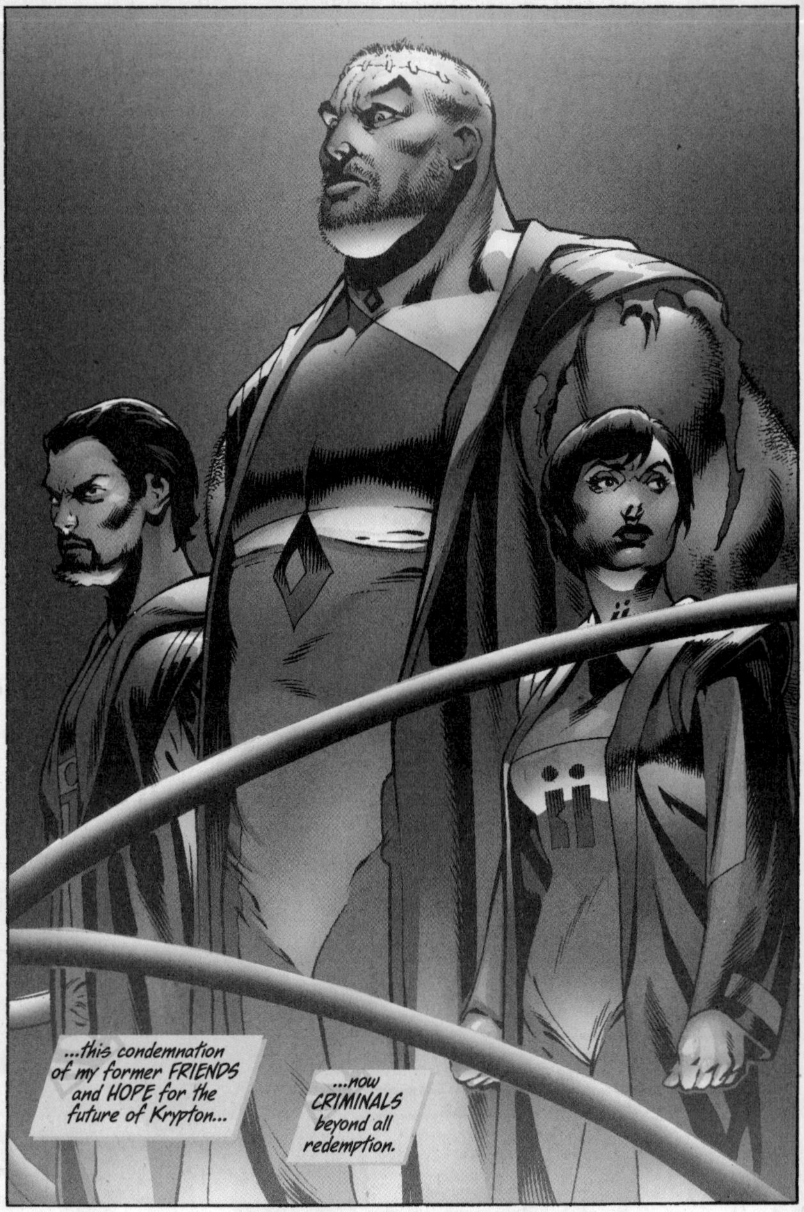
...this condemnation of my former FRIENDS and HOPE for the future of Krypton...
...now CRIMINALS beyond all redemption.

The Criminals of Krypton

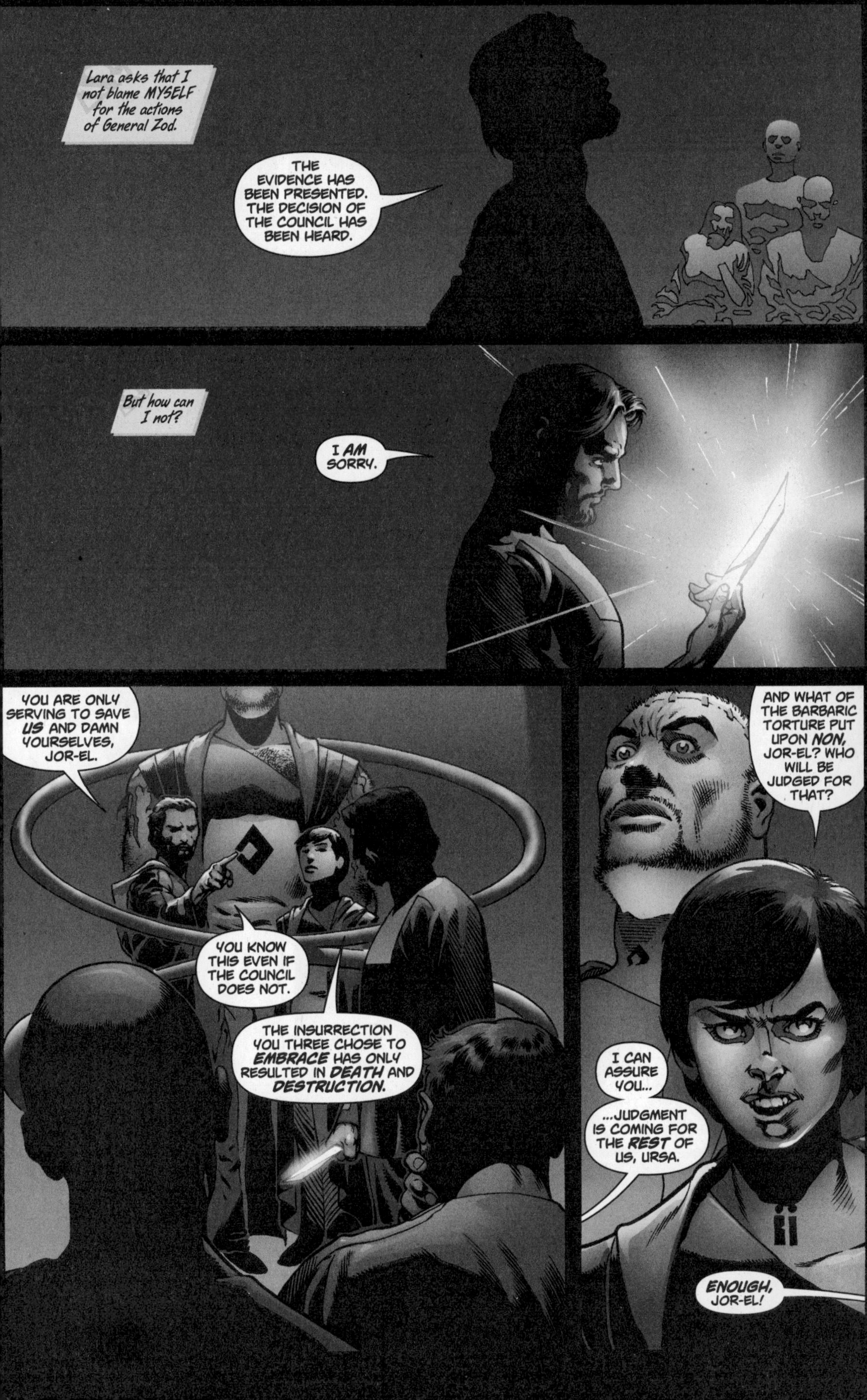
Lara asks that I not blame MYSELF for the actions of General Zod.
THE EVIDENCE HAS BEEN PRESENTED. THE DECISION OF THE COUNCIL HAS BEEN HEARD.
But how can I not?
I AM SORRY.
YOU ARE ONLY SERVING TO SAVE US AND DAMN YOURSELVES, JOR-EL.
YOU KNOW THIS EVEN IF THE COUNCIL DOES NOT.
THE INSURRECTION YOU THREE CHOSE TO EMBRACE HAS ONLY RESULTED IN DEATH AND DESTRUCTION.
AND WHAT OF THE BARBARIC TORTURE PUT UPON NON, JOR-EL? WHO WILL BE JUDGED FOR THAT?
I CAN ASSURE YOU...
...JUDGMENT IS COMING FOR THE REST OF US, URSA.
ENOUGH, JOR-EL!

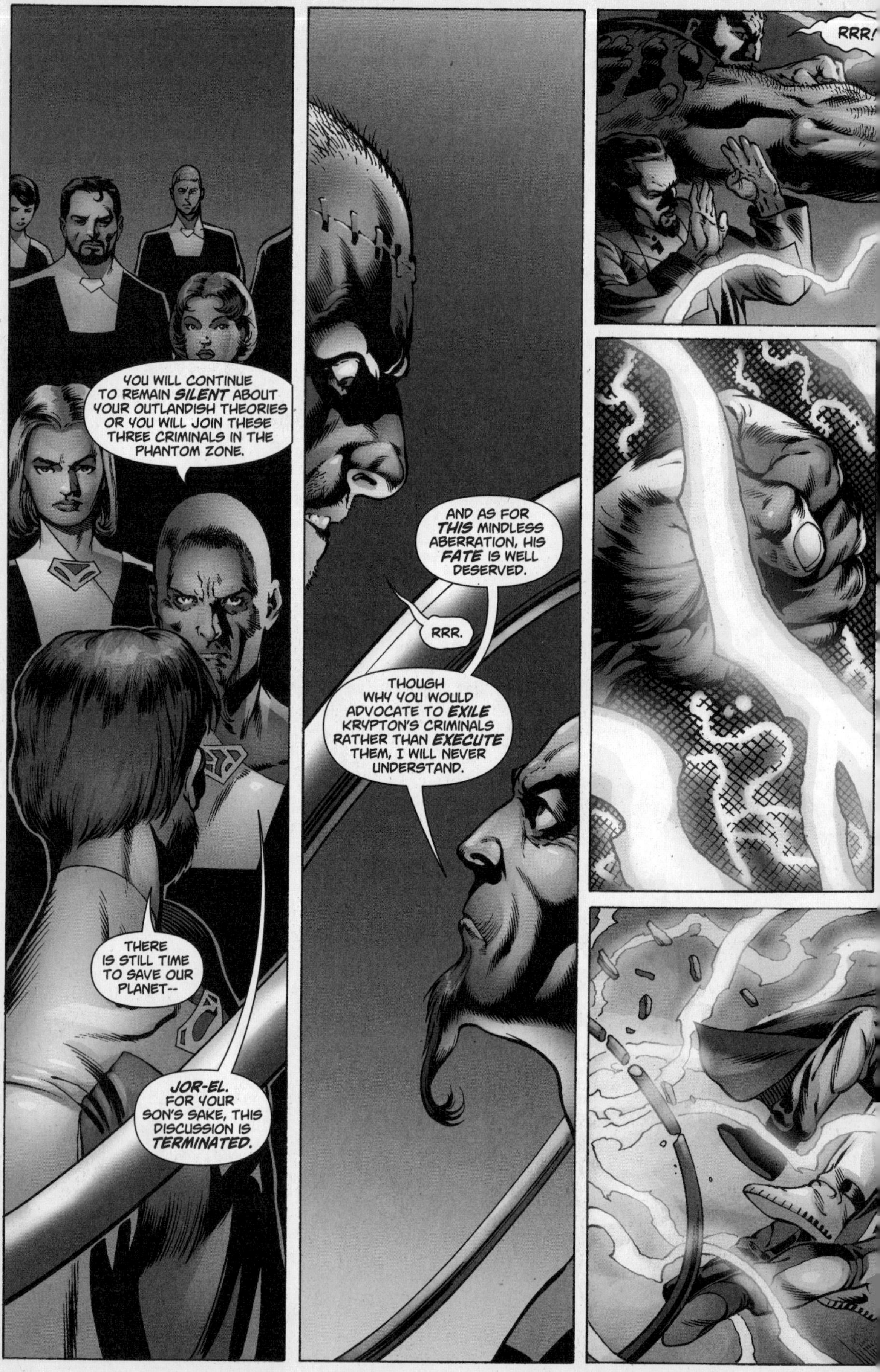
YOU WILL CONTINUE TO REMAIN SILENT ABOUT YOUR OUTLANDISH THEORIES OR YOU WILL JOIN THESE THREE CRIMINALS IN THE PHANTOM ZONE.
THERE IS STILL TIME TO SAVE OUR PLANET--
JOR-EL. FOR YOUR SON'S SAKE, THIS DISCUSSION IS TERMINATED.
AND AS FOR THIS MINDLESS ABERRATION, HIS FATE IS WELL DESERVED.
RRR.
THOUGH WHY YOU WOULD ADVOCATE TO EXILE KRYPTON'S CRIMINALS RATHER THAN EXECUTE THEM, I WILL NEVER UNDERSTAND.
RRR!

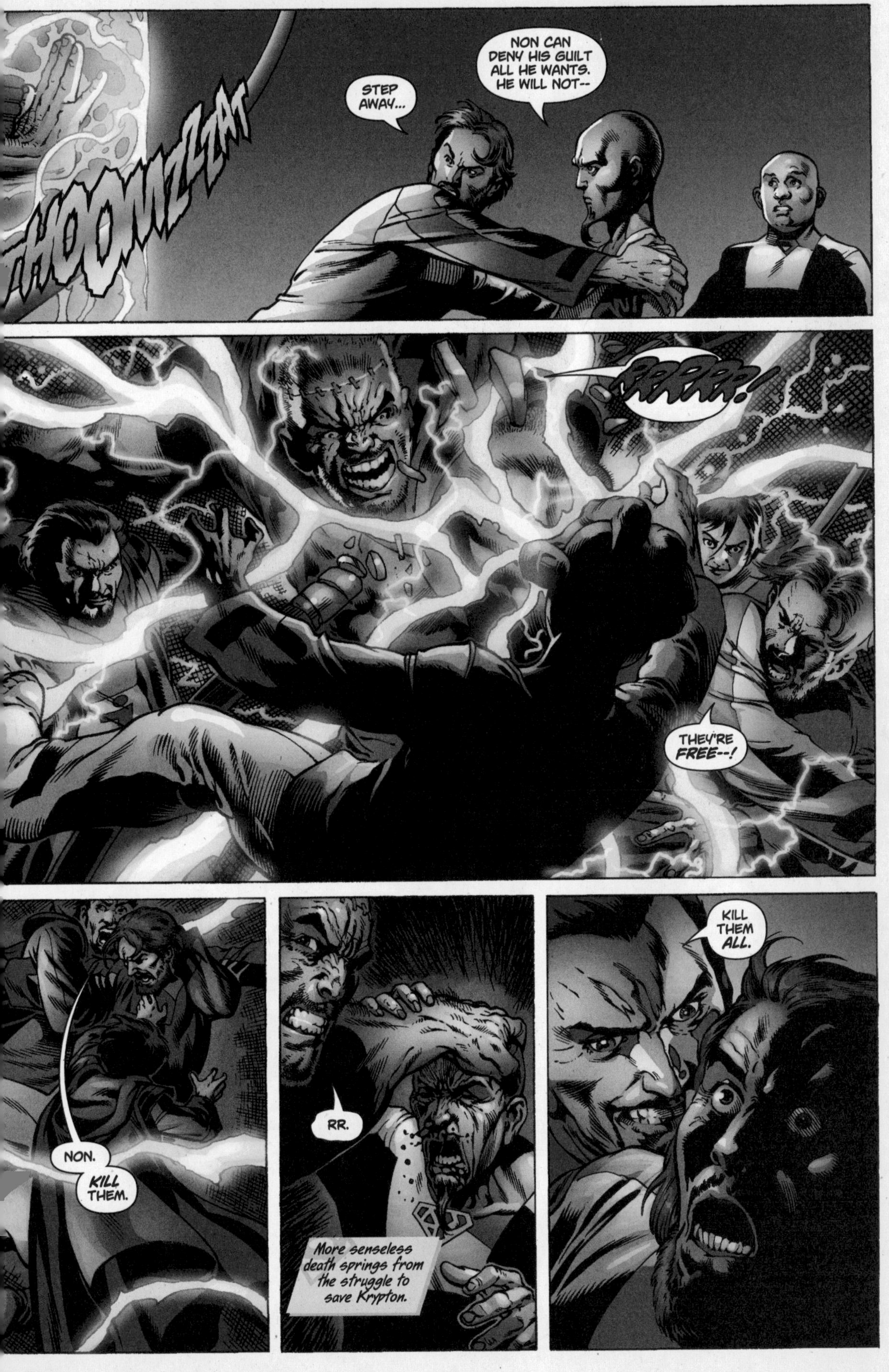
THOOMZZZAT
STEP AWAY...
NON CAN DENY HIS GUILT ALL HE WANTS. HE WILL NOT--
RRRRR!
THEY'RE FREE--!
NON.
KILL THEM.
RR.
More senseless death springs from the struggle to save Krypton.
KILL THEM ALL.

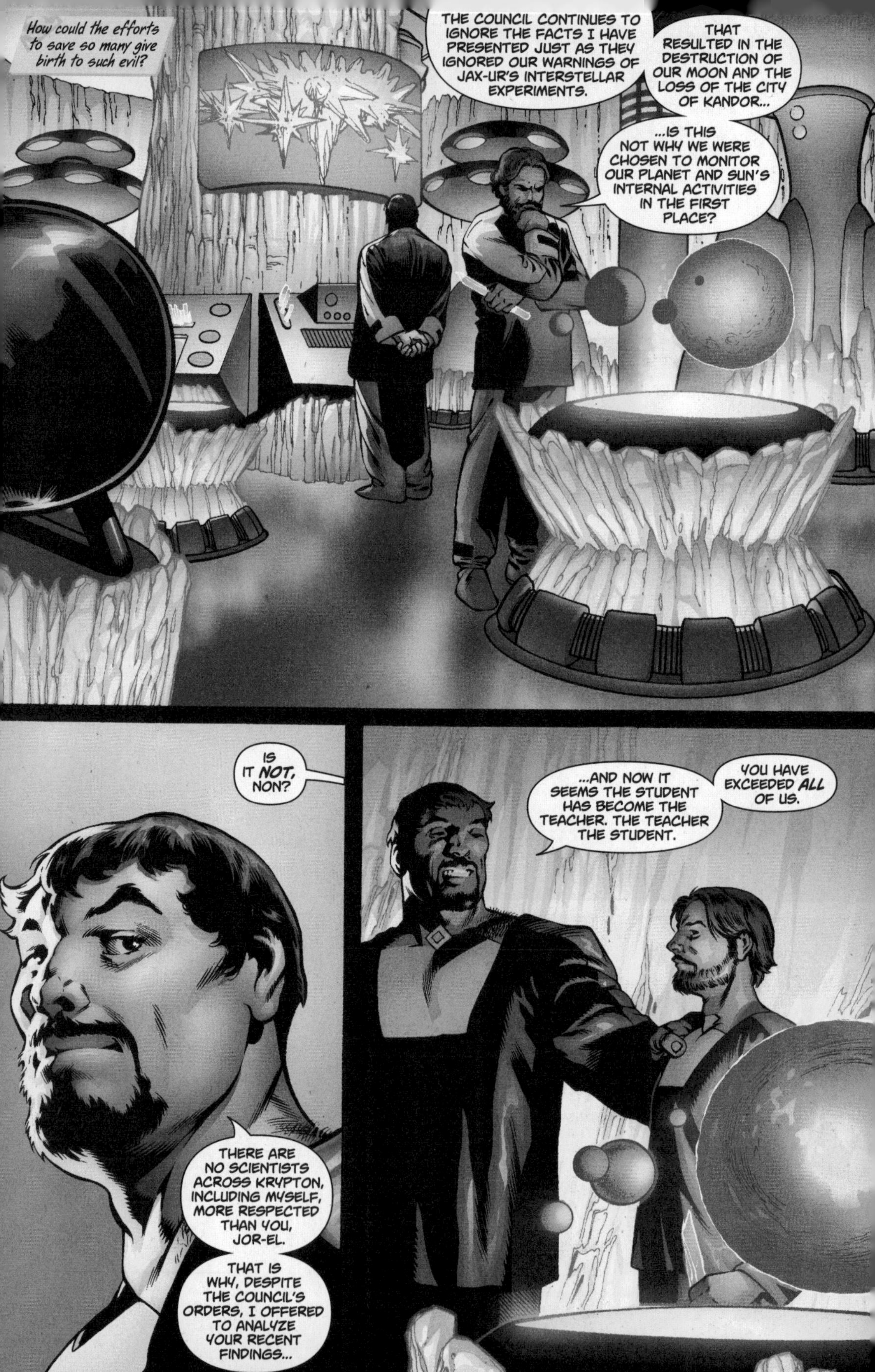
How could the efforts to save so many give birth to such evil?
THE COUNCIL CONTINUES TO IGNORE THE FACTS I HAVE PRESENTED JUST AS THEY IGNORED OUR WARNINGS OF JAX-UR'S INTERSTELLAR EXPERIMENTS.
THAT RESULTED IN THE DESTRUCTION OF OUR MOON AND THE LOSS OF THE CITY OF KANDOR...
...IS THIS NOT WHY WE WERE CHOSEN TO MONITOR OUR PLANET AND SUN'S INTERNAL ACTIVITIES IN THE FIRST PLACE?
IS IT NOT, NON?
THERE ARE NO SCIENTISTS ACROSS KRYPTON, INCLUDING MYSELF, MORE RESPECTED THAN YOU, JOR-EL.
THAT IS WHY, DESPITE THE COUNCIL'S ORDERS, I OFFERED TO ANALYZE YOUR RECENT FINDINGS...
...AND NOW IT SEEMS THE STUDENT HAS BECOME THE TEACHER. THE TEACHER THE STUDENT.
YOU HAVE EXCEEDED ALL OF US.

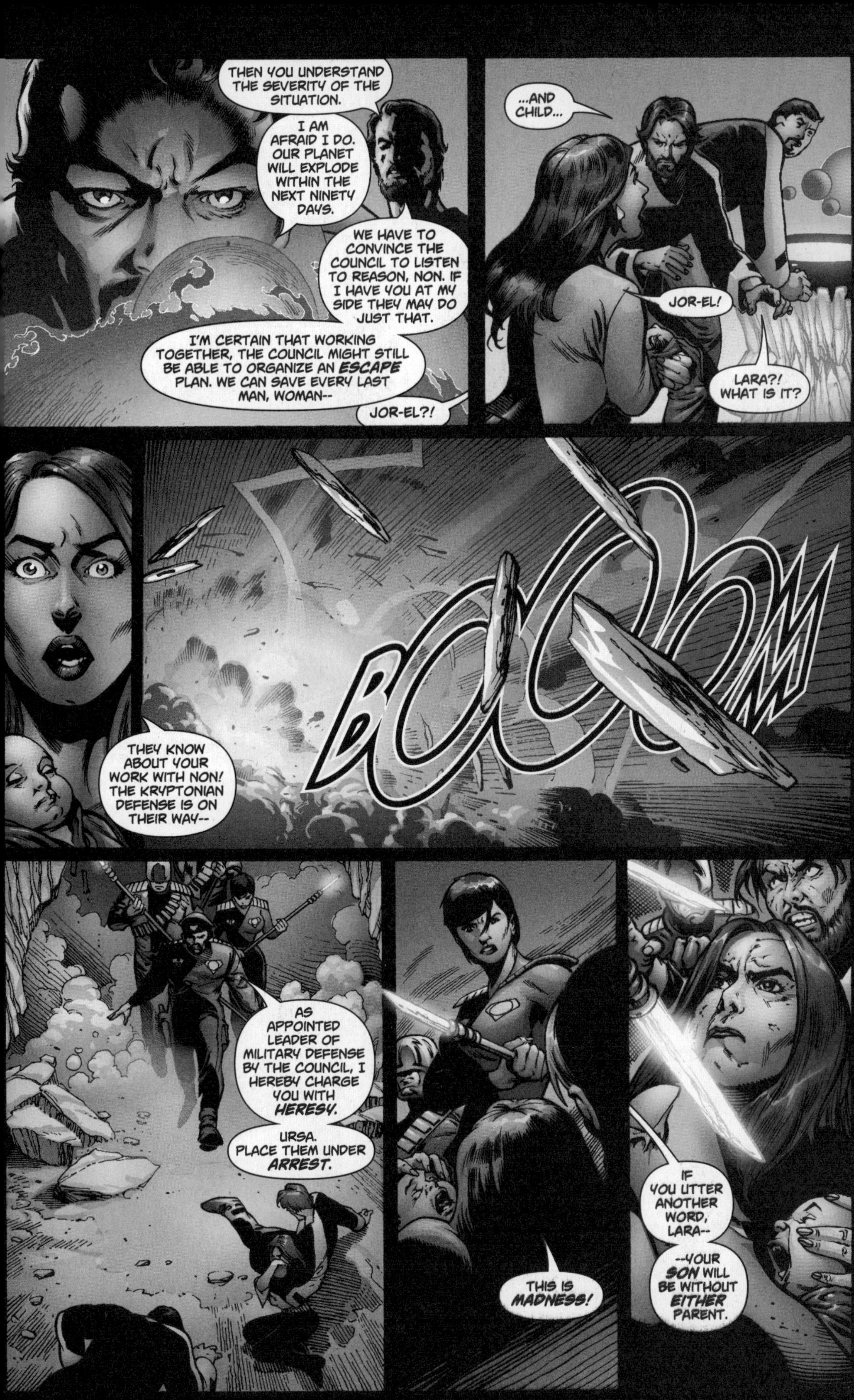
THEN YOU UNDERSTAND THE SEVERITY OF THE SITUATION.
I AM AFRAID I DO. OUR PLANET WILL EXPLODE WITHIN THE NEXT NINETY DAYS.
WE HAVE TO CONVINCE THE COUNCIL TO LISTEN TO REASON, NON. IF I HAVE YOU AT MY SIDE THEY MAY DO JUST THAT.
I'M CERTAIN THAT WORKING TOGETHER, THE COUNCIL MIGHT STILL BE ABLE TO ORGANIZE AN ESCAPE PLAN. WE CAN SAVE EVERY LAST MAN, WOMAN--
JOR-EL?!
...AND CHILD...
JOR-EL!
LARA?! WHAT IS IT?
BOOOM
THEY KNOW ABOUT YOUR WORK WITH NON! THE KRYPTONIAN DEFENSE IS ON THEIR WAY--
AS APPOINTED LEADER OF MILITARY DEFENSE BY THE COUNCIL, I HEREBY CHARGE YOU WITH HERESY.
URSA. PLACE THEM UNDER ARREST.
THIS IS MADNESS!
IF YOU UTTER ANOTHER WORD, LARA--
--YOUR SON WILL BE WITHOUT EITHER PARENT.

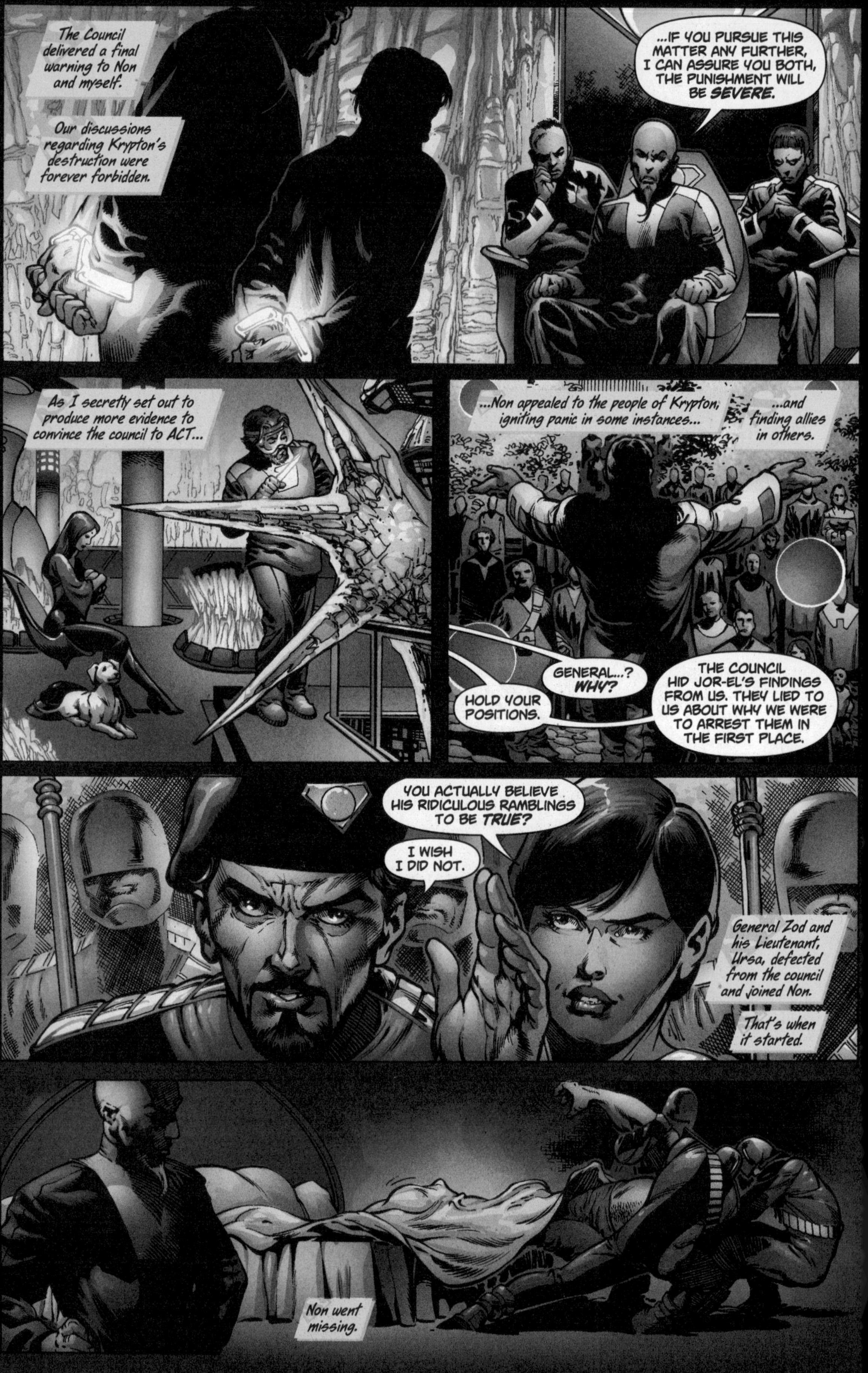

The Council delivered a final warning to Non and myself.
Our discussions regarding Krypton's destruction were forever forbidden.
...IF YOU PURSUE THIS MATTER ANY FURTHER, I CAN ASSURE YOU BOTH, THE PUNISHMENT WILL BE SEVERE.
As I secretly set out to produce more evidence to convince the council to ACT...
...Non appealed to the people of Krypton, igniting panic in some instances...
...and finding allies in others.
GENERAL...? WHY?
HOLD YOUR POSITIONS.
THE COUNCIL HID JOR-EL'S FINDINGS FROM US. THEY LIED TO US ABOUT WHY WE WERE TO ARREST THEM IN THE FIRST PLACE.
YOU ACTUALLY BELIEVE HIS RIDICULOUS RAMBLINGS TO BE TRUE?
I WISH I DID NOT.
General Zod and his Lieutenant, Ursa, defected from the council and joined Non.
That's when it started.
Non went missing.

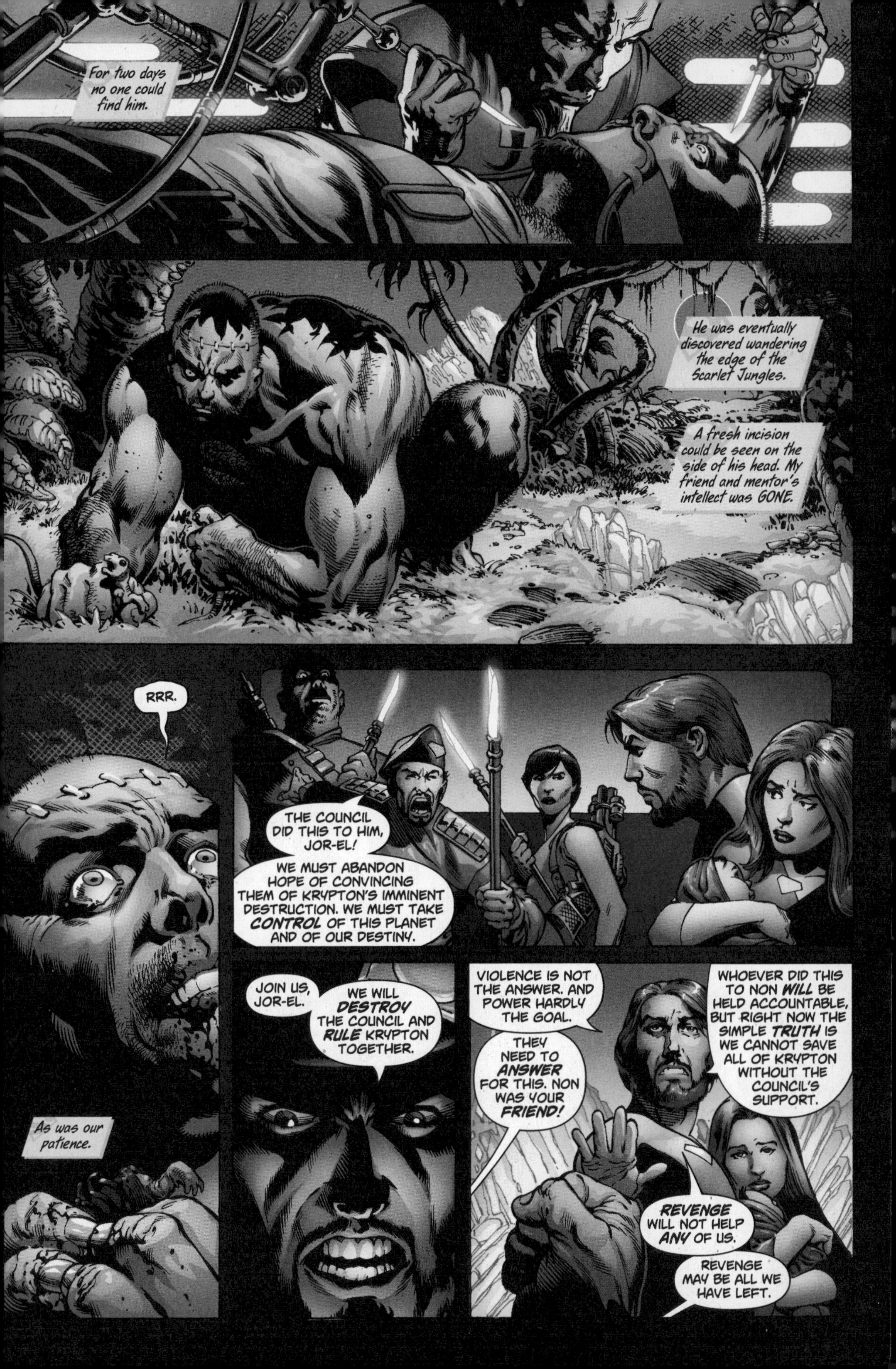
For two days no one could find him.
He was eventually discovered wandering the edge of the Scarlet Jungles.
A fresh incision could be seen on the side of his head. My friend and mentor's intellect was GONE.
RRR.
THE COUNCIL DID THIS TO HIM, JOR-EL!
WE MUST ABANDON HOPE OF CONVINCING THEM OF KRYPTON'S IMMINENT DESTRUCTION. WE MUST TAKE CONTROL OF THIS PLANET AND OF OUR DESTINY.
As was our patience.
JOIN US, JOR-EL.
WE WILL DESTROY THE COUNCIL AND RULE KRYPTON TOGETHER.
VIOLENCE IS NOT THE ANSWER. AND POWER HARDLY THE GOAL.
THEY NEED TO ANSWER FOR THIS. NON WAS YOUR FRIEND!
WHOEVER DID THIS TO NON WILL BE HELD ACCOUNTABLE, BUT RIGHT NOW THE SIMPLE TRUTH IS WE CANNOT SAVE ALL OF KRYPTON WITHOUT THE COUNCIL'S SUPPORT.
REVENGE WILL NOT HELP ANY OF US.
REVENGE MAY BE ALL WE HAVE LEFT.

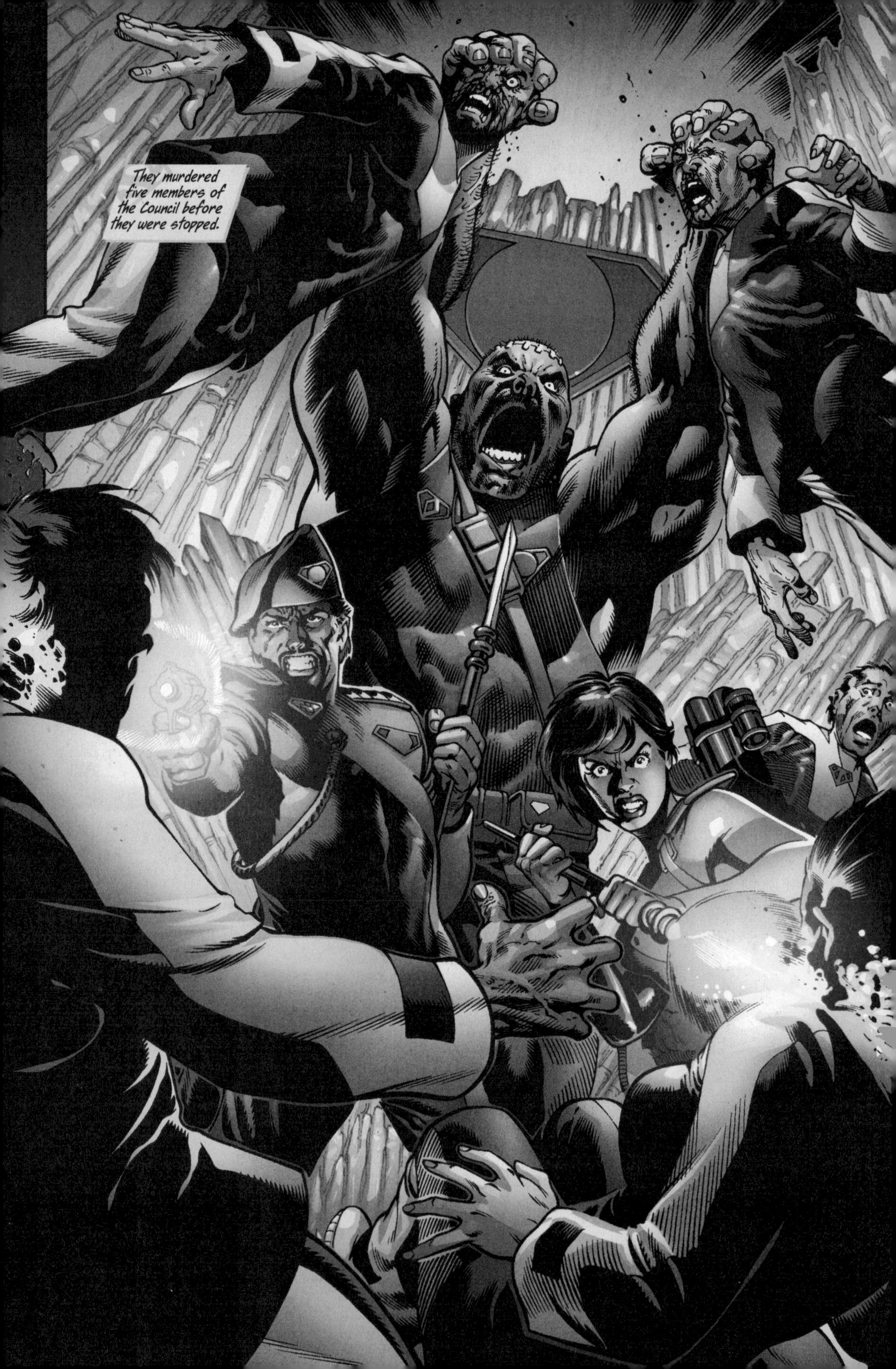
They murdered five members of the Council before they were stopped.

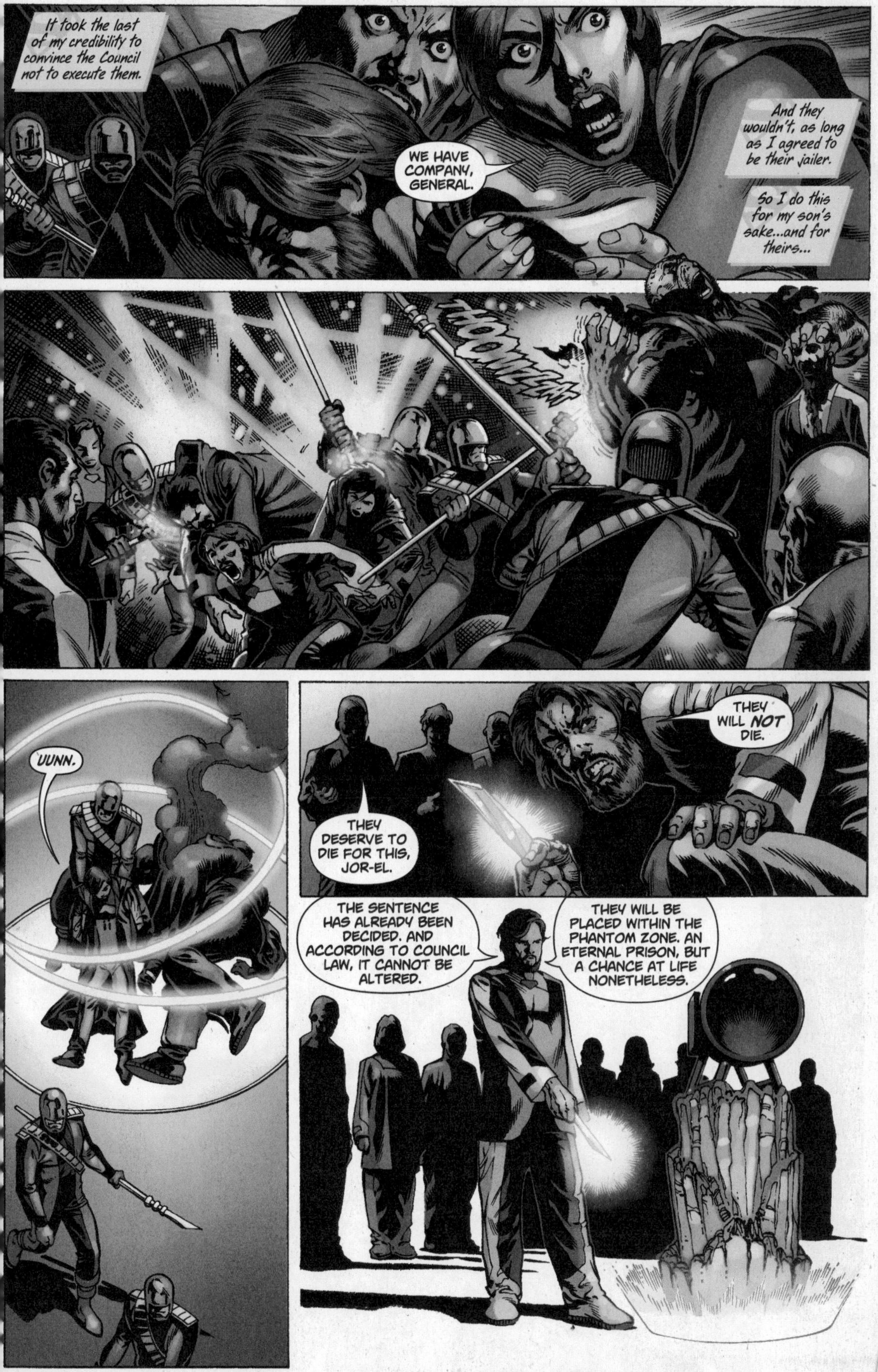
It took the last of my credibility to convince the Council not to execute them.
WE HAVE COMPANY, GENERAL.
And they wouldn't, as long as I agreed to be their jailer.
So I do this for my son's sake...and for theirs...
THOOMMM
UUNN.
THEY WILL NOT DIE.
THEY DESERVE TO DIE FOR THIS, JOR-EL.
THE SENTENCE HAS ALREADY BEEN DECIDED. AND ACCORDING TO COUNCIL LAW, IT CANNOT BE ALTERED.
THEY WILL BE PLACED WITHIN THE PHANTOM ZONE. AN ETERNAL PRISON, BUT A CHANCE AT LIFE NONETHELESS.

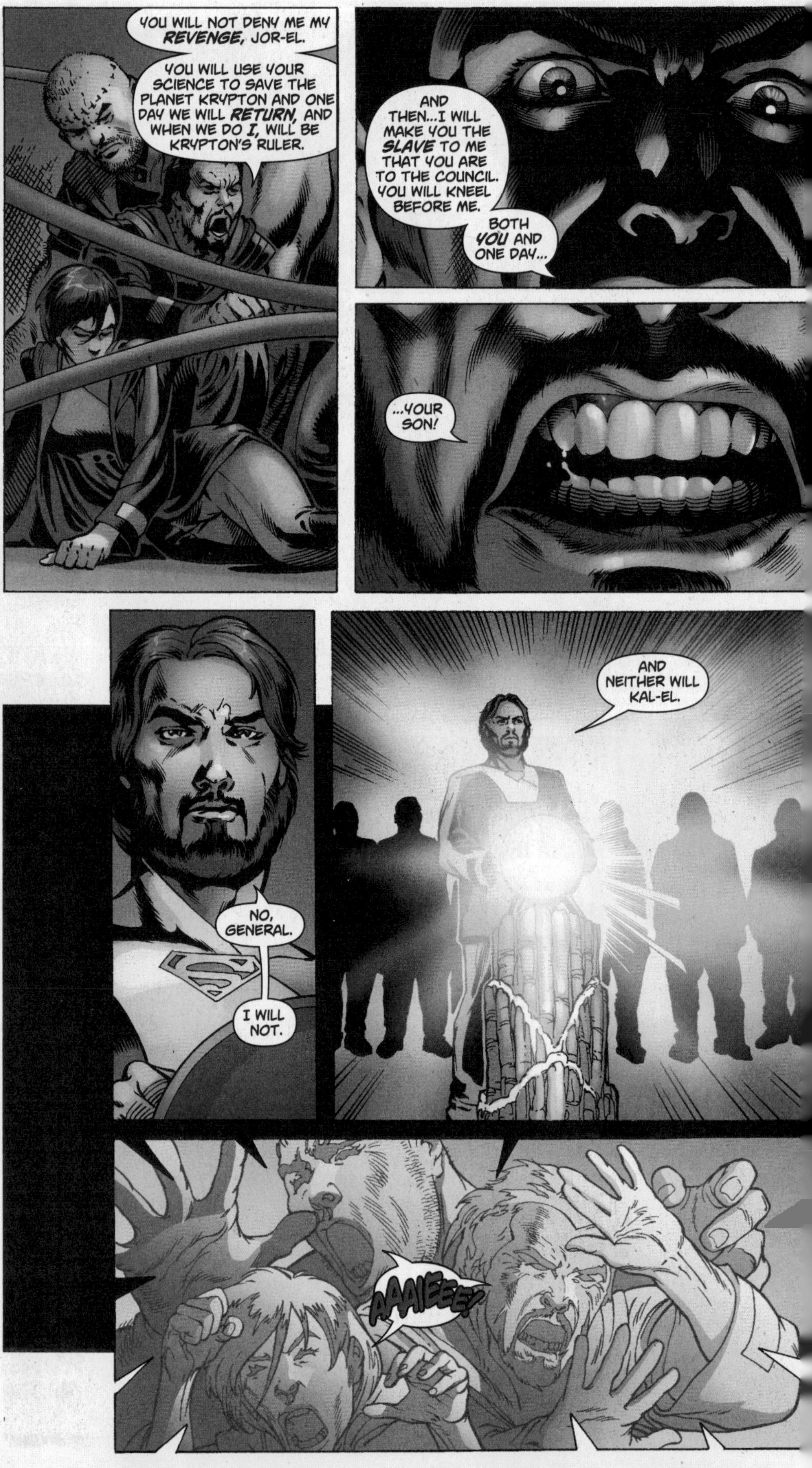
YOU WILL NOT DENY ME MY REVENGE, JOR-EL.
YOU WILL USE YOUR SCIENCE TO SAVE THE PLANET KRYPTON AND ONE DAY WE WILL RETURN, AND WHEN WE DO I, WILL BE KRYPTON'S RULER.
AND THEN...I WILL MAKE YOU THE SLAVE TO ME THAT YOU ARE TO THE COUNCIL. YOU WILL KNEEL BEFORE ME.
BOTH YOU AND ONE DAY...
...YOUR SON!
NO, GENERAL.
I WILL NOT.
AND NEITHER WILL KAL-EL.
AAAIEEE!

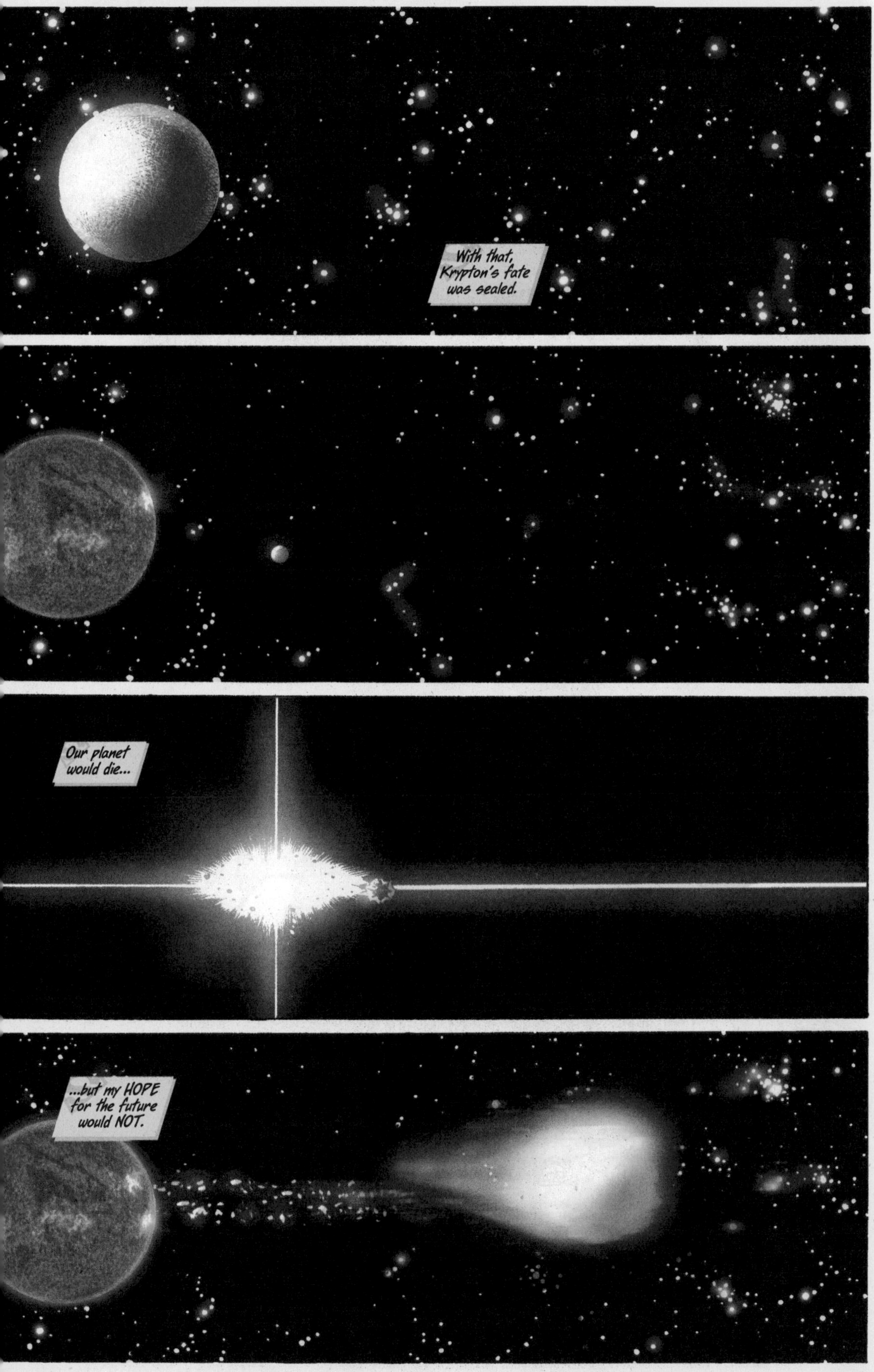
With that, Krypton's fate was sealed.
Our planet would die...
...but my HOPE for the future would NOT.

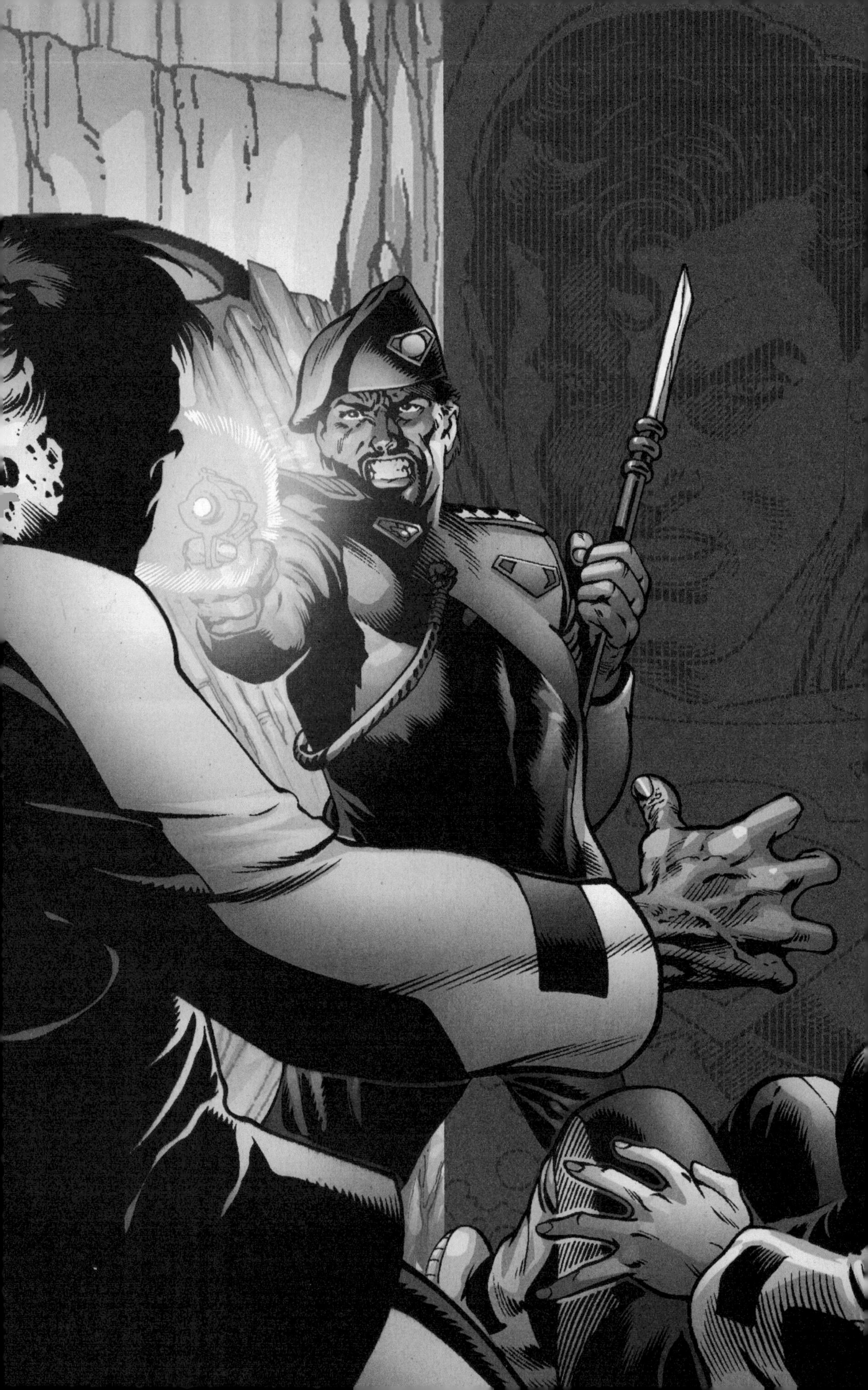

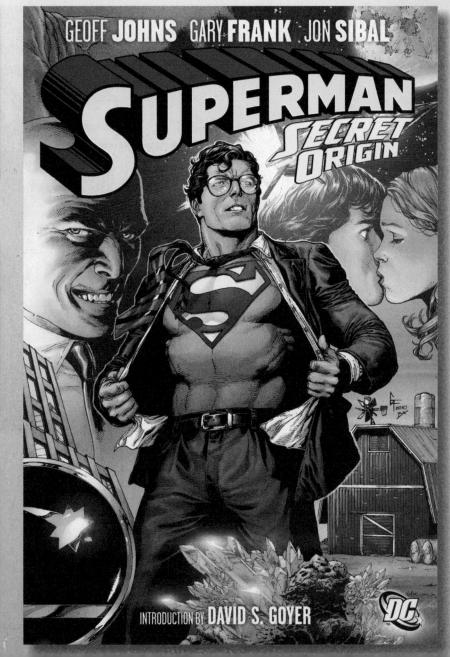

DC COMICS™

"It's fresh air. I like this all-too-human Superman, and I think a lot of you will, too."
—SCRIPPS HOWARD NEWS SERVICE

START AT THE BEGINNING!

SUPERMAN: ACTION COMICS VOLUME 1: SUPERMAN AND THE MEN OF STEEL

SUPERMAN VOLUME 1: WHAT PRICE TOMORROW?

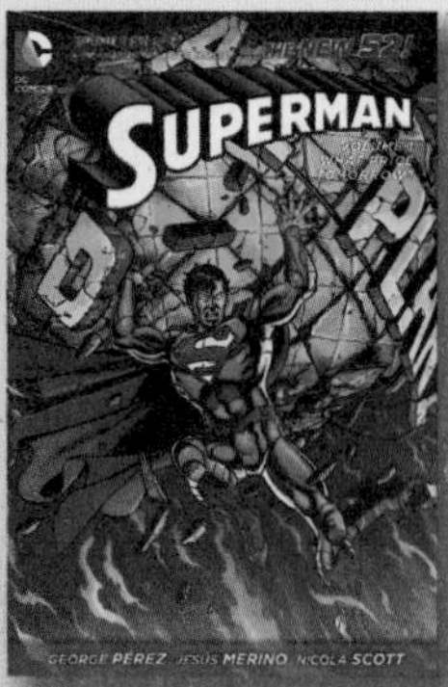
THE NEW 52!
SUPERMAN
GEORGE PÉREZ JESUS MERINO NICOLA SCOTT

SUPERGIRL VOLUME 1: THE LAST DAUGHTER OF KRYPTON

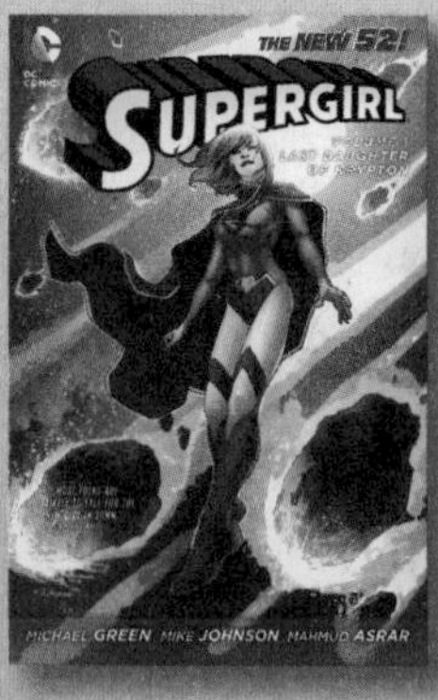
THE NEW 52!
SUPERGIRL
MICHAEL GREEN MIKE JOHNSON MAHMUD ASRAR

SUPERBOY VOLUME 1: INCUBATION

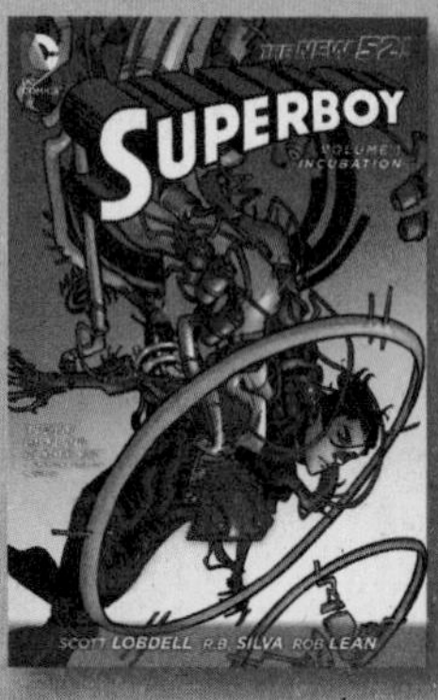
THE NEW 52!
SUPERBOY
VOLUME 1 INCUBATION
SCOTT LOBDELL R.B. SILVA ROB LEAN

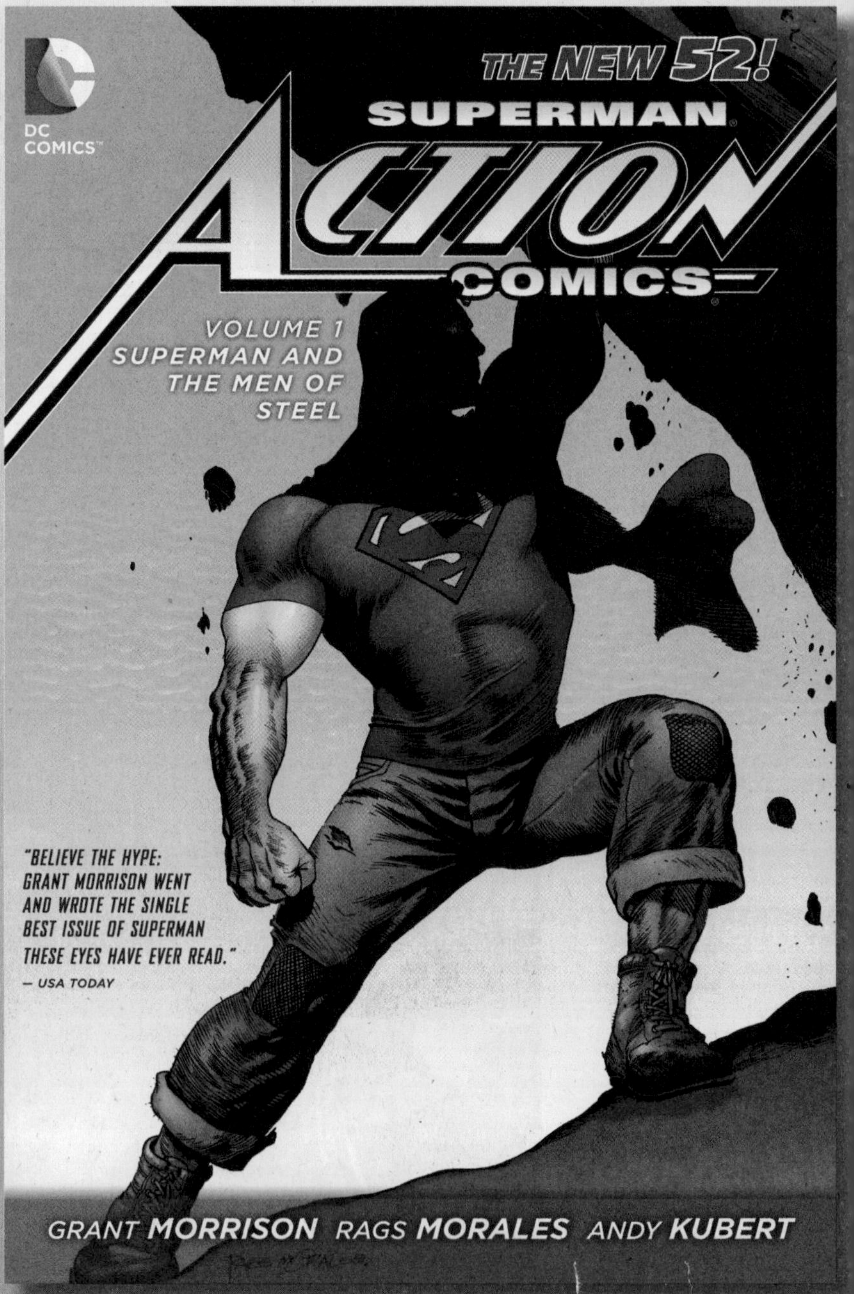
DC COMICS™
THE NEW 52!
SUPERMAN
ACTION COMICS
VOLUME 1
SUPERMAN AND THE MEN OF STEEL
"BELIEVE THE HYPE: GRANT MORRISON WENT AND WROTE THE SINGLE BEST ISSUE OF SUPERMAN THESE EYES HAVE EVER READ."
– USA TODAY
GRANT MORRISON RAGS MORALES ANDY KUBERT